MW0126896

THE POLITICO-LEGAL DYNAMICS OF JUDICIAL REVIEW

Comparative scholarship on judicial review has paid a lot of attention to the causal impact of politics on judicial decision-making. However, the slower-moving, macro-social process through which judicial review influences societal conceptions of the law/politics relation is less well understood. Drawing on the political science literature on institutional change, *The Politico-Legal Dynamics of Judicial Review* tests a typological theory of the evolution of judicial review regimes – complexes of legitimating ideas about the law/politics relation. The theory posits that such regimes tend to conform to one of four main types – democratic or authoritarian legalism, or democratic or authoritarian instrumentalism. Through case studies of Australia, India, and Zimbabwe and a comparative chapter analyzing ten additional societies, the book then explores how actually existing judicial review regimes transition between these types. This process of ideational development, Roux concludes, is distinct both from the everyday business of constitutional politics and changes to the formal constitution.

Theunis Roux is Professor of Law at UNSW Sydney. He was the founding director of the South African Institute for Advanced Constitutional, Public, Human Rights and International Law and is a former Secretary General of the International Association of Constitutional Law. He is the author of *The Politics of Principle* (Cambridge University Press, 2013) and coeditor, with Rosalind Dixon, of a recent anthology of papers assessing the triumphs and disappointments of postapartheid South African constitutionalism.

COMPARATIVE CONSTITUTIONAL LAW AND POLICY

Series Editors

Tom Ginsburg *University of Chicago*
Zachary Elkins *University of Texas at Austin*
Ran Hirschl *University of Toronto*

Comparative constitutional law is an intellectually vibrant field that encompasses an increasingly broad array of approaches and methodologies. This series collects analytically innovative and empirically grounded work from scholars of comparative constitutionalism across academic disciplines. Books in the series include theoretically informed studies of single constitutional jurisdictions, comparative studies of constitutional law and institutions, and edited collections of original essays that respond to challenging theoretical and empirical questions in the field.

Books in the Series

The Invisible Constitution in Comparative Perspective edited by Rosalind Dixon and Adrienne Stone

Constituent Assemblies edited by Jon Elster, Roberto Gargarella, Vatsal Naresh, and Bjorn Erik Rasch

Judicial Review in Norway Anine Kierulf

The DNA of Constitutional Justice in Latin America: Politics, Governance, and Judicial Design Daniel M. Brinks and Abby Blass

The Adventures of the Constituent Power: Beyond Revolutions? Andrew Arato

Constitutions, Religion and Politics in Asia: Indonesia, Malaysia and Sri Lanka Dian A. H. Shah

Canada in the World: Comparative Perspectives on the Canadian Constitution edited by Richard Albert and David R. Cameron

Courts and Democracies in Asia Po Jen Yap

Proportionality: New Frontiers, New Challenges edited by Vicki C. Jackson and Mark Tushnet

Constituents Before Assembly: Participation, Deliberation, and Representation in the Crafting of New Constitutions Todd A. Eisenstadt, A. Carl LeVan, and Tofigh Maboudi

Assessing Constitutional Performance edited by Tom Ginsburg and Aziz Huq

Buddhism, Politics and the Limits of Law: The Pyrrhic Constitutionalism of Sri Lanka Benjamin Schonthal

Engaging with Social Rights: Procedure, Participation and Democracy in South Africa's Second Wave Brian Ray

Constitutional Courts as Mediators: Armed Conflict, Civil–Military Relations, and the Rule of Law in Latin America Julio Ríos-Figueroa

Perils of Judicial Self-Government in Transitional Societies David Kosař

Making We the People: Democratic Constitutional Founding in Postwar Japan and South Korea Chaihark Hahm and Sung Ho Kim

The Politico-Legal Dynamics of Judicial Review

A COMPARATIVE ANALYSIS

THEUNIS ROUX

University of New South Wales, Sydney

CAMBRIDGE
UNIVERSITY PRESS

CAMBRIDGE
UNIVERSITY PRESS

University Printing House, Cambridge CB2 8BS, United Kingdom

One Liberty Plaza, 20th Floor, New York, NY 10006, USA

477 Williamstown Road, Port Melbourne, VIC 3207, Australia

314–321, 3rd Floor, Plot 3, Splendor Forum, Jasola District Centre, New Delhi – 110025, India

79 Anson Road, #06–04/06, Singapore 079906

Cambridge University Press is part of the University of Cambridge.

It furthers the University's mission by disseminating knowledge in the pursuit of education, learning, and research at the highest international levels of excellence.

www.cambridge.org
Information on this title: www.cambridge.org/9781108425421
DOI: 10.1017/9781108340977

© Theunis Roux 2018

First published 2018

Printed in the United States of America by Sheridan Books, Inc.

A catalogue record for this publication is available from the British Library.

Library of Congress Cataloging-in-Publication Data
NAMES: Roux, Theunis, author.
TITLE: The politico-legal dynamics of judicial review : a comparative analysis / Theunis Roux, University of New South Wales, Sydney.
DESCRIPTION: Cambridge [UK] ; New York, NY : Cambridge University Press, [2018] | Includes bibliographical references and index.
IDENTIFIERS: LCCN 2018012357 | ISBN 9781108425421
SUBJECTS: LCSH: Judicial review. | Judicial review – Political aspects. | Constitutional law.
CLASSIFICATION: LCC K3175 .R68 2018 | DDC 347/.012–dc23
LC record available at https://lccn.loc.gov/2018012357

ISBN 978-1-108-42542-1 Hardback

For Hannah and Sarah

Contents

Figures

Tables

Acknowledgments

Australia is a place where writing a scholarly treatise is generally thought to be a missed opportunity to do other, more important things, like investing in the property market or hitting a red ball across a green field. If you foolishly admit over the barbecue flame to being an academic, the look of puzzled confusion on your interlocutor's face can incapacitate you for a week.

If this is true of Australia generally, it is also true of its tertiary education sector in particular. The neoliberal, managerialist assault on the humanities and social sciences, which British universities have had the good sense to attenuate and elite American universities the private funding to ignore, is in the Antipodes still a topic of anxious conversation. Australian universities' usually very admirable desire to prove their international standing has made them particularly susceptible to the cult of the rankings lists, as though something as intrinsically important as the pursuit of truth could be reduced to a SNIP index. In this measurable-outcomes-oriented world, the writing of a scholarly treatise, and especially one that takes four years to complete, is generally seen as being akin to playing test cricket when all the money and crowd support is in the shorter versions of the game.

The word "generally," however, implies that there are exceptions, and it is in the community of the exceptional that a book like this gets written. First and foremost, I would like to acknowledge the support of my home institution, UNSW Law, which has fearlessly defended its research culture in the face of serious challenges. From the time of his appointment in 2016, George Williams has been a brave and exemplary Dean and the most committed democrat one could ever wish for. Carolyn Penfold and Andrew Lynch, as successive Heads of School, have been friendly puncturers of my surly disposition. My extraordinarily gifted colleague, Rosalind Dixon, has honored me with a sustained interest in my work. Her standing in the comparative constitutional law community has ensured a steady flow of international visitors to UNSW Law that has made up for my tendency to plough my own furrow – sometimes, it seems, on my own planet.

In the section of these acknowledgments that I might have given the subheading "camaraderie-cum-collegiality," I should mention first the friendship of Martin Krygier, who has stuck with me through dark times, for only some of which he bears responsibility. As this book was nearing completion, Adam Czarnota welcomed me into his home, fed me flavorful Polish food, and reminded me what devotion to a life of the intellect means. Simon Halliday shared his advice on how to make the most of cooking for one, and occasionally roused himself from his Scottish Presbyterian bleakness to think of good names for cycling teams. To these three mates, who also read and commented on my work, I shall be eternally grateful.

Lastly, to my daughters, Hannah and Sarah, to whom this book is dedicated, I am sorry for what I have put you through, but I hope that reading this book, or just leafing through it, you will get some sense of the madness that possessed me.

Various iterations of this book have been presented at seminars in Australia, India, and the United States. The typology on which this study is based was first presented in a different form at a comparative constitutional law symposium organized by Rosalind Dixon at UNSW Law in November 2013. I presented an early draft of the Australian case study chapter at the Australian Political Studies Conference in Sydney in September 2014. In April 2016, Kevin Walton kindly invited me to present what turned out to be an initial version of Chapter 2 at the Julius Stone Institute at the University of Sydney. In October of that year, Erin Delaney and Rosalind Dixon hosted a Conference on Comparative Judicial Review at Northwestern University Pritzker School of Law at which I again presented the theoretical framework for this study. I presented the redrafted paper I eventually wrote for Erin and Rosalind's edited anthology at the Centre for Comparative Constitutional Studies *Constitutional Theory Workshop* at the University of Melbourne in July 2017. Chapter 6 was presented in near-final form at the UNSW Law *Comparative Constitutional Law Roundtable* in August 2017 (again organized by Rosalind Dixon) and at the Australian National University *Troubling the Rule of Law* Conference at Kioloa, New South Wales, in September 2017 (organized by Nick Cheesman). In November 2017, Alexander Fischer of Jindal Global Law School organized a workshop at which the Indian case study chapter was presented. Finally, in December 2017, Rosalind Dixon helped me to organize a book manuscript review workshop at UNSW Law at which I presented the penultimate draft of this book. I am grateful to the organizers of these events for the opportunity to discuss my work and to the commentators for their feedback: Madhav Khosla, James Stellios, David Landau (three times), Tom Daly, Bjoern Dressel, Raul Sanchez-Urribarri, Javier Couso, Mark Graber, Michaela Hailbonner, Rehan Abeyratne, Heinz Klug, and Gabrielle Appleby. Aside from these formally designated commentators, Jeffrey Goldsworthy sent me extremely helpful comments on the Australian case study chapter, Pratap Bhanu Mehta and Satya Prateek helped with the Indian chapter, Jason Brickhill corrected various oversights and oversimplifications in the Zimbabwe chapter, and Sharon Cowan picked up some errors and inconsistencies in the first two chapters.

In the course of writing this book, I tested out parts of the argument in published papers. Some passages from these papers have been republished in this volume, as indicated in parentheses after the citation: "Reinterpreting the Mason Court Revolution: An Historical Institutionalist Account of Judge-Driven Constitutional Transformation in Australia" (2015) 43 *Federal Law Review* 1 (a couple of paragraphs from Chapter 4); "Trajectories of Curial Power: The Rise, Fall and Partial Rehabilitation of the Indonesian Constitutional Court" (2016) 17 *Australian Journal of Asian Law* 1 (sections of Chapter 7); "Comparative Constitutional Studies: Two Fields or One?" (2017) 13 *Annual Review of Law & Social Science* 123 (parts of Chapter 1); "How, When and Why Does Faith in Law's Autonomy Decline? A Comparative Constitutional-Cultural Analysis" in Erin F. Delaney and Rosalind Dixon (eds.), *Comparative Judicial Review* (Edward Elgar, forthcoming) (small portions of Chapter 6); and "In Defence of Empirical Entanglement: The Methodological Flaw in Waldron's Case against Judicial Review" in Ron Levy and Graeme Orr (eds.), *The Cambridge Handbook of Deliberative Constitutionalism* (Cambridge University Press, 2018) 203 (some of the argument in Chapter 7). I am grateful to the editors and publishers of these papers for permission to republish the relevant extracts here.

Introduction

The adoption of a system of "strong-form"[1] judicial review poses the perennial question of law's relationship to politics in a particularly stark form. Complex in its origins,[2] morally controversial,[3] and yet remarkably popular over the last thirty years,[4] the most striking feature of this institution is that it thrusts the judiciary into the center of politics while at the same time requiring judges to rationalize their decision-making processes in ways sufficiently different from politics to justify the powers given to them. Unless and until judicial review is disestablished, the judiciary may assert final decision-making power over aspects of public policy formerly reserved to the political branches. Political actors, in turn, may either embrace this move, cognizant of judicial review's legitimating potential, or push back against it, arguing that the judiciary has overreached its authority.

According to "dialogue theory"[5] and conceptualizations of judicial review as "separation-of-powers games,"[6] the back-and-forth interaction of judicial and political-branch interpretations of the constitution is an iterative policy-

---

[1] The precise meaning of this term is defined in Chapter 1.
[2] The two leading comparative studies of this issue are Tom Ginsburg, *Judicial Review in New Democracies: Constitutional Courts in Asian Cases* (New York: Cambridge University Press, 2003) and Ran Hirschl, *Towards Juristocracy: The Origins and Consequences of the New Constitutionalism* (Cambridge, MA: Harvard University Press, 2007).
[3] The leading, non-jurisdiction specific critique is Jeremy Waldron, "The Core of the Case against Judicial Review" (2006) 115 *Yale Law Journal* 1346.
[4] See Tom Ginsburg, "The Global Spread of Constitutional Review" in Gregory A. Caldeira, R. Daniel Kelemen, and Keith E. Whittington (eds.), *The Oxford Handbook of Law and Politics* (Oxford: Oxford University Press, 2008) 85.
[5] Peter W. Hogg and Allison A. Bushell, "The Charter Dialogue between Courts and Legislatures (Or Perhaps the Charter of Rights Isn't Such a Bad Thing after All)" (1997) 35 *Osgoode Hall Law Journal* 75.
[6] See Jeffrey A. Segal, "Separation-of-Powers Games in the Positive Theory of Courts and Congress" (1997) 91 *American Political Science Review* 28.

making process: judicial decisions and legislative and executive responses to them are conversational gambits or strategic moves in which each branch of government tries to influence public policy in line with its prerogatives. These accounts are instructive as far as they go, but they focus on slice-in-time events rather than the slower-moving, sociological process that underlies them. Beneath the contest over the constitutionality of particular legislative provisions or executive acts there may be a long tradition in the society concerned of thinking about law's claim to authority and its relationship to political authority. It is this tradition to which legal and political actors appeal when justifying their actions. In older constitutional democracies, for example, there will usually be a well-developed tradition of thinking about the role of judges in checking the abuse of political power and securing the conditions for free democratic competition. In authoritarian societies, the traditions on which legal and political actors draw are different, but may be no less powerful or deep.[7] The real story of judicial review, on this view of things, is not the surface-level contestation between the judiciary and the political branches for control of aspects of public policy, but the constantly evolving complex of legitimating ideas through which legal and political actors make their respective claims to authority.

Each society, of course, has its own, idiosyncratic tradition of thinking about law and its relationship to politics. The adoption of a system of judicial review will both influence that tradition and be influenced by it – in the institutional form that it takes and the constitutional politics to which it gives rise. For comparative purposes, however, traditions of thinking about the law/politics relation may be conceptualized as varying according to the extent to which, on the one hand, law is thought of as being autonomous from politics and, on the other, legitimate political authority is thought to derive from a democratic mandate. Depending on the time that they have had to codetermine each other, these two aspects of a tradition, even when they are called on to justify divergent outcomes, may be mutually supporting. This may occur, for example, where judicial rights enforcement legitimates claims to political authority based on the authenticity of a democratic mandate. In situations like that, the judicial resolution of politically controversial questions need not undermine, and may in fact reinforce, settled understandings of the law/politics relation. In other circumstances, however, where unprecedented threats to national

---

7   See, for example, Tamir Moustafa, *The Struggle for Constitutional Power: Law, Politics, and Economic Development in Egypt* (New York: Cambridge University Press, 2009); Jothie Rajah, *Authoritarian Rule of Law: Legislation, Discourse, and Legitimacy in Singapore* (New York: Cambridge University Press, 2012); Mark Tushnet, "Authoritarian Constitutionalism" (2015) 100 *Cornell Law Review* 391.

security, say, prompt democratic legislatures to limit individual rights to a greater extent than they have before, such settled understandings may unravel. In this scenario, the external development, perhaps aided by inherent tendencies in the existing tradition, may open the way to societal reconsideration of law's claim to authority and its relationship to political authority.

The primary aim of this book is to develop a typological theory of this phenomenon that may be used in the comparative study of *judicial review regimes* ("JR regimes") – clusters of legitimating ideas about the law/politics relation in societies that have adopted a system of judicial review. At a conceptual level, the theory claims, the historical development of judicial review in such societies may be understood as a process of consolidation, transformation, and incremental development of their JR regimes. While such regimes are infinitely various, in practice they tend to conform to one of four main ideal types: democratic legalism, authoritarian legalism, authoritarian instrumentalism, and democratic instrumentalism.

The first type denotes a situation in which a constitutional culture that is committed to the ideal of law's autonomy from politics coexists with a well-functioning democratic system. In this style of regime, judicial review is conceived as the politically impartial enforcement of the constitution's prescriptions for democratic government. The second ideal type, authoritarian legalism, denotes a situation in which a commitment to the autonomy of law from politics has become distorted in the sense that it functions to separate social life into spheres where law rules and spheres where politics rules. The stability of this kind of JR regime comes from the residual legitimating role that law continues to play in those circumstances coupled with a political authority claim that justifies the repression of democratic rights by reference to some or other overarching goal that the power holder claims to be pursuing. Authoritarian instrumentalism, the third ideal type, denotes a situation in which law acts as a mere instrument of politics, and where law and politics are thus not separate social systems in any real sense. Here, stability is a function of the success of a sustained, state-sanctioned ideological presentation of law as necessarily subordinate to the pursuit of important societal goals. Finally, democratic instrumentalism describes a situation in which law's claim to authority is premised, not on the alleged impartiality of judicial reasoning techniques, but on judicial review's capacity to serve as a vehicle for competing, ideologically motivated conceptions of constitutional justice. In JR regimes that approximate this ideal type, the political system has either for some reason adjusted to tolerate this more politicized kind of legal authority claim or is unable to resist it.

The fact that actually existing JR regimes tend to approximate these ideal types makes it possible to compare the historical evolution of conceptions of the law/politics relation in different societies and to look for recurrent patterns. In some societies, for example, the process of JR-regime consolidation is driven by increasing returns as contingently chosen conceptions of the law/politics relation are politically accepted and legitimated. JR-regime transformation, too, exhibits certain patterned qualities that may be expressed in the form of an underlying causal mechanism. Understanding these processes and the politico-legal dynamics of each JR-regime type provides an empirical basis for normatively assessing them. Insights into the conditions for JR-regime change may also assist judges, legal practitioners, and democratic activists to influence the practice of judicial review in the society in which they find themselves.

In presenting this typological theory, the secondary aim of this study is to contribute to the burgeoning, but still a little uncertain-of-itself, field of "comparative constitutional studies" aka "comparative constitutional law" or "comparative judicial politics."[8] The absence of an agreed name for the field betrays its participants' ongoing and perhaps futile search for a uniform identity. It is that line of scholarly research, at any rate, which is devoted to describing, explaining, and normatively assessing the "global expansion of judicial power"[9] – the tremendous growth in both the coverage and the influence of judicially enforced constitutionalism in the wake of the end of the Cold War. The constitutional democracies that were established in the first decade after that momentous event have lost their youthful allure and are now entering a different phase of their institutional life, some strengthening and others showing signs of weakness. In Hungary, for example, the 1949 Constitution – as amended in 1989 to provide for judicial review – was replaced in 2011 and again amended in 2013 in ways that curtail the Constitutional Court's powers.[10] In Colombia, by contrast, the

---

[8] The term "comparative constitutional studies" was coined by Ran Hirschl in his book, *Comparative Matters: The Renaissance of Comparative Constitutional Law* (Oxford: Oxford University Press, 2014). See Chapter 1 for a discussion of the suitability of this term and for this study's understanding of the field.

[9] C. Neal Tate and Torbjörn Vallinder (eds.), *The Global Expansion of Judicial Power* (New York: New York University Press, 1995).

[10] See Miklós Bánkuti, Gábor Halmai, and Kim Lane Scheppele, "Hungary's Illiberal Turn: Disabling the Constitution" (2012) 23 *Journal of Democracy* 138; András Jakab and Pál Sonnevend, "Continuity with Deficiencies: The New Basic Law of Hungary" (2013) 9 *European Constitutional Law Review* 102; Bojan Bugarič, "A Crisis of Constitutional

Constitutional Court's forcefulness and popularity appear to have no limits, with each year bringing another raft of decisions that test conventional wisdom about the role of constitutional courts in national politics.[11] These and other similar developments present new opportunities for research and reflection. If the initial phase of comparative scholarship was directed at the causes of the judicialization of politics, the time is now ripe to consider the long-term effects and evolutionary dynamics of this phenomenon.

The most obvious of these effects is the contribution that judicial review is making to the quality of democracy in the countries concerned. That was, after all, the promise of the new constitutionalism – that far from detracting from democracy, judicial review would help to enhance and consolidate it. Contrasting opinions on this question are already emerging, with Samuel Issacharoff's somewhat optimistic account competing with Tom Daly's call for caution.[12] This conversation is just beginning and more scholars are sure to enter the debate. Beneath the complex question of constitutional courts' role in democracy building, however, lies an even deeper question about the process of ideational development that the adoption of a system of judicial review sets in motion – not just in democratic societies, but in authoritarian ones as well. In the end, if we are to understand the full potential and moral worth of this institution, we need to understand its impact on conceptions of the law/politics relation in the societies in which judicial review has been introduced.

Clearly, for judicial review to be established at all, there has to be some political rationale for it, whether that be the provision of "insurance" to reluctant democratizers,[13] the preservation by legal, political, and judicial elites of their "hegemony,"[14] or something as seemingly mundane as getting a federal constitutional system off the ground.[15] Whatever the rationale, however, judicial review becomes significant only to the extent that it acts as an effective counterweight to, and source of legitimacy for, claims to political authority. The battleground on which this drama is played out is essentially an ideological one – a clash of ideas in which competing conceptions of the law/

Democracy in Post-Communist Europe: 'Lands in-between' Democracy and Authoritarianism" (2015) 13 *International Journal of Constitutional Law* 219.

[11] See Manuel José Cepeda Espinosa and David Landau (eds.), *Colombian Constitutional Law: Leading Cases* (New York: Oxford University Press, 2017).

[12] Samuel Issacharoff, *Fragile Democracies: Contested Power in the Era of Constitutional Courts* (New York: Cambridge University Press, 2015); Tom Daly, *The Alchemists: Questioning our Faith in Courts as Democracy-Builders* (Cambridge: Cambridge University Press, 2017).

[13] See Ginsburg, *Judicial Review in New Democracies*.

[14] See Hirschl, *Towards Juristocracy*.

[15] This is true of the 1900 Australian Constitution, for example, as discussed in Chapter 3.

politics relation are invoked and continually revised. To the extent that judicial review has real consequences – for the protection of individual freedom and the distribution of material resources – its effectiveness as an institution depends on the extent to which, and the manner in which, the judiciary's power to strike down legislative and executive conduct is accepted, institutionalized, and made real in the national political life of the country concerned. That, at root, is a question of constitutional culture – of the way in which the formal promise of law's social-systemic distinctiveness from politics is embedded in societal conceptions of the law/politics relation.

Researching this issue calls for a different combination of approaches to the ones that have thus far been deployed in comparative constitutional studies (to use, for the moment, the most capacious term for the field). On the one hand, the evolution of societal conceptions of the law/politics relation is something that is amenable to the historical case study method in comparative politics.[16] On the other, the process through which law in certain circumstances establishes its autonomy from politics is something with which sociologists of law have long been preoccupied.[17] The changing nature of law's claim to authority, for its part, is a question of the presentational style of judicial decisions and other public documents, for which the techniques of close textual analysis developed by legal academics are best suited. Finally, the normative dimension of the question requires sensitivity both to the way in which concepts like "authority" and "legitimacy" are understood in legal and political theory and to the more specific literature around the moral justification for judicial review. Blending all these approaches together is no simple task, but it is made easier by using a typological theory that allows, first, for rigorous definition of the core concepts and, second, for comparative exploration of a complex sociological process in which there are multiple lines of causation that cannot be reduced to a simple set of independent and dependent variables.

The first motivation for writing this book, then, is to extend the field of comparative constitutional studies into an area where it has yet to go – to provide a theoretical framework within which the historical development of competing ideas about the purpose and moral legitimacy of judicial review in different societies may be compared. While there are several studies of the evolution of judicial review in this sense in older constitutional democracies –

---

[16]   See Alexander L. George and Andrew Bennett, *Case Studies and Theory Development in the Social Sciences* (Cambridge, MA: MIT Press, 2005).

[17]   See the discussion of the literature in Chapter 2, Section 2.1.

like the US,[18] Germany,[19] and India[20] – the field at present lacks a conceptual vocabulary and framework for considering the general nature of this phenomenon.

The second motivation is to correct some of the American bias in the field. As will be stressed over the course of this study, there are numerous ways in which the relationship between law and politics is understood in different constitutional cultures. To date, however, much of the field has been premised on the unconscious scientization of the specifically American conception of this relationship. That has had a profoundly distorting effect on the field that is in urgent need of remedying. Indeed, it will be one of the main contentions of this study that comparative work on judicial review, if it is to be at all persuasive, must take questions of constitutional culture into account. This is an old insight from comparative law, but one that appears to have been lost in the search for generalizable theories of judicial behavior.

The third motivation for this study is a desire to reconnect legal-academic research on constitutionalism and judicial review to perspectives from comparative law and legal sociology. As the broader field of comparative constitutional studies has developed, academic lawyers have been sucked into a conversation with political scientists that has seen them abandon, or fail even to take up, many of the intellectual resources available to them in these older and arguably more appropriate disciplines. Comparative constitutional lawyers thus tend to be national constitutional scholars in the first instance, who began to work comparatively as judicial review spread and threw up recurrent problems of doctrinal interpretation, moral justification, and constitutional design. They are not, with rare exceptions,[21] comparative lawyers who happen to have chosen to specialize in comparative *constitutional* law. This has had an impact on how comparative constitutional law is conducted and on the kinds of interdisciplinary conversations that have developed. Driven by the need to respond to political scientists, comparative constitutional

[18]   See, for example, Morton J. Horwitz, *The Transformation of American Law, 1870–1960: The Crisis of Legal Orthodoxy* (New York: Oxford University Press, 1992).

[19]   Michaela Hailbronner, *Traditions and Transformations: The Rise of German Constitutionalism* (Oxford: Oxford University Press, 2015).

[20]   Manoj Mate, "Public Interest Litigation and the Transformation of the Supreme Court of India" in Diana Kapiszewski, Gordon Silverstein, and Robert A. Kagan (eds.), *Consequential Courts: Judicial Roles in Global Perspective* (New York: Cambridge University Press, 2013) 262.

[21]   See, for example, Jacco Bomhoff, *Balancing Constitutional Rights: The Origins and Meanings of Postwar Legal Discourse* (Cambridge: Cambridge University Press, 2013).

lawyers have mostly lost contact with comparative law and legal sociology.[22]

The latter discipline, in particular, has several qualities that could be of assistance. One is its openness to understanding law as a motivating ideal and a constitutive influence on judicial decision-making.[23] Another quality is its long-established tradition of operationalizing law as a comparative variable – whether that be law in the form of legal culture or law in the form of traditions of legal reasoning.[24] While there are some concerns in the sociological literature about the extent to which the concept of legal culture may be deployed comparatively,[25] these concerns are addressed by the typological approach used here. When the focus falls on competing conceptions of the law/politics relation, what matters is the extent to which the constitutional culture concerned remains committed to the ideal of law's autonomy from politics. Fine-grained variations in the strength of this ideal, of course, are not measurable in any practical way. But much sociological work on law uses a broad distinction between, on the one hand, legal cultures in which the ideal of law's autonomy from politics is hegemonic and, on the other, legal cultures where this ideal has either never had much purchase or has significantly declined in strength.[26] For the typological approach pursued in this study, that simple distinction suffices.

The turn to sociology, it is hoped, may help to correct the current obsession in the field with the direct causal influence of politics on judicial decision-making. This emphasis is essentially a hangover from the American debate

[22] See Stephen Gardbaum, "How Do We and Should We Compare Constitutional Law" in Samantha Besson, Lukas Heckendorn, and Samuel Jube (eds.), *Comparing Comparative Law* (Geneva: Schulthess, 2017).

[23] As discussed in Chapter 1, the historical institutionalist school in political science is also open to this understanding, as indeed was one of the leading legal realists, Karl Llewellyn. (See particularly Karl N. Llewellyn, *The Common Law Tradition: Deciding Appeals* (Boston, MA: Little Brown, 1960).) In the nature of things, however, historical institutionalism has been difficult to deploy comparatively, and thus has not exerted a great deal of influence on comparative constitutional studies to date.

[24] See Martin Krygier, "Law as Tradition" (1986) 5 *Law and Philosophy* 237.

[25] See Roger Cotterrell, "The Concept of Legal Culture" in David Nelken (ed.), *Comparing Legal Cultures* (Aldershot: Dartmouth, 1997) 13; David Nelken, "Using the Concept of Legal Culture" (2004) 29 *Australian Journal of Legal Philosophy* 1; David Nelken, "Comparative Legal Research and Legal Culture: Facts, Approaches, and Values" (2016) 12 *Annual Review of Law and Social Science* 45.

[26] See, for example, Max Weber, *Economy and Society*, ed. Günther Roth and Claus Wittich (New York: Bedminister Press, 1968); C. Roberto Mangabeira Unger, *Law in Modern Society* (New York: Free Press, 1976) 52–3; Phillippe Nonet and Philip Selznick, *Toward Responsive Law: Law & Society in Transition* (New Brunswick, NJ: Transaction Publishers, 2001 [1978]); Niklas Luhmann, *Law as a Social System* trans. K. A. Ziegert (2004) 112.

about the determinacy of law, which may be traced all the way back to the legal realist critique of formalist modes of legal reasoning in the 1920s and 1930s. While important, and used in this study in a self-consciously disruptive way,[27] that historical episode is what lies behind the constitutional cultural bias in the field alluded to earlier. US political scientists and comparative lawyers, socialized as they are in a postrealist conception of the law/politics relation, have constructed the field of comparative constitutional studies on those foundations, seldom interrogating the extent to which their constitutional-cultural assumptions affect the research questions they are asking. In consequence, much research in comparative constitutional studies either leeches out relevant constitutional-cultural differences, or strains to fit complex social processes under general covering laws, in the process flattening out, homogenizing, and draining those processes of color.[28]

A similar criticism may be made of the contribution of legal and political theory to the field. One might mention here particularly Jeremy Waldron's presentation of the "Core of the Case against Judicial Review." In that highly influential paper, Waldron expresses a desire to "identify a core argument against judicial review that is independent of both its historical manifestations and questions about its particular effects."[29] No enterprise could be more destined to fail from a sociological perspective, according to which everything hinges on how judicial review is instantiated in practice and what social processes it actually triggers. In any case, Waldron's project fails on its own terms because the assumptions that he says must hold if his normative argument is to apply are assumptions that depend on assessments that are no less sociologically complex than the ones he wants to avoid.[30] Even where one's interests are principally normative, there is no way of escaping the need to assess judicial review in all its empirical complexity.

[27] See Chapter 2.
[28] Again, rare exceptions are Javier A. Couso, Alexandra Huneeus, and Rachel Sieder (eds.), *Cultures of Legality: Judicialization and Political Activism in Latin America* (Cambridge: Cambridge University Press, 2010) and Hailbronner, *Traditions and Transformations*.
[29] See Jeremy Waldron, "The Core of the Case against Judicial Review" (2006) 115 *Yale Law Journal* 1346, 1351.
[30] Waldron's assumptions include, for example, the assumption that democratic institutions should be in reasonably good working order (ibid 1360). For a full critique of the way in which Waldron's assumptions undermine his argument, see Theunis Roux, "In Defence of Empirical Entanglement: The Methodological Flaw in Waldron's Case against Judicial Review" in Ron Levy and Graeme Orr (eds.), *The Cambridge Handbook of Deliberative Constitutionalism* (Cambridge: Cambridge University Press, 2018) 203. Chapter 7 develops this critique of Waldron's argument.

In short, this study is theoretically informed, empirically grounded, and normatively inflected. It takes as its main concern the evolutionary dynamics of JR regimes, understood as complexes of legitimating ideas about the law/politics relation in societies that have adopted a system of judicial review. The aim is to investigate: first, whether this abstract concept provides a useful lens through which to examine the historical development of judicial review in different societies; second, to examine whether there are any systematic patterns in the way JR regimes change character over time; and, third, to assess the strengths and weaknesses of the different types of JR regimes from the standpoint of a commitment to liberal democracy. Those three topics may be expressed in the form of the following research questions: What drives the development of JR regimes and what different forms do they take? Do JR regimes, once stabilized, ever change their fundamental character? If so, what causes that to happen – their internal developmental logic or exogenous factors? Are some types of JR regime more normatively attractive than others? And, finally, what are the practical implications of the answers to these questions for judges, legal practitioners, democracy activists, and others engaging with the practice of judicial review?

Chapter 1 starts by assessing the current state of comparative constitutional law/comparative judicial politics, both with a view to situating this study in this line of research and to flesh out some of the observations made in this overview about its limitations. The chapter first defines the institutional scope of this study and what its main aims and objectives are. It then explains how comparative research on constitutionalism and judicial review has come to be formed around a pair of mutually reinforcing blind spots: political scientists' relative inattention to the ideational dimension of judicial review and academic lawyers' lack of interest in general theorizing. The chapter ends by explaining the methodology to be followed and the choice of case studies.

Chapter 2 presents the typological theory of JR-regime change that grounds the entire study. The adoption of a system of judicial review, the theory goes, sets in train a dynamic, interactive process in which legal and political actors lay claim to distinct forms of authority. The interaction of these claims is structured by competing understandings of law's legitimate claim to authority and its relationship to political authority. The process is dynamic in so far as societal understandings of the law/politics relation, even as they are called upon to justify particular outcomes, are constantly evolving. Three such evolutionary processes are identified: the *consolidation* of a JR regime, which describes the emergence of a relatively stable, dominant societal understanding of the law/politics relation; the *transformation* of a JR regime, which describes a situation where one dominant societal understanding of the law/

politics relation transitions to another; and *incremental change* to a JR regime, which refers to any observable change in societal understandings of the law/politics relation short of wholesale transformation.

Chapters 3–5 develop this theory through in-depth case studies of the evolution of societal conceptions of the law/politics relation in Australia, India, and Zimbabwe. Each case study both uses the theory as a heuristic device and refines it, in this way creating a dialogue between the theory and the local literature on judicial review in the country concerned.

A detailed explanation for the choice of case studies is given in Chapter 1. In essence, the drivers were the need to find a relatively small number of societies whose JR regimes could be used to illustrate the four ideal-typical JR regimes and the processes of consolidation, transformation, and within-regime incremental change. The fact that these three societies evince very different histories of JR-regime change, notwithstanding their shared status as former British colonies with legal systems based on the common law, at the same time helps to eliminate those two background factors as explanatory variables. By demonstrating in the detailed case studies that the historical development of judicial review in Australia, India, and Zimbabwe may be represented in terms of the evolution of their respective JR regimes, Chapters 3–5 show that the typological theory has real-world application.

Chapter 6 conducts a comparative analysis of JR-regime change in ten additional countries: Colombia, Chile, Singapore, Germany, Myanmar, South Africa, Hungary, Indonesia, Egypt, and the OPT. These countries were chosen for reasons explained at the beginning of that chapter: to populate the typology and demonstrate its application beyond the former British colonial context, and to provide a richer empirical basis for exploring the processes of consolidation, transformation, and incremental change. After demonstrating the geographic coverage of the theory, Chapter 6 identifies four recurrent pathways to JR-regime consolidation and the causal mechanism driving JR-regime transformation.

Chapter 7 summarizes this study's main findings and sets out its normative and practical implications for those engaged in designing, implementing, and utilizing systems of judicial review.

1

Preliminaries

Every society that adopts a system of judicial review draws on an existing set of ideas about the appropriate relationship between law and politics. At the same time, the establishment of judicial review influences the development of these ideas in profound ways. Understanding the dynamics of this process should be one of the core questions of comparative research. After all, our interest in the post-1945 "global spread of constitutionalism and judicial review"[1] emanates not just from a desire to explain the causes and practical policy consequences of this phenomenon. It also has to do with the impact of judicial review on the constitutional culture of the societies concerned. If judicial review is to achieve its object of holding political actors to account, it needs to be institutionalized in the national political life of the society concerned.[2] That means that support for judicial review needs to stem not just from political actors' rational self-interest, but also from deep-seated, value-laden commitments. And yet the ideational dimension of judicial review in this sense has not been adequately researched. We know a lot about the political factors that influence judicial decision-making under various conditions, but very little about the process through which societal understandings of the law/politics relation evolve and change character over time.

The principal reason for this gap in our understanding, this chapter argues, is that the comparative study of constitutionalism and judicial review has been dominated by two groups of scholars who, for different reasons, have paid insufficient attention to ideational questions. Comparative constitutional lawyers, for their part, have been preoccupied with the impact of the global spread of judicial review on the practice of constitutional law. While the role

---

[1] Ran Hirschl, *Comparative Matters: The Renaissance of Comparative Constitutional Law* (Oxford: Oxford University Press, 2014) 1.

[2] On the sense of the term "institutionalization" used here, see Philip Selznick, *The Moral Commonwealth: Social Theory and the Promise of Community* (Berkeley, CA: University of California Press, 1992) 232.

of constitutional culture has been raised in the context of understanding why certain doctrines have migrated from one country to another and what happens to them when they get there, few comparative constitutional lawyers have thought systematically about how to compare constitutional cultures or how to analyze their development over time. On the part of comparative judicial politics scholars, the problem has been a tendency to see law, and thus judicial review, as a subsystem of politics. Proceeding from a postrealist premise about the inevitable politicization of law in systems of judicial review, comparative judicial politics scholars have focused their efforts on exploring the measurable causal influence of politics on constitutional adjudication. They have consequently been inattentive to variations both within and between societies in the way the relationship between law and politics is conceived, and how such variations may affect the practical operation of judicial review.

This chapter makes the detailed case for this assessment of the literature while at the same time situating this study within – and to a certain extent, *across* – the fields of comparative constitutional law and comparative judicial politics. Section 1.1 begins by delimiting the institutional scope of this study. Section 1.2 then reflects on the work that comparativists have been doing on the global spread of constitutionalism and judicial review and explains how it has come about that so little attention has been paid to ideational questions. Section 1.3 outlines this study's theoretical framework, methodological approach, and the solution it proposes to the challenge of generating comparative insights about the politico-legal dynamics of judicial review. Finally, Section 1.4 explains the reasons behind the choice of this study's three main case studies.

1.1 INSTITUTIONAL SCOPE

The scope of this study is circumscribed in the first instance by its focus on a distinct institutional arrangement, one in which the judiciary has been given the power to decide whether challenged conduct conforms to the requirements of a written constitution and to enforce its decisions by handing down orders with which its addressees are legally obliged to comply. For the purposes of this study, that arrangement encompasses situations where: (1) the power to enforce the constitution has been entrusted either to a specialist constitutional court or to another kind of national high court or group of national high courts; (2) the power to enforce the constitution is exercised in relation to legislative or executive conduct or both and may also extend to the conduct of private actors; (3) the power to review legislation is exercised either before the legislation has taken effect or after it has entered into force, or both; (4) the judiciary's power to interpret the constitution is final in the sense that the addressees of its orders are not legally free to disregard or overturn them except by way of constitutional amendment; and (5) the major grounds of unconstitutionality are the challenged conduct's lack of conformity to the standards set by a bill of rights or a list of legislative competences.

Defined in this way, the institutional scope of this study is quite broad.[3] It encompasses judicial review in both its "concrete" and "abstract" forms,[4] centralized and decentralized review,[5] fundamental rights and federalist review,[6] and the vertical and horizontal application of rights.[7] There is, however, one significant exclusion, and that is "weak-form" judicial review of the kind found in the United Kingdom, New Zealand, and (more debatably) Canada.[8] In those countries the judiciary does not have the power to finally determine the constitutionality of legislative or executive conduct, either because the addressees of the court's orders are legally free to disregard them (as in the United Kingdom and New Zealand) or because there is some means, short of constitutional amendment, through which decisions enforcing the constitution may be overridden (as in Canada).[9] While there is a view in the literature that weak-form judicial review may not be all that different, for practical purposes, from its strong-form cousin,[10] the distinction between these two types of system in theory signals a fundamentally different approach to the allocation of constitutional power between the judicial and political branches. That difference may be significant enough to drive real differences in the way the law/politics distinction is conceived and, in turn, how such conceptions impact on the practical operation of judicial review. Since examining whether

---

[3] See David S. Law and Mila Versteeg, "The Declining Influence of the US Constitution" (2012) 87 *New York University Law Review* 762, 766 (reporting that "almost 90 percent of all countries possess written constitutional documents backed by some kind of judicial enforcement").

[4] In systems of concrete review, the reviewing court exercises its powers in relation to an allegation by one of the parties to a dispute that law sought to be applied to that dispute is unconstitutional. In systems of abstract review, the constitutionality of a law may be challenged before it takes effect.

[5] In centralized systems, judicial review is performed by a specialist constitutional court. In decentralized systems, several different courts or layers of the judiciary may be able to perform this function.

[6] Australia is the main example of an exclusively federalist review system.

[7] The distinction concerns whether private parties may be held accountable for rights violations.

[8] On the operation of weak-form systems of judicial review, see Stephen Gardbaum, *The New Commonwealth Model of Constitutionalism: Theory and Practice* (New York: Cambridge University Press, 2012); Mark Tushnet, *Weak Courts, Strong Rights: Judicial Review and Social Welfare Rights in Comparative Constitutional Law* (Princeton, NJ: Princeton University Press, 2009) 24–33.

[9] The reference here is to Canada's famous "notwithstanding clause."

[10] See Tushnet, *Weak Courts, Strong Rights* 27.

this is in fact so is not the main purpose of this study, it is simpler to leave weak-form systems out of its scope. In any case, they comprise only a small proportion of the whole.[11]

Note also two points of terminology up front. First, the term "constitutional court" will be used here to refer both to constitutional courts proper – i.e., courts whose jurisdiction is restricted to constitutional matters – and to national high courts (like the US Supreme Court) which perform judicial review functions alongside other original-jurisdiction and appellate functions. While there are important differences between those two types of situation, the term "constitutional court" captures what is common to both and will be used here to refer to nonspecialist constitutional courts insofar as they exercise the power of judicial review. Secondly, the American term "judicial review" will be used in preference to the English term "constitutional review" to describe the function courts perform when reviewing public or private conduct for conformance to a supreme-law constitution.[12] In its usage here, in other words, "judicial review" does not include the process through which judges test the conformance of administrative action to the terms of an authorizing statute.

1.2 INATTENTION TO IDEATIONAL QUESTIONS

There is an ongoing debate about how best to understand the scholarly work that is being done on constitutionalism and judicial review. In a recent influential treatment, Ran Hirschl argued that this body of work should be seen as belonging to the multidisciplinary field of "comparative constitutional studies."[13] Though taking a variety of forms, Hirschl proposed there was enough commonality of purpose to think of the research being conducted in this field as a single enterprise.

This study's approach is somewhat different. While sympathetic to Hirschl's call for interdisciplinary conversations, the position taken here is that the work that legal academics and political scientists have been doing is conceptually and methodologically quite distinct.[14] For comparative constitutional lawyers,

---

[11] See Mila Versteeg and Tom Ginsburg, "Why Do Countries Adopt Constitutional Review?" (2013) 29 University of Virginia School of Law Public Law and Legal Theory Research Paper Series 2 (reporting that strong-form judicial review has been adopted in 150 of 194 United Nations member countries).

[12] See Mark Tushnet, *Advanced Introduction to Comparative Constitutional Law* (Cheltenham: Edward Elgar, 2014) 6.

[13] Ran Hirschl, *Comparative Matters: The Renaissance of Comparative Constitutional Law* (Oxford: Oxford University Press, 2014).

[14] For the full version of this argument, see Theunis Roux, "Comparative Constitutional Studies: Two Fields or One?" (2017) 13 *Annual Review of Law and Social Science* 123. For related

the primary purpose of research in this area is to understand the way that the global spread of constitutionalism and judicial review is changing the practice of constitutional law in the jurisdictions they study. For comparative judicial politics scholars, on the other hand, the focus is on explaining the causes of this phenomenon and its impact on contemporary modes of governance. In that line of research, normative questions about the appropriateness of what is happening tend to be pushed to one side. Rather, the concern is to explain and theorize the ongoing political dynamics.

When research on comparative constitutionalism is understood as consisting of two distinct enterprises in this way, it is immediately apparent why there has been so little work done on the ideational dimension of judicial review. Comparative constitutional lawyers, though more alive to the influence of constitutional culture, lack the theory-building ambitions of political scientists. Their treatment of ideational questions has thus tended to be directed either at improving the use of foreign law for doctrinal purposes or at understanding how legal doctrines in different societies have come to take the form they have. Comparative judicial politics scholars, by contrast, *are* interested in theory building. But the predominance of behavioralist and rational choice approaches in US political science has led to a focus on interests rather than ideas and on measurable causal effects rather than the structuring influence of societal conceptions of the law/politics relation. As we shall see, there have been exceptions on both sides of the disciplinary divide. But these have been the main preoccupations in each case. In consequence, there have been very few attempts, on the one hand, to theorize the impact of judicial review on the historical development of societal conceptions of the law/politics relation, and, on the other, to investigate how variations within and between societies in such conceptions affect the practical operation of judicial review.

Comparative constitutional lawyers, to start on that side of the divide, have been engaged in three main types of research.[15] The first type (CCL Type 1) is purely doctrinal inasmuch as it uses foreign law to give content to constitutional norms in a particular jurisdiction. Exactly how this is done depends on the roles legal scholars play in the legal system concerned and on what the rules governing reference to foreign law are. For continental European legal scholars, used as they are to being at the center of the legal system, comparative

---

critiques of Hirschl's take on the field, see Katharine G. Young, "On What Matters in Comparative Constitutional Law: A Comment on Hirschl" (2016) 96 *Boston University Law Review* 1375; Vicki C. Jackson, "Comparative Constitutional Law, Legal Realism, and Empirical Legal Science" (2016) 96 *Boston University Law Review* 1359.

[15]   Parts of this discussion reproduce passages from Theunis Roux, "Comparative Constitutional Studies: Two Fields or One?"

constitutional law as "doctrinal constructivism" comes naturally.[16] Scholars working in this tradition think of themselves as participating in the construction of constitutional law doctrine – not just describing it from without, but "shap[ing] it from within."[17] Anglo-American legal scholars, by contrast, tend to position themselves as somewhat more detached "observers" of the way judges draw on foreign law.[18] Rather than participating in the construction of doctrine, they prefer to reflect on the methods judges use when relying on foreign law. The exact form that CCL Type 1 takes also depends on whether reliance on foreign law is explicitly endorsed by the constitutional order in question (as is the case in South Africa, for example) or a more contested practice that needs to be justified (as is the case in the United States).

Closely related to this type of research is research on the way judges in different jurisdictions have responded to the demand that they take account of foreign law in constitutional decision-making (CCL Type 2). This form of research is a logical extension of Anglo-American legal scholars' more detached role in doctrinal construction. Starting in the late 1990s in the United States with the controversy over Justice Breyer's reference to foreign law in his dissenting opinion in *Printz v. United States*,[19] CCL Type 2 has broadened into the study of the way in which judges in different parts of the world have responded to the globalization of judicial review.[20] Although doctrinally oriented in one sense – knowledge generated by this form of research may conceivably be fed back into the practice of constitutional law in a particular jurisdiction – the point of CCL Type 2 is to contribute to a legal-system-independent body of knowledge about the characteristic ways judges respond to the demand to take account of foreign law and, by extension, to

---

[16] Armin Von Bogdandy, "Comparative Constitutional Law: A Continental Perspective" in Michel Rosenfeld and András Sajó (eds.), *The Oxford Handbook of Comparative Constitutional Law* (Oxford: Oxford University Press, 2012) 25, 26.

[17] Ibid.

[18] Michel Rosenfeld, "Comparative Constitutional Analysis in United States Adjudication and Scholarship" in Michel Rosenfeld and András Sajó (eds.), *The Oxford Handbook of Comparative Constitutional Law* (Oxford: Oxford University Press, 2012) 38, 39.

[19] 521 US 898 (1997). See, for example, Mark Tushnet, "The Possibilities of Comparative Constitutional Law" (1999) 108 *Yale Law Journal* 122; Jeremy Waldron, "Foreign Law and the Modern *Ius Gentium*" (2005) 119 *Harvard Law Review* 129; Vicki C. Jackson, "Constitutional Comparisons: Convergence, Resistance, Engagement" (2005) 119 *Harvard Law Review* 109; Sujit Choudhry, "Migration as a New Metaphor in Comparative Constitutional Law" in Sujit Choudhry (ed.), *The Migration of Constitutional Ideas* (Cambridge: Cambridge University Press, 2006) 1; Rosalind Dixon, "A Democratic Theory of Constitutional Comparison" (2008) 56 *American Journal of Comparative Law* 947.

[20] Cheryl Saunders, "The Use and Misuse of Comparative Constitutional Law" (2006) 13 *Indiana Journal of Global Legal Studies* 37; Vicki C. Jackson, *Constitutional Engagement in a Transnational Era* (Oxford: Oxford University Press, 2010).

contribute to transnational understanding of the methodologies of doctrinally oriented comparison.[21]

Neither CCL Type 1 nor CCL Type 2 is concerned with systematically researching variations in constitutional culture. To be sure, in seeking to contribute to the construction of constitutional law doctrine, CCL Type 1 proceeds from within the argumentative frameworks, value-laden commitments, and reasoning practices of a particular legal tradition. The best comparative work of this kind also takes constitutional-cultural variations into account in the process of utilizing foreign doctrines. But there is rarely any attempt to think systematically about these variations or to analyze their development over time. Rather, attention to constitutional culture in the case of CCL Type 1 is directed at extracting the maximum legal-interpretive value from the comparison. Likewise, CCL Type 2 pays some attention to variations in the way different legal systems have responded to the challenge of referring to foreign law, but the focus is on classifying these various types of response, rather than the constitutional-cultural differences that may be driving them.

The third major type of CCL research (CCL Type 3) concerns research into the way in which particular constitutional doctrines, reasoning methodologies, structures, and rights are instantiated in different legal orders. For a time it was contended that constitutional law in different jurisdictions was converging on a core set of principles,[22] or that there might even be such a thing as a body of "generic constitutional law."[23] This is no longer the dominant view, however. Rather, in line with the ascendance of conceptions of reference to foreign law as forms of transnational engagement or dialogue,[24] the purpose of CCL Type 3 is today seen as being to clarify the way in which local constitutional cultures and institutional settings influence the meaning given to similar-seeming norms and practices. This form of research, in other words,

---

[21] Vicki Jackson has been particularly influential here in distinguishing between "postures" of "resistance," "convergence," and "engagement" – responses that are notionally applicable to all jurisdictions in which recourse to foreign law occurs (Jackson, *Constitutional Engagement in a Transnational Era*). On this approach, neither a universalist faith in the eventual emergence of a common understanding of all constitutional structures and doctrines, nor an expressivist denial of the value of constitutional comparison, is winning or should win the day.

[22] Norman Dorsen, Michel Rosenfeld, András Sajó, Sandra Baer (eds.), Comparative Constitutionalism: Cases and Materials 1ed (St Paul, MN: Thomson West, 2003); David M. Beatty, *The Ultimate Rule of Law* (Oxford: Oxford University Press, 2004).

[23] David S. Law, "Generic Constitutional Law" (2005) 89 Minnesota Law Review 652.

[24] Jackson, *Constitutional Engagement in a Transnational Era*; Sujit Choudhry, "Globalization in Search of Justification: Toward a Theory of Comparative Constitutional Interpretation" (1999) 74 *Indiana Law Journal* 819; Ruti Teitel, "Comparative Constitutional Law in a Global Age" (2004) 117 *Harvard Law Review* 2570.

takes the expressivist insight that constitutional law, like all law, needs to be viewed through the lens of legal culture,[25] and uses this insight not as a basis to give up on the enterprise of CCL, but to drive the project of enhanced understanding through contrast and comparison.

In its attention to issues of legal culture, CCL Type 3 clearly takes account of the ideational dimension of judicial review. As they pass between societies, legal doctrines are seen as taking on different meanings according to the convictions judges hold about their institutional role and legitimate forms of legal reasoning. Several illuminating studies have thus shown how the doctrine of proportionality takes on the color of the background constitutional culture to which it migrates.[26] In Australia, for example, there was for a long time strong resistance to proportionality as a potentially open-ended, value-laden form of inquiry. Even after proportionality's endorsement in the *McCloy* case,[27] debates have continued over how best to reconcile the doctrine with prevailing modes of legal reasoning and conceptions of law's appropriate relationship to politics.[28] Similar debates took place in Germany in the 1950s and 1960s as the Federal Constitutional Court worked out how to reconcile proportionality with Germany's long-standing tradition of legalism.[29] Recent research on the constitutional-cultural reasons for the US Supreme Court's distrust of proportionality is also exemplary of this trend.[30]

The value of CCL Type 3 is thus that it draws attention to the way in which constitutional-cultural variations impact on the meaning given to transnational constitutional concepts. This style of research, however, has generally not progressed to the systematic study of how these variations affect the practice of judicial review and how constitutional cultures develop and change character over time. Rather, the concern is to understand why certain doctrines have travelled and others not, and how similar-seeming doctrines take on different forms in different constitutional cultures.

---

[25] Roger Cotterrell, "Comparative Law and Legal Culture" in M. Reimann and R. Zimmermann (eds.), *The Oxford Handbook of Comparative Law* (Oxford: Oxford University Press, 2006) 710.

[26] Jacco Bomhoff, *Balancing Constitutional Rights: The Origins and Meanings of Postwar Legal Discourse* (Cambridge: Cambridge University Press, 2013); Moshe Cohen-Eliya and Iddo Porat, "American Balancing and German Proportionality: The Historical Origins" (2010) 8 *International Journal of Constitutional Law* 263.

[27] *McCloy v New South Wales* (2015) HCA 34.

[28] Adrienne Stone, "Proportionality: Between Substance and Method" draft paper presented at Comparative Constitutional Law Roundtable, UNSW Law (August 2017).

[29] Michaela Hailbronner, *Traditions and Transformations: The Rise of German Constitutionalism* (Oxford: Oxford University Press, 2015).

[30] Bomhoff, *Balancing Constitutional Rights*; Cohen-Eliya and Porat, "American Balancing and German Proportionality."

There are some exceptions to this generalization, and the work of these scholars comes closest to what is being attempted here. Michaela Hailbronner, for example, argues that it is impossible to understand the postwar development of German constitutionalism without appreciating the character of the constitutional culture in which judicial review was embedded.[31] To this end, she develops a comparative typology of constitutional cultures based on varying "concepts of law" ("reactive" and "activist") and "models of authority" ("hierarchical" and "coordinate").[32] The development of this typology constitutes a major advance in using the concept of constitutional culture to understand the evolution of constitutional orders over time. Hailbronner herself uses it to identify the characteristic features of contemporary German constitutionalism and to explain how these features developed from their pre-1950 origins. In the course of that explanation, she contrasts the peculiar German combination of activist law and hierarchical authority with concepts of law and models of authority in the US, Japan, and South Africa.[33] In keeping with most comparative constitutional lawyers, however, Hailbronner does not in the end attempt to present a general theory of constitutional development across all her ideal types. Her typology is rather a heuristic that is used to illuminate one particular case.

The other major study that deploys constitutional culture as a comparative variable, this time by a political scientist, is Gary Jacobsohn's work on "constitutional identity."[34] One of Jacobsohn's central claims is that the fundamental political commitments of a society – its "self-understanding" – are different from, and may be in tension with, its formal written constitution.[35] He then uses that fertile idea to explore such issues as cross-country variation in receptiveness to the doctrine of unconstitutional constitutional amendments,[36] the different approaches that constitutional courts in Ireland, India, and Israel have taken to the use of foreign law,[37] and the distinction between "militant" and "acquiescent" models of constitutionalism.[38] Jacobsohn's study is illuminated by a subtle understanding of the dynamic development of constitutional traditions within the parameters of more fixed national characteristics.[39] In chapter 2 he presents a conceptual framework for this understanding, likening the development of

[31] Ibid.
[32] Hailbronner, *Traditions and Transformations* 14–39.
[33] Ibid.
[34] Gary Jeffrey Jacobsohn, *Constitutional Identity* (Cambridge, MA: Harvard University Press, 2010).
[35] See particularly ibid 149 ("disjuncture between a constitution and a society").
[36] Ibid 34–83.
[37] Ibid 136–212.
[38] Ibid 213–70.
[39] Ibid 104.

constitutional identity to the development of human personality – open to change but tied in some ways to past commitments and influenced by the contingency of unforeseen events.[40] In this way, Jacobsohn powerfully demonstrates how we might go about comparing general patterns in the development of constitutional orders that appear at first to be idiosyncratic expressions of a contested national political identity. Like Hailbronner, however, he does not seek to test the generalizability of his framework. Rather, he is content to use it as a guideline to aid understanding of a particular society's constitution.

This characteristic reluctance on the part of comparative constitutional lawyers and some interpretive political scientists to build testable theories is in stark contrast to the often ambitious theorizing in which the bulk of comparative judicial politics scholars have engaged. From the origins of the spread of constitutionalism and judicial review to the impact of party-political diffusion on judicial independence, there is now an impressive array of causal-explanatory political science theorizing on judicial review. The problem in this instance is not a lack of theoretical ambition, but inattention to ideational questions.

Despite one early objection,[41] research by American political scientists on the global spread of constitutionalism and judicial review has almost exclusively taken the form of causal-explanatory inquiry into the political origins and ongoing dynamics of this phenomenon. Within that focus, behavioralist and rational choice approaches have prevailed over historical institutionalist and ethnographic approaches of the sort advocated by Rogers Smith and Kim Lane Scheppele.[42] The reasons for this have not been examined but presumably have to do with the higher status of the first two approaches in US political science and with the difficulty of developing an in-depth, ethnographic understanding of long-run constitutional developments in more than a handful of countries. Whatever the cause, the consequence of this epistemological slant has been that comparative judicial politics scholars have tended not to stress the constitutive and constraining role of shared *societal* conceptions of the law/politics relation.[43] Rather, constitutional courts are modeled as political

---

[40] Ibid 84–135.
[41] Howard Gillman, "On Constructing a Science of Comparative Judicial Politics: Tate & Haynie's 'Authoritarianism and the Functions of Courts'" (1994) 28 *Law & Society Review* 355.
[42] Kim Lane Scheppele, "Constitutional Ethnography: An Introduction" (2004) 38 *Law & Society Review* 389; Rogers M. Smith, "Historical Institutionalism and the Study of Law" in Gregory A. Caldeira, R. Daniel Kelemen, and Keith E. Whittington (eds.), *The Oxford Handbook of Law and Politics* (Oxford: Oxford University Press, 2008) 46.
[43] Lisa Hilbink, "From Comparative Judicial Politics to Comparative Law and Politics" (2008) 18(12) *Law & Politics Book Review* 1098, 1099–1100.

institutions whose judges are motivated by a combination of their *personal* ideological values and institutional power-building aspirations.

Within this interest-based framework, there have been three main areas of concern: (1) the political origins of the global spread of constitutionalism and judicial review; (2) the conditions under which constitutional courts build their institutional legitimacy and play consequential roles in national political systems; and (3) the relative influences of law and politics on constitutional decision-making.

The two major contributions to the first area are Tom Ginsburg's "insurance theory" of judicial empowerment[44] and Ran Hirschl's "hegemonic preservation theory" of the judicialization of politics.[45] While these two theorizations technically fall outside the scope of this study because they are concerned with the political origins of judicial review rather than its post-establishment dynamics, they are relevant insofar as the political origins of judicial review continue to influence the subsequent evolution of this institution. Research in this area also usefully illustrates the way in which inattention to ideational questions leads to incomplete theorizations of the phenomenon being studied. It is accordingly worth spending a little time on each of the two main theorizations.

Ginsburg's insurance theory, for its part, posits that rational ruling elites and aspirant political power holders will adopt judicial review as a form of insurance against future electoral defeat.[46] It further posits that the strength of the judicial review system adopted will correlate to the degree of political uncertainty at the time of adoption.[47] Thus, a threatened political elite that fears an electoral loss, but which still has considerable bargaining power at the time of adoption, will insist on relatively strong judicial review powers. That demand may be conceded by an aspirant political power holder that sees constitutional negotiations as the most likely route to power and which in any case reckons on its capacity to control judicial review after power has been transferred.[48] The situation is reversed where the incumbent power holder does not fear electoral defeat, or where the aspirant power holder has greater bargaining power at the time of adoption and foresees an uncontested political future.[49]

---

[44]   Tom Ginsburg, *Judicial Review in New Democracies: Constitutional Courts in Asian Cases* (New York: Cambridge University Press, 2003).

[45]   Ran Hirschl, *Towards Juristocracy: The Origins and Consequences of the New Constitutionalism* (Cambridge, MA: Harvard University Press, 2007).

[46]   Ginsburg, *Judicial Review in New Democracies* 18.

[47]   Ibid.

[48]   Ibid 55–7 (discussing the South African experience as a "textbook illustration of the insurance theory").

[49]   Ibid 24.

Either way, the common idea is that negotiating parties will adopt a system of judicial review that calibrates the strength of the judiciary's review powers to the role they see judges playing in the protection of their fundamental political interests.[50]

Ginsburg explores this theory through three case studies of the adoption of judicial review in East Asia (Taiwan, Mongolia, and Korea), investigating in each case whether the strength of the judicial review system adopted and later institutionalized conforms to his theorization. And, indeed, the insurance theory explains the different powers given to constitutional courts in these instances. Ginsburg's theory has also subsequently been supported by other studies.[51] Nevertheless, the generalizability of his findings is undermined by his focus on three countries with weakly developed traditions of judicial independence. The methodological reason for that choice was to keep this variable constant, allowing the examination of the independent effects of political uncertainty.[52] But that way of proceeding eliminates by fiat the possibility that a country's legal culture, and culturally embedded notions of law's separateness from politics in particular, might make a difference to the timing and nature of a transition to constitutional democracy. In a highly legalist society like South Africa, for example, the 1991–4 constitutional negotiations proceeded in stages as political bargains were reduced to precise legal formulations that the parties were confident would be enforced. South Africa's strong tradition of legalism also explains why the negotiating parties were able to use (what was until that point) a unique two-stage constitution-making process to overcome political deadlocks.[53] That only occurred because the parties placed a particular kind of trust in law – not the strategic trust that Ginsburg posits, but a culturally conditioned trust of a sort that could have developed only from a long process of ideational development during which law came to

---

[50] Ibid.

[51] See Jodi S Finkel, *Judicial Reform as Political Insurance: Argentina, Peru, and Mexico in the 1990s* (Notre Dame, IN: University of Notre Dame Press, 2008) (applying Hirschl's theory to explain the judicialization process in these three countries). For an argument that the insurance theory fails to explain judicialization in Indonesia, see Hendrianto, "Institutional Choice and the New Indonesian Constitutional Court" in Andrew Harding and Pip Nicholson (eds.), *New Courts in Asia* (London: Routledge, 2009) 158, 162. See also Simon Butt, *The Constitutional Court and Democracy in Indonesia* (Leiden, NL: Brill Nijhoff, 2015) 16 n 13.

[52] See Hirschl, *Comparative Matters* 248–9.

[53] Ginsburg mentions this solution as a "key point" in the negotiations process (ibid 55, citing Heinz Klug, *Constituting Democracy: Law Globalism and South Africa's Political Reconstruction* (Cambridge: Cambridge University Press, 2000) 140). He does not go on to explain, however, precisely why it worked.

be seen as a distinctive and relatively autonomous social system.[54] In a country like Myanmar, by contrast, where this process has not occurred,[55] constitutional negotiations have repeatedly failed to get off the ground. By leaving out such differences, Ginsburg's insurance theory misses important aspects of the dynamics of constitution making that may continue into the postadoption politico-legal dynamics of judicial review.[56]

Hirschl's hegemonic preservation theory of judicial empowerment similarly downplays the structuring influence of ideas. The central claim in the case of this theory is that the adoption of judicial review may be explained as a function of strategic action on the part of political, economic, and judicial elites to respectively "preserve or enhance their political hegemony," "promot[e] a free market," and "enhance their political influence and international reputation."[57] To this end, Hirschl conducts a comparative study of the judicialization of politics in Canada, Israel, South Africa, and New Zealand, giving a detailed and interwoven analysis of each. Hirschl's skepticism about the possibility that an attachment to the ideal of law's autonomy from politics might ever be sincere, however, weakens his analysis, and leads him to interpret empirical facts in ways that support his thesis when other readings are possible.

It is not at all clear, for example, that South Africa fits Hirschl's theory. In that country, there was a significant break between the judicial elite that existed prior to the transition and the elite that took charge of the enforcement of the new constitutional order. In fact, if one is going to examine the matter in terms of material interests, it was precisely members of the oppositional group in the legal-professional community that the transition benefitted most. Whether it is accurate to describe what happened in these self-interested terms is, however, questionable. Constitutional Court justices Albie Sachs and Arthur Chaskalson, and other members of the new judicial elite, were motivated by principled political commitments and an admittedly idealistic, but nevertheless genuinely felt, conception of law as a bulwark against the

---

54 Jens Meierhenrich, *The Legacies of Law: Long-Run Consequences of Legal Development in South Africa, 1652–2000* (Cambridge: Cambridge University Press, 2008) (explaining the transition to constitutional democracy in South Africa as a function of South Africa's "dual state" in which confidence in law in the normative dimension of the state facilitated the transition).

55 See Nick Cheesman, *Opposing the Rule of Law: How Myanmar's Courts Make Law and Order* (Cambridge: Cambridge University Press, 2015).

56 See Theunis Roux, *The Politics of Principle: The First South African Constitutional Court, 1995–2005* (Cambridge: Cambridge University Press, 2013) (explaining the ongoing role of legalism in the South African case).

57 Hirschl, *Towards Juristocracy* 12.

abuse of political power.[58] To describe their positions on the Constitutional Court after the transition to democracy as amounting to the realization of their quest for "political influence and international reputation"[59] misrepresents their actual motivations.

Hirschl's analysis also fails to mention the rich tradition of thinking about rights within South Africa's dominant political party, the African National Congress (ANC). This leads him into a strained analysis of the adoption of the 1996 South African Constitution's property clause, in which the motivations of key actors are read as supporting his thesis that constitutionalized property rights are the lynchpins of elite attempts to maintain a position of privilege.[60] The real story behind the adoption of the property clause is a much more complex one than that. In brief, the ANC's decision to support the adoption of a property clause was not legally compelled by the two-stage constitution-making process. Rather, it had to do with its attempt to reconcile two rival conceptions of the social function of property in its internal political tradition going all the way back to the Freedom Charter.[61] That attempt is reflected in the text of the provision, which is anything but a neoliberal manifesto.[62] It is this nuanced compromise that the Constitutional Court has subsequently been at pains to draw out.[63] That South Africa's land reform process and social and economic transformation agenda more generally have been stymied by the ANC elite's co-optation by global capitalism is not a function of the constitutionalization of property rights, but of much larger political and economic forces. Indeed, the real story of South Africa's transition to democracy may be the inability of liberal-democratic constitutionalism to contain these forces.

The great virtue of Hirschl's work, to be sure, is that it challenges the simple idea that the adoption of a liberal-democratic constitution necessarily promotes human freedom. But his own theorization commits the opposite error of assuming that such constitutions are necessarily some sort of confidence trick through which legal and political elites give the impression of conceding a demand for democracy when in fact denying it. The truth is somewhere in between – in South Africa's case, a situation in which sincerely motivated actors, inspired by liberal-legalist ideals, established judicial review in the

---

[58] Roux, *Politics of Principle* 191–231.
[59] Hirschl, *Towards Juristocracy* 12.
[60] Ibid 94.
[61] See Roux, *Politics of Principle* 305–8 for the detailed argument on this point.
[62] Section 25 of the 1996 Constitution, for example, does not guarantee the payment of market value compensation in the event of expropriation.
[63] See Roux, *Politics of Principle* 312–31.

hope that it would help to drive social and economic transformation, but in which influential members of the liberation movement cynically manipulated the constitutional transition to serve their material interests.[64]

It is not surprising that interest-based theories have dominated the literature on the political origins of judicial review; if they are going to work anywhere, it is during the moment of constitutional pacting, which most closely fits these theories' rational-strategic assumptions. As soon as the focus shifts to the second area of concern – the conditions under which constitutional courts are able to build their institutional legitimacy and play a consequential role in national politics – the theorizations become more diverse. Here, the literature includes research on the consolidation of judicial review, particularly in new or fragile democracies – a topic that can be studied historically for older democracies, as it has been in US and Australia, for example.[65] Other major questions include the surprising forcefulness of some of the post-1989 constitutional courts,[66] the contribution constitutional courts may make to democratic stabilization,[67] and the phenomenon of political backlash or authoritarian backsliding, which has to do with the fate of initially forceful courts whose powers are reined in.[68] There is now also a new and burgeoning literature on judicial review in dysfunctional democracies and authoritarian settings.[69]

[64] For a similar critique, see Lisa Hilbink, "The Constituted Nature of Constituents' Interests: Historical and Ideational Factors in Judicial Empowerment" (2009) 62 *Political Research Quarterly* 781.

[65] Jack Knight and Lee Epstein, "On the Struggle for Judicial Supremacy" (1996) 30 *Law & Society Review* 87; Brian Galligan, *The Politics of the High Court* (Brisbane: University of Queensland Press, 1987).

[66] Samuel Issacharoff, *Fragile Democracies: Contested Power in the Era of Constitutional Courts* (New York: Cambridge University Press, 2015).

[67] Nancy Maveety and Anke Grosskopf, "'Constrained' Constitutional Courts as Conduits for Democratic Consolidation" (2004) 38 *Law & Society Review* 463; Christopher J. Walker, "Toward Democratic Consolidation: The Argentine Supreme Court, Judicial Independence, and the Rule of Law" (2008) 4 *High Court Quarterly Review* 54; Marcus Mietzner, "Political Conflict Resolution and Democratic Consolidation in Indonesia: The Role of the Constitutional Court" (2010) 10 *Journal of East Asian Studies* 397; Tom Ginsburg, "The Politics of Courts in Democratization: Four Junctures in Asia" in Diana Kapiszewski, Gordon Silverstein, and Robert A. Kagan (eds.), *Consequential Courts: Judicial Roles in Global Perspective* (New York: Cambridge University Press, 2013) 45.

[68] Miklós Bánkuti, Gábor Halmai, and Kim Lane Scheppele, "Hungary's Illiberal Turn: Disabling the Constitution" (2012) 23 *Journal of Democracy* 138; David Landau, "Abusive Constitutionalism" (2013) 47 *UC Davis Law Review* 189.

[69] Lisa Hilbink, *Judges beyond Politics in Democracy and Dictatorship: Lessons from Chile* (New York: Cambridge University Press, 2007); Tom Ginsburg and Tamir Moustafa (eds.), *Rule by Law: The Politics of Courts in Authoritarian Regimes* (New York: Cambridge University Press, 2008).

The common concern underlying all this research is to investigate the factors that influence constitutional courts' ongoing forcefulness or lack thereof. Why do democratically elected politicians tolerate judicial review given its anti-majoritarian features, and why do authoritarian regimes sometimes allow courts to act in seemingly independent ways?

According to the first major theorization in this area, the "regime politics" approach,[70] constitutional courts, even in mature democracies, have little capacity to contradict the policy preferences of powerful political actors. While not wholly denying constitutional courts' capacity to exert an independent influence on politics, regime theorists conceive of them as marginal policy makers at best, with some scope to fine-tune regime preferences, but rarely able to thwart those preferences for long. The implicit explanation for the forcefulness of constitutional courts according to this view is that this phenomenon is more apparent than real – an artifice of a focus on the short-term effects rather than the longer-term policy influence of judicial review.

In its extreme form, the regime politics approach, as Mark Graber has noted,[71] denies altogether the possibility of judicial "agency" – the idea that judges might be able to exert an independent influence on the course of a society's politics. But that extreme view is mostly attributed to the theory by its opponents.[72] However dominant a political coalition, there are always likely to be schisms within it, or parts of the political system that it does not control. Just as competition between political parties produces space for courts to act, so too might competition within a dominant coalition. There are in any case self-interested reasons why even a dominant coalition might promote a degree of judicial independence. These have to do with the capacity of independent judicial review to legitimate political decision-making – a capacity that may be exploited only if judges actually are given some genuinely independent influence over policy.[73] This is true both of

---

[70] This approach originates in Robert A. Dahl's well-known study of the US Supreme Court (see Robert A. Dahl, "Decision-making in a Democracy: The Supreme Court as a National Policy-Maker" (1957) 6 *Journal of Public Law* 279). For a helpful discussion, see Mark A. Graber, "Constitutional Politics in the Active Voice" in Diana Kapiszewski, Gordon Silverstein, and Robert A. Kagan (eds.), *Consequential Courts: Judicial Roles in Global Perspective* (New York: Cambridge University Press, 2013) 363, 368–71.

[71] Graber, "Constitutional Politics in the Active Voice" 368.

[72] Ibid.

[73] This point is connected to E. P. Thompson's well-known argument about the rule of law. See E. P. Thompson, *Whigs and Hunters: The Origin of the Black Act* (New York: Pantheon Books, 1975).

democracies in which there is a single dominant political party[74] and of authoritarian societies.[75]

Outside the United States, regime politics theory has largely given way to the "political fragmentation" thesis, which holds that an important condition for the expansion of judicial power, especially in new or otherwise fragile democracies, is the existence of significant political competition. The more fragmented the political system, the argument goes, the more likely it is that multiple political players will look to the judiciary, first, to protect their fundamental political interests and, secondly, to safeguard the democratic rights required to ensure a fair electoral process. Rebecca Bill Chavez, for example, has argued that variations in judicial independence at the national and provincial level in Argentina may be attributed to fluctuations in the concentration of political and economic power.[76] Tom Ginsburg similarly points to political diffusion as an important condition for the emergence of strong constitutional courts in Asia.[77]

The political fragmentation thesis is a logical extension of Ginsburg's insurance theory insofar as it posits that the uncertainty that drives the establishment of judicial review might also drive political actors' ongoing toleration of a court's powers. It accordingly suffers from the same weakness as that theory – an inability to differentiate between situations where law might warrant that trust and situations where law's autonomy from politics is too weakly developed to fulfil the expectations placed on it. In highly competitive but democratically unstable political settings, where the temptation to use the courts to marginalize political opponents is strong, it is not at all clear why the judiciary should be expected to safeguard the conditions for free political competition. And, indeed, a large-N empirical study has found that political competition is positively correlated to judicial independence only in developed democracies.[78] In less stable democracies, as Maria Popova's study of Russia and Ukraine

---

[74] See Meierhenrich, *The Legacies of Law* (on the National Party in apartheid South Africa).

[75] Tamir Moustafa, *The Struggle for Constitutional Power: Law, Politics, and Economic Development in Egypt* (New York: Cambridge University Press, 2009).

[76] Rebecca Bill Chavez, *The Rule of Law in Nascent Democracies: Judicial Politics in Argentina* (Stanford: Stanford University Press, 2004); Rebecca Bill Chavez, "The Rule of Law and Courts in Democratizing Regimes" in Gregory A. Caldeira, R. Daniel Kelemen, and Keith E. Whittington (eds.), *Oxford Handbook of Law and Politics* (New York: Oxford University Press, 2008) 63.

[77] Ginsburg, *Judicial Review in New Democracies*.

[78] Aylin Adin, "Judicial Independence across Democratic Regimes: Understanding the Varying Impact of Political Competition" (2013) 47 *Law & Society Review* 105.

attests,[79] political actors have moved to control the judiciary as a means of maintaining power.

Though not yet properly explored, the differential impact of political competition on judicial independence in stable and unstable democratic settings likely has something to do with the correlation between law's relative autonomy from politics in the first instance and its subordination to politics in the second. In stable settings, political competition supports judicial independence because the political costs of subordinating the judiciary are high. In unstable settings, where there are few political costs entailed by subordinating the judiciary and much to gain, the strategic calculus is different. Once again, therefore, it seems that an important theorization fits the facts only when account is taken of law's potential to develop into an autonomous social system with its own distinctive claim to authority.

The next set of theorizations of the conditions under which constitutional courts become forceful actors in national politics directly addresses the question of judicial agency and asks whether there is anything constitutional courts may do, assuming a reasonably favorable political context, to build their institutional legitimacy. Are constitutional courts purely political constructions, in the sense that their power waxes and wanes with changes in the political environment for judicial review, as both the regime politics and political fragmentation theories appear to suggest, or is there something that constitutional judges may do to exploit propitious political circumstances to promote their court's role?

The leading approach in this respect is Lee Epstein, Jack Knight, and Olga Shvetsova's "tolerance interval" theory of judicial empowerment,[80] which also features in Ginsburg's work[81] and in the so-called strategic approach to judicial decision-making.[82] On this approach, constitutional judges may and do act strategically to build their court's institutional legitimacy. They do this

---

[79] Maria Popova, *Politicized Justice in Emerging Democracies: A Study of Courts in Russia and Ukraine* (Cambridge: Cambridge University Press, 2014). Cf. Brad Epperly, "Political Competition and De Facto Judicial Independence in Non-Democracies" (2017) 56 *European Journal of Political Research* 279.

[80] Lee Epstein, Jack Knight, and Olga Shvetsova, "The Role of Constitutional Courts in the Establishment and Maintenance of Democratic Systems of Government" (2001) 35 *Law & Society Review* 117.

[81] Ginsburg, *Judicial Review in New Democracies*.

[82] Georg Vanberg, *The Politics of Constitutional Review in Germany* (New York: Cambridge University Press, 2005); Jeffrey K. Staton, *Judicial Power and Strategic Communication in Mexico* (New York: Cambridge University Press, 2010); Gretchen Helmke, *Courts under Constraints: Judges, Generals, and Presidents in Argentina* (New York: Cambridge University Press, 2012).

principally by anticipating the likely political response to their decisions and adjusting them to maximize the chances that they will be enforced.[83] According to Epstein, Knight, and Shvetsova's version of the theory, this kind of strategic behavior may produce a virtuous cycle in terms of which each decision that is enforced widens the policy "interval" into which a decision may be placed, making it easier and easier to avoid negative political repercussions.[84]

Once again, there is a slight difference in the thrust of these theories between stable and unstable settings. In stable settings, the purpose of strategic decision-making is said to be to maximize the court's policy influence,[85] whereas in unstable settings, strategic decision-making is targeted at building the court's institutional legitimacy, or at least at averting some or other institution-threatening attack or personal judicial setback.[86] The common thread, however, is the notion that judges may take their court's institutional fate into their hands to a certain extent, and exploit whatever political space exists to maximize their influence in national politics. This set of theories is thus distinctly different from, but not necessarily incompatible with, the political fragmentation thesis. Whereas the latter stresses external political factors, the former stresses judicial choices. But they may be reconciled insofar as the capacity for judicial action is seen to be structured by the external political environment.

The problem with tolerance interval theory and the strategic approach more generally is that judges are modelled as purely political actors.[87] While the legal plausibility of a decision is sometimes factored into the analysis,[88] judges are typically treated as having a purely political choice in the sense that the constraints under which they operate are constraints of politics rather than law. The idea that law might impose its own constraints on judicial choice, of a kind that run across a purely political calculus, is mostly anathema to these approaches.[89] This blind spot gives rise to the anomaly that courts are seen to build their institutional legitimacy on the back of decision-making practices that at face value are only likely to reinforce their reputation as political actors.

[83]   Epstein, Knight, and Shvetsova, "The Role of Constitutional Courts" 128; Ginsburg, *Judicial Review in New Democracies* 65–89.
[84]   Epstein, Knight, and Shvetsova, "The Role of Constitutional Courts" 128.
[85]   Lee Epstein and Jack Knight, *The Choices Justices Make* (Washington, DC: Congressional Quarterly 1998).
[86]   Helmke, *Courts under Constraints*; Jeffrey K. Staton, *Judicial Power and Strategic Communication in Mexico* (New York: Cambridge University Press, 2010).
[87]   See Roux, *Politics of Principle* 31–2 for a longer version of this argument.
[88]   See Epstein, Knight, and Shvetsova, "The Role of Constitutional Courts" 129–30.
[89]   Brian Z. Tamanaha, *Beyond the Formalist-Realist Divide: The Role of Politics in Judging* (Princeton, NJ: Princeton University Press, 2010) 112–23.

But if courts are purely political actors, there is no reason in principle why the public should support them or why the power of judicial review should be conferred on them. At most, strategic power building of this kind may help to win a court a measure of legitimacy for as long as the political factors supporting its independence remain relatively stable. More enduring forms of judicial independence, however, likely require constitutional courts to build a reputation as a legally constrained actor. At least, that is a proposition worth exploring.

Samuel Issacharoff's work on the forcefulness of some of the post-1989 constitutional courts backs up this conjecture to some degree.[90] On this view, constitutional judges in new democracies do not have to be particularly strategic given that their courts are by definition deliberately established to act in countermajoritarian ways and may be protected by a groundswell of public support for the new constitutional order.[91] This insight certainly explains some well-known decisions in which constitutional courts have acted without seeming regard for the preferences of powerful political actors. The problem with Issacharoff's argument, however, is that he supports it by citing a series of single instances rather than tracking the fate of constitutional courts over the medium to long term. In the result, the instances of forcefulness he refers to do not tell us much about the ongoing dynamics of judicial review in the countries concerned.[92] Marcus Mietzner's study of the Indonesian Constitutional Court,[93] which attributes its early forcefulness in the post-authoritarian era to the Court's public support as a seemingly incorruptible institution together with the boldness of that country's first democratic Chief Justice, Jimly Asshiddiqie, is more richly contextualized. In Indonesia's case, however, the political fragmentation thesis provides a competing explanation for the Court's early forcefulness that is hard to disentangle from the effects of the way it initially approached its mandate.[94]

There has been surprisingly little work done on the role of constitutional courts in democratic consolidation. While Mietzner offers an explanation for the Indonesian case, he does not seek to generalize it.[95] The same is true of Nancy Maveety and Anke Grosskopf's work on the Estonian Supreme

---

[90] Issacharoff, *Fragile Democracies*.

[91] Ibid.

[92] This is true of his discussion of the Ukrainian Supreme Court, for example (ibid 200–1).

[93] Mietzner, "Political Conflict Resolution and Democratic Consolidation in Indonesia."

[94] See Donald L. Horowitz, *Constitutional Change and Democracy in Indonesia* (New York: Cambridge University Press, 2013). As noted earlier, not everyone agrees with this analysis of the Indonesian case. See note 47.

[95] Mietzner, "Political Conflict Resolution and Democratic Consolidation in Indonesia."

Court.[96] The closest thing to a general theory is Tom Ginsburg's account of the role of constitutional courts in democratic consolidation in four Asian countries. By examining common themes in the constitutional politics of South Korea, Taiwan, Thailand, and Pakistan, Ginsburg provides support for a tripartite classification of constitutional courts as "upstream triggers of democracy," "downstream guarantors" of authoritarian "exit bargains," and "downstream democratic consolidators."[97] This classificatory scheme is a useful start. As Ginsburg's himself notes, however, it is less than a "complete theory."[98] Rather, it provides a way of distinguishing the types of roles constitutional courts may play, thereby facilitating exploration of such issues as the mutual compatibility of the roles and their particular contribution to the consolidation of democracy.

The final area in the literature of relevance to this study is the voluminous statistical work investigating the influence of legal and political factors on judicial decision-making.[99] In its comparative dimension, this work largely consists of attempts to test whether the three main empirical models of US Supreme Court adjudication – the legalist, attitudinal, and strategic models – can explain judicial decision-making in other parts of the world. The conclusion emerging from this work is that these models all need to be significantly adjusted before they attain any kind of descrip-

---

[96]   See Maveety and Grosskopf, "'Constrained' Constitutional Courts as Conduits for Democratic Consolidation."

[97]   Ginsburg, "The Politics of Courts in Democratization."

[98]   Ibid 63.

[99]   See Matías Iaryczower, Pablo T. Spiller, and Mariano Tommasi, "Judicial Decision Making in Unstable Environments, Argentina 1935–1998" (2002) 46 *American Journal of Political Science* 699; Clifford Carruba, Matthew Gabel, and Charles Hankla, "Judicial Behavior under Political Constraints: Evidence from the European Court of Justice" (2008) 102 *American Political Science Review* 435; Sofia Amaral-Garcia, Nuno Garoupa, and Veronica Grembi, "Judicial Independence and Party Politics in the Kelsenian Constitutional Courts: The Case of Portugal" (2009) 6 *Journal of Empirical Legal Studies* 381; Nuno Garoupa, Veronica Grembi, and Shirley Ching-pin Lin, "Explaining Constitutional Review in New Democracies: The Case of Taiwan" (2011) 20 *Pacific Rim Law & Policy Journal* 1; Diana Kapiszewski, "Tactical Balancing: High Court Decision-making on Politically Crucial Cases" (2011) 45 *Law & Society Review* 471; Laarni Escresa and Nuno M. Garoupa, "Judicial Politics in Unstable Democracies: The Case of the Philippine Supreme Court, an Empirical Analysis 1986–2010" (2012) 3 *Asian Journal of Law & Economics* 1; Nuno Garoupa, Fernando Gomez-Pomar, and Veronica Grembi, "Judging under Political Pressure: An Empirical Analysis of Constitutional Review Voting in the Spanish Constitutional Court" (2013) 29 *Journal of Law and Economic Organization* 513; Laarni Escresa and Nuno Garoupa, "Testing the Logic of Strategic Defection: The Case of the Philippine Supreme Court – An Empirical Analysis (1986–2010)" (2013) 21 *Asian Journal of Political Science* 189.

tive accuracy.[100] The reason for this, as one would expect, is the differing institutional and political circumstances of judicial decision-making outside the US. That conclusion is valuable for current purposes because it points to the way these models need to be reconceptualized if they are to serve as guides to comparative research. The value of this research for this study, in other words, lies less in whether the decision-making models accurately describe decision-making outside the US, and more in what the adjustments that need to be made to improve their descriptive accuracy reveal about the politico-legal dynamics of judicial review in different settings.[101]

In summary, the comparative politics literature on judicial review, despite its theoretical ambition and considerable achievements, suffers from the following deficiencies:

Downplaying variations in conceptions of the law/politics relation: Most studies simply assume that law is a subsystem of politics and proceed from there to analyze the political dynamics of judicial review taking account of other variables, such as the degree of political fragmentation and the strategic behavior of judges. This approach is homogenizing and reductive. To say that law is a subsystem of politics in Germany and a subsystem of politics in Russia, for example, clearly leaves out significant differences between these two societies and the extent to which law is thought of as being autonomous from politics. Even if, empirically, it could be shown that constitutional adjudication is purely a function of political factors in all societies – that either the dominant political power holder so determines the outcomes of constitutional decisions that law could not be said to play any kind of independent role or, conversely, that judicial independence is a function of the degree of political competition – underlying societal ideas and values would still affect the meaning given to judicial review and the ideational development of judicial review as an institution in that sense.

Contradictory tensions: The regime politics and political fragmentation theories are hard to reconcile insofar as the first contends that constitutional courts, even in competitive democracies like the US, never stray too far from the policy preferences of the dominant coalition, whereas the second holds that political fragmentation drives judicial independence, at least in stable democracies. Those propositions cannot both be true. There are also

---

[100] See further Theunis Roux, "American Ideas Abroad: Comparative Implications of US Supreme Court Decision-Making Models" (2015) 13 *International Journal of Constitutional Law* 90.

[101] Ibid.

numerous examples where constitutional courts in dominant-party regimes or authoritarian settings have asserted their independence, suggesting that political fragmentation is not a necessary condition for courts to play a forceful role in national politics. Some notion of law's legitimating potential as a distinct source of authority needs to be inserted into these theorizations to enhance their explanatory power.

Lack of generalizability: Most of the research considered, apart from Hirschl's and Ginsburg's studies of the political origins of judicial review and Chavez's work on political fragmentation, takes the form of single-country case studies or at most regional studies. The generalizability of these theories has consequently not been properly tested.

Failure to integrate normative dimension: In those parts of the literature dominated by political scientists, there is almost no normative evaluation of the merits and demerits of different models of judicial review. And yet this is vitally important when considering such phenomena as authoritarian retrenchment and constitutional courts' role in addressing democratic pathologies. There is also a sense in which much of the literature has lost touch with what the point of establishing judicial review is, and thus with what practical purposes research might serve. The quest is clearly not for the conditions that support curial power for curial power's sake, but for the conditions that support constitutional courts' playing a role in promoting democracy and human freedom.

1.3 THIS STUDY'S APPROACH

In its concern for developing a general theory of the factors driving the evolution of societal conceptions of the law/politics relation, this study falls within the field of comparative judicial politics broadly conceived. The premise is that, notwithstanding the wide variety of societies in which judicial review has been adopted, the evolution of JR regimes follows recurrent patterns and is driven by processes that are amenable to comparative analysis. Unlike much of the research being done in this field, however, this study is not concerned with the measurable causal influence of politics on constitutional adjudication. Rather, the concern is for the structuring role of ideas. The goal is a generalizable theory of the process through which societal conceptions of the law/politics relation evolve, stabilize around a dominant conception, and occasionally change character.

At the same time, this study's treatment of societal conceptions of the law/politics relation as a comparative variable puts it in conversational range of some of the work being done in comparative constitutional law and the more interpretive areas of political science. In keeping with the work of scholars such as Gary Jacobsohn and Michaela Hailbronner, this study focuses on the ideas that lie beneath the formal written constitution and the everyday business of constitutional politics. Just as Jacobsohn argues that societies have a "constitutional identity" that is in some ways more resistant to change than their formal constitutional arrangements,[102] and akin to Hailbronner's contention that societal commitments to a particular concept of law and model of authority structure the path of constitutional development,[103] so this study contends that the historical development of judicial review influences, and is influenced by, societal conceptions of the law/politics relation. Unlike the work of those scholars, however, this study aims to develop generalizable insights. Not content to use its conceptual framework as a heuristic to understand the operation of judicial review in different settings, this study sets itself the task of building a typological theory of the phenomenon studied. The specific contention is that claims to legal and political authority lock into each other in standardized ways, and that the processes through which societal conceptions of the law/politics relation consolidate, transform, and incrementally develop follow recurrent patterns that are observable across a diverse range of societies.

Of all the various approaches in the literature, the approach best suited to pursuing these research goals is the historical institutionalist approach in political science insofar as that approach has been applied to judicial review.[104] As here, historical institutionalists are interested in the development of judicial review as an institution,[105] the path-dependent effects of contingent doctrinal choices,[106] and the factors that trigger major periods of constitutional development and change.[107] To date, however, historical institutionalist research on judicial review has seldom been comparative. Rather, most of

[102] See Jacobsohn, *Constitutional Identity* (discussed in Section 1.2).

[103] See Hailbronner, *Traditions and Transformations.*

[104] See Rogers M. Smith, "Historical Institutionalism and the Study of Law" in Gregory A. Caldeira, R. Daniel Kelemen, and Keith E. Whittington (eds.), *Oxford Handbook of Law and Politics* (New York: Oxford University Press, 2008) 46.

[105] See, for example, Keith E. Whittington, *Political Foundations of Judicial Supremacy: The Presidency, the Supreme Court, and Constitutional Leadership in U.S. History* (Princeton, NJ: Princeton University Press, 2007); Barry Friedman, *The Will of the People: How Public Opinion Has Influenced the Supreme Court and Shaped the Meaning of the Constitution* (New York: Farrar, Straus and Giroux, 2009).

[106] Karen Orren, *Belated Feudalism: Labor, the Law, and Liberal Development in the United States* (New York: Cambridge University Press, 1991).

[107] Although not self-identifying as an historical institutionalist, Bruce Ackerman's work is exemplary here. See his three-volume study: *We the People: Foundations* (Cambridge, MA: Harvard University Press, 1991); *We the People: Transformations* (Cambridge, MA: Harvard

the work done in this vein has been directed at the development of the US Supreme Court's power of judicial review.[108] While there have been some non-US applications of this approach,[109] these studies are not strictly speaking comparative insofar as they focus on the development of judicial review in a single country or region.[110]

As noted in Section 1.2, the reasons why historical institutionalism has not been much utilized in comparative research have to do partly with intramural priorities and trends in US political science and partly with the difficulty of applying this approach's ethnographic, thick-description methods to the study of more than one country. Particularly for single researchers,[111] it is extremely difficult to develop the kind of familiarity with historical trends that is required to pursue this method for more than a handful of countries, and limitations of space and readers' patience in any case preclude extending this method to multiple-country case studies.

This does not mean, however, that there is no way forward. Elsewhere in political science and sociology, the last 10–15 years have seen major advances in the comparative study of the dynamics of institutional change. Coming together in the field of "comparative historical analysis" (CHA),[112] scholars engaged in this line of research have developed sophisticated methods for studying institutional change of various sorts, from high-level regime transformation to more micro-level changes in social policy. The methods developed in this line of research demonstrate how the work that historical

University Press, 1998); *We the People: The Civil Rights Revolution* (Cambridge, MA: Harvard University Press, 2014).

[108] See works cited in notes 105–106.

[109] See Alec Stone, *The Birth of Judicial Politics in France: The Constitutional Council in Comparative Perspective* (New York: Oxford University Press, 1992); Alec Stone Sweet, *Governing with Judges: Constitutional Politics in Europe* (Oxford: Oxford University Press, 2000); Lisa Hilbink, *Judges beyond Politics in Democracy and Dictatorship: Lessons from Chile* (New York: Cambridge University Press, 2007); Jens Meierhenrich, *The Legacies of Law: Long-Run Consequences of Legal Development in South Africa, 1652–2000* (New York: Cambridge University Press, 2008).

[110] In chapter 8 of his study of legal development in South Africa, Jens Meierhenrich conducts a "plausibility probe" extending his claims about path dependence and the law to Chile, but he explicitly disavows any "attempt at universal generalization" (Meierhenrich, *The Legacies of Law* 295).

[111] For a successful example of collective research using something like this method, see Terence C. Halliday, Lucien Karpik, and Malcolm Feeley (eds.), *Fates of Political Liberalism in the British Post-Colony: The Politics of the Legal Complex* (New York: Cambridge University Press, 2012).

[112] See James Mahoney and Dietrich Rueschemeyer (eds.), *Comparative Historical Analysis in the Social Sciences* (New York: Cambridge University Press, 2003); James Mahoney and Kathleen Thelen (eds.), *Advances in Comparative-Historical Analysis* (New York: Cambridge University Press, 2015).

institutionalists have been doing on judicial review could be extended comparatively. At the same time, extending CHA to the comparative study of judicial review broadens the reach of this approach to a globally significant institution. The rest of this section provides more detail on historical institutionalism and CHA, and then explains how this study proposes to bring them together.

Together with rational choice institutionalism, historical institutionalism was one of two main lines of research triggered by the publication of James March and Johan Olsen's celebrated article on "The New Institutionalism: Organizational Factors in Political Life."[113] Whereas rational choice institutionalists used March and Olsen's insights to explore the way institutions function as contexts for self-interested strategic action, historical institutionalists began distinguishing themselves in the 1990s by their concern for institutions as vehicles for the transmission of values and ideas. Institutionalized values and ideas, they argued, constitute preferences in ways not explained by the utility-maximizing models of rational choice theory, and their structuring influence needs to be studied over time.[114]

The next phase of historical institutionalism's development involved a search for greater methodological rigor. In the early 2000s, Paul Pierson, James Mahoney, and other scholars began applying ideas from path dependency theory in historical sociology and economics to the study of politics.[115] According to this body of work, "contingent" events may set in train institutional trajectories that have moderately deterministic properties. The key concept is the idea of a "critical juncture" – a reasonably compressed period, typically following an "exogenous shock,"[116] during which a choice or event is relatively underdetermined by existing institutional

---

[113] James G. March and Johan P. Olsen, "The New Institutionalism: Organizational Factors in Political Life" (1984) 78 *American Political Science Review* 734. For comprehensive overviews of historical institutionalism see Kathleen Thelen, "Historical Institutionalism in Comparative Politics" (1999) 2 *Annual Review of Political Science* 369; Paul Pierson and Theda Skocpol, "Historical Institutionalism in Contemporary Political Science" in Ira Katznelson and Helen Milner (eds.), *Political Science: The State of the Discipline* (New York: W. W. Norton, 2002) 693; Elizabeth Sanders, "Historical Institutionalism" in Sarah A. Binder, R. A. W. Rhodes, and Bert A. Rockman (eds.), *The Oxford Handbook of Political Institutions* (New York: Oxford University Press, 2008) 39.

[114] Rogers M. Smith, "Historical Institutionalism and the Study of Law" in Gregory A. Caldeira, R. Daniel Kelemen, and Keith E. Whittington (eds.), *The Oxford Handbook of Law and Politics* (New York: Oxford University Press, 2008) 46.

[115] See James Mahoney, "Path Dependence in Historical Sociology" (2000) 29 *Theory and Society* 507; Paul Pierson, "Increasing Returns, Path Dependence, and the Study of Politics" (2000) 94 *American Political Science Review* 251.

[116] Mahoney, "Path Dependence in Historical Sociology" 521.

traditions.[117] That choice or event may define an institutional trajectory that would have been entirely different had some other choice been made or event occurred. In just the same way that the contingent choice of a particular technology may increase the chances of that technology's achieving market dominance,[118] so might the contingent choice of a particular social practice increase the chances of that practice's being accepted.[119] "Increasing returns" processes of this kind may eventually lead to "equilibria" – relatively stable economic or social patterns that "lock in" and reward particular types of behavior, making them difficult to change absent another exogenous shock to the system, after which the process begins again.

In the more sociological applications of this approach, one of the important mechanisms of increasing-returns processes is said to be the legitimation of past contingent choices through their acceptance by significant social actors and the public.[120] According to this insight, the contingent choice of a particular social practice may be reinforced by a developing sense of the appropriateness or moral correctness of that practice, which in turn enhances the legitimacy of any future conduct consistent with it, eventually leading to its institutionalization.[121] Self-reinforcing trajectories of this kind are relevant to the study of judicial decision-making insofar as they may be used to explain the way contingently adopted legal norms are legitimated over time. Karen Orren's study of the surprisingly late demise of the law of master and servant in the US, for example, argues that this area of law was a remnant of European feudalism brought over to the US in the eighteenth century, and then legitimated through judicial decision-making and political acceptance.[122]

Historical institutionalism's so-called punctuated equilibrium[123] model of development has been challenged by scholars whose empirical findings have

---

[117]   Giovanni Capoccia and R. Daniel Kelemen, "The Study of Critical Junctures: Theory, Narrative, and Counterfactuals in Historical Institutionalism" (2007) 59 *World Politics* 341, 348.

[118]   The fact that efficiency does not come into it is important because market dominance would otherwise be explicable on those grounds.

[119]   W. Brian Arthur, *Increasing Returns and Path Dependence in the Economy* (Ann Arbor, MI: University of Michigan Press, 1994) 6–7.

[120]   Mahoney, "Path Dependence in Historical Sociology" 523–4.

[121]   Ibid.

[122]   Orren, *Belated Feudalism*.

[123]   The term was coined in Niles Eldredge and Stephen Jay Gould, "Punctuated Equilibria: An Alternative to Phyletic Gradualism" in Thomas J. M. Schopf (ed.), *Models in Paleobiology* (San Francisco: Freeman, Cooper & Co, 1972) 82. It was introduced into the political science literature by Stephen D. Krasner, "Approaches to the State: Alternative Conceptions and Historical Dynamics" (1984) 16 *Comparative Politics* 223.

suggested that institutions may be fundamentally transformed over time in the absence of an exogenous shock. Kathleen Thelen and Wolfgang Streeck have been particularly influential here in developing a typology of forms of incremental change that may be transformational over the long run, including "displacement," "layering," "drift," and "conversion."[124] While restricted to formal institutions (i.e., institutions whose governing norms are formally stated) and thus not conclusively refuting the punctuated equilibrium model in all instances, this line of research at the very least suggests that anyone studying institutional change should be open to the possibility of change occurring through incremental, endogenous processes of adaptation and internal challenge.

From the very beginning, as exemplified by Orren's work,[125] historical institutionalist methods were used to study law and legal institutions. As a distinct subfield within the American political science field of "law and courts,"[126] however, historical institutionalism's status was confirmed in 1999 with the publication of two anthologies of papers edited by Howard Gillman and Cornell Clayton.[127] While including some contributions from the rational choice strand of the new institutionalism,[128] most of the papers in these two anthologies were concerned with the way institutional norms have structured the evolution of judicial review in the US, including the way different doctrinal innovations took root and determined the course of later events.[129] Howard Gillman's contribution to the first of these volumes, for example, argued that the development of judicial review on the US Supreme Court was better understood as having been driven by the justices' socialized sense of

---

[124] Kathleen Thelen, *How Institutions Evolve: The Political Economy of Skills in Germany, Britain, the United States, and Japan* (New York: Cambridge University Press, 2004); Wolfgang Streeck and Kathleen Thelen, "Introduction: Institutional Change in Advanced Political Economies" in Wolfgang Streeck and Kathleen Thelen (eds.), *Beyond Continuity: Institutional Change in Advanced Political Economies* (New York: Oxford University Press, 2005) 1.

[125] Orren, *Belated Feudalism.*

[126] "Law and Courts" is an official section of the American Political Science Association.

[127] Howard Gillman and Cornell W. Clayton, *The Supreme Court in American Politics: New Institutionalist Interpretations* (Lawrence, KS: University of Kansas Press, 1999); Cornell W. Clayton and Howard Gillman (eds.), *Supreme Court Decision-Making: New Institutionalist Approaches* (Chicago: University of Chicago Press, 1999).

[128] See, for example, Lee Epstein and Jack Knight, "Mapping Out the Strategic Terrain: The Informational Role of Amici Curiae" in Clayton and Gillman (eds.), *Supreme Court Decision-Making* 215.

[129] See, for example, Elizabeth Bussiere, "The Supreme Court and the Development of the Welfare State: Judicial Liberalism and the Problem of Welfare Rights" in Cornell W. Clayton and Howard Gillman (eds.), *Supreme Court Decision-Making: New Institutionalist Approaches* (Chicago: University of Chicago Press, 1999) 155.

their "mission" rather than their strategic choices as rational actors. The distinct advantage of the former approach, at least, was that it allowed for the examination of a wider range of "institutional effects on judicial decision-making ... that are not best characterized in the language of self-interest."[130]

Since the publication of the Clayton and Gillman anthologies, major contributions to this line of inquiry have included Mark Graber's study of the place and continuing ideational significance of the *Dred Scott* decision in American constitutional law,[131] Keith Whittington's examination of the way successive American presidents have supported the Supreme Court's assertion of its final decision-making powers,[132] and Barry Friedman's historical analysis of the role of public opinion in shaping and supporting judicial review in the US.[133] While pursuing their own scholarly agendas, all of these studies are committed to examining the development of judicial review as an institution over time. Whittington's study, for example, is directed at showing how judicial review has developed as a powerful political institution, not through judicial usurpation of democratic decision-making, but as a function of the self-interested choices of successive presidents. Barry Friedman, for his part, argues that US Supreme Court decisions have never strayed far from public opinion, and that judicial review in the US owes much of its stability to this fact.

Insofar as it addresses the historical development of American constitutionalism, and particularly the factors that drive transitions from periods of relative stability ("ordinary politics") to periods of more fundamental change ("constitutional moments"), Bruce Ackerman's three-volume analysis of the American "higher law-making system" also fits under the broad rubric of historical institutionalism, although Ackerman does not explicitly identify his work as belonging to this school.[134] Like other scholars working in this

---

[130]   Howard Gillman, "The Court as an Idea, Not a Building (or a Game): Interpretive Institutionalism and the Analysis of Supreme Court Decision-Making" in Howard Gillman and Cornell W. Clayton, *The Supreme Court in American Politics: New Institutionalist Interpretations* (Lawrence, KS: University of Kansas Press, 1999) 65.

[131]   Mark A. Graber, *Dred Scott and the Problem of Constitutional Evil* (New York: Cambridge University Press, 2006).

[132]   Keith E. Whittington, *Political Foundations of Judicial Supremacy: The Presidency, the Supreme Court, and Constitutional Leadership in U.S. History* (Princeton, NJ: Princeton University Press, 2007).

[133]   Barry Friedman, *The Will of the People: How Public Opinion Has Influenced the Supreme Court and Shaped the Meaning of the Constitution* (New York: Farrar, Straus and Giroux, 2009).

[134]   See Bruce Ackerman, *We the People: Foundations* (Cambridge, MA: Harvard University Press, 1991); Bruce Ackerman, *We the People: Transformations* (Cambridge, MA: Harvard University Press, 1998); Bruce Ackerman, *We the People: The Civil Rights Revolution*

area, Ackerman is interested in the factors that drive major periods of constitutional change, such as that which occurred during the civil rights movement in the 1960s.[135] In particular, Ackerman suggests that the American "higher law-making system" is not restricted to the formal amendment process under Article V, but includes situations where the US Supreme Court, political leaders, and a "mobilized" public combine to drive a fundamental transformation in conceptions of the nation's founding commitments.[136]

Outside the US, contributions that adopt a broadly historical institutionalist approach include Alec Stone Sweet's work on judicial review in France and Europe,[137] Jason Pierce's study of the "Mason Court revolution" in Australia,[138] Lisa Hilbink's examination of constitutional politics in Augusto Pinochet's Chile,[139] and Jens Meierhenrich's study of legal development in South Africa.[140] None of these studies are truly comparative.[141] Rather, they all deploy Geertzian "thick description" methods,[142] or what Kim Lane Scheppele has called a "constitutional ethnographic" approach,[143] to give richly detailed accounts of the functioning of judicial review in the particular country or region chosen for analysis. Such methods ordinarily do not lend themselves to cross-country comparison – both as a matter of scale and because they tend to favor local and contingent explanations over

(Cambridge, MA: Harvard University Press, 2014). For a review of the first two volumes of Ackerman's work by a political scientist, see Walter Dean Burnham, "Constitutional Moments and Punctuated Equilibria: A Political Scientist Confronts Bruce Ackerman's *We the People*" (1999) 108 *Yale Law Journal* 2237.

[135] Ackerman, *We the People: The Civil Rights Revolution.*

[136] Ibid. Note that, despite Ackerman's inventiveness in forcing those interested in constitutional change to think beyond the formal amendment process, his focus remains the development of the normative constitution.

[137] Alec Stone Sweet, *Governing with Judges: Constitutional Politics in Europe* (Oxford: Oxford University Press, 2000). See also Alec Stone, *The Birth of Judicial Politics in France: The Constitutional Council in Comparative Perspective* (New York: Oxford University Press, 1992).

[138] Jason L. Pierce, *Inside the Mason Court Revolution: The High Court of Australia Transformed* (Durham, NC: Carolina Academic Press, 2006). See also Brian Galligan, *Politics of the High Court: A Study of the Judicial Branch of Government in Australia* (Brisbane: University of Queensland Press, 1987).

[139] Lisa Hilbink, *Judges beyond Politics in Democracy and Dictatorship: Lessons from Chile* (New York: Cambridge University Press, 2007).

[140] Meierhenrich, *The Legacies of Law.*

[141] Stone Sweet's various studies are comparative, but restricted to the European system of judicial review.

[142] Clifford Geertz, *The Interpretation of Cultures: Selected Essays* (New York: Basic Books, 1973) 3–30.

[143] Kim Lane Scheppele, "Constitutional Ethnography: An Introduction" (2004) 28 *Law & Society Review* 389.

generalizable ones. As noted above, however, the methodologies developed in the closely related field of CHA provide a potentially fruitful basis on which the historical institutionalist study of judicial review could be extended comparatively.

CHA may be understood as a narrower enterprise than historical institutionalism inasmuch as it is concerned with the systematic comparison of the development of a defined institution in more than one society.[144] But CHA is also broader in another sense because, although identified as a field in the 2000s, it in fact traces its lineage all the way back to the comparative research that was conducted by the grand masters of social science, including Adam Smith, Alexis de Tocqueville, Karl Marx, and Max Weber.[145] CHA's breadth is also apparent in the fact that, as it is conceived today, this field is not tied to a particular theoretical tradition or set of methodologies. Rather, it is a loose label for research that shares three basic characteristics, namely, a concern for "causal analysis, an emphasis on process over time, and the use of systematic and contextualized comparison."[146]

Framed by this set of concerns, CHA scholars trade off the advantages of a richly contextualized account of the development of institutions in a single country against the benefits of analyzing the development of those institutions in several countries in a more schematic way.[147] Comparison is driven by the use of a common conceptual vocabulary to draw out similarities and differences between the societies studied. In Theda Skocpol's classic study of social revolutions, for example, the French, Russian, and Chinese revolutions were compared as examples of a single, specified type of revolution with shared dynamics, notwithstanding considerable differences in political and institutional contexts.[148] As with all comparative approaches, CHA is a compromise inasmuch as any attempt to schematize the development of institutions so as to facilitate cross-country comparison is inevitably going to be reductive.[149] As Michael Coppedge puts the point, even so simple a categorization as treating the British House of Lords as a species of upper chamber of

---

[144] James Mahoney and Dietrich Rueschemeyer, "Comparative Historical Analysis: Achievements and Agendas" in James Mahoney and Dietrich Rueschemeyer (eds.), *Comparative Historical Analysis in the Social Sciences* (New York: Cambridge University Press, 2003) 1, 11.

[145] Ibid 1.

[146] Ibid 10.

[147] See Michael Coppedge, *Democratization and Research Methods* (New York: Cambridge University Press, 2012) 115–57.

[148] Theda Skocpol, *States and Social Revolutions: A Comparative Analysis of France, Russia, and China* (New York: Cambridge University Press, 1979).

[149] Coppedge, *Democratization and Research Methods*.

parliament distorts the actual situation to some extent.[150] Nevertheless, the advantage of CHA is that it is "less myopic" than single-country case studies and "more likely to call attention to structural macrocauses."[151]

The clear advantage for the current study of combining historical institutionalist approaches with CHA is that the latter provides a ready-made set of methodologies that can be used as the basis for comparing the way conceptions of the law/politics relation have evolved in different societies. From qualitative comparative analysis using "fuzzy sets,"[152] to Boolean algebra[153] and Millian methods of agreement and difference,[154] CHA scholars use a range of tools to cast light on the development of complex macrosocial processes that are not amenable to multivariate regression analysis. The common thread running through all this research is an interest in explaining the causal mechanisms that lead to significant social outcomes. In order to do this, CHA scholars use process tracing to delineate the pathway to the defined outcome in a particular society,[155] and various methods of cross-case comparison to build towards more generalizable propositions about the common causal mechanisms that could be said to be responsible for the defined outcome across a range of societies.[156]

To date, no comparative study of judicial review has used these sorts of methodologies. Clearly, however, the historical development of judicial review is amenable to such treatment. If judicial review is conceived as an institution that both emerges from and influences an evolving complex of legitimating ideas about the law/politics relation, it is possible that the development of judicial review might evince path-dependent properties. Choices made at the stage of constitutional design or during the early establishment period of judicial review might structure the development of societal conceptions of the law/politics relation in ways that eventually become difficult to

---

[150] Ibid 141.
[151] Ibid 140.
[152] Charles C. Ragin, *Fuzzy-Set Social Science* (Chicago: University of Chicago Press, 2000).
[153] See the discussion in James Mahoney, "Strategies of Causal Assessment in Comparative Historical Analysis" in James Mahoney and Dietrich Rueschemeyer (eds.), *Comparative Historical Analysis in the Social Sciences* (New York: Cambridge University Press, 2003) 337, 343–6.
[154] John Stuart Mill, *A System of Logic* (Toronto: University of Toronto Press, 1974) (first published in 1843).
[155] Andrew Bennett, "Process Tracing and Causal Inference" in Henry E. Brady and David Collier (eds.), *Rethinking Social Inquiry: Diverse Tools, Shared Standards* (Plymouth: Rowman & Littlefield, 2010) 207.
[156] See Tulia G. Falletti and James Mahoney, "The Comparative Sequential Method" in James Mahoney and Kathleen Thelen (eds.), *Advances in Comparative-Historical Analysis* (New York: Cambridge University Press, 2015) 211.

change. The contingent choice of a particular legal-interpretive approach, for example, might produce a line of decisions that is accepted by political power holders for self-interested reasons. Where that happens, conceptions of legal and political authority might coalesce into a comprehensive legitimating ideology. Provided judicial review did not present an absolute hurdle in the way of pressing political initiatives, an accommodation might be reached between the judiciary and major political actors in terms of which each respected the other's legitimate sphere of operation. In ideational terms, such an accommodation would manifest itself as a relatively stable societal conception of the law/politics relationship, with conceptions of legal and political authority taking on a discernible form, and the ideational substructure as a whole characterized by the distinctive ways in which those authority claims locked into and mutually supported one another.

In theory, there could be numerous different equilibria of this sort depending on the contingent choices that set the regime's trajectory in motion. If, however, there are only a finite number of ways in which legal and political actors may assert their authority, the number of equilibria might be more limited. At least, we should be able to identify a manageable number of ideal-typical equilibria depending on the distinctive authority claims that the literature suggests legal and political actors typically make, and the way in which these claims could in theory be combined.

This study presents and tests a theory of this sort. In particular, it suggests that there are four main forms of law/politics accommodation that have the potential to produce relatively stable (though not necessarily morally desirable) equilibria or JR regimes. Those four ideal types, together with the typological theory that connects them to each other, are then used as a framework to explore actually existing JR regimes, and to compare their dynamics and the factors that drive transitions between them.

The concluding section of this chapter explains the methods that this study adopts to pursue this approach and the reasons behind the choice of the three main case studies.

1.4 METHODS AND CASE SELECTION

This study's solution to the methodological challenge of comparing the evolution of conceptions of the law/politics relation across a range of societies in which judicial review has been adopted is, first, to use a typological approach to reduce the "property-space" (i.e., the number of independent variables) in play[157] and, secondly, to combine detailed historical case studies with more schematic process tracing in a medium-N comparative case study. Instead of trying to account for all the possible influences on the development of judicial review as an institution, this study conceives of that process as a function of the dynamic interaction of law and politics as potentially autonomous social subsystems associated with distinct claims to authority.

Chapter 2 justifies the choice of this study's key independent variables (forms of legal and political authority claim) and explains how they are conceptualized. At the outset, the process is an inductive one of beginning with the best-known example of JR-regime change – the transformation of the American JR regime during the course of the *Lochner* era – and then extracting potentially generalizable concepts from this example. From that point, induction turns to deduction as the conceptual logic of the identified variables and social processes is used to devise a testable typological theory.[158]

This approach produces four ideal-typical forms of law/politics accommodation that represent relatively stable states or equilibria. Each of these ideal types is then used to explore the dynamics of actually existing JR regimes and the processes that prompt major changes in the way legal and political authority claims interact. The detailed case studies use a thick, ethnographic method to trace the evolution of the studied regimes, while the medium-N comparative case study in Chapter 6 relies on existing findings in the secondary literature to examine the three sociological processes posited by the theory in a wider range of societies.

The normative dimension of the study has to do with assessing whether one of the ideal types represents a form of law/politics accommodation that could be said to be more morally attractive than the others. There are really just two contenders here: democratic legalism and democratic instrumentalism. The relative merit of those two ideal types in other guises has enjoyed a fair amount of attention in the literature,[159] and each has well-known strengths and weaknesses. Thus, the democratic legitimacy flowing from democratic

---

[157] See Arend Lijphart, "Comparative Politics and the Comparative Method" (1971) 65 *American Political Science Review* 682, 687 (explaining how the "property-space" of an analysis may be reduced in this way).

[158] Although presented in this linear way, the movement between induction and deduction in the actual research process was obviously iterative in the sense that earlier tentative versions of the theory were first trialled and then revised.

[159] See Patrick S. Atiyah and Robert S. Summers, *Form and Substance in Anglo-American Law: A Comparative Study of Legal Reasoning, Legal Theory, and Legal Institutions* (Oxford: Clarendon Press, 1987); Nonet and Selznick, *Law and Society in Transition*; Brian Z. Tamanaha, *Law as a Means to an End: Threat to the Rule of Law* (New York: Cambridge University Press, 2007).

legalism's claim to be implementing the commands of a higher-law political mandate comes at the cost of doing justice in the individual case. Democratic instrumentalism's relative strengths and weaknesses are just the reverse: attentiveness to substantive justice in the individual case at the cost of departing from the strict terms of a higher-law mandate. What the typology brings to this well-rehearsed debate is an understanding of the processes that lead to the stabilization of these two regimes, greater clarity as to their internal dynamics and legitimating effects, and a specification of the broader jurisprudential debate to the moral justifiability of judicial review.

The advantage of the typological approach is that it reduces the complex reality of actually existing JR regimes to a more manageable set of ideal types. As with any such approach, however, there are risks of distortion. The persuasiveness of the approach depends, first, on the plausibility of depicting the evolution of JR regimes as a function of the interaction of legal and political authority claims and, secondly, on the plausibility of further dividing each of these authority claims into two main variants. If either of those moves is distorting, the approach will have little validity or utility. Even if both moves are plausible, there is a risk that subsuming all the various influences on the evolution of JR regimes into the interaction of two macro-variables will obscure more than it illuminates. Finally, since the classification of actually existing JR regimes depends on the application of a set of qualitative indicators, there is a danger of error through misclassification. None of these risks can be entirely avoided. The persuasiveness of the approach will in the end depend on whether the four ideal types have some intuitive connection to actually existing states of affairs and on whether the classificatory judgments that are made group together JR regimes that seem to share certain essential characteristics. If that part of the argument succeeds, the normative aspect will stand or fall on its own terms.

So much for the risks attendant on this study's approach. The last part of this chapter briefly explains how the case studies were chosen. The main requirement was to find a paradigmatic example of each ideal type together with examples of the three causal processes posited by the theory: consolidation, transformation, and within-regime incremental change. The secondary goal was to eliminate background factors such as legal tradition and type of political system.

With those goals in mind, the three countries chosen – Australia, India, and Zimbabwe – are all former British colonies whose legal systems are based on the common law and whose political systems were based on the Westminster tradition of parliamentary democracy before transition to judicially enforced constitutionalism. The specific reasons driving the choice of each country were as follows:

Australia: Despite being a well-developed, English-speaking constitutional democracy, Australia is seldom included in comparative studies of judicial review because of the well-known idiosyncrasies of its constitutional system. As one of the last holdouts against the global trend towards judicially enforced bills of rights, Australia seems peripheral to many of the phenomena that comparative constitutionalists study. Nevertheless, Australia does have an active and politically consequential High Court with the power to review questions of federalism and other structural matters. These features put it within the institutional scope of this study. In addition to this, the Australian case presents several empirical puzzles and methodological challenges that make it more interesting from the point of view of theory development than initially appears.

First, while seemingly foreordained by the strong aversion to rights review that informed the design of its 1900 Constitution, Australia's democratic legalist regime took a surprisingly long time to develop, achieving stability only in the 1950s. What should be a straightforward case of culturally and institutionally determined JR-regime consolidation, therefore, turns out to be anything but. Understanding why that is so promises to add empirical nuance to the theoretical idea of JR-regime consolidation presented in Chapter 2.

Second, the Australian JR regime, once it consolidated in the 1950s, has proven to be very durable, resisting a major judge-led attempt to transform it in the 1980s and early 1990s. Since then, the Australian regime has incrementally adapted to modern global trends, such as the emergence of proportionality as a judicial technique for resolving conflicts between constitutional values. Both these features suggest that the Australian case, despite its peripheral status, may be instructive in understanding the conditions for JR-regime consolidation and the adaptive capacity of JR regimes once consolidated.

India: India was chosen, first, as a paradigmatic case of democratic instrumentalism and, second, because the development of its JR regime provides a rich and well-documented empirical setting in which to refine the typological theory. The particular value of the Indian case is that the existing literature on the Supreme Court periodizes the development of judicial review in a more or less standard way. From the early conflict between the Court and the Congress Party over the *zamindari* abolition laws, to the Court's performance during the 1975–7 Emergency and its rehabilitation after that, the Indian case presents itself as a ready-made series of chapters. Refracting the typological theory through the prism of these chapters promises to achieve two things: first, to illustrate the explanatory power of the typology through demonstrating its capacity to reinterpret a well-known story in a refreshing and instructive way and, second, to enhance the theory by exposing it to, and requiring it to accommodate, a number of well-known empirical reference points.

The Indian case is also helpful for demonstrating how the theory resolves the age-old question of structure and agency. The standard Indian story thus gives a starring role to certain charismatic justices who are said to have rehabilitated the Supreme Court's reputation after its disastrous performance during the Emergency. What the Indian case study adds to this well-known story is a clearer sense of what collapsed – public confidence in a particular conception of the law/politics relation – and how the justices were able to refashion a new conception in an iterative process of doctrinal development, procedural innovation, and political acceptance.

Today, the Supreme Court of India is famously "one of the most powerful constitutional courts in the world,"[160] but questions are increasingly being asked about whether the influence it exerts in national politics is healthy from a democratic point of view. That aspect allows for rich exploration of the normative questions underpinning this study. Finally, the largely English-language literature on the Indian Supreme Court makes it an easily accessible case to study. While this means that India is a "usual suspect" country in Hirschl's sense,[161] it is too important an example to ignore for that reason alone.

Zimbabwe: The Zimbabwe case study provides an interesting illustration of the typological theory's application to authoritarian settings while at the same time allowing for examination of the development of societal conceptions of the law/politics relation that, as in India, have gone through several different stages. From its postindependence authoritarian legalist regime, which evinced strong continuities with the way law and politics were conceived under colonialism, to the descent into instrumentalism from 2000 to 2008, and the reversion back to authoritarian legalism after that, the Zimbabwean case provides a rich empirical backdrop against which to assess the causal mechanisms driving the evolution of conceptions of the law/politics relation in authoritarian societies.

The methods and case selection criteria used in Chapter 6, the chapter that tests the typological theory against a wider range of cases, are explained in that chapter.

---

[160] Manoj Mate, "Public Interest Litigation and the Transformation of the Supreme Court of India" in Diana Kapiszewski, Gordon Silverstein, and Robert A. Kagan (eds.), *Consequential Courts: Judicial Roles in Global Perspective* (New York: Cambridge University Press, 2013) 262, 262.

[161] Hirschl, *Comparative Matters* 211.

2

A Typological Theory of JR-Regime Change

This chapter presents a typological theory of JR-regime change that will be refined in the case studies to follow. The adoption of a system of judicial review, the theory goes, triggers a dynamic, interactive process in which legal and political actors lay claim to distinct forms of authority. The interaction of these claims is structured by prevailing conceptions of the appropriate relationship between law and politics – the society's JR regime. These conceptions supply ideational resources on which actors draw in the conflicts of constitutional politics. The central claim of the theory is that, however intense these conflicts, the fact that actors disagree over how the constitution ought to be interpreted does not necessarily destabilize the ideational foundations of the relevant JR regime. That is because the successful deployment of the regime's ideational resources in the resolution of constitutional conflicts helps to reinforce extant understandings of the law/politics relation. Only under certain conditions, as explored by the theory, do the ideational foundations of a JR regime become destabilized. Where that happens, the JR regime is susceptible to more rapid and significant change.

Three distinct processes are identified: the *consolidation* of a JR regime, which refers to a situation in which a hegemonic conception of the law/politics relation emerges and begins to provide a stable and ideologically powerful account of the legitimate scope of judicial review; the *transformation* of a JR regime, which refers to the process through which a JR regime breaks down and transitions to another regime; and the *incremental development* of a JR regime, which refers to any change to a JR regime short of wholesale transformation.

Conceptions of law's authority, the theory posits, vary both within and across societies according to the centrality to those conceptions of the ideal of law's autonomy from politics. Conceptions of political authority, in turn, vary according to the centrality to those conceptions of the idea that legitimate

49

political authority depends on an open and competitive democratic mandate. Treating each of these variables as dichotomous, and positing further that each element in each dichotomous pair may be associated with each element in the other pair, this conceptualization generates four ways in which claims to legal and political authority may in theory be reconciled: democratic and authoritarian legalism, and democratic and authoritarian instrumentalism. Each of these ideal types is defined by its own legitimation logic – reasons for stability that are associated with the distinctive way legal and political authority claims lock into and mutually support one another.

Actually existing JR regimes, the theory continues, are infinitely various but typically approximate one of these ideal types more than the others. At least, that is a question to be investigated, together with the causal mechanisms driving the processes of consolidation, transformation, and incremental change in the real world.

So much for the theory in outline. The first task is to shore up the main assumptions underlying it. In what sense, Section 2.1 asks, do legal and political actors make claims to distinct forms of authority, and how much violence to reality does conceiving of the evolution of JR regimes as the product of competing legal and political authority claims do? While law's autonomy from politics, the section notes, is a controversial question in political science accounts of judicial review, it is less so in sociological theorizations of the nature of law in modern society. The reason for this is that the two lines of inquiry conceive of law's autonomy from politics in distinct ways: in the first case, as an empirically testable claim about the causal influence of politics on judicial decision-making, while in the second case as a legal-cultural ideal that may become ideologically ascendant in certain societies under certain conditions. Since the theory presented here conceives of JR regimes as clusters of legitimating ideas about the law/politics relation, the second conception is more appropriate. The degree of law's autonomy from politics, on this view, is coterminous with the salience of this ideal in the relevant constitutional culture.

With this preliminary point clarified, Section 2.2 gets the theory off the ground by giving a stylized account of one of the best-known examples of JR-regime change – the transformation of conceptions of the law/politics relation that occurred over the course of the so-called *Lochner* era in US constitutional politics. While the transformation that occurred during this time, the section acknowledges, was broader and deeper than a mere change to the American JR regime, the *Lochner* era still serves as a paradigmatic example of what is meant by this idea: a period of ideational instability during which legal and political actors drove significant changes to the dominant societal conception of the appropriate relationship between law and politics.

Section 2.3 considers how the *Lochner* story might be generalized to account for other instances of JR-regime change. The central argument here is that the evolution of JR regimes is characterized by changing conceptions of legal and political authority and thus that it is variation in those conceptions that the theory needs to capture. In particular, the section argues, law's authority in JR regimes is conceived of in one of two characteristic ways: either law is seen as a politically neutral transmitter of the framers' vision for a just society or it is modeled as a politically useful instrument for the promotion of the best contemporary understanding of constitutional justice. Political authority claims are more diverse in nature, but it is nevertheless possible to divide them into two main variants as well: those that depend on the openness and competitiveness of the democratic system in the society concerned, and those that, while perhaps partly reliant on the maintenance of the outward appearance of democracy, place greater store in political power holders' capacity to promote some other important societal goal, such as the preservation of ethnic harmony, the promotion of economic prosperity, or the maintenance of national security.

At a conceptual level, Section 2.4 argues, claims to legal and political authority lock into each other in four distinctive ways, each of which represents a theoretically stable legitimating ideology. Under democratic legalism, the authority of law is founded on public confidence in the existence of a set of legal reasoning methods capable of excluding the influence of judicial policy preferences on constitutional decision-making. This conception of law's authority is paired with a conception of legitimate political authority as contingent on the authenticity of a democratic mandate. Authoritarian legalism, on the other hand, describes a situation in which the alleged separability of law and politics operates, not as the legitimate basis on which law speaks truth to political power, but as a reason for the exercise of political power to be put beyond the reach of law. Authoritarian instrumentalism describes a situation where law functions as a mere instrument of politics, and where law is therefore not autonomous from politics in any real sense. Finally, democratic instrumentalism returns full circle to a legitimating ideology in which political authority is founded on the openness and competitiveness of the democratic system. In contrast to democratic legalism, however, law's authority in this style of JR regime is premised not on the strenuous denial of judicial review's immersion in politics but on the frank embrace or at least grudging acceptance of this fact.

The final substantive section of the chapter, Section 2.5, considers the process through which societal conceptions of the law/politics relation might come to consolidate around one or another of these four legitimating ideologies and the factors that might drive a JR regime, once consolidated, to change character. The central issue here is whether transformation between the regime types is best conceived of as the product of the relevant JR regime's internal susceptibilities to change or as contingent on an exogenous shock of some kind. While that question cannot be answered at a purely theoretical level, it is possible to press down on the conceptual logic of the typology to suggest certain lines of transformation that may be more likely than others.

The concluding section, Section 2.6, sets out the main theoretical propositions that will be refined in the case studies and then tested in the comparative chapter, Chapter 6.

2.1 LAW'S AUTONOMY: LEGAL-CULTURAL IDEAL NOT EMPIRICALLY TESTABLE CLAIM

The main assumption underlying the theory presented in this chapter – that legal and political actors in systems of judicial review lay claim to distinct forms of authority – is relatively controversial in comparative judicial politics. For most scholars working in this tradition, as we saw in Chapter 1, law is best viewed as a subsystem of politics. The establishment of judicial review on this account is the establishment of a special kind of political institution,[1] and any contestation between a constitutional court and other organs of government will be a contestation between political actors, working either individually or collectively to maximize their or their institution's power. On this view, constitutional judges behave largely as other political actors behave – strategically asserting their interests. Where they fail, they likewise fail for primarily political reasons – because they have misjudged the strategic environment in which they are operating.

As soon as we shift the disciplinary lens from political science to sociology, however, the idea that law might achieve some degree of autonomy from politics is less controversial – indeed, taken to be a defining characteristic of law in modern society. There is thus a very long tradition of sociological theorizing about law's autonomy – from Max Weber's study of the role of

---

[1] See, for example, Martin Shapiro and Alec Stone Sweet, *On Law, Politics, and Judicialization* (New York: Oxford University Press, 2002) 5; Ran Hirschl, "The Judicialization of Politics" in Gregory A. Caldeira, R. Daniel Kelemen, and Keith E. Whittington (eds.), *The Oxford Handbook of Law and Politics* (New York: Oxford University Press, 2008) 119, 134.

logically formal rationality in differentiating Western law from the rival normative orders of politics and religion;[2] to Niklas Luhmann's idea of law as an autonomous social system capable of processing the communications of other social systems, including politics, according to its own, self-reproducing logic;[3] Roberto Mangabeira Unger's notion of law in modern society as characterized by four distinct forms of autonomy;[4] and Phillippe Nonet's and Philip Selznick's idea of "autonomous law" as an intermediate stage of legal development between "repressive" and "responsive" law.[5] In addition to these accounts there is a separate literature concerned with the specifically Marxist conception of law, and in particular the debate sparked by E. P. Thompson's controversial (for a Marxist historian) claim that the rule of law is "an unqualified human good."[6] In this extensive body of sociological theorizing, law's autonomy from politics is sometimes held up as one of the major achievements of Western society, while at other times as a perverse development that hides the reality of oppressive class relations. The fact that law might be seen at certain times and in certain places as autonomous from politics, however, is not seriously doubted.

How to explain this difference? Why is it that for sociologists a proposition that comparative judicial politics scholars find relatively controversial is taken to be a defining feature of law in modern society? The answer, of course, lies in the different nature of their respective inquiries. For judicial politics scholars, the question of law's autonomy from politics is a question of the causal

---

[2] Max Weber, *Economy and Society*, eds. Günther Roth and Claus Wittich (New York: Bedminister Press, 1968). For an accessible introduction to Weber's account, see David M. Trubek, "Max Weber on Law and the Rise of Capitalism" (1972) *Wisconsin Law Review* 720.

[3] Niklas Luhmann, *Law as a Social System* trans. Klaus A. Ziegert (Oxford: Oxford University Press, 2004) 112.

[4] Roberto Mangabeira Unger, *Law in Modern Society* (New York: Free Press, 1976) 52–3. Unger goes on to argue that law in postliberal society (the welfare state) loses this autonomy (192–200).

[5] Phillippe Nonet and Philip Selznick, *Toward Responsive Law: Law & Society in Transition* (New Brunswick, NJ: Transaction Publishers, 2001 [1978]).

[6] Edward P. Thompson, *Whigs and Hunters: The Origin of the Black Act* (New York: Pantheon Books, 1975) 266. Some of the responses to Thompson's argument include Morton Horwitz, "The Rule of Law: An Unqualified Human Good?" (1977) 86 *Yale Law Journal* 561; Isaac D. Balbus, "Commodity Form and Legal Form: An Essay on the 'Relative Autonomy' of Law" (1977) 11 *Law & Society Review* 571; Robert Fine, "The Rule of Law and Muggletonian Marxism: The Perplexities of Edward Thompson" (1994) 21 *Journal of Law and Society* 193; and Daniel H. Cole, "'An Unqualified Human Good': E.P. Thompson and the Rule of Law" (2001) 28 *Journal of Law and Society* 177. For all the controversy Thompson's remarks generated, the contributors to this literature all accept the premise that an ideology of law's autonomy from politics may under certain conditions become ascendant. Their disagreement concerns whether the triumph of this ideal masks the reality of capitalist class relations or whether adherence to this ideal may under certain conditions restrain the exercise of arbitrary power.

independence of judicial decision-making from political influence. When Robert Dahl, for example, asserts that the justices of the US Supreme Court never depart too far from the policy preferences of the dominant political coalition,[7] what he means is that there is an empirically detectable causal link between the political content of the justices' decisions and the political commitments of the dominant coalition. When Weber, Luhmann, Unger, and Nonet and Selznick talk of the emergence of "autonomous law," by contrast, what is being described is the process through which, in certain societies at certain times, the ideal of law's autonomy from politics becomes the dominant ideological frame through which the law/politics relation is understood.[8] While this process may be impacted by societal conceptions of the actual causal influence of politics on judicial decision-making, it is not in the end dependent on the empirical verifiability of such influence. Rather, it depends on the degree of public commitment to this ideal, its instantiation in practice, and its tendency to legitimate arguments that rely on it for support.

This is not to say that these ideological effects are not real or not in any way empirically detectable. It is simply to say that the causal independence of law from politics as an empirical matter is not the be all and end all of the sociological understanding of law's autonomy. For social theorists, law's autonomy from politics is an ideal that has real animating power, and may influence both individual actions and broader social processes in ways that cannot always be detected by multivariate regression analysis. As Unger put the point, "[a]n adequate understanding of the legal system must . . . avoid the errors of either an idealist or a behaviorist approach to legal order."[9] It must, he said, steer a middle path between the twin misconceptions of assuming that law operates exactly as the ideology of law's separation from politics says it operates and "the tendency to treat the generality and autonomy of a legal order as merely ideological pretenses that ought simply to be set aside by one who would understand how law operates."[10]

According to this sociological understanding, law's autonomy from politics is one possible outcome of, and animating ideal in, complex social processes that may take centuries to unfold. Those processes are partly a function of interests – of support received from social actors who are either sincerely committed to, or have something to gain from, the ideological ascendance of this ideal – and partly a function of contingent events that set in train a

[7]   Robert A. Dahl, "Decision-making in a Democracy: The Supreme Court as a National Policy-Maker" (1957) 6 *Journal of Public Law* 279, 285.
[8]   See, for example, Luhmann, *Law as a Social System* 357–80.
[9]   Unger, *Law in Modern Society* 57.
[10] Ibid 56.

trajectory of institutional development that may become self-reinforcing.[11] One of the reasons why such a trajectory might take hold, for example, is that the notion that law is autonomous from politics has the capacity to legitimate political authority.[12] As artificial and mystifying as it may seem, an ideology of law's autonomy from politics may be better than the other alternatives on offer: in democratic societies, better than a constant and destabilizing questioning of the impartiality of law, and in authoritarian societies, better than the mental and material costs of ruling by force alone.

In societies in which a system of judicial review has been established, claims about law's autonomy from politics are typically founded on a subsidiary claim about the impartiality of the reasoning methods judges use to decide constitutional cases. While the general public will not usually be well versed in the specifics of these methods, the broader claim to law's autonomy becomes ascendant when there is a sufficient degree of public confidence in the existence of some such set of methods and their capacity to exclude the influence of judicial policy preferences on constitutional decision-making, or at least to bring this influence within acceptable limits. Legal professionals, and especially legal academics, may play an intermediary role in this respect – their technical debates and robust critique of judicial decisions reassuring the public that judicial adherence to the relevant methods is being properly policed. In the end, however, public confidence in these methods is not a matter of technical understanding, but of their association with the broader claim to law's autonomy that has become ascendant at an ideological level.

There is an admitted circularity in all of this. The reasoning methods that ostensibly support law's autonomy from politics are themselves accepted only to the extent that the ideal of law's autonomy from politics achieves some degree of ideological salience. But what kind of support is that? If the credibility of the claim that these methods constrain the influence of judicial policy preferences on constitutional decision-making depends on the ideological ascendance of the ideal of law's autonomy, we have at best the support of two sticks leaning against each other – at worst, a dog chasing its tail.

A full answer to this conundrum will be given in the course of this study. For the moment, the point is that claims about law's autonomy in systems of judicial review are not made in thin air, but are attached to a subsidiary

---

[11] On path dependence effects in the development of legal institutions, see Alec Stone Sweet, "Path Dependence, Precedent, and Judicial Power" in Martin Shapiro and Alec Stone Sweet (eds.), *On Law, Politics, and Judicialization* (New York: Oxford University Press, 2002) 112; Karen Orren, *Belated Feudalism: Labor, the Law, and Liberal Development in the United States* (New York: Cambridge University Press, 1991).

[12] See Trubek, "Max Weber on Law and the Rise of Capitalism" 749.

claim about the impartiality of the reasoning methods through which this autonomy is instantiated in practice. The broader claim makes use of the existence of these methods in the battle of ideas over law's autonomy, and those methods in turn come to stand in for law's autonomy to the extent that the broader claim succeeds. The important consequence of this dynamic – however empirically unfounded and however circular the claim about law's causal independence from politics might be – is that perceived adherence to the set of reasoning methods that has come to be associated with this claim has the power to legitimate a judicial decision. Once a claim about law's autonomy becomes ascendant, debates over the irreducible politicality of judicial decision-making decline in relative terms, and attention turns instead to whether a disputed decision in fact adheres to the methods that have come to be associated with the successfully asserted claim to law's autonomy.

There is no standard set of reasoning methods through which law's claim to autonomy is everywhere supported. While there may be some commonalities among different legal traditions,[13] every society in which the ideal of law's autonomy from politics has achieved some degree of ideological salience will have its own tradition of legal reasoning that defines the boundary between law and politics. In some societies, for example, law's claimed autonomy may be associated with a tradition of legal reasoning that gives primacy to formalist methods. In other societies this claim may be associated with a tradition that allows at least some recourse to more substantive, policy-oriented methods. Different traditions of legal reasoning may combine these methods in different ways, and there may be internal contestation over the legitimacy of particular methods. No two legal traditions will be the same in this respect. Instead, each will have its own unique combination of ever-evolving and contestable methods. Provided that public confidence in the capacity of these methods to constrain judicial decision-making is maintained, however, the existence of some such tradition will support law's claim to autonomy.

It is this variation in the extent of different societies' commitment to the ideal of law's autonomy and the reasoning methods that instantiate it that comparative studies of judicial review need to take into account. On the one hand, public confidence in law's autonomy from politics is not everywhere the

---

[13] This study uses the term "legal tradition" to refer to a tradition of legal reasoning associated with the institutional practice of law in a particular society. See Martin Krygier, "Law as Tradition" (1986) 5 *Law and Philosophy* 237. The term "legal culture," by contrast, will be used to refer to public understandings, not just within the legal profession, but more broadly, of the law/politics relation. See Roger Cotterrell, "The Concept of Legal Culture" in David Nelken (ed.), *Comparing Legal Cultures* (Aldershot: Dartmouth, 1997) 13; David Nelken, "Using the Concept of Legal Culture" (2004) 29 *Australian Journal of Legal Philosophy* 1.

same. In some societies, as explained later on,[14] law's autonomy may be compartmentalized in the sense that only certain forms of public power are believed to be subject to meaningful judicial control while others are not. On the other hand, even where the ideal of law's autonomy is ideologically ascendant, the reasoning methods associated with this ideal vary from society to society. Nor is the strength of public confidence in law's autonomy or the methods with which this confidence is associated static. Public confidence in law's autonomy may founder in the face of some supervening event, such as a national emergency during which the imperatives of law are subordinated to the imperatives of politics. And legal reasoning methods may evolve over time, so that methods that previously may have been regarded as unacceptably political may win acceptance and come to be seen as legitimate. A final possibility, famously explored by Nonet and Selznick,[15] is that a legal culture committed to the ideal of law's autonomy may undergo some sort of transformation process, so that the authority of law comes to depend less on the ideological salience of this ideal and more on some other social function that law is said to perform. In such legal cultures, faith in law's autonomy from politics may effectively collapse, making them in one sense like legal cultures in which law's autonomy has never been established. In another sense, however, legal cultures in which a previously strong faith in law's autonomy has been abandoned will be significantly different from legal cultures in which such a faith has never existed. They may even be superior in some normative sense to legal cultures in which the authority of law is still tied to an empirically unprovable and formalistically maintained faith in law's autonomy from politics.

As noted, the claim that law is causally independent of politics in systems of judicial review has been disputed as an empirical matter, and merely stating that an ideology of law's autonomy from politics may triumph at a legal-cultural level says nothing about the actual relationship between law and politics in practice. But this problem may be dealt with methodologically. Nothing in treating the ideal of law's autonomy from politics as having the potential to become ascendant assumes that this potential will be realized in every society, or that every constitutional decision taken in a society in which this ideal has triumphed will be free from political influence. Indeed, it may be that judicial decision-making is nowhere causally independent of the influence of politics. However, this does not matter when the focus of attention is not on the causal influence of politics on judicial decision-making but

---

[14] Section 2.3.1.
[15] Nonet and Selznick, *Law and Society in Transition*.

rather on how societal conceptions of the law/politics relation evolve, some-times consolidate around a dominant conception, and at other times transi-tion to a new conception. When that is the focus, what matters is how law's relationship to politics is understood at an ideological level and the way this understanding is instantiated in official discourse, judicial decisions, popular conceptions, and formal and informal institutional practices.

The question to which this chapter now turns is how best to conceptualize the interaction of competing legal and political authority claims in JR regimes. If the central issue is not the causal independence of judicial decision-making from political influence, but changing societal conceptions of the law/politics relation, how should claims to legal and political authority be conceived as macrovariables for the purposes of this study? The next section starts to address this issue by drawing on what is probably the best-known example of JR-regime change in the comparative literature – the transformation of societal concep-tions of the law/politics relation that took place in the United States in the first half of the last century.

2.2 JR-REGIME TRANSFORMATION DURING THE *LOCHNER* ERA

Consider the famous *Lochner* era in American constitutional politics,[16] a period of heightened judicial activism during which the US Supreme Court declared nearly 200 pieces of state economic legislation unconstitutional against a laissez-faire reading of the Fourteenth Amendment's due process clause.[17] Before this period began in the 1890s, the Supreme Court's authority to countermand the wishes of a democratic majority was premised on a dominant conception of law as "a structure of impartial and self-executing norms."[18] On this view, law (then principally associated with the common law) had its own internal logic and immanent values that were relatively impervious to the influence of democratic politics. By the period's end in 1937, this faith in law's autonomy had declined, and instead law (now princi-pally in the form of legislation) was viewed as a malleable instrument of public policy that, with the assistance of social science, could be put to use in service

---

[16] The period is named after *Lochner* v. *New York* 198 US 45 (1905) although the era technically began in the 1890s. See Richard H. Fallon, Jr., *The Dynamic Constitution: An Introduction to American Constitutional Law* (New York: Cambridge University Press, 2004) 81.

[17] See Robert G. McCloskey, *The American Supreme Court* (4th ed.) revised by Sanford Levinson (Chicago: University of Chicago Press, 2005) 101.

[18] Morton J. Horwitz, *The Transformation of American Law, 1870–1960: The Crisis of Legal Orthodoxy* (New York: Oxford University Press, 1992) 4.

of partisan political goals.[19] On this view, democratic politics was about winning the right to use law in this way; judicial review, in turn, was a politically significant institution that could be used to thwart the wishes of a contemporary democratic majority. Clearly, societal conceptions of the law/ politics relation changed character during this time. But what drove those changes? And is it possible to use the *Lochner* example to construct a more general account of the evolution of JR regimes?

The standard explanation for the *Lochner* period ascribes the Supreme Court's heightened activism to the justices' ideologically motivated resistance to the rise of the welfare state. A majority group of conservative justices, this explanation goes, applied the Court's past decisions on the unconstitutionality of class-based legislation to veto a range of state initiatives aimed at regulating the basic conditions of employment. Those initiatives were backed by legislative majorities responding to profound structural changes in the American economy.[20] Over the course of the nineteenth century, what had been a largely agricultural society changed into an urban, industrialized society. Conditions of employment in the new cities were exploitative and unhealthy, and state legislatures responded by attempting to set minimum wages, maximum hours of work, and other standards. These new forms of regulation challenged existing laissez-faire understandings of the freedom of contract and, associated with those, received doctrinal understandings of the legitimate reach of state legislatures' police power.[21] In striking down many of the new statutes, the justices were enforcing these received understandings, which they reasoned were protected by the Fourteenth Amendment's due process clause.

In 1935, after 40 years of this rearguard action, things were driven to a head when a new conservative majority on the Supreme Court turned its attention to President Franklin Roosevelt's New Deal program and sought to declare certain types of *federal* economic legislation permanently off-limits.[22] Emboldened by his decisive 1936 election victory, Roosevelt responded by announcing a plan to appoint an additional justice for every justice over seventy years of age. If implemented, the plan would have seen the Court's membership enlarged from nine to as many as fifteen – enough to defeat the conservative majority. Faced with this prospect, Justice Owen Roberts switched sides and the Court's substantive due process reading of the Fourteenth Amendment was effectively overruled in a series of decisions in

---

[19] Ibid, 6.

[20] Horwitz, *The Transformation of American Law* 4.

[21] See Howard Gillman, *The Constitution Besieged: The Rise and Demise of Lochner Era Police Powers Jurisprudence* (Durham, NC: Duke University Press, 1993).

[22] McCloskey, *The American Supreme Court* 101.

1937.[23] There was no simple returning to the pre-*Lochner* era, however. Democrats, previously skeptical of judicial review, had learned the value of an ideologically committed Court and sought to exploit its newfound influence and activism to support their own political agenda.[24] It was this bipartisan embrace of the Court's politicized role that paved the way for the decision in *Brown* v. *Board of Education*[25] and the Warren Court's liberal activism that followed it.[26]

In addition to the bipartisan embrace of the Court's new role, any notion of returning to the pre-*Lochner* era was negated by a significant transformation of American legal culture that occurred at roughly the same time as the *Lochner* line of cases was playing itself out. While the exact causes and nature of this transformation are disputed, there is broad agreement that the legal realist movement, which came to prominence in the 1920s and 1930s, succeeded in fundamentally shaking Americans' faith in the determinacy of law.[27] Part of this transformation was directly associated with the *Lochner* line of cases. Thus, Justice Oliver Wendell Holmes, who had been a protorealist before joining the Court and who had dissented in *Lochner*, became a leading voice for the movement from the Bench.[28] It was also Justice Holmes's famous quip in *Lochner* that the Fourteenth Amendment did not "enact Mr. Herbert Spencer's Social Statics"[29] that eventually came to be vindicated in *Carolene Products*,[30] the case that put the

---

[23]   The most famous of these being *West Coast Hotel Co* v. *Parrish* 300 US 379 (1937).
[24]   Thomas C. Grey, "Judicial Review and Legal Pragmatism" (2003) 38 *Wake Forest Law Review* 473, 508.
[25]   *Brown* v. *Board of Education* 347 US 483 (1954).
[26]   See G. Edward White, *Earl Warren: A Public Life* (Oxford: Oxford University Press, 1987); Morton J. Horwitz, *The Warren Court and the Pursuit of Justice* (New York: Hill and Wang, 1998); Lucas A. Powe, Jr., *The Warren Court and American Politics* (Cambridge, MA: Harvard University Press, 2000).
[27]   For the most comprehensive treatment, see Horwitz, *The Transformation of American Law, 1870–1960*. For a revisionist account that argues that the formalism of the earlier period has been talked up too much, see Brian Z. Tamanaha, *Beyond the Formalist-Realist Divide: The Role of Politics in Judging* (Princeton, NJ: Princeton University Press, 2010). In his review of Tamanaha's book, Brian Leiter, while agreeing that Tamanaha has identified various instances where earlier writers' work has been misrepresented, argues that Tamanaha overstates his conclusions and that there was indeed a significant transformation of views about the adjudicative process (Brian Leiter, "Legal Formalism and Legal Realism: What is the Issue?" (2010) 16 *Legal Theory* 111).
[28]   See Horwitz, *The Transformation of American Law* 109–43; see also Jacco Bomhoff, *Balancing Constitutional Rights: The Origins and Meanings of Postwar Legal Discourse* (Cambridge: Cambridge University Press, 2013); G. Edward White, *Oliver Wendell Holmes: Law and the Inner Self* (Oxford: Oxford University Press, 1996).
[29]   *Lochner* v. *New York* 198 US 45, 76 (1905).
[30]   *United States* v. *Carolene Products Co* 304 US 144 (1938).

final nail in the coffin of the Supreme Court's power substantively to review economic legislation.

As Brian Leiter has been at pains to point out, legal realism was not centrally about demystifying the politics of constitutional adjudication. Rather, it was about exposing the indeterminacy of rule-based decision-making and explaining how various extralegal norms, such as those prevailing in the business community, influenced judicial decisions.[31] The transformation of American legal culture that occurred during the *Lochner* period is therefore not reducible to a transformation of societal conceptions of the law/politics relation. Nevertheless, at the level of constitutional culture, public faith in the autonomy of law from politics did decline – not because of the triumph of a positive thesis about the necessary influence of politics on constitutional adjudication, but rather because of the recognition that legal reasoning, as an indeterminate science, was conceivably open to political influence. In consequence, judicial review could no longer be justified as the impartial implementation of the higher-law commands of a political sovereign. Rather, judicial review had to be justified either on the basis that, in cases of indeterminacy, the justices could always defer to contemporary political mandates or on the basis that, in a system of regularly rotating political power, each side of politics would eventually have an opportunity to appoint its own ideologically loyal justices.

What does this well-known story tell us about how societal conceptions of the law/politics relation evolve? Is it possible to reframe it in more general terms? Note, first, that the majority justices in *Lochner* offered their reading of the Fourteenth Amendment's due process clause as a legally authorized interpretation. Though the public policy implications of that interpretation were clear, the argument that state economic legislation was class-based redistributive legislation had a solid basis in precedent.[32] The majority justices' vetoing of these statutes was in this sense an assertion of legal authority over the policy issues in question – an attempt to carve out a space within which law would rule. Had their decisions been accepted and enforced, they would have been legitimated and depoliticized – accepted as a legally required reading of the Fourteenth Amendment. Only this did not happen. Instead, the legal correctness of the majority justices' reading was contested by state politicians,

---

[31]   See Brian Leiter, "Rethinking Legal Realism: Toward a Naturalized Jurisprudence" (1997) 76 *Texas Law Review* 267.

[32]   See Mark Tushnet, *The Constitution of the United States: A Contextual Analysis* (Oxford: Hart Publishing, 2009) 26–7.

the public media, and progressive forces more generally.[33] Eventually, the Court's substantive due process doctrine was dramatically opposed by President Roosevelt, claiming the political authority of his overwhelming 1936 election mandate.

With Justice Roberts's switch, the majority justices' reading was defeated and now stands in history as an illegitimate authority claim – a legally unjustified and never-to-be-repeated interpretation of the Fourteenth Amendment. But societal understandings of the law/politics relation, upon resolution of this conflict, did not simply return to their previous position. Over the course of the *Lochner* era, the genie of ideologically motivated Supreme Court decision-making had been let irretrievably out of the bottle. At the period's end, no one sought to deny that what had been going on was an attempt on the part of the majority justices to write their subjective political values into law. And, indeed, the end of that period saw the appointment of liberal justices in their stead – a reaction to, but also acceptance of, this approach to constitutional decision-making.[34] To the extent that societal conceptions of the law/politics relation stabilized again, in other words, they stabilized around a new understanding of the legitimate basis for judicial review. If law's authority before *Lochner* had been founded on the assumed existence of politically neutral, technocratic reasoning methods through which abstract constitutional expressions could be applied to the assessment of public policy, the new accommodation rested on the recognition of the potential role of subjective political values in US Supreme Court decision-making. This was more than just a slight adjustment. It was a tectonic shift in societal conceptions of the law/politics relation – from a conception that had previously been grounded in public confidence in law's autonomy from politics to its exact opposite – a conception founded on the acknowledgment of law's susceptibility to political influence.

2.3 GENERALIZING THE *LOCHNER* STORY

The transformation of conceptions of the law/politics relation that occurred during the *Lochner* era is the most familiar example of this phenomenon. But there are parallels in other societies as well. One of these is the constitutional-

---

[33] See Barry Friedman, *The Will of the People: How Public Opinion Has Influenced the Supreme Court and Shaped the Meaning of the Constitution* (New York: Farrar, Straus and Giroux, 2009) 175–94.

[34] See Noah Feldman, *Scorpions: The Battles and Triumphs of FDR's Great Supreme Court Justices* (New York: Twelve, 2010).

cultural transformation that took place in India after the 1975–7 Emergency.[35] According to the now-familiar story, the Indian Supreme Court's public reputation changed during the 1980s from that of a technocratic court enforcing the terms of the written constitution to that of a politically progressive court correcting deficiencies in India's democratic system.[36] This process was associated with the adoption of new interpretive methodologies, procedural rules, and doctrinal norms. But it also involved changing conceptions of the legitimate basis for judicial review. Before the transformation began, the Court's claim to authority had been founded on the alleged objectivity of its interpretive methods. By the late 1980s, its authority had come to be founded on its role in giving a voice to the poor and the marginalized.

Another familiar example of this sort of process is the development of German constitutionalism after the end of World War II. As recently retold by Michaela Hailbronner, the story of that process is one of "transformations and traditions" – of the emergence of an understanding of the legitimate basis for judicial review that both drew on and refashioned Germany's long-standing tradition of legalism.[37] Here, again, it is impossible to tell this story without knowing something about past societal conceptions of the law/politics relation and the way legal and political elites adapted these conceptions to justify the Federal Constitutional Court's role under the Basic Law.

One final example of this phenomenon is the so-called "Mason Court revolution" in Australia – a period during which a group of High Court justices attempted to articulate and enforce the unwritten political values informing the Australian Constitution.[38] In pursuit of that goal, the High Court developed several new doctrines that purported to change its institutional role.[39] The new doctrines were resisted by more traditionally minded justices and the constitutional-cultural revolution that the Mason Court sought to effect was in the end not fully achieved. In this sense, the Australian case may be thought of as a negative example of the sort of transformation process witnessed in the US between 1890 and 1937. Nevertheless, it again illustrates how the American experience might serve as the basis for comparative theorizing. The remainder of this section mines

---

[35] See Upendra Baxi, *The Indian Supreme Court and Politics* (Lucknow: Eastern Book Co, 1980).
[36] See the detailed discussion in Chapter 4.
[37] Michaela Hailbronner, *Traditions and Transformations: The Rise of German Constitutionalism* (Oxford: Oxford University Press, 2015).
[38] See Jason L. Pierce, *Inside the Mason Court Revolution: The High Court of Australia Transformed* (Durham, NC: Carolina Academic Press, 2006).
[39] See further the discussion in Chapter 3.

the *Lochner* example for the generalizable concepts that this study proposes to use in this exercise.

2.3.1 *The Core Concept: JR Regimes*

What was it exactly that transformed during the *Lochner* era? In a review of the second volume of *The Transformation of American Law*,[40] Richard Posner criticized Horwitz's account of the changes that took place during this period for abandoning the successful formula he had used in the first volume.[41] Horwitz's object of study, Posner disparagingly remarked, was no longer the evolution of doctrinal law or the development of formal institutions. It had become "the discourse of law professors and jurists."[42]

Posner was certainly right to note a change in the nature of Horwitz's project, and the second volume of the *Transformation of American Law* is more fragmented than the first – a collection of essays rather than a single narrative. But Posner was too quick to dismiss as unimportant Horwitz's newfound concern for ideational change. At least, the claim that such matters are not worthy of scholarly attention seems a little dogmatic.[43] There clearly is a story to be told about the transformation of American law over the first half of the last century. It could be about the collapse of substantive due process or about the institutional power struggle between the Court and the President. But it could equally well be about how Americans lost their faith in the impartiality of judicial reasoning processes and about how a new understanding of the relationship between law and politics gradually developed to replace it. In its very dismissiveness, then, Posner's critique of Horwitz's book helps to clarify what this study's dependent variable might be – the complex of legitimating ideas about the law/politics relation in a society in which a system of judicial review has been introduced.

Defined in that way, the idea of a JR regime is an admittedly fuzzy, abstract concept that is not statistically measurable in any way.[44] Unlike, say, judicial independence, societal conceptions of the law/politics relation cannot be

---

[40] Horwitz, *The Transformation of American Law, 1870–1960.*
[41] Morton J. Horwitz, *The Transformation of American Law, 1780–1860* (Cambridge, MA: Harvard University Press, 1979).
[42] Richard A. Posner, "Law as Politics: Horwitz on American Law, 1870–1960" (1992) 6 A *Critical Review* 559, 563.
[43] For a more sympathetic account of Horwitz's project, see Michael R. Belknap's review in (1993) 98 *American Historical Review* 970.
[44] On the difficulties, but also the rewards, of studying "fuzzy" ideas, see Sheri Berman, *The Social Democratic Moment: Ideas and Politics in the Making of Interwar Europe* (Cambridge, MA: Harvard University Press, 1998) 19–24.

assigned a numerical value. Such conceptions are also complex and contested, and the best that we can do is to say where we should look to discern
the character of a society's JR regime. Drawing again on the American
experience during the *Lochner* era, the suggested sources of information
about a society's JR regime are: (1) a variety of forms of culturally influential
public discourse (judicial decisions, extracurial judicial statements, statements by other public office bearers, legal-academic writing, and, especially
in authoritarian regimes, official state ideology); (2) public attitudes towards
the law/politics relation (as gleaned from social surveys); and (3) formal and
informal institutional practices to the extent that they reveal something about
underlying societal conceptions of the law/politics relation (for example, the
judicial appointments process in the society concerned).

None of these sources provides anything more than qualitative information
about the character of a society's JR regime. The specification of an actually
existing regime is an interpretive matter that is only as persuasive as the
argument made out. Nevertheless, varying conceptions of the law/politics
relation are empirically real in some sense. They are the stuff both of internal
contestation within a JR regime and the reason for intuited differences
between JR regimes. We know, for example, that when we travel in our
comparative constitutional armchairs from the US to Germany, or from
Singapore to Pakistan, we are moving between different constitutional cultures and that one aspect of the difference we discern is the way the law/
politics relation is conceived. In the US, for example, widespread cynicism
prevails about whether the justices of the Supreme Court are capable of
privileging their good-faith interpretation of the law over their ideological
loyalties in high-profile constitutional cases like those involving abortion,[45] or
the right to bear arms,[46] or same-sex marriage,[47] or the election of a president.[48] Even when the justices appear to stray from their known ideological
commitments, as famously happened when Chief Justice Roberts announced
his opinion in the *Obamacare* case,[49] public discussion turns to what their
strategic motivations might have been. In contrast, in Germany, the idea that
there exist quasi-scientific legal reasoning techniques, like proportionality,
through which members of the Federal Constitutional Court might be able
to accord appropriate weight to competing political values is less controversial.
Judges and legal professionals really do seem to believe this, and they argue

[45] *Roe* v. *Wade* 410 U.S. 113 (1973).
[46] *District of Columbia* v. *Heller* 554 U.S. 570 (2008).
[47] *Obergefell* v. *Hodges* 576 U.S. (2015).
[48] *Bush* v. *Gore* 531 U.S. 98 (2000).
[49] *National Federation of Independent Business* v. *Sebelius* 567 U.S. 519 (2012).

and reason on the assumption that these techniques effectively constrain the influence of subjective political values on judicial decision-making.

Conceptions of the law/politics relation are, of course, contested in any reasonably sophisticated constitutional culture. There will be degrees of faith in law's autonomy, rival theories of the legitimacy of judicial review, different views about which reasoning methods best conform to a morally defensible conception of law's authority, and so on. But at some higher level of abstraction, many constitutional cultures have a dominant conception of this kind, so that it makes sense (and everybody understands what we mean) when we say that German constitutional culture is founded on a strong faith in law's autonomy from politics and US constitutional culture on a comparatively weak one. That does not mean that every German lawyer buys into that conception as a true believer, or that there are not US legal theorists, like Frederick Schauer, for example,[50] who have more confidence in the autonomy of law than others. But it does mean that, at this higher level of abstraction, we may be able to identify a dominant conception that serves as a rough identifier of a constitutional culture, in the same way that we might think of Italians as being stylish dressers or Australians as being easygoing and relaxed. These are caricatures, but there is a grain of truth in them and they are thus useful as starting points for comparison.

The significance of these dominant conceptions, the *Lochner* example suggests, is their legitimating power. Judicial decisions and political conduct that conform to them have a greater chance of being accepted than judicial decisions or political conduct that do not. Judicial decisions, of course, must also conform to accepted methods of legal reasoning, and there is a complex link between those methods and dominant societal conceptions of the law/politics relation that this study will explore. Political actors likewise may appeal to a specifically political tradition of thinking about the value of democracy and the extent to which a democratic mandate should be constrained by law. But, at a higher level of abstraction, a society's legal and political traditions may under certain conditions coalesce into a dominant conception of the appropriate relationship between law and politics.

2.3.2 *The Evolution of JR Regimes*

The fact that there may be such a dominant conception does not mean that it is static, of course. Every time a controversial political decision or assertion of judicial authority is accepted as legitimate, societal conceptions of the law/

---

[50]   See, for example, Frederick Schauer, "Formalism" (1988) 97 *Yale Law Journal* 509.

politics relation subtly change. This follows from the nature of JR regimes as complexes of legitimating ideas that provide the resources for argumentation about issues in dispute. The evolution of JR regimes is not a story of endless, deterministic conformity, but a story about competition between legal and political actors, each appealing to the same complex of legitimating ideas, but in the process developing them.

How best to conceive of this competition and how might it drive the evolution of JR regimes? Again, drawing on the *Lochner* example, we might say that the driving force behind the development of a JR regime is the fact that legal and political authority claims conflict with each other in two distinct ways. One way is the ordinary stuff of constitutional politics – the daily contestation over public policy, with legal actors laying claim to the authority of law and political actors laying claim to the authority of a democratic mandate or some other allegedly compelling justification for their actions. Provided those two sets of claims appeal to the same dominant conception of the law/politics relation, they reinforce that conception even as actors disagree over the correct answer to the question at hand. In other situations, however, such as the US after 1890, when rapid urbanization and industrialization required state legislatures and eventually Congress to demand greater powers in the name of their democratic mandates to regulate certain aspects of social and economic life, an external event may drive a fundamental change in the scope of the authority claimed by either legal or political actors. When that happens, the changed scope of the relevant authority claim may trigger a deep-structural conflict that cannot be resolved by the existing legitimation structure. Thus, in the US, state legislatures' claims about the legitimate scope of their democratic mandates ran up against claims of legitimate legal authority to enforce the limits of the police power as that doctrine had traditionally been understood. In circumstances of deep-structural conflict like that, the tension between rival legal and political authority claims has the capacity to drive fundamental changes in societal conceptions of the law/politics relation, such that we might be able to discern, over time, a profound change in the dominant conception.[51]

We are dealing here, in other words, with a legitimating complex of ideas that is constantly evolving through contestation between actors speaking in the name of law and actors speaking in the name of politics. In situations of

---

[51] The distinction between the normal law/politics conflict that reinforces a JR regime and the heightened law/politics conflict that may drive the transformation of a JR regime is similar to Bruce Ackerman's notion of "dualistic democracy." See Ackerman, "Constitutional Law/Politics" (1989) 99 *Yale Law Journal* 453, 456. The difference is that Ackerman is referring to the normative Constitution, while the reference here is to an ideational complex.

relative stability, those conflicting claims are contained within the existing legitimation structure and the JR regime develops slowly and incrementally. But there are also periods of more rapid and profound transformation, such as that in the US between 1890 and 1937.

In the American case, the period of transformation is reasonably determinate inasmuch as most scholars agree that it began in the late nineteenth century and ended when the bubble burst on the substantive due process doctrine in *West Coast Hotel* v. *Parrish*.[52] It was as though the Supreme Court had sustained an increasingly implausible impression of itself as a politically neutral institution until suddenly things switched, and *Lochner* became a negative example – of what not to do – around which a new dominant societal conception of the law/politics relation began to develop. Similarly, in Australia, the Mason Court revolution is said to have ended in the *Lange* case,[53] when the High Court issued a *per curiam* opinion reconciling the Court's new doctrines with traditional conceptions of legitimate legal reasoning. There, too, periodization is relatively easy. That need not be the case, however, and in certain societies the most that we might be able to say is that over time one dominant societal conception progressively comes to replace another.

Any comparative theory of the evolution of JR regimes needs to take account of this difference between significant shifts in societal conceptions of the law/politics relation and more incremental developments. It also needs to distinguish exogenously driven change of the sort depicted in the *Lochner* story (the industrialization and urbanization shocks to Classical Legal Thought) from endogenous change of the kind stressed in the Australian story (of Sir Anthony Mason's internal judicial challenge to the complex of legitimating ideas that had stabilized around the middle of the last century). Either way, the dynamic quality of this evolutionary process flows from the fact that legal and political actors appeal to distinct forms of authority and that, under certain conditions, rather than reinforcing the existing JR regime, these authority claims may conflict with each other in ways that open the regime to change.

2.3.3 *The Key Independent Variables: Changing Conceptions of Legal and Political Authority*

The key variables that interact in this process are societal conceptions of the legitimate basis for law's authority, on the one hand, and societal conceptions

---

[52]   300 US 379 (1937).
[53]   *Lange* v. *Australian Broadcasting Corporation* (1997) 189 CLR 520 (discussed in Chapter 3).

of the legitimate basis for political authority, on the other. In a consolidated JR regime, these conceptions are by definition in a stable relationship with each other – indeed, they mutually support each other in a composite legitimating ideology. At the same time, however, each variable is also in theory capable of being impacted by exogenous factors or internal ideational (i.e., endogenous) challenges and changing in ways that put it in tension with the other.

Continuing to draw on the *Lochner* example, we might stipulate that the legal variable concerns public faith in the ideal of law's autonomy from politics. Actually existing JR regimes occupy a continuum of possibilities between the absolute ascendance of this ideal and complete disillusionment with it. For comparative purposes, however, two main possibilities may be distinguished: (1) JR regimes in which the ideal of law's autonomy from politics is hegemonic; and (2) JR regimes where a commitment to, or a faith in this ideal, has either never been established or is in significant decline. In the first instance, law's authority is defended on the basis that judicial review provides a politically impartial mechanism for enforcing the requirements of a supreme-law constitution against the wishes of a contemporary political power holder. In the second instance, law either enjoys little autonomous authority and is essentially treated as a subsystem of politics, or law is seen as deeply implicated in politics and yet as still authoritative for another reason – its usefulness as an instrument for the promotion of political goals and, in the case of judicial review, the best contemporary understanding of constitutional justice.

The first of these two bases for law's authority commonly goes under the rubric of legalism.[54] In democratic societies, the primary advantage of this conception is that it purports to meet the democratic objection to judicial review. To the charge that judicial review is about countermanding the will of the contemporary majority, legalism replies that this function is carried out in furtherance of a superior political mandate – the will of the people at the founding moment as discerned through impartial judicial reasoning methods.[55] The further advantage of this conception in democratic societies is that it provides a ready basis for the legitimation of political authority. If law truly is

[54] See Judith N. Shklar, *Legalism: Law, Morals, and Political Trials* (Cambridge, MA: Harvard University Press, 1964). Shklar's definition of legalism as "an ethical attitude that holds moral conduct to be a matter of rule following" (at 1) is directed at the legalist underpinnings of analytic legal philosophy. Nevertheless, there is much in Shklar's argument that also addresses legalism as a political ideology with varying degrees of strength (see especially 117).

[55] In practice, this defense thus tends to be associated with originalist methods of interpretation, although it is possible, as we shall see, for a faith in law's autonomy from politics to coexist with other methods.

an impartial mechanism for the enforcement of a superior political mandate, then democratic leaders who submit themselves to the discipline of judicial review may claim not just that their mandate is that much more legitimate for having been produced according to constitutional prescriptions, but also that all the policies they adopt and which are not challenged, or which survive constitutional scrutiny, are legitimate, too. Indeed, so powerful is this legitimation logic that it is readily apparent how a legalist conception of law's authority might emerge, accommodate itself to democratic political authority, and become entrenched.[56]

Legalism as a legitimating ideology also holds several advantages in authoritarian societies. Where the political content of law is antidemocratic or otherwise immoral, legalism offers judges a way of distancing themselves from that content.[57] "It is not we the judges, who are doing this, but the holders of political power, whose servants we merely are." There is some awkwardness to this stance, and judges who are committed to democracy and social justice might consider themselves to be morally obliged to resign – all the more so because their presence on the Bench helps to legitimate the unjust political order to which they are opposed.[58] But there are usually enough judges who find reasons to stay on: not all areas of the law are necessarily antidemocratic or unjust, and there might be opportunities to hold political power holders to account in areas where they are prepared to accept this. Under such conditions, legalism fulfils a legitimation function for authoritarian power holders even as it tempers the worst excesses of their rule. In E. P. Thompson's well-known formulation, authoritarian power holders who wish to benefit from autonomous law's legitimating power must on occasion submit themselves to law's authority.[59]

The second advantage of legalism in authoritarian settings is that it supports the bifurcation of social life into areas where law rules and areas where it does not.[60] The distinction between law and politics – which in democratic

---

[56]   Whatever the merits of Jeremy Waldron's moral-philosophical argument against judicial review (Waldron, "The Core of the Case against Judicial Review"), this is the basis for judicial review's sociological legitimacy in Western liberal democracies.

[57]   See David Dyzenhaus, *Hard Cases in Wicked Legal Systems: South African Law in the Perspective of Legal Philosophy* (Oxford: Clarendon Press, 1991); Robert M. Cover, *Justice Accused: Antislavery and the Judicial Process* (New Haven, Yale University Press, 1975).

[58]   There was a long debate over this question in apartheid South Africa, for example. For a survey, see Stephen Ellmann, "To Resign or Not to Resign" (1997) 19 *Cardozo Law Review* 1047.

[59]   Thompson, *Whigs and Hunters* 266.

[60]   See Ernst Fraenkel, *The Dual State: A Contribution to the Theory of Dictatorship* (Oxford: Oxford University Press, 2017 [1941]); Jens Meierhenrich, *The Legacies of Law: Long-Run*

societies is a distinction based on the distinctive purposes, methods, and organizing logic of these two social systems – becomes in authoritarian societies a basis for defining certain areas of social life as exclusively political. Law in authoritarian societies with a commitment to legalism is not all pervasive in this sense. There are areas of social life where law holds sway, and the existence of these areas provides a source of legitimation for political power holders. But there are also areas where politics holds sway, and the existence of these areas enhances political power holders' control over actors who might want to challenge their continued rule and over the means to protect their core interests unfettered by law's constraints.

For all these strengths, legalism – and particularly that version of it that attaches itself to democratic political authority – also has two major vulnerabilities. First, it is vulnerable to instances of apparent existential threat to the nation. This vulnerability is apparent in the state-of-emergency exception – the allowance that in cases where national security comes under extreme threat law's reach into certain areas of social life may be suspended. That provision for exceptionalism, as the burgeoning literature on Giorgio Agamben's work attests,[61] exposes legalism in democratic societies to the possibility of the normalization of emergency rule. Where that occurs, law may lose its capacity to speak truth to political power in precisely those areas of social life where it matters the most. In extreme circumstances, the normalization of emergency rule, especially where it affects the exclusion of law from the enforcement of democratic rights, may become the basis for a transition to the sort of bifurcated legalism characteristic of authoritarian societies.

Legalism's second vulnerability lies in the difficulties actors appealing to this ideology experience in accommodating the need for judicial creativity in systems of judicial review. Modelling law as it does as an impartial set of reasoning techniques for discerning the will of a political sovereign, a legalist conception of law's authority inhibits judges from adapting the constitution in line with evolving societal understandings of constitutional justice. Legalism's stock response when confronted with a tension between what the law requires and the demands of constitutional justice is to return the problem to the political sovereign for a fresh command. That approach may work in some instances, but it is not convenient in rigid constitutional systems where formal amendment is difficult. As the gap between the constitution's original

---

Consequences of Legal Development in South Africa, 1652–2000 (New York: Cambridge University Press, 2008).

[61] See Giorgio Agamben, *State of Exception* trans. Kevin Attell (Chicago: University of Chicago Press, 2005).

meaning and the constitutional law made by judges in response to the demands of constitutional justice grows, the denial of judicial law-making may come to seem increasingly improbable.

If legalism's first vulnerability is a vulnerability to regression into bifurcated legalism, this second vulnerability provides space for a different conception of law's authority to develop – one premised on the open embrace or at least grudging acceptance of law's immersion in politics, and on an appreciation for law's usefulness as an instrument for the promotion of the best contemporary understanding of constitutional justice. This alternative basis for law's authority at first seems anomalous. Why should unelected judges have the power to strike down democratically mandated legislation by reference to the best contemporary understanding of constitutional justice when that understanding will inevitably be affected by their own subjective political values? But the US experience after the *Lochner* period suggests that judges might well be able to reassert law's authority on this more instrumental basis.[62]

First, there is something intrinsically appealing about being more candid about the influence of subjective political values on constitutional decision-making. In place of the strained formalism of attempts to deny judges' creative role, defenders of law's claim to authority as an instrument for the promotion of the best contemporary understanding of constitutional justice celebrate the value of candor – of levelling with the public about how judicial review actually works.[63] While this admission raises concerns, on the one hand, about judicial review's countermajoritarian function, on the other, there is something fundamentally liberating about fessing up to law's politicality. "We have been deluded all these years and have in turn been deluding others," it is as though those who appeal to this conception of law's authority are saying. "We concede that judicial review's claimed impartiality is a myth and now we seek to legitimate judicial review on a new and more transparent footing – its capacity to justify the exercise of public power by providing, first, a forum within which the reasons for policies and other decisions may be challenged and scrutinized, and second, a forum within which the most attractive

---

[62] Instrumentalism is not a completely satisfactory term for this alternative basis, but is used here because it has some resonance with the way the post-*Lochner* basis for law's authority in the US has been understood. See Robert S. Summers, "Pragmatic Instrumentalism in Twentieth Century American Legal Thought – A Synthesis and Critique of our Dominant General Theory about Law and its Use" (1981) 66 *Cornell Law Review* 861. "Instrumentalism" is also capacious enough to cover the way law is used in authoritarian societies where an ideology of law's autonomy from politics plays little or no legitimating role.

[63] See Scott Altman, "Beyond Candor" (1990) 89 *Michigan Law Review* 296; Leslie Gielow Jacobs, "Even More Honest than Ever Before: Abandoning Pretense and Recreating Legitimacy in Constitutional Interpretation" (1995) 2 *University of Illinois Law Review* 363.

understanding of our political traditions and the legitimate basis for the exercise of coercive political power may be openly debated."

As public confidence in law's autonomy from politics recedes, in other words, what replaces it is a growing sense that a more instrumentalist conception of law, though harder to defend in many ways, provides certain advantages. Whereas under legalism, law is constantly in tension with the requirements of constitutional justice – as general rules fail to speak to particular circumstances and profound social and economic changes upset the framers' best-laid plans for a just society – instrumentalism allows this tension to be periodically resolved. Judicial legislation becomes the device through which broad political mandates are adapted to the case at hand, and the elaboration of new and unforeseen constitutional doctrines the means through which the constitution's connection to social justice is continually refreshed. The price to be paid for this flexibility is a blurring of the line between the production and application of law, but this is reduced where the reasons for judicial value choices are laid bare and exposed to public scrutiny. In Rawlsian terms, the constitutional court because a forum for "public reason" in which contending political values are debated in a more rarefied atmosphere than is possible in Parliament.[64]

To the extent that there is reasonable disagreement about how conflicting political values ought to be reconciled, instrumentalism stakes its claim to authority on procedural justice. The provision of procedural justice is also, of course, part of legalism's ideological armory, but here the emphasis is different. Whereas under legalism procedural justice is about blindly applied and thus impartial procedures, on an instrumentalist conception of law's authority, procedural justice is a way of accommodating disagreement over political values, and the indeterminacy of rights adjudication in particular, once the interpenetration of law and politics has been conceded. Law's claim to authority in this guise, as the legal process school in the US explained,[65] centers on its provision of mechanisms for "reasoned elaboration" in which general principles, which are concededly indeterminate and politically charged, are applied to the resolution of concrete disputes. This conception of law's authority also underpins democratic experimentalism and dialogue

---

[64] John Rawls, "The Idea of Public Reason Revisited" (1997) 64 *University of Chicago Law Review* 765. Jeremy Waldron has, of course, contested this portrayal of legislatures in a sustained body of work (see, for example, Jeremy Waldron, *The Dignity of Legislation* (Cambridge: Cambridge University Press, 1999)), but the point for now is simply to articulate it.

[65] Henry M. Hart and Albert M. Sacks, *The Legal Process: Basic Problems in the Making and Application of Law* (Foundation Press, 1994 [1958]).

theory – both of which hold that law's claim to authority may be justified on the basis that judicial decisions are merely provisional statements of the constitution's requirements.[66] In this way, law paradoxically claims authority by becoming less authoritarian.

The pursuit of substantive justice, too, is not the exclusive preserve of an instrumentalist conception of law. Legalism promises constitutional justice in the form of the purity and logical coherence of the framers' vision for a just society. Once public confidence in law's autonomy declines, however, judges are no longer thought to be capable of discerning that vision without interposing their own political values. It is accordingly preferable, on the instrumentalist view, that judges present what they are doing as appealing to some or other extralegal conception of constitutional justice. In relation to rights adjudication, for example, the court's work ceases to be about discerning the internal philosophical logic of the framers' scheme, and more about the moral persuasiveness of the court's decisions on their own terms. When this shift in the basis of law's claim to authority occurs, constitutional rights become moral rights pure and simple, and judges become moral reasoners in all but name.

In authoritarian societies in which public confidence in law's autonomy has either collapsed or has never been established, law has no independent claim to authority as such. Here, law's authority is entirely fused with the authority of the political order it claims to be implementing. This is an instrumentalist conception of law, but one according to which law has no autonomy and thus no independent capacity to legitimate political authority. This does not necessarily mean that law serves no role in such societies. As a basic means of communicating political commands and ensuring order, law still might serve a valuable social function. But the absence of any real faith in the distinction between law and politics means that the strength of law's claim to authority is entirely parasitic on the strength of political power holders' claim to authority.

The second key variable, political authority, is a notoriously slippery concept and its distinction from political legitimacy is not always consistently drawn.[67] In some usages, political authority is a purely descriptive term that refers to the *de facto* power of a political regime to direct the behavior of its

---

[66]   On dialogue theory, see Peter W. Hogg and Allison A. Bushell, "The Charter Dialogue between Courts and Legislatures (Or Perhaps the Charter of Rights Isn't Such a Bad Thing after All)" (1997) 35 *Osgoode Hall Law Journal* 75. On democratic experimentalism, see Michael C. Dorf and Charles F. Sabel, "A Constitution of Democratic Experimentalism" (1998) 98 *Columbia Law Review* 267.

[67]   See, for example, John T. Sanders, "Political Authority" (1983) 66 *The Monist* 545.

subjects and to enforce obedience to its commands.[68] In other usages, political authority connotes the normative appropriateness or justifiability of the exercise of political power in respect of a particular issue. For example, in the expression, "by what authority is this done?" the assumption is that the power being exercised must have some legitimate basis for it to be authoritative. Legitimacy conditions authority in this usage and there is no political authority that is not also legitimate political authority.[69] For the sake of clarity, the term "political authority" will be used here to refer to rightful or legitimate political authority, and "political authority claim" will mean a claim that the political regime as a whole, or the exercise of a particular political power, is legitimate. In this usage, claiming political authority is synonymous with seeking political legitimacy.

Today, political authority claims are usually supported by at least the pretense of democracy – by the holding of elections that solicit the consent of the governed in some form. This situation is testament to the status of democracy as the major source of political legitimacy after 1989. But that still leaves an important difference between power holders that claim authority on the basis of their commitment to a competitive, multiparty democratic system and power holders that offer an attenuated form of democracy as part of a package of legitimating devices.[70] In Singapore, for example, regular elections have been held ever since the break from Malaysia in 1965. But political rights are not actively enforced by the courts and only one political party – the People's Action Party (PAP) – has ever been in power.[71] While the holding of regular elections is thus part of what confers legitimacy on the PAP government, it also claims authority on other bases, including the preservation of ethnic harmony, which is seen as integral to the survival of the Singaporean state, and its ability to deliver continued economic prosperity.[72]

---

[68] See Tom Christiano, "Authority" in *The Stanford Encyclopedia of Philosophy* (Spring 2013 Edition), Edward N. Zalta (ed.), Retrieved from URL <http://plato.stanford.edu/archives/spr2013/entries/authority/>.

[69] See David M. Estlund, *Democratic Authority: A Philosophical Framework* (Princeton, NJ: Princeton University Press, 2007) 2.

[70] Freedom House's *Freedom in the World Report* 2016 (https://freedomhouse.org/report/freedom-world/freedom-world-2016) listed 145 out of 195 countries as free or partly free on the basis, inter alia, of their commitment to "electoral democracy." Of the remaining 50 countries, seven hold no elections at all. That suggests that there are 43 countries in the world where democratic elections are part of a package of authoritarian legitimation devices.

[71] PAP was founded by Lee Kuan Yew and is now led by his son Lee Hsien Loong.

[72] See Jothie Rajah, *Authoritarian Rule of Law: Legislation, Discourse, and Legitimacy in Singapore* (New York: Cambridge University Press, 2012).

The range of these alternative, nondemocratic bases for political authority is extremely diverse. To Max Weber's original list of legal-rational, traditional, and charismatic bases[73] may be added such things as redistributive economic reforms (think Venezuela and Bolivia),[74] law and order and the maintenance of a hegemonic ethnic identity (Myanmar),[75] and the continuation of a national democratic revolution linked to the ruling party's role in securing independence from a colonial settler regime (Zimbabwe).[76] What all these other ways of claiming political authority have in common is that they present some alternative to fully competitive, multiparty democracy. While power holders may also offer democratic elections, those elections fall short of being fully competitive, either because political rights are restricted in some way, or because the results are doctored after the event. The outward form of democracy in this sense is maintained and constitutes part of power holders' claim to political authority, but this claim is supplemented by their capacity to deliver on certain other substantive benefits.

Some of these alternative bases for political authority also feature in fully democratic regimes, of course. Thus, the maintenance of national security in the face of the threat posed by international terrorism currently provides an additional basis for political authority in most Western liberal democracies. Nevertheless, there is a crucial difference between societies in which political power holders' authority rests on the mandate they have received from the people voting in a fully competitive, multiparty democratic election and societies in which something less than full democracy forms part of a package of legitimating devices. In the former case, a political power holder's right to govern is contingent on its capacity to convince a majority of the voting public that its conception of the public interest and its capacity effectively to pursue

---

[73] See Max Weber, *Economy and Society*, ed. Günther Roth and Claus Wittich (New York: Bedminister Press, 1968). Christian von Soest and Julia Grauvogel expand Weber's list to the following six dimensions of a regime's legitimation strategy: "(1) ideology, (2) foundational myth, (3) personalism, (4) international engagement, (5) procedural mechanisms, and (6) performance (i.e., claims to success in producing desirable political, social, or economic outcomes)" (Von Soest and Grauvogel, "How Do Non-Democratic Regimes Claim Legitimacy?" German Institute of Global and Area Studies (August 2015) available at www.isn.ethz.ch/Digital-Library/Articles/Detail/?lng=en&id=193255). See also Tom Ginsburg and Tamir Moustafa, "Introduction" in Tom Ginsburg and Tamir Moustafa (eds.), *Rule by Law: The Politics of Courts in Authoritarian Regimes* (New York: Cambridge University Press, 2008) 5 (listing "income redistribution, land reform, economic growth, or political stability in post-conflict environments" as alternatives to the "possibility of legitimation at the ballot box").

[74] See Raul A. Sanchez-Urribarri, "Courts between Democracy and Hybrid Authoritarianism: Evidence from the Venezuelan Supreme Court" (2011) 36 *Law & Social Inquiry* 854.

[75] The Myanmar case is discussed in Chapter 6.

[76] On Zimbabwe, see Chapter 5.

that conception warrants its accession to, or continuation in, power. To the extent that this claim to political authority is supplemented by the alternative bases just listed, therefore, it is still open to other political parties to contest the rational basis for those claims and to win the right to govern accordingly. Where a political power holder's authority rests on manipulating the outward form of democracy as part of a package of legitimating devices, by contrast, the rational connection between these alternative bases for its authority and the public interest is not open to genuine democratic discussion. Rather, these alternative bases are used precisely to justify the denial of political rights – to supplement and shore up a weak democratic claim to authority.

A cardinal distinction running through the wide variety of political systems on the continuum from democracy to authoritarianism is thus the distinction between systems in which political authority rests on a genuine commitment to fully competitive, multiparty democracy and those in which the primary basis for political power holders' claim to authority is something else. It is this difference that allows us to distinguish situations that might otherwise appear superficially similar. In both South Africa and Zimbabwe, for example, the current ruling party (the African National Congress (ANC) and the Zimbabwe African National Union-Patriotic Front (ZANU-PF) respectively) claims political authority on the basis of its status as a former national liberation movement. South Africa differs from Zimbabwe, however, to the extent that the ANC's claim to political authority on this basis is relatively more open to political contestation than ZANU-PF's claim – to the ability of rival political parties to contest the relevance of the ANC's status as a former liberation movement to its current capacity to promote the public interest.

As soon as a genuine commitment to competitive, multiparty democracy is absent or lacking in some way, a complex array of political authority claims opens up. There are many varieties of less than fully democratic political systems in this sense, some of which rely on the outward form of democracy as a legitimating device and some of which do not. There is a vast literature in comparative democratization studies on this topic and each major scholar working in this area has their own way of distinguishing the range of political systems short of full democracy. The terms "hybrid regime," "electoral authoritarianism," and "competitive authoritarianism" have all been used, with each one subtly different from the others.[77] Nevertheless, the common feature of all

---

[77] See, for example, Larry Jay Diamond, "Thinking About Hybrid Regimes" (2002) 13 *Journal of Democracy* 21; Steven Levitsky and Lucan A. Way, "The Rise of Competitive Authoritarianism" (2002) 13 *Journal of Democracy* 51; Steven Levitsky and Lucan A. Way, *Competitive Authoritarianism: Hybrid Regimes after the Cold War* (New York: Cambridge University Press, 2010).

these forms of political system is that power holders' claim to authority is premised on something less than a mandate derived from a fully competitive democratic system. Rather, political authority is claimed by appealing to some overarching conception of the public interest to which democracy is in the end subordinate.

There are good reasons to be skeptical about dichotomies that simplify what is in fact a continuum of possibilities.[78] For the purposes of this study, however, a bipartite classification of political authority claims into "fully democratic" and "less than fully democratic" is not too reductive. As we shall see in the next section, when combined with the two main conceptions of law's authority, this bipartite classification generates four ideal types, two of which capture reasonably stable forms of the law/politics accommodation in less than fully democratic systems. The first of these describes a situation in which political power holders rely on a distorted conception of law's autonomy from politics to legitimate their claim to authority and the second a situation in which law is essentially subordinated to politics. The typology in this way accommodates an important distinction in the literature on authoritarian constitutionalism between systems in which law plays a significant legitimating role and those in which it does not.[79]

2.4 FOUR IDEAL-TYPICAL JR REGIMES

The intersection of the two key variables discussed in the previous section generates four ideal-typical JR regimes, as depicted in Table 2.1.

2.4.1 *Democratic Legalism*

Under democratic legalism, law's authority is founded on the claimed capacity of legal reasoning methods to exclude the influence of judges' personal political values and partisan political commitments on judicial decision-making. This understanding of law's authority is paired with a conception of political authority as stemming from a democratic mandate received under conditions of free and fair political competition. Once consolidated, the ongoing stability of this type of JR regime depends on the judiciary's observance of the reasoning methods that have come to be associated with the ideal

---

[78] See Gary Goertz and James Mahoney, *A Tale of Two Cultures: Qualitative and Quantitative Research in the Social Sciences* (Princeton, NJ: Princeton University Press, 2012) 161–73.

[79] See, for example, Mark Tushnet, "Authoritarian Constitutionalism" (2015) 100 *Cornell Law Review* 391; Ginsburg and Moustafa (eds.), *Rule by Law*.

TABLE 2.1: *Typology of JR regimes*

	Political authority based on the legitimacy of a mandate derived from a fully competitive democratic system that respects liberal political rights	Political authority based on asserted need to subordinate the democratic system to some overarching and democratically nonnegotiable conception of the public interest
Law's authority based on public commitment to separability of law and politics	Democratic Legalism	Authoritarian Legalism
Law's authority based on its usefulness as an instrument for the pursuit of political goals	Democratic Instrumentalism	Authoritarian Instrumentalism

of law's autonomy from politics. Provided the judiciary is seen to stay within these limits, or develops these reasoning methods only incrementally, its power of judicial review is respected. More than this, judicial review serves an important legitimating function in the construction of political authority. Judicial review fulfils this function, first, by authenticating electoral mandates as the product of a fair and competitive democratic process, and secondly, by legitimating those laws and executive acts that are not struck down for lack of conformance to the constitution.[80]

Judges in democratic legalist regimes deny that the often vague, open-ended and value-laden language of constitutions, especially their bill of rights provisions, means that judicial decision-making is inevitably political. Instead, judges and their supporters in the legal profession and legal academia insist, in public statements and occasionally also in the text of judicial decisions, that strict adherence to recognized methods of legal reasoning acts as an effective constraint on judges' personal political values and any tendency to political partisanship. Judges and other legal professionals in such regimes also typically insist that legal reasoning is different in kind from political reasoning –

---

[80] Cf. David M. Trubek, "Complexity and Contradiction in the Legal Order: Balbus and the Challenge of Critical Social Thought about Law" (1977) 11 *Law & Society Review* 529, 540 (the "neutrality and autonomy of law forms one basis for the claims of political systems in capitalist societies to legitimate authority" (citing Weber, *Economy and Society* 941–54)).

that it is based on a good-faith search for the correct legal answer – and that judges who are socialized to decide cases in this way are relatively immune to improper political influence.

Public confidence in the separability of law and politics is harder to sustain in systems of rights-based judicial review than it is in systems of federalist judicial review because the value-laden nature of decisions about rights renders judicial decision-making in the former case more susceptible to charges of political bias. Those defending law's autonomy deal with this challenge in a range of ways. One approach is to assert that constitutional rights constitute a philosophically well-ordered system that, when understood properly, produces predictable and "objective" answers to questions about what rights people have. While difficult to sustain in highly open-textured systems, such as the American, such protestations of law's neutrality may be more convincing in postauthoritarian constitutional democracies where the political values informing constitutional rights are specified in greater detail, and where the recent memory of an authoritarian past provides additional contextual material for understanding how these rights are to be applied.

An alternative device for democratic legalism when confronted by the discretionary, value-laden nature of rights-based judicial review is to convert rights-based inquiries into rule-based inquires. Thus, judges who are required to enforce a vaguely worded right to equality and nondiscrimination, say, may decide early on that claims based on this right should be dealt with in a structured, step-by-step way. While not eliminating the intrusion of political values into the inquiry, such devices may succeed in giving the appearance of a more rule-bound choice, and thus do enough to sustain a faith in the neutrality of legal reasoning methods.[81] Alternatively, judges may adopt an incremental, precedent-based style of reasoning so that seemingly open-ended rights inquiries become steadily more determinate over time.[82] Where the composition of the Bench in ideological terms does not change (perhaps because judges are all appointed by the same political party), such an approach may succeed in giving greater specificity to vaguely worded constitutional rights. At least, the difficulty of distinguishing precedent-based from political decision-making in such cases may be enough to sustain a constitutional-cultural faith in the neutrality of law's methods.

Three brief examples illustrate the wide variety of forms of democratic legalism. As discussed in Chapter 3, Australia's JR regime is based on a strong

[81] See Bomhoff, *Balancing Constitutional Rights.*
[82] See Wil J. Waluchow, *A Common Law Theory of Judicial Review: The Living Tree* (Cambridge: Cambridge University Press, 2007).

but qualified faith in law's autonomy. Adopted in 1900, the Australian Constitution drew on both the British tradition of parliamentary sovereignty and the American tradition of supreme-law federalism. This led to a distinctive form of democratic legalism that combines aspects of each tradition. At a rhetorical level, judges and other legal professionals are quick to deny the legitimacy of reasoning by reference to subjective political values. In practice, however, the adjudication of political values, particularly where these may be said to relate to the maintenance of the federal structure or the system of representative government, is increasingly countenanced. In contrast, Germany has managed to marry the same strong attachment that Australians have to legalism with substantive rights review. What in Australia is a reason to keep rights out of the Constitution is in Germany a reason to work harder to harmonize rights review with a conception of law as separate from politics. Finally, Chile represents a society in which a strong legalist tradition has consistently led to deferential rights review. Chilean legalism famously worked in General Pinochet's favor after the 1973 coup, as judges accommodated the slide into authoritarianism by treating it as political matter beyond their purview.[83] Even after the restoration of democracy, Chile has taken some time to develop a tradition of robust rights review.

2.4.2 *Authoritarian Legalism*

Authoritarian legalism describes a situation in which a public commitment to the separability of law and politics functions, not as the legitimate basis on which law speaks truth to political power, but as a pretext for certain areas of social life to be put beyond the reach of law.[84] In such JR regimes, judicial review continues to operate, and may in fact flourish in certain areas, but is ineffective in the crucial sense that it provides few resources for proponents of a more open and competitive democratic system to challenge authoritarian power holders. While not necessarily dispensing with the holding of elections, power holders' claim to authority in authoritarian legalist regimes rests on some alternative basis, such as the preservation of ethnic harmony, the promotion of economic prosperity, or the provision of security from some or other

---

[83] Lisa Hilbink, *Judges beyond Politics in Democracy and Dictatorship: Lessons from Chile* (New York: Cambridge University Press, 2007).

[84] Cf. Terence C. Halliday and Lucien Karpik, "Political Liberalism in the British Post-Colony: A Theme with Three Variations" in Terence C. Halliday, Lucien Karpik, and Malcolm Feeley (eds.), *Fates of Political Liberalism in the British Post-Colony: The Politics of the Legal Complex* (Cambridge: Cambridge University Press, 2012) 3, 15 (analyzing the path of "despotic order" in British postcolonial states).

external threat. The stability of this JR regime comes from the residual legitimating role that law plays in these circumstances, together with power holders' skill in prosecuting their alternative, less than fully democratic claim to authority.

Judicial review's legitimating role in authoritarian legalist regimes is what distinguishes this regime from authoritarian instrumentalism. In authoritarian legalist regimes, an ideology of law's autonomy from politics provides crucial cover for political power holders' denial of the full panoply of democratic political rights. In order to enable law to function in this way, it is important for power holders to accord judges a significant measure of independence in areas that are deemed not to threaten their hold on power. Thus, for example, a power holder that premises its claim to political authority on promoting economic prosperity, may give a constitutional court significant independent decision-making powers in respect of property rights.[85] Indeed, there may be an elaborate system of independent courts that are given great latitude in many areas. Authoritarian legalist regimes maintain a commitment to the autonomy of law to that extent. It is just that this commitment is informed by an underlying power preservation rationale.[86]

The distinguishing feature of authoritarian legalism is that law's autonomy is suppressed in precisely those areas where it would threaten power holders' claim to less than fully democratic political authority – rights to political participation, organization, and communication – the enforcement of which might provide opportunities for groups with alternative visions of the public interest to compete for power. In those areas, assertions of the separability of law and politics are deployed to exactly the opposite ends to those to which they are deployed under democratic legalism – to justify the relegation of sensitive matters, such as the suppression of free speech or the incarceration of political opponents, to the judicial no-go area of "politics." Instead of recognizing law's autonomy from politics as the legitimate basis for holding power holders to account in these areas, authoritarian legalism either justifies the exclusion of judges from enforcing democratic rights or, where these rights remain formally available, incentivizes judges to decline to hear or properly entertain cases on the grounds that the matters raised are "political" and thus beyond their remit. Judges acquiesce in this process, not necessarily out of support for the power holder, but because their legal-professional socialization

---

[85] See Tamir Moustafa, *The Struggle for Constitutional Power: Law, Politics, and Economic Development in Egypt* (New York: Cambridge University Press, 2009).

[86] Cf. Mark Tushnet, "Authoritarian Constitutionalism" 391 (arguing that "where constitutionalism exists in authoritarian systems, it does so because the rules have a modest normative commitment to constitutionalism").

inclines them to agree with this understanding of their role. Indeed, the less actual political control power holders need to exert over the judiciary, the more valuable the legitimating role of judicial review becomes.

2.4.3 *Authoritarian Instrumentalism*

Authoritarian instrumentalism describes a situation where law operates as a mere instrument of authoritarian rule, and where law is thus not autonomous from politics in any meaningful sense. Here, stability is a function of naked force and non-legal forms of legitimation, with law acting as a projection of political power rather than a constraint on it. Law has no legitimating role in such regimes. Because there are virtually no significant areas of social life over which judges exert independent control, law's claim to being autonomous from politics has no credibility. In such regimes, law really does function as a subsystem of politics in the sense that it is a fully subordinated system with no autonomous capacity to thwart or even significantly regulate the abuse of political power.[87] While judicial review formally exists, it functions neither to legitimate nor to check political power. Rather, judicial review serves a series of purely instrumental functions, such as the extension of central political control over regional areas, the provision of information to central power holders, and the transmission and implementation of centralized political commands.[88]

Constitutional judges in such regimes are nothing more than stooges of political power holders; they are appointed by them, loyal to them, and entirely beholden to them for their positions. Because law in situations of authoritarian instrumentalism is a subsystem of politics, judges do not experience a socialized pull towards deciding cases according to law, except perhaps in those areas that are politically insignificant to the regime. Instead, they see their function as being to discern the will of the contemporary power holder or, in the event this power holder's rule is threatened, the will of its likely successor.[89] Through these sorts of strategies, judges in such regimes may be able to enhance their court's powers to some degree.[90] In doing so, however,

---

[87] This ideal type reveals the weakness of accounts that treat law as invariably a subsystem of politics.

[88] See Tamir Moustafa and Tom Ginsburg "Introduction" 4–11; Martin Shapiro, *Courts: A Comparative and Political Analysis* (Chicago: University of Chicago Press, 1986).

[89] See Gretchen Helmke, *Courts under Constraints: Judges, Generals, and Presidents in Argentina* (New York: Cambridge University Press, 2012).

[90] See Lee Epstein, Jack Knight, and Olga Shvetsova, "The Role of Constitutional Courts in the Establishment and Maintenance of Democratic Systems of Government" (2001) 35 *Law & Society Review* 117.

they behave as an ordinary political actor might behave – strategically calculating how far they are able to expand the limited powers they have. Such strategies sometimes succeed in broadening the political space in which the judiciary is able to act, but they are in the nature of things incapable of enhancing law's authority as an autonomous social system capable of controlling the abuse of political power.

As with authoritarian legalist regimes, situations of authoritarian instrumentalism are not incompatible with the existence of democratic elections in some form. It is just that the power holder does not derive its authority from the openness and competitiveness of the democratic system and thus does not tolerate its proper operation in that sense. Indeed, the power holder might deploy the judiciary precisely to nullify the effects of any democratic elections that might be held by, for example, banning candidates said to be threatening to national unity or upholding corruption charges against its more popular opponents. When the judiciary acts in this way, no one believes that it is exercising any independent authority and thus no legitimacy is conferred. But this does not matter since the point of deploying the judiciary in this way is not to legitimate the power holder's oppression of its opponents but to provide the thinnest of pretexts for the exercise of naked political power.

2.4.4 *Democratic Instrumentalism*

The final ideal type, democratic instrumentalism, brings us back full circle to a relatively stable form of law/politics accommodation that arises where political authority is founded on the authenticity of a democratic mandate. As with democratic legalism, no political party is able to compete for, let alone hold, political power in such a regime without expressing its commitment to multiparty democracy, and all major political players accept that they must relinquish power if defeated in a democratic election. This does not mean that the democratic system actually is free from corruption and the influence of moneyed interests. It simply means that all parties are outwardly committed to the principle of free and fair elections. What distinguishes this type of JR regime from democratic legalism is that law's authority is premised, not on the strenuous denial of the irreducibly political nature of constitutional adjudication, but on the frank embrace, or at least grudging acceptance, of this fact. In place of the denial of law's politicality, law's authority is premised on its claimed capacity to promote substantively just outcomes and on decision makers' candor about the politics of constitutional adjudication, which is dealt with by foregrounding rather than suppressing the value-laden choices that are being made.

The different basis for law's authority in democratic instrumentalist regimes is reflected in reasoning methods that pay less attention to the semantic scope of legal rules and more attention to the policy consequences of the various rule choices open to the judge. Indeed, the distinction between legal reasoning and policy reasoning becomes quite blurred in such regimes, with legal professionals well versed, and law students openly trained, in how to present all-things-considered policy arguments. The process of judicial selection is typically very politicized in such regimes, with rival political parties using every opportunity to stock the Bench with judges who are seen to be ideologically loyal (while not obviously politically partisan). Legal practitioners in turn worry as much about the ideological composition of the Bench as they do about the technical legal quality of their arguments, and spend considerable time poring over a judge's decision-making record to try to discern how an argument might best be pitched to the judge in policy terms so as to win their vote.

2.5 CONSOLIDATION, TRANSFORMATION, AND INCREMENTAL CHANGE

The four JR regimes just presented are conceptual constructs – theoretical forms of law/politics accommodation whose significance at this point in the argument rests on their logical coherence and intuitive plausibility. Actually existing JR regimes do not conform exactly to these ideal types. Indeed, as soon as one considers real-world examples, it is immediately apparent that in every society that has adopted a system of judicial review there is a unique and constantly evolving set of societal conceptions of the law/politics relation. Nevertheless, the idea of JR regimes may be used to understand periods of relative stability in the evolution of these conceptions in the real world – periods, that is, where legal and political authority claims, even as they conflict in the daily business of constitutional politics, mutually legitimate each other at some deeper level.

The idea of JR regimes may also be used as an explanatory tool for examining the processes through which actually existing JR regimes evolve and change character over time. Drawing again on the *Lochner* story, three evolutionary subprocesses may be distinguished: (1) the consolidation of a JR regime, which describes the emergence of a relatively stable, dominant societal conception of the law/politics relation; (2) the transformation of a JR regime, which describes a situation where one dominant conception of the law/politics relation transitions to another; and (3) the incremental development of a JR regime, which refers to any observable change in societal understandings of the law/politics relation short of wholesale transformation.

This section presses down on the conceptual logic of the typology to explore, first, the consolidation process for each ideal type and, secondly, whether there is anything that suggests that certain kinds of transformation might be more likely than others. Does the conceptual logic of democratic instrumentalism, for example, suggest that this form of regime arises only after a slow-moving process of constitutional-cultural change, or is a more rapid transition to democratic instrumentalism possible? The purpose of this exercise is to illustrate how the conceptual logic of the typology not only provides a basis for classifying and comparing actually exiting JR regimes. It also provides a basis for converting the typology into a testable typological *theory* of JR-regime change. In particular, by pressing down on the conceptual logic of the typology, each of the three processes of consolidation, transformation, and incremental development may be expressed as an empirically testable conjecture about how actually existing JR regimes evolve.

As noted, democratic legalism is sustained by judicial respect for the reasoning methods that have come to be associated with law's claim to autonomy from politics. With the element of political authority added, we may think of the consolidation process for this ideal type as the process through which a political demand for a legitimate democratic mandate supports law's claim to separateness from politics as an autonomous sphere of authority capable of guaranteeing the background conditions for fair and equal political competition. Absent an exogenous shock, the continued political acceptance of judicial decisions premised on the relevant reasoning methods sustains the public's faith in law's autonomy.

The stabilization of democratic legalism around the continued use of a particular set of judicial reasoning methods does not preclude the possibility of incremental development of those methods. An aversion to implied constitutional rights, for example, might soften over time as more rigorous ways of inferring such rights from the text and structure of the constitution are found. In this way, judges might be able to adapt extant methods to changes in the political environment. But there are limits to such adaptations, or at least on the pace of such adaptations, and these limits might constrain democratic legalism's ability to respond to very sudden or significant exogenous shocks. The party-political structure in the society concerned, for example, might consolidate around two dominant parties in ways that prevented other parties from effectively competing for power. If the constitution contained no formal provisions for addressing this type of problem, judges in democratic legalist regimes might be unable to develop the doctrines required to respond to it.

Nothing might come of this in the sense that the regime might remain stable, though operating suboptimally from the point of view of some or other normative conception of democracy. If serious enough, however, this kind of challenge might eventually force a change in the form of the law/politics interaction, with political authority claims shifting to a broader set of legitimation strategies and judges acquiescing in the repression of political rights. A similar process might occur in a dominant-party democracy in which outsider groups became increasingly militant in their demand for political representation and posed a plausible enough security threat to legitimate the repression of political rights.

One possible line of transition for democratic legalism, then, is towards authoritarian legalism. Another, already described in the *Lochner* example given earlier, is in the direction of democratic instrumentalism. This occurs when a period of heightened politico-legal conflict over the right to shape a particular aspect of public policy ends in bipartisan embrace of ideologically motivated decision-making. This line of transition might also be driven by the factors Nonet and Selznick stress in their discussion of the development from Autonomous to Responsive Law – recognition that democratic legalism's suspension of disbelief in the existence of apolitical, technocratic reasoning methods entails certain costs in terms of the delivery of substantive justice.[91] A direct diagonal transition (in spatial terms) from democratic legalism to authoritarian instrumentalism, on the other hand, is harder to imagine at a conceptual level. Unless the exogenous shock to the regime were of a very high order, staged transition to authoritarian instrumentalism through either authoritarian legalism or democratic instrumentalism would appear more likely.

Authoritarian legalism stabilizes in one of two scenarios. Either there is an existing commitment to law's separateness from politics (democratic legalism) that is shaken by some or other national emergency to which judges fail to respond adequately, prompting a shift in the basis of political authority towards nondemocratic claims (as set out above), or authoritarian legalism emerges out of an authoritarian regime's strategic deployment of autonomous law in defined areas as a legitimating device (a shift from authoritarian instrumentalism, thus). Whether transitioning from democratic legalism or trading up from authoritarian instrumentalism, stabilization occurs when the legitimating role of law sufficiently supplements the political regime's

---

[91]   Phillippe Nonet and Philip Selznick, *Law and Society in Transition: Towards Responsive Law* (Harper Torch, 1978).

nondemocratic claim to authority to reduce the need for overt reliance on violence and other nonlegal legitimation devices.

Under the former scenario, there might be a remembered ideal of the role of law in defending democracy that provided resources for a return to democratic legalism. But one could also plausibly imagine that law's capitulation to political power in the transition from democratic legalism might destroy an always delicate legal-cultural faith in law's separability from politics. If so, one of two possibilities would open up. Most obviously, declining faith in law's autonomy from politics might prompt a further transition to authoritarian instrumentalism as the political power holder tightened its grip and dispensed altogether with law as a legitimating device. This would also be a possible line of transition under the second scenario, where the shift to authoritarian legalism had been prompted by an authoritarian power holder's search for legitimation and judges, say, overreached into forbidden areas, such as the enforcement of political rights, to the point where they needed to be curbed. The second (less likely) possibility is a diagonal movement across to democratic instrumentalism as judges, exploiting the legal-cultural space provided by declining faith in law's autonomy, worked to refashion law's authority as a politically malleable instrument for the pursuit of the best contemporary understanding of constitutional justice.

Authoritarian instrumentalism is in one sense the conceptual ground zero for all the other regimes – a situation in which law has yet to build any significant autonomy from politics or, having done so, is pushed back into subsystem status. To say that authoritarian instrumentalism is a conceptual ground zero, however, does not necessarily mean that every, or even the majority of, JR regimes start here. Clearly, it is possible to construct a JR regime in a mature democracy and for that regime to approximate democratic legalism from the get-go. The typology is not developmental in that sense. Rather, describing authoritarian instrumentalism as the conceptual ground-zero regime is a statement about the ideological simplicity of this regime in its crude subsumption of law into politics.

Authoritarian instrumentalism's ground-zero status also need not imply that it is the most stable or frequently occurring JR regime in practice.[92] In the absence of legal legitimation, this regime needs to deliver at least some substantive benefits – economic growth or at least the prevention of famine,

---

[92]   Tamir Moustafa, "Law and Courts in Authoritarian Regimes" (2014) 10 *Annual Review of Law and Social Science* 281, 282 ("courts rarely serve as mere pawns of their regimes").

and defense against external military aggressors. In consequence, such regimes experience certain well-known problems of social control and efficiency.[93] At a conceptual level, there is thus an inherent tendency in such regimes to transition to authoritarian legalism through the provision of at least some courts and forms of law enforcement.[94] Methodologically, it may be impossible to distinguish the boundary line between authoritarian instrumentalism and authoritarian legalism – the exact point at which the instrumental use of law flips into something more substantial and legitimating. But this does not mean that there are not clear examples of each ideal type.

One possible line of transition for authoritarian instrumentalism, then, is towards authoritarian legalism. Another might be towards democratic instrumentalism as judges work to build their court's institutional legitimacy. The problem with this conjecture, though, is how exactly judges could trigger the required shift in the political power holder's authority claim. Perhaps by asserting their institutional independence courts might be able to create the space for political competition to drive this shift. More likely, such a transition would require an exogenous trigger, such as the power-holder's military defeat or an economic crisis.

2.6 CONCLUSION: REFINING AND TESTING

The typological theory of JR-regime change set out in this chapter generates a number of empirically testable conjectures or "observable implications."[95] The first is that JR regimes evolve on the back of competing legal and political authority claims. The second is that such regimes may stabilize in ways that resemble one of four ideal types. And the third is that, once stabilized, JR regimes are relatively resistant to change absent an exogenous shock, although certain internal susceptibilities in the regime to change may help to facilitate a transformation once started by an external trigger.

---

[93] See Ginsburg and Moustafa (eds.), *Rule by Law*, 4–11.

[94] See Mark Fathi Massoud, *Law's Fragile State: Colonial, Authoritarian, and Humanitarian Legacies in Sudan* (New York: Cambridge University Press, 2013) (showing that even very repressive states may provide some autonomous law).

[95] Gary King, Robert O. Keohane, and Sidney Verba, *Designing Social Inquiry: Scientific Inference in Qualitative Research* (Princeton, NJ: Princeton University Press, 1994). By citing "KKV" this study does not mean to align itself with all the propositions these authors make about the extent to which quantitative methods may be applied to qualitative case studies. On some of the problems with the KKV approach, see James Mahoney "After KKV: The New Methodology of Qualitative Research" (2010) 62 *World Politics* 120. On the enduring differences, but also possibilities for productive dialogue, between qualitative and quantitative social science research cultures, see Goertz and Mahoney, *A Tale of Two Cultures*.

In addition to refining the theory in these respects, the case study chapters that follow illustrate the typology's explanatory power in three ways: first, by using the typology to contribute to existing debates about the evolution of societal conceptions of the law/politics relation in the countries studied; second, by providing a basis for collecting insights about the internal dynamics of each ideal type and more generally about the way JR regimes stabilize around and transition between each type; and finally, by facilitating the normative assessment of different forms of stable and mutually legitimating forms of law/politics accommodation – not necessarily so as to decide which of them is the best in some abstract moral sense, but so as to enable us to see what is won and what is lost in each case. Those insights may in turn inform debates about how to reform actually existing JR regimes so as to maximize their advantages and minimize their disadvantages, either as a matter of constitutional design, judicial practice, or social-movement-led, public impact litigation strategy.

3

Australian Democratic Legalism: Constant Cultural Cause or Path-Dependent Trajectory?

There is little doubt that Australia's JR regime warrants classification as a central case of democratic legalism. But the reasons for this situation seem at first somewhat obvious and thus unpromising for theory development. In contrast to the other societies considered in this study, Australia does not have a justiciable bill of rights in its Constitution.[1] Rather, its High Court's powers of judicial review are primarily federalist in nature.[2] Given this institutional setting, the consolidation of Australia's JR regime around something approximating democratic legalism hardly seems surprising. The Constitution's framers, after all, deliberately chose to deny the High Court the power to review laws against a bill of rights to keep the judiciary away from what they regarded as an impermissibly political function. In this sense, the Constitution was both informed by a long-standing tradition of thinking about the appropriate role of the judiciary in democratic politics and intended to preserve it. While the need for judicial review of the Constitution's federal structure was conceded, the rest of the system was carefully designed to limit the High Court's role to what were thought to be safely legal functions. That the dominant conception of the law/ politics relation in Australia conforms to the democratic legalist ideal type, it might be thought, is mainly attributable to the ongoing influence of this constitutional-design choice and the constitutional culture that informed it rather than anything that happened after the Constitution was adopted.[3]

---

[1] Commonwealth of Australia Constitution Act 1900 (Imp) (in effect from 1 January 1901).

[2] For a recent, accessible introduction to Australian constitutional law, see Cheryl Saunders, *The Constitution of Australia: A Contextual Analysis* (Oxford: Hart Publishing, 2011).

[3] On "constant cause explanations," see Kathleen Thelen, "How Institutions Evolve: Insights from Comparative Historical Analysis" in James Mahoney and Dietrich Rueschemeyer (eds.), *Comparative Historical Analysis in the Social Sciences* (New York: Cambridge University Press, 2003) 208, 214ff.

As soon as one delves beneath the surface of things, however, a more complex picture begins to emerge. For one thing, the notion that federalist judicial review is inherently more technical and determinate than rights-based judicial review, and therefore somehow more naturally compatible with legalism, is a little dubious. As Adrienne Stone has most recently shown, decision-making under the Australian Constitution is just as "discretionary" and "evaluative" as it is in other systems.[4] From the methodology for characterizing Commonwealth laws to the interpretation of express and implied limits on legislative power, Australian constitutional law is shot through with vague and malleable standards.[5] That being so, the consolidation of democratic legalism in Australia after the adoption of its federal Constitution in 1900 was anything but foreordained. It depended on the dynamic interaction and mutual accommodation of distinct legal and political authority claims in precisely the sense in which this study is interested.

Second, the notion that federalist judicial review is less prone to the sort of competing legal and political authority claims that characterize the evolution of rights-based systems is not borne out by the history of constitutional politics in Australia, which includes several turbulent periods during which the legitimate scope of law's authority has been called into question. The best known of these is the 1920 *Engineers* case,[6] in which the High Court dramatically cast off two established doctrines that had been used to secure a large measure of autonomy for the states in the federal system. That about-turn, which presaged the strongly centralist interpretation of the Constitution that has been maintained ever since, was justified by the labelling of the reasoning methods that the earlier Court had used as impermissibly political in nature.[7]

Nor was the *Engineers* case the only dramatic episode in this unfolding story. Apart from the changes in judicial style that one would expect to see in a constitutional system as enduring as the Australian, there has also been one period of wholesale reexamination of the appropriate relationship between

---

[4] Adrienne Stone, "Judicial Review without Rights" (2008) 28 *Oxford Journal of Legal Studies* 1 (arguing that judicial review in federalist systems may be just as indeterminate as in systems of rights-based review).

[5] The High Court, for example, has accepted that one aspect of its standard test for characterization, which requires it to decide whether a law that is not within the core of a head of power is nevertheless "sufficiently connected" to it, involves "questions of degree" (*Burton* v. *Honan* (1952) 86 CLR 169 at 179). See further Jeffrey Goldsworthy, "Australia: Devotion to Legalism" in Jeffrey Goldsworthy (ed.), *Interpreting Constitutions: A Comparative Study* (Oxford: Oxford University Press, 2007) 106, 114–15.

[6] *Amalgamated Society of Engineers* v. *Adelaide Steamship Co Ltd* (1920) 28 CLR 129 (hereafter "the Engineers case").

[7] See the discussion in Section 3.1.

law and politics in the late 1980s and early 1990s. Led by then Chief Justice, Sir Anthony Mason, and influenced by global constitutional developments and Australia's final move to legal independence from the United Kingdom, the High Court embarked on an ambitious attempt to transform the way it decided cases.[8] In essence, the call was one for greater candor in the judicial reasoning process – for judges to foreground the hidden premises that drive their decisions and by this device to enter into a more honest relationship with the Australian people.[9] Drawing in part on the teachings of Julius Stone, a University of Sydney legal academic who had worked with Roscoe Pound at Harvard,[10] the Mason Court attacked the formalism of the Court's methods and called on the judiciary to articulate the political values informing their decisions. Unlike the earlier instance of judge-led transformation, however, this attempt is generally seen to have been only partially successful. While the Mason Court did succeed in introducing new doctrines that would have been unthinkable at the time of federation,[11] it did not go so far as to trigger a wholesale transformation of the prevailing JR regime.

In short, the absence of a bill of rights does not mean that the Australian case cannot be examined through the lens of the typological theory set out in Chapter 2. While the stubborn persistence of the peculiarly Australian version of democratic legalism does have a lot to do with the aversion to judicial involvement in politics that was expressed in the Constitution's design, it is still an interesting question how Australian constitutional culture's commitment to a strict conception of the separability of law and politics has been maintained in the face of serious doubts about the determinacy of the High Court's reasoning methods. In addition, while the basic form of the Australian JR regime has not changed much since the consolidation of democratic legalism in the 1950s, there have been several subtler changes to conceptions of the relationship between law and politics. To this extent, Australia provides fertile ground for examining interstitial adjustments within mature and highly stable JR regimes.[12]

---

[8] Haig Patapan, *Judging Democracy: The New Politics of the High Court of Australia* (Cambridge: Cambridge University Press, 2000); Jason L. Pierce, *Inside the Mason Court Revolution: The High Court of Australia Transformed* (Durham, NC: Carolina Academic Press, 2006). See also David Solomon, *The Political High Court* (Sydney: Allen & Unwin, 1999).

[9] See Section 4.4.

[10] See Leonie Starr, *Julius Stone: An Intellectual Life* (Melbourne: Oxford University Press, 1992) 29–32.

[11] See Section 3.4.

[12] See Thelen, "How Institutions Evolve" 209 (calling for attention to "institutional changes that fall short of actual breakdown").

A final interesting question worth exploring is how it came about that the High Court was able, from the 1920s, to transform a strongly federalist Constitution into a weakly federalist one, but that its later attempt to transform Australia's democratic legalist regime was only partially successful. Was it just the case that the first transformation process was about the balance of power in the federal system whereas the latter was about the JR regime that had grown up around it? Or does the Australian experience tell us something about the imperviousness to change of JR regimes in settled constitutional democracies, especially those that have experienced few exogenous shocks in the nature of, say, the external economic and social changes that drove "the transformation of American law" in the early twentieth century?[13]

The next section begins the exploration of these questions by examining the seminal *Engineers* decision and what it was about that decision that made it such a focal point for the consolidation of Australian democratic legalism. The central argument here is that the *Engineers* decision operated on three distinct levels: its rhetorical claim about the law/politics relation, its endorsement of a distinct approach to constitutional interpretation, and its practical policy effects in expanding the scope of the Commonwealth's legislative powers. Only be separating out those three aspects and examining their interaction can the influence of *Engineers* be properly appreciated. Section 3.2 considers the major period of conflict between the High Court and the Australian Labor Party (ALP) in the late 1940s, during which the Court came perilously close to being packed in anticipation of its opposition to the ALP's socialization program. Section 3.3 explains the process through which Australia's most influential twentieth-century justice, Sir Owen Dixon, helped to restore the Court's institutional legitimacy around an ideology of legalism, and how *Engineers* came to be subsumed under that ideology, notwithstanding significant differences between the reasoning methods that it advocated and those that Dixon preferred. Section 3.4 examines the Mason Court era, the challenge it posed to democratic legalism, the major cases in which the Court tried to push its transformation agenda, and the reasons why it only partially succeeded. Section 3.5 discusses how the Australian JR regime operates today as a form of democratic legalism that is increasingly open to purpose-oriented, substantive reasoning methods, including multifactor balancing and structured proportionality, albeit still within a constitutional culture steadfastly committed to a strict conception of the separability of law and

---

[13] See the sources cited in Chapter 2 and particularly Morton J. Horwitz, *The Transformation of American Law 1870–1960: The Crisis of Legal Orthodoxy* (New York: Oxford University Press, 1992).

politics. Section 3.6 ends by summarizing what this chapter's account of the development and stabilization of Australia's JR regime adds to the typological theory set out in Chapter 2.

3.1 THE THREE LEVELS OF *ENGINEERS*

The *Engineers* case is such an icon in the literature on Australian constitutionalism that it is hard to approach it without going over well-trodden ground.[14] For purposes of this study, the main point to emphasize is that the decision was as much concerned with judicial reasoning methods as it was with the doctrinal question at issue. Indeed, the High Court famously went further than required to resolve the dispute in order to make its larger methodological point. Whether the Court was motivated in this respect by a political agenda – by a desire to use the case as an opportunity to expand the Commonwealth's legislative powers at the expense of the states – or by sincere legal-professional conviction, has been fiercely debated.[15] The consensus today is that at least two of the majority judges (Isaacs and Higgins JJ) might have had such an agenda while the others likely did not.[16] That particular point in any event does not need to be resolved for current purposes. The interesting issue from the perspective of this study is not what motivated the *Engineers* decision, but how it came to be a focal point for the later consolidation of Australian democratic legalism.

As a purely doctrinal matter, the question in *Engineers* was whether an award made under Commonwealth industrial relations legislation could bind so-called state instrumentalities, i.e., employers that were part of the state government. According to one of the two doctrines that the Court had developed before *Engineers* – the implied immunity of instrumentalities doctrine – the Commonwealth and the states were reciprocally immune from each

---

[14]   For a collection of essays exploring the significance of the case, see Michael Coper and George Williams (eds.), *How Many Cheers for Engineers?* (Sydney: Federation Press, 1997).

[15]   The thesis that the *Engineers* Court's commitment to legalism was part of a grand political strategy was, as explained below, first put by Brian Galligan in *Politics of the High Court: A Study of the Judicial Branch of Government in Australia* (Brisbane: University of Queensland Press, 1987). It was strongly critiqued at the time by Jeffrey Goldsworthy, "Realism about the High Court" (1989) 18 *Federal Law Review* 27. Galligan's reply to Goldsworthy was published as "Realistic 'Realism' and the High Court's Role" (1989) 18 *Federal Law Review* 40 and Goldsworthy's rejoinder as "Reply to Galligan" (1989) 18 *Federal Law Review* 50. See also Cheryl Saunders, "Book Review" (1988) 18 *Publius* 133.

[16]   See Anne Twomey, "The Knox Court" in Rosalind Dixon and George Williams, *The High Court, the Constitution and Australian Politics* (Melbourne: Cambridge University Press, 2015). The other majority justices were Knox CJ and Rich and Starke JJ. Gavan Duffy J was in dissent.

other's law-making power.[17] This doctrine, however, had been progressively weakening in the ten years before the decision, with the Court accepting that at least some state instrumentalities were too far removed from the traditional business of government to come under the doctrine's ambit.[18] One available and relatively uncontroversial way of resolving the case, therefore, would have been for the Court to have decided that the state employers in question (the Western Australian sawmills, implement and engineering works, and Minister for Trading Concerns) fell under this developing exception.

The other main doctrine that *Engineers* is typically said to have "exploded"[19] – the reserved state powers doctrine – was strictly speaking not at issue in the case. That doctrine held that each head of power in s 51 of the Constitution should be understood as a complete statement of the Commonwealth's legislative power over the topic in question. Thus, if a particular head of power purported to deal with interstate trade and commerce, say, that was the Commonwealth's only power in respect of that topic, with all other powers not explicitly covered by it reserved to the states. In *Engineers*, however, there was no dispute over whether the Commonwealth had the power to enact the industrial relations legislation in question or over the constitutionality of the award made under it.[20] The question was whether the employers joined in the litigation were bound by the award.

Notwithstanding the irrelevance of the reserved state powers doctrine for this reason, and the fact that the instrumentalities question might have been resolved by a narrower holding, the Court in *Engineers* overruled both doctrines in their entirety. In a sweeping and highly polemical main judgment, Knox CJ and Isaacs, Rich and Starke JJ held that the two doctrines were founded on impermissibly "political" reasoning methods.[21] In particular, their derivation depended on a theory of the nature of Australian federalism that was nowhere to be found in the "text" of the Constitution.[22] Rather, the judges responsible for developing the two doctrines had imputed their own

---

[17]   The leading cases were *D'Emden v. Pedder* (1904) 1 CLR 91 and *Federated Amalgamated Government Railway and Tramway Service Association v. New South Wales Railway Traffic Employees Association* (1906) 4 CLR 488.

[18]   See the discussion in George Williams, Sean Brennan, and Andrew Lynch, *Blackshield and Williams Australian Constitutional Law and Theory: Commentary and Materials* 6th ed. (Sydney: Federation Press, 2014), 246–7.

[19]   See the authorities cited in Twomey, "The Knox Court" 106 n 60.

[20]   The legislation at issue was within the Commonwealth's conciliation and arbitration power under s 51(xxxv) and the particular industrial dispute had crossed state boundaries.

[21]   *Engineers* 151.

[22]   Ibid 142.

"personal opinions"[23] and "individual conception[s]"[24] into the Constitution under the guise of necessary "implication[s]."[25] That style of reasoning, and the American precedents on which the Court had relied, were inappropriate to the interpretation of an Imperial British statute that sought to give expression to English constitutional doctrines, like that of the indivisibility of the Crown and responsible government.[26] Far better, the main judgment reasoned, to use ordinary English statutory interpretation methods to interpret what was in the end an ordinary English statute.[27] In short, what was required was "to read [the Constitution] naturally, in the light of the circumstances in which it was made, with knowledge of the combined fabric of the common law and the statute law that preceded it."[28] If that were done, "*lucet ipsa per se* [the thing would shine by its own light]."[29]

This entire section of the main judgment, Australian constitutional scholars now agree, amounted to rhetorical overreaching, if not plain irrationality. First, to use the English doctrine of responsible government as a justification for the exclusive use of English statutory interpretation methods was to fixate on just one part of the Australian Constitution's heritage and moreover a part that was not even relevant to the case.[30] Secondly, to dismiss wholesale the appropriateness of American precedents, when they, for their part, *were* relevant to the question in issue, was clearly wrong.[31] The fact of the matter was that the Australian Constitution was a hybrid of English and American influences, with the indivisibility of the Crown and responsible government coming from the English side and federalism and the power of judicial review from the American.[32] Accordingly, both English and American precedents were likely to be relevant in some cases and irrelevant in others.[33]

---

[23]   Ibid.

[24]   Ibid 145.

[25]   Ibid.

[26]   Ibid 146.

[27]   Ibid 148–53.

[28]   Ibid 152.

[29]   Ibid.

[30]   This point was made in a famous commentary on the case by R. T. E. Latham, *The Law and the Commonwealth* (Oxford: Oxford University Press, 1949 [1937]) 563.

[31]   The immunity of instrumentalities doctrine had drawn on *McCulloch* v. *Maryland* 17 US (4 Wheat) 316 (1819) and the reserved state powers doctrine on *Collector* v. *Day* 78 US (11 Wall) 113 (1870).

[32]   The classic study of the Constitution's dual inheritance is Elaine Thompson, "The 'Washminster' Mutation" in Patrick Weller and Dean Jaensch (eds.), *Responsible Government in Australia* (Richmond: Drummond, 1980) 32.

[33]   See Goldsworthy, "Australia" 115.

As to judicial reasoning methods, it was clear that, although technically an enactment of the Imperial Parliament, this did not mean that the Constitution was an ordinary English statute that fell to be interpreted according to ordinary English statutory interpretation methods. More important than its formal provenance was the fact that it was a *constitution*, and a fairly open-textured one at that. If anything, this meant that American judicial decisions were more relevant than the English. As the Court later came to acknowledge,[34] it is virtually impossible to interpret an open-textured constitution that is meant to endure for a long time without resorting to the derivation of implied terms. This is true of most constitutions, but especially so of the relatively short and elliptical Australian one. To judge by the text, the Australian Constitution has a rather limited purpose – to delineate the powers and functions of the new Commonwealth legislature, executive, and judiciary, and to define their relationship *inter se* and collectively with the former Australian colonies, renamed states. Whole parts of the operational, small "c" constitution, including the nature of the concurrent powers of the states and even the workings of Cabinet government at the federal level, are simply left unstated – taken to be so settled by established convention as not to be worth mentioning.[35]

Given these considerations, the *Engineers* Court's choice of English statutory interpretation methods was both unjustified and highly distorting. It led to an interpretation of the scope of the Commonwealth's legislative powers that was far broader than anyone present at the constitutional conventions would have imagined. In case after case, the Court's insistence that the derivation of implied limits on the Commonwealth's powers was an impermissibly political method of interpretation resulted in the expansion of the Commonwealth's legislative powers.[36] Given the operation of s 109 of the Constitution, in terms of which Commonwealth legislation renders inoperative any state legislation found to be inconsistent with it, this expansion greatly tilted the balance of power in the federation in favor of the Commonwealth.

Why was this accepted? Why was an understanding of the scope of the Commonwealth's powers based on a contestable method of constitutional

---

[34] See, for example, *West* v. *Commissioner of Taxation* (NSW) (1937) 56 CLR 657 (discussed in Section 4.3 below).

[35] See Helen Irving, *Five Things to Know about the Australian Constitution* (Cambridge: Cambridge University Press, 2004).

[36] Some of the most notable post-*Engineers* cases upholding an expanded understanding of the limits of Commonwealth power are *R* v. *Burgess; Ex parte Henry* (1936) 55 CLR 608, *Strickland* v. *Rocla Concrete Pipes Ltd* (1971) 124 CLR 468, and *Commonwealth* v. *Tasmania* (1983) 158 CLR 1 (the *Tasmanian Dam* case).

interpretation allowed to wreak such havoc on the original constitutional design?

There are two main answers to this question in the Australian literature. The first stresses the fit between the Court's expansionary reading and external political developments. Decided as it was in 1920, this answer goes, the *Engineers* case resonated with a developing sense of Australian nationhood that had been forged in World War I and reinforced by growing economic integration. For one influential early commentator, this was the inarticulate major premise of the decision.[37] It accordingly stands to be criticized for failing to disclose that premise and for giving impetus to a decision-making style in which the substantive policy grounds for case outcomes are hidden behind legalist rhetoric. For a later commentator, *Engineers* stands for a nobler tradition of living constitutionalism in which the Court adapts the Constitution to changing circumstances.[38] Its influence as a decision is bound up with the success of this flexible constitutional-interpretive methodology. While this version of the first answer thus takes a different view of the merits of the Court's lack of candor, the two versions come together in explaining the acceptance of *Engineers* as a decision that gave the nation what it wanted: a federal government adequately empowered to promote the national interest. That the decision needed to transform the original meaning of the Constitution to achieve this result was part of its talismanic charm.

The second main answer to the question of why *Engineers* was accepted, by political scientist Brian Galligan, adapts aspects of the first, but accords much greater importance to the justices' conscious awareness of what they were doing and to the bipartisan appeal of the outcome of their decision.[39] The major threat to the institutionalization of judicial review in Australia, Galligan argues, was the divergence between the Constitution's conservative, small-government conception of federal powers and the newly emergent Australian Labor Party's socialization program.[40] The ALP, he reminds us, had not been a significant player in the Constitutional Conventions that took place during the 1890s. The absence of any significant ALP influence meant that the Constitution mainly reflected nineteenth-century, laissez-faire beliefs. As it emerged in the early twentieth century, the ALP's political program was

---

[37] See Latham, *The Law and the Commonwealth* 563 (criticizing the *Engineers* decision for failing to state its major premise, namely that Australia's growing sense of nationhood required a stronger Commonwealth).

[38] *Victoria* v. *Commonwealth* (1971) 122 CLR 353 per Windeyer J (explaining the acceptance of *Engineers*).

[39] Galligan, *Politics of the High Court* 96–7.

[40] Ibid 4, 26–30, 37, 72, 97, 119.

fundamentally at odds with this style of constitution – its goal of introducing federal industrial relations and social welfare legislation contradicted by the Constitution's relegation of significant legislative powers in respect of these issues to the states. The ALP accordingly made the amendment of the Constitution one of its explicit policy goals.[41]

Against this background, Galligan continues, the *Engineers* Court's embrace of legalism must be understood as part of a deliberate "political strategy" to bring the ALP into the constitutional fold.[42] Appreciating that judicial review would never be properly institutionalized unless the ALP accepted it, the *Engineers* Court chose an interpretive method that it knew would lead inexorably to the expansion of the Commonwealth's powers. In the decision itself, that meant getting rid of a doctrine (the implied immunity of instrumentalities) that prevented Commonwealth industrial awards from benefitting state employees – an important section of the work force. But beyond that immediate result, the Court appreciated that its interpretive methodology would expand the Commonwealth's powers sufficiently to allow the ALP to pursue its socialization program at the federal level. By blunting the ALP's opposition to judicial review in this way, the Court was able to win bipartisan support for its role as an impartial arbiter of intergovernmental disputes. In short, the acceptance of *Engineers* may be put down to its success in building a broad political constituency for the Constitution and with that, for the Court.

Both these answers are instructive as far as they go. Each one of them, however, is also limited. The problem with the first answer is that it does not really explain the causal link between the external political developments that it highlights and the consolidation of legalism as an ideological claim about the law/politics relation. To be sure, the *Engineers* Court's expansionist read-ing of Commonwealth powers eventually came to suit a nation bound together by great trials. But how exactly did that process of acceptance work? How did the Court's reasoning methods in *Engineers* come to be associated with an ideological claim about the law/politics relation that succeeded in legitimating the Court's institutional function? And what does the Australian experience tell us in general about how these sorts of processes work – how JR regimes come to stabilize around a certain understanding of the law/politics relation?

The second answer fares better in explaining the process through which the Court's judicial review function came to be institutionalized. Galligan thus

[41]   Ibid 23–4, 26–30, 87.
[42]   Ibid 39.

clearly shows why the results of the Court's decisions were accepted by the ALP and how this acceptance served the Court's quest for legitimacy. But the weakness of Galligan's account is that he presents this result as the fulfilment of a deliberate political strategy when only two of the *Engineers* Court's members were centralizers as a matter of political conviction.[43] Another problem for Galligan is that the English statutory interpretation methods the Court endorsed in *Engineers* did not, as we shall see,[44] always produce outcomes favorable to the ALP. In relation to the freedom of interstate trade and commerce in s 92 of the Constitution, for example, those methods drove an individual rights interpretation that thwarted the ALP's attempt to nationalize the airlines and banking industries in the 1940s. Was that also foreseen and somehow built into the Court's strategy? Galligan argues that these setbacks did not really matter because the policies concerned were at the extreme left of the ALP's socialization program and the Court in any case quickly balanced them out with its decision in the *Communist Party* case,[45] which in turn undermined a central plank in the Liberal Party's political program.[46] But that attempt to rescue the argument, as Jeffrey Goldsworthy has shown,[47] reveals its essential weakness. Legalism as a conscious political strategy on the part of the Court explains things when it explains them, and doesn't when it doesn't; it explains the general trajectory of the Court's jurisprudence that proved appealing to the ALP, but also some decisions that weren't that appealing. Also, the evenhanded thwarting of the Liberal Party's program in the *Communist Party* case was achieved in part through the evocation of a broad, textually unsupported rule of law principle that prevented the Commonwealth from using the preamble to an Act to "recite itself into power."[48] So apparently legalism as a conscious political strategy can just be cast off when it proves inconvenient. But how then has legalism retained its status as both methodological and constitutional-cultural orthodoxy?

A final problem for Galligan is that the doctrinal repercussions that the *Engineers* case set in motion were highly complex and took the best part of a century to work through, if they are not still being worked through to this day. It is simply not plausible that the *Engineers* majority could have foreseen and consciously willed all those repercussions. To be sure, the two justices who were centralizers by political conviction might have foreseen the immediate

43 See note 13.
44 Section 4.2.
45 *Australian Communist Party v. Commonwealth* (1951) 83 CLR 1 ("*Communist Party* case").
46 Galligan, *Politics of the High Court* 203–7.
47 Goldsworthy, "Realism about the High Court" 34.
48 *Communist Party* case 205–6 (per McTiernan J).

advantages to their project of rejecting the two implied limits on the Commonwealth's legislative power. But to describe that as a conscious political strategy of *legitimation* (as opposed to a doctrinal strategy to reorient the federal balance) seems a little far-fetched, especially given that the two justices concerned were not in control of the Court. Rather, the process through which the doctrinal about-face in *Engineers* came to legitimate the Court's institutional function is likely to have been more contingent than that – a function of the way the *Engineers* decision interacted with the kind of external political developments stressed by the first main answer.

The key to understanding *Engineers* and its influence, it is suggested, is to see that the decision operated on at least three distinct levels. First, there is what we might call the *rhetorical dimension* of the decision – the claim that previous judicial-reasoning methods were illegitimate because they were too dependent on the judges' personal, politically motivated theories of federalism. That claim is undeniably legalist in tone because, in condemning past decisions as being too political, it suggests that law can in theory distinguish itself from politics, if only the judges approach their task in the right way.

The second distinct level on which *Engineers* operates is the level of *reasoning methods* – the principles and techniques of English statutory interpretation that the decision vindicates and claims to be implementing. There has been endless debate in Australia over what exactly these methods are – whether the Court, in its constant references to the need for a textual basis for its decisions, was advocating pure literalism, or whether the Court was promoting a richer and more complex method than that, one that included references to context, legislative intention, and the background common-law rules against which the Constitution was enacted.[49] The consensus now is that something broader than mere literalism was intended.[50] The main judgment, after all, summarized the approach it was advocating as including reference to "the circumstances in which [the Constitution] was made ... the combined fabric of the common law, and the statute law which preceded it."[51] The common idea underpinning that formulation is the assumption that there is a set of authoritative legal materials to which judges may refer when interpreting the Constitution – more than merely just the text of the Constitution itself, but at the same time not unlimited and not including

---

[49]　Former Chief Justice Barwick, for example, famously gave a more literalist gloss to *Engineers* in a speech delivered on his retirement from office (reported in (1981) 148 CLR v).

[50]　See Williams, Brennan, and Lynch (eds.), *Australian Constitutional Law and Theory*, 170–2, quoting JD Heydon, "Theories of Constitutional Interpretation: A Taxonomy" (2007) (Winter) *Bar News: The Journal of the New South Wales Bar Association* 12, 26.

[51]　*Engineers* 152.

supposedly extralegal materials, like the judges' preferred theory of federalism. This is the second sense, then, in which the *Engineers* decision is said to stand for legalism – not just legalism as legitimating ideology, but also legalism as a set of judicial reasoning methods that purport to provide judges with an apolitical basis on which to decide the great questions of constitutional law.

The complication here is that there is a difference between what the main judgment says these preferred methods are and the reasoning methods that it itself deploys. As noted already, having inveighed against the drawing of implications based on political necessity, the main judgment relies on two implied principles – the indivisibility of the Crown and the principle of responsible government – neither of which can be found in so many words in the text of the Constitution. The purpose of invoking those two principles, it will be recalled, was to build a foundation for rejecting the Court's past reliance on American authorities. That move was disingenuous because the main judgment was itself doing what it condemned previous judges for doing, and arguably with less justification (because the two principles it called up were not immediately relevant to the decision). By itself making use of two implied principles, *Engineers* is open to being read not as a wholesale rejection of the legitimacy of drawing implications, but only as denying the legitimacy of drawing certain kinds of implications. It was this feature of the *Engineers* decision, as we shall see,[52] which was later exploited by Sir Owen Dixon to claw back some ground from the English statutory interpretation methods that the Court advocated.

The third level on which the *Engineers* decision operated was its *doctrinal and policy consequences*: the overruling of the implied immunity of instrumentalities and reserved state powers doctrines, and the narrower holding that Commonwealth industrial relations legislation may bind state instrumentalities. The overruling of the two doctrines was clearly the more far-reaching doctrinal point because it had such wide ramifications beyond the industrial relations context. As noted already, the two implied doctrines had operated in a crosscutting way that limited all the heads of power. In dispensing with them, the Court thus not only expanded the Commonwealth's conciliation and arbitration power in s 51(xxxv). It also extended the reach of all the other heads of power. It is this aspect of the decision that has made *Engineers* such a consequential decision, to the point of changing the overall balance of power between the Commonwealth and the states, at least as that balance had been understood in 1900.

---

[52] Section 4.3.

One part of understanding the influence of *Engineers* is to see that it operates on these three distinct levels. The other part is that the influence of the decision on the first two levels has, in large measure, occurred on the back of the influence of the decision on the third level. This is because, as far as the political acceptance of the decision was concerned, the third level mattered much more than the first two. Political actors the world over are generally not concerned with the technical niceties of judicial reasoning methods. Rather, they are concerned with the policy consequences of a decision. Of course, if political actors do not like the policy consequences, and respected legal professionals tell them the decision was badly reasoned, they will use that as political ammunition. But equally, if they like the consequences, they will not be too bothered about how the Court got there. In the case of *Engineers*, the policy consequences of the decision were crystal clear and desirable from a Commonwealth perspective – the enlargement of federal power. That was especially pleasing to the ALP given its socialization program, but it was also not unpleasing to the conservative side of politics, which also sought to impose its conception of government at the federal level.

As the doctrinal logic of *Engineers* worked itself out in area after area, the expansionary effect of the decision only became clearer and more desirable from a Commonwealth point of view. In a self-reinforcing, iterative process of the sort modelled by path dependency theory,[53] political acceptance of the Court's decisions legitimated the approach taken in *Engineers* as doctrinal orthodoxy. Neither of the two main Australian political groupings – the ALP, on the one hand, and the conservative side of politics, on the other – had any reason to object to the approach the Court was taking. To the extent that the state governments might have been aggrieved by their concomitant loss of power, there was very little they could do about it. For most of the last century, the states had very little say in the selection of High Court judges.[54] Instead, judges of the High Court were selected by the Commonwealth government, without involvement of the upper house, and drawing principally on barristers from the Sydney and Melbourne bars.[55] As with the *Engineers* Court itself, justices from these two main cities were either favorably disposed to strong Commonwealth government or socialized in the ideology and techniques of

---

[53] See the discussion in Chapter 1, Section 1.3.
[54] Consultation with the states over the appointment of High Court justices has only been formally required since a change to the applicable federal legislation in 1979.
[55] See Simon Evans, "Appointment of Justices" in Tony Blackshield, Michael Coper, and George Williams, *The Oxford Companion to the High Court of Australia* (Melbourne: Oxford University Press, 2001) 19, 20 (giving a list of justices of the High Court with their states of residence).

legalism. Either way, the Commonwealth's power of judicial appointment perpetuated the process that the *Engineers* Court had started.

In this way, the doctrinal aspect of *Engineers* became entrenched, extending the Commonwealth's power over the states even further as it coalesced into a reasonably coherent set of principles. At a certain point in the self-reinforcing process through which the *Engineers* approach became legitimated, the doctrinal logic of *Engineers* took over, in the sense of becoming less dependent on the political acceptance of the approach and more capable of relying on internal legal principles of adherence to precedent, consistency of approach, and coherence of doctrine. Thus, for example, the principle of "dual characterization," which holds that the Commonwealth need only show that its legislation is supported by at least one head of power for it to be valid, and that that head of power need not be connected to the legislation's dominant or "true character,"[56] flows naturally from the doctrinal logic of *Engineers*. The *Engineers* decision in that sense gathered up other principles in its doctrinal wake, which together compounded the overall effect of expanding the Commonwealth's power at the expense of the states.

As the doctrinal logic of *Engineers* played itself out in this way, the two other levels of the decision – its rhetorical claim and the reasoning methods it advocated – were carried along with it. Having adopted a rhetorical posture of legalism (without using that term in so many words), the acceptance of *Engineers* and entrenchment of its doctrinal logic gave that claim tremendous constitutional-cultural salience. It was as though the political acceptance of *Engineers* as doctrine meant also the political acceptance of the conceptual premise of the decision – the separability of law and politics. There had, of course, already been a strong predisposition in Australian constitutional culture towards that view. This is precisely why the *Engineers* Court called it up in aid of its decision. And legalism as legitimating ideology, as noted, also underlay the constitutional-design choice not to give the High Court the power to review legislation for conformance to the prescriptions of a bill of rights. Thus, *Engineers* could hardly be said to have invented this understanding of law's authority. But it did give powerful impetus to it as the rhetorical posture through which judges would seek to legitimate their function and accommodate the rival authority claim of democratic politics.

The effect of the political acceptance of *Engineers* on the reasoning methods that the decision advocated was more complex. English statutory interpretation methods never became quite as dominant as one might have anticipated. Rather, they continued to vie for ascendancy with more purposive

---

[56] One of the leading cases is *Fairfax v. Federal Commissioner of Taxation* (1965) 114 CLR 1.

methods, including the drawing of structural implications. One reason for this, as we have seen, was *Engineers'* self-contradictory quality in not itself applying the methods it advocated. The other was that the English statutory interpretation methods vindicated in *Engineers* were not all that relevant to the working out of the decision's expansionary logic as soon as the work of exploding the two implied limits on Commonwealth power was done.[57] Rather, the authority for giving a broad interpretation to the heads of power was *Jumbunna Coal*,[58] a case that had been decided 12 years before *Engineers* at a time when a more American style of reasoning was still being used.[59]

Jumbunna Coal had concerned the meaning of "industrial disputes" in s 51 (xxxv), the same head of power that was later at issue in *Engineers*. The *Conciliation and Arbitration Act* 1904 (Cth) had defined industry very broadly to include service occupations, in addition to heavy industry. The appellants had sought to attack the Act in part on the basis that this definition was too broad and not supported by s 51(xxxv). Citing the US case of *McCullogh* v. *Maryland* and its classic injunction that it should never be forgotten that "it is *a constitution* we are expounding,"[60] the *Jumbunna* Court held that "where the question is whether the Constitution has used an expression in the wider or the narrower sense, the Court should ... always lean to the broader interpretation unless there is something in the context or in the rest of the Constitution to indicate that the narrower interpretation will best carry out its object and purpose."[61] That dictum in isolation is reconcilable with *Engineers* inasmuch as English statutory interpretation methods also allow for references to context. But the interpretive ethos of *Jumbunna* is clearly that of the American authorities whose style of reasoning *Engineers* rejected. It is thus somewhat ironic that the full development of the expansionary logic of *Engineers* did not occur on the back of the reasoning methods advocated in that case, but rather through recitation of a case that stood for a diametrically opposed method of interpretation.

In consequence, it has never been entirely clear what legalism *as a set of reasoning methods* stands for. As Leslie Zines, one of Australia's leading constitutional scholars, explained, over the High Court's history different

---

[57] See Leslie Zines, "*Engineers* and the 'Federal Balance'" in Coper and Williams, *How Many Cheers for Engineers?* 81, 82.
[58] *Jumbunna Coal Mine NL* v. *Victorian Coal Miners' Association* (1908) 6 CLR 309.
[59] Much later, the dictum in *R* v. *Public Vehicles Licensing Appeal Tribunal (Tas); Ex parte Australian National Airways Pty Ltd* (1964) 113 CLR 207, 225 that heads of power should be "construed with all the generality which the words admit" came to be added to *Jumbunna Coal*, but this occurred once the main effects of *Engineers* had already worked themselves out.
[60] 17 US (4 Wheat) 316 (1819).
[61] *Jumbunna Coal* 368.

justices have deployed different methods, with some known for greater literalism than others, some for attention to policy consequences, and most using
a variety of different methods over their careers.[62] Insofar as legalism has been
central to the consolidation of the Australian JR regime, therefore, this is not
because it connotes a coherent and consistently applied set of methods.
Rather, the consolidation of democratic legalism in Australia has been
a function of three interrelated factors: (1) the doctrinal centrality of
Engineers in reshaping the federalist system and the political acceptance of
that development; (2) the ascendance in Australian constitutional culture of
legalism as an ideological claim about the law/politics relation; and (3) the
association of this claim with the rejection of "political" reasoning methods in
Engineers.

By the end of the 1930s all three of these factors were in play, but they had
not yet coalesced into a coherent JR regime. The expansionary logic of
Engineers, for its part, had begun to make itself felt in several cases. In *R* v.
Burgess; *Ex parte Henry*, for example, Evatt and McTiernan JJ cited *Engineers*
in holding that the scope of the external affairs power could not to be restricted
on the basis of an assumption that certain legislative topics were purely
domestic and therefore reserved to the states.[63] This decision eventually led
to the external affairs power becoming one of the most important sources of
Commonwealth legislation. In other areas, however, most notably the interaction of the corporations and trade and commerce powers, the full doctrinal
effects of *Engineers* had not been explored.[64] The main reason for this was that
the ALP, the most inclined of the two major political groupings to push the
boundaries of Commonwealth legislative power, had not, apart from a brief
and ineffectual period from 1929 to 1932, been in government.[65] In the absence
of Commonwealth legislation actually exploiting the expansionary logic of
Engineers, its influence at this stage was still latent.

Legalism, in turn, was well on its way to becoming the main ideological
frame through which the legitimacy of judicial review would be defended. Sir
John Latham, in particular, had, from his appointment as Chief Justice in
1935, done much to promote the idea that legal reasoning in constitutional
matters was a technical discipline distinct from, and therefore capable of
disciplining, politics.[66] But legalism had not yet been properly tested – called

---

[62] See Leslie Zines, *The High Court and the Constitution* 5th ed. (Sydney: Federation Press, 2008) 599–610.
[63] (1936) 55 CLR 608, 680.
[64] *Strickland* v. *Rocla Concrete Pipes Ltd* (1971) 124 CLR 468.
[65] See Galligan, *Politics of the High Court* 104–5.
[66] See Zines, *The High Court and the Constitution* 599–602.

on in the course of a major constitutional conflict to support law's claim to authority. In consequence, legalism at the end of the 1930s had yet to lock into a matching democratic political authority claim in the manner explained in Chapter 2. For that, both a more serious constitutional conflict and a more effective public advocate were required, someone who could show how an ideology of law's autonomy from politics might legitimate not just judicial review, but also the exercise of political power.

Finally, the third factor, the process through which legalism came to be associated with the rejection of "political" reasoning methods in *Engineers*, was also underway but not yet complete. While feeding into the steady rise of legalism as constitutional-cultural orthodoxy, *Engineers* had yet to take on the full ideological resonance that it has today. Instead, what Australia had was a leading decision associated with a malleable set of reasoning methods that had produced results pleasing to both major political groupings. Over the next decade, that happy marriage would first flourish and then come under severe strain.

3.2 THE POSTWAR CASES AND THE FAILED COURT-PACKING PLAN

Australia entered World War II on September 3, 1939. As had happened during the Great War, the Commonwealth's primary responsibility for coordinating the nation's military effort accelerated the weakening of the federal system. The added feature on this occasion was the ALP's determination, on assuming power in October 1941,[67] to exploit the circumstances of war to justify greater centralized control of the economy.[68] For the most part, the High Court cooperated in this endeavor. Its decisions under the defense power, in particular, licensed the Commonwealth's entry into areas of regulation that had traditionally been thought to be reserved to the states.[69]

At the height of the war, in the *First Uniform Tax* case,[70] the Court upheld a package of legislation through which the Commonwealth effectively wrested control of the levying of income tax from the states. Relying on two earlier

---

[67] The Curtin ALP government lasted four years. On Curtin's death at the end of the war, the Chifley ALP government was in office for a further four years. The combined total of eight years constituted the longest period of ALP government at the federal level until the Hawke/Keating governments which were in office from 1983 to 1996.

[68] See Fiona Wheeler, "The Latham Court" in Rosalind Dixon and George Williams (eds.), *The High Court, the Constitution, and Australian Politics* (Melbourne: Cambridge University Press, 2015) 159, 161–4.

[69] Ibid.

[70] *South Australia v. Commonwealth* (1942) 65 CLR 373 (First Uniform Tax Case).

cases in which the grants power in s 96 of the Constitution had been generously interpreted,[71] the Commonwealth raised the rate of its own income tax to a level that matched the rate previously imposed by the states and the Commonwealth together. It then conditioned the distribution back to the states of their share of Commonwealth revenue on their refraining from levying income tax themselves. The scheme was clearly coercive but structured in such a way as to satisfy the standard set by past precedents, provided that the Court was prepared to overlook the substantive impact of the scheme on the states' financial autonomy.

In what has generally been seen as a formalistic judgment,[72] Latham CJ began by reaffirming the Court's autonomy from politics:

> [T]he controversy before the Court is a legal controversy, not a political controversy. It is not for this or any court to prescribe policy or to seek to give effect to any views or opinions upon policy. We have nothing to do with the wisdom or expediency of legislation. Such questions are for Parliaments and the people.[73]

The Chief Justice then proceeded to assess the constitutionality of each plank in the legislative scheme separately.[74] On the crucial question of whether the distribution back to the states of their share of revenue could be conditioned on their not levying their own income tax, Latham CJ maintained that there was a difference between an "inducement" to act and "legal compulsion."[75] Since the Commonwealth had not actually attempted formally to deprive the states of their power to levy income tax, there could be no constitutional complaint.[76]

The confluence in the *First Uniform Tax* case of the Court's appeal to the specifically legal nature of its function and the ALP's interest in centralized control of the economy brought Australian democratic legalism close to consolidation. The two elements of a mutually legitimating pair of authority claims were by this time clearly in place. On one side stood the Court, heavily invested in justifying its decisions as the outcome of impartial reasoning

---

[71] *Victoria v. Commonwealth* (*Federal Roads* case) (1926) 38 CLR 399; *Deputy Federal Commissioner of Taxation* (*NSW*) v. *WR Moran Pty Ltd* (1939) 61 CLR 735.

[72] See Cheryl Saunders, "The Uniform Income Tax Cases" in H. P. Lee and George Winterton (eds.), *Australian Constitutional Landmarks* (Melbourne: Cambridge University Press, 2003) 62; Wheeler, "The Latham Court" 165 (referring to the Court's "legalistic analysis"); Zines, *The High Court and the Constitution* 601.

[73] *First Uniform Tax* case 409.

[74] Ibid 411.

[75] Ibid 417.

[76] Ibid 416.

processes, on the other, the ALP, for the first time in receipt of a clear democratic mandate to act on its long-term socialization objective. Immediately after the end of World War II, however, the two elements came apart. The ALP, emboldened by two successive federal election victories – the first, a very emphatic one in 1943, and the second, in 1946, less emphatic but still convincing[77] – introduced a sweeping range of nationalization and social welfare measures. Though long part of the ALP's political program, the measures went further than expected, and pushed Australians' tolerance for state interference in the market to the limit. The Court responded by using the same malleable set of interpretive methods that it had used to facilitate the expansion of Commonwealth power to block the ALP's plans.

The two major planks in the ALP's socialization program challenged in the Court were its attempted nationalization of the airline and banking industries and its scheme for providing free pharmaceutical benefits.[78] Both planks relied on the extensive understanding of federal power that had been developing since *Engineers*: the two nationalization initiatives on a reading of the banking and trade and commerce powers as permitting the Commonwealth to take control of whole industries, and the pharmaceutical benefits scheme on a broad understanding of the appropriations power in s 81. In its decisions on the nationalization initiatives the Court upheld the broad understanding of the two powers but struck the initiatives down under the freedom of interstate trade and commerce in s 92. In its decisions on the pharmaceutical benefits scheme, the Court's holding on the breadth of the power was inconclusive, but restrictive enough to invalidate the legislation.

All four of the Court's decisions in this group of cases deployed the interpretive techniques that it had developed in expanding the Commonwealth's powers, albeit on this occasion to limit them. In the *Australian National Airlines*[79] and *Bank Nationalization* cases,[80] the Court held that s 92 conferred an individual right to freedom of interstate trade and commerce. Thus, while the Commonwealth was in principle at liberty under the banking and trade and commerce powers to take over entire industries, the prohibition on private banks' and airlines' capacity to trade interstate was constitutionally fatal. Although the individual rights reading of s 92 had been doing the rounds for a long time, the *Airlines* and *Bank Nationalization* cases conclusively

---

[77]   In the election of August 21, 1943, the ALP won 49 of 74 seats in the House of Representatives and all 19 Senate seats contested.
[78]   The cases are discussed later on in this section.
[79]   *Australian National Airways Pty Ltd* v. *Commonwealth* (1945) 71 CLR 29.
[80]   *Bank of New South Wales* v. *Commonwealth* (1948) 76 CLR 1.

vindicated it over the rival interpretation of s 92 as conferring a more limited immunity against discriminatory protectionist legislation. As it had in *Engineers*, the Court focused on a narrow literal reading of the text of the Constitution to the exclusion of its original meaning.

In the first of the two *Pharmaceutical Benefits* cases,[81] the Court was confronted with an argument that the Commonwealth lacked the power under s 51 to provide free access to pharmaceuticals, and that the appropriations power in s 81 could not be used to regulate this issue in the absence of an independent head of power. Section 81 provides, in the relevant part, that Commonwealth revenues can be "appropriated for the purposes of the Commonwealth." On the broad view of this power, which was supported by McTiernan J, one of two controversial Labor appointments to the Court in 1930,[82] those purposes were essentially unlimited. This meant that s 81 sanctioned the funding of any policy initiatives that the Commonwealth wished to pursue, even if those initiatives were not countenanced in the list of Commonwealth legislative powers in s 51.[83] Latham CJ agreed in principle with this view. However, in invalidating the Act on the grounds that it was really about the regulation of access to pharmaceuticals, rather than the appropriation of revenue, he effectively restricted the appropriations power to situations where the main purpose of the legislation was the appropriation of funds.[84] Dixon and Rich JJ adopted a similar view to this,[85] while Starke and Williams JJ rejected altogether the idea that s 81 could be used for purposes not specified elsewhere in the Constitution.[86]

Inconclusive as it was, the result in the *First Pharmaceutical Benefits* case cast doubt on a range of Labor's social welfare programs, many of which depended on the broad reading of s 81.[87] A referendum to amend the Constitution was accordingly hastily arranged. Unusually for Australia, but proving the popularity of the social welfare measures, the referendum passed. On being reenacted, however, the pharmaceutical benefits legislation was once again challenged, this time on the grounds that it provided for the

---

[81] *Attorney-General (Vic); Ex rel Dale v. Commonwealth* (1945) 71 CLR 237 (*First Pharmaceutical Benefits* case).

[82] The other was H. V. Evatt, who left the Court in 1940.

[83] *First Pharmaceutical Benefits* case 273–4.

[84] Ibid 252–6.

[85] Ibid 269, 271–2.

[86] Ibid 266, 281–2.

[87] Geoffrey Sawer, *Australian Federal Politics and Law 1929–1949* (Melbourne: Melbourne University Press, 1963) 173; Galligan, *Politics of the High Court* 153–4; Wheeler, "The Latham Court" 168 n 94.

conscription of doctors.[88] The window for this challenge had been opened by political lobbying from the Liberal Party, which had seen the constitutional amendment specifically disallowing "any form of civil conscription."[89] In another highly formalistic judgment, the Court held that the requirement that doctors use a specific Commonwealth form when prescribing medicines under the scheme violated this prohibition.[90]

It is possible to read all four of these decisions as having been influenced by a judicial aversion to state interference in the market.[91] From 1940, the Court had been staffed by judges drawn mostly from the Melbourne and Sydney bars.[92] Their legal-professional backgrounds naturally inclined them to be distrustful of the ALP's capacity to manage complex industries. Their approach in these cases may thus be read as a reflection of their conservative views. Equally, however, the decisions in the *Bank Nationalization*, *Airlines*, and *Pharmaceutical Benefits* cases were a natural product of the reasoning methods the Court had long been developing. The charge that these decisions were ideologically motivated is therefore hard to demonstrate conclusively. What mattered from the point of regime stability was that the very methods that had been used to facilitate the expansion of Commonwealth power in the 1920s and 1930s were now limiting it.

The inconclusiveness of the ideological charge perhaps explains why Australia's version of Roosevelt's court-packing plan led to very different results. In June and July 1945, when the bill to nationalize the airlines industry was being debated in Parliament, but before the *First Pharmaceutical Benefits* case had been decided,[93] the Chifley ALP government proposed to increase the size of the Court from six to nine judges in order to secure a majority for its nationalization plans. A proposal to this effect was approved by Cabinet on October 2, 1945, but implementation was delayed until the return of the Attorney General, Dr H. V. Evatt, from an overseas trip.[94] Evatt was a former justice of the High Court whose own appointment had ironically been somewhat controversial because the then Attorney General had been away

[88] *British Medical Association* v. *Commonwealth* (1949) 79 CLR 201 (*Second Pharmaceutical Benefits* case).

[89] Section 51(xxiiiA).

[90] It is notable that Dixon J dissented from this judgment on the grounds of its formalism.

[91] See the illuminating discussion of this point in Wheeler, "The Latham Court" 175.

[92] Of the justices serving from 1940 to 1950, all apart from William Webb, who served on the Court from 1946 to 1958, were from either New South Wales or Victoria.

[93] Wheeler, "The Latham Court" 173.

[94] Galligan, *Politics of the High Court* 145–6.

overseas.[95] In the event, on Evatt's return, he strongly objected to the plan and persuaded the Cabinet to amend its decision to provide for increasing the size of the Court by one judge only, effectively back to prewar levels.[96]

As noted, Galligan sees this episode as the key moment when the Court was able to ward off the ALP's threat to the Constitution. His explanation for the Court's ability to survive this period emphasizes both Evatt's legal-professional socialization, as a former High Court justice,[97] and the Court's later even-handed rejection of the Liberal Party's Communist Party dissolution legislation.[98] Both of those factors were undoubtedly important, but the first tends to undermine Galligan's overarching thesis that the Court's embrace of legalism was part of a conscious political strategy. On his own account, Evatt's refusal to endorse the ALP's court-packing plan, despite his own deep conviction that the Court's reading of s 92 was wrong, points to a sincere commitment to legalism as a governing judicial philosophy.

It is also far from clear that legalism was finally vindicated by the Court's decision in the *Communist Party* case.[99] While the Court's rejection of a central plank in the Liberal Party's political platform did much to allay fears about its political evenhandedness, the *Communist Party* case, with the two nationalization cases and the two *Pharmaceutical Benefits* cases, constituted the fifth major policy reversal for a sitting government in six years. That left the Court more exposed than it had ever been before to the charge that it was a countermajoritarian institution whose decisions lacked democratic legitimacy. Although the Court continued to deny the political nature of its function, the reasoning methods that had served it so well in the past now seemed like a liability. Legalism's association with the Court's ahistorical, literalist reading of s 92 in the *Bank Nationalization* case, in particular, posed considerable challenges to law's claim to authority as an impartial device for the resolution of political conflicts.

By the end of 1951, therefore, Australia's democratic legalist regime could not be said to have been finally consolidated. That process required one last intervention – that of Australia's most influential twentieth-century justice, Sir Owen Dixon.

---

[95] See Peter Bayne, "Herbert Vere Evatt" in Tony Blackshield, Michael Coper, and George Williams (eds.), *The Oxford Companion to the High Court of Australia* (Melbourne: Oxford University Press, 2001) 251, 251–2.

[96] Wheeler, "The Latham Court" 173.

[97] Galligan, *Politics of the High Court* 146.

[98] Ibid 203–7.

[99] *Australian Communist Party* v. *Commonwealth* (1951) 83 CLR 1.

3.3 THE DIXONIAN CONSOLIDATION OF LEGALISM

As noted, the *Engineers* decision itself did not use the word "legalist" to describe its methods. While the main judgment's rhetorical posture certainly was legalist in arguing that the methods used in prior decisions had been impermissibly "political," the terms "legalism" and its cognate "legalist" do not appear in the judgment.[100] The prominence of those terms to describe the Court's methods is rather attributable to a speech made by Sir Owen Dixon when he was sworn in as Chief Justice in 1952. On that occasion, as all Australian constitutional law students are taught, Sir Owen proclaimed that "[t]here is no other safe guide to judicial decisions in great conflicts than a strict and complete legalism."[101] Ever since then, the Court's reasoning methods, whether they are being defended or attacked, have been described as legalist. There is thus no question that legalism serves as a shorthand description for what the dominant reasoning style on the Court is taken to be.[102] That the particular methods of reasoning advocated by the main judgment in *Engineers* should be so described, however, is somewhat misleading. If there is one *other* thing that every Australian law student is taught, it is that Sir Owen was responsible for clawing back some of the methodological ground claimed in *Engineers* by a purely English, statutory interpretation approach. In the years after his appointment as a High Court justice in 1929, he thus worked assiduously to construct a new version of the implied immunity of instrumentalities doctrine, in part by relying on implications drawn from the federal structure of the Constitution.[103] To that extent, Dixon's methods were emphatically not the methods that the *Engineers* Court had

---

[100] A search of the AustLII database of Commonwealth decisions revealed that the earliest use of the word "legalism" by the High Court was in 1939 in the case of *Peters' American Delicacy Co Ltd v. Heath* (1939) 61 CLR 457.

[101] Swearing in of Sir Owen Dixon as Chief Justice (1952) 85 CLR xi.

[102] See Goldsworthy, "Australia: Devotion to Legalism."

[103] The new version of the doctrine was announced in *Melbourne Corporation v. Commonwealth* (1947) 74 CLR 31. A decade before that decision, in *West v. Commissioner of Taxation* (NSW) (1937) 56 CLR 657, 681 Dixon J wrote that "[s]ince the *Engineers'* case a notion seems to have gained currency that in interpreting the Constitution no implications can be made. Such a method would defeat the intention of any instrument, but of all instruments a written constitution seems the last to which it could be applied." He then went on to explain why he thought that the majority judgment in *Engineers* did not mean to "propound such a doctrine" (at 682). See also Dixon J's judgment, shortly after arriving at the Court, in *Australian Railways Union v. Victorian Railways Commissioners* (1930) 44 CLR 319, 390 (restating *Engineers* as authorizing the Commonwealth Parliament to make laws affecting the states and their agencies so long as, inter alia, "the Parliament confines itself to laws which do not discriminate against the States or their agencies"). Dixon generally held an extremely negative view of Engineers, and "never mentioned it without a touch of asperity"

advocated. We are accordingly confronted with an intriguing paradox: a decision (*Engineers*) has come to be understood as standing in for a legitimating ideology and associated set of reasoning methods (legalism) that the fiercest critic of that decision (Dixon) had the greatest hand in developing. The resolution of this paradox, this section argues, provides the key to understanding the post-1952 consolidation of Australian democratic legalism.

The explanation has to start first with Dixon's stature as a judge and the most influential constitutional-cultural actor in mid-twentieth-century Australia. Appointed at the age of 42 in 1929, he served on the High Court as an ordinary justice for 23 years, and then for 12 years as Chief Justice.[104] Despite his comparative youth, Dixon was intellectually dominant at the Court from the outset, often single-handedly writing joint judgments and even on several occasions ghostwriting the judgments of his fellow judges.[105] He had very fixed views of the Constitution and, as his work in restating the *Engineers* decision shows, he was prepared to spend a number of years gradually building support for his view so that when he made his move the outcome would have an air of inevitability about it.[106]

As Chief Justice, Dixon in fact presided over a fairly quiet period on the Court insofar as its relationship with the political branches was concerned. Partly this had to do with the correspondence between his personal political views and those of the long-serving Prime Minister Robert Menzies, whose period in office his chief justiceship largely overlapped.[107] But Dixon was also a canny diplomat, who knew how to present the Court's work in public speeches in ways apt to legitimate its function. The speech at his swearing in was the best-known example of this, but there were others too.[108]

In contrast to his tenure as Chief Justice, Dixon's 1952 swearing-in speech was delivered in the aftermath of one of the most turbulent periods in the

---

(Geoffrey Sawer, *Australian Federalism in the Courts* (Melbourne: Melbourne University Press, 1967) 133).

[104] See Helen Irving, "The Dixon Court" in Rosalind Dixon and George Williams, *The High Court, the Constitution and Australian Politics* (Melbourne: Cambridge University Press, 2015) 179. See also Kenneth Hayne "Owen Dixon" in Tony Blackshield, Michael Coper, and George Williams (eds.), *The Oxford Companion to the High Court of Australia* (Melbourne: Oxford University Press, 2001) 218. The best-regarded biography is Philip Ayres, *Owen Dixon* (Melbourne: The Miegunyah Press, 2003).

[105] Irving, "The Dixon Court" 181.

[106] This is true of Dixon's approach to s 92, for example, although here he was in the company of a number of other justices.

[107] Ibid 180–1.

[108] Dixon's public speeches are collected in *Jesting Pilate and Other Papers and Addresses* (Melbourne: Law Book Co, 1965).

Court's institutional life. As we have seen, the mid-1940s and early 1950s had seen the decisions in the *Airlines* case,[109] the two *Pharmaceutical Benefits* cases,[110] the *Bank Nationalization* case,[111] and the *Communist Party* case.[112] Dixon had participated in all these decisions, voting on the side of the majority except in the *Second Pharmaceutical Benefits* case.[113] In appointing him Chief Justice, therefore, Menzies was not appointing someone with a record for judicial deference. But Dixon's stature was such that his appointment as Chief Justice was virtually automatic.[114] Most of the controversial cases, in any event, had been decided against the ALP rather than the Liberal Party, and Dixon's credentials as a political conservative on economic matters were assured. Nevertheless, the 1952 swearing-in speech was delivered with the conflict over the attempted dissolution of the Communist Party still fresh in the public mind. There had been enough tension between the Court and the political branches, at least, to require Dixon at his swearing-in to calm the waters a little – to reassure the political branches and the Australian public that the Court would respect the limits of its power.[115] As it turned out, Dixon's speech turned into the seminal legal-cultural moment in Australian history – the moment at which the legitimacy of judicial review was nailed firmly to the mast of legalism, from which the Court has only once subsequently (and unsuccessfully) sought to detach it.

When one looks at the longer passage in the speech from which the "strict and complete legalism" quote is drawn, it is significant that, while clearly identifying legalism as a reasoning method, the new Chief Justice was not very clear about what that method actually entailed. The full passage thus reads:

> [xiii] Federalism means a demarcation of powers and this casts upon the court a responsibility of deciding whether legislation is within the boundaries of allotted powers. Unfortunately that responsibility is very widely misunderstood, largely by the popular use and misuse of terms which are not applicable, and it is not sufficiently recognized that the court's sole function is to

---

[109] *Australian National Airways Pty Ltd* v. *Commonwealth* (1945) 71 CLR 29.

[110] *Attorney-General (Vic); Ex rel Dale* v. *Commonwealth* (1945) 71 CLR 237; *British Medical Association* v. *Commonwealth* (1949) 79 CLR 201.

[111] *Bank of New South Wales* v. *Commonwealth* (1948) 76 CLR 1.

[112] *Australian Communist Party* v. *Commonwealth* (1951) 83 CLR 1.

[113] *British Medical Association* v. *Commonwealth* (1949) 79 CLR 201.

[114] The only rival contender was rumored to be the Prime Minister himself. See Irving, "The Dixon Court" 181.

[115] See William Gummow, "Law and the Use of History" in Justin T. Gleeson and Ruth C. A. Higgins (eds.), *Constituting Law: Legal Argument and Social Values* (Sydney: Federation Press, 2011) 75 (explaining Dixon's speech as an attempt to "mollify resentment in the other branches of government at recent decisions").

interpret [xiv] a constitutional description of power or restraint upon power and say whether a given measure falls on one side of a line consequently drawn or on the other, and that it has nothing whatever to do with the merits or demerits of the measure.

Such a function has led us all I think to believe that close adherence to legal reasoning is the only way to maintain the confidence of all parties in Federal conflicts. It may be that the court is thought to be excessively legalistic. I should be sorry to think that it is anything else. There is no other safe guide to judicial decisions in great conflicts than a strict and complete legalism.[116]

Legalism, this passage implies, means "close adherence to legal reasoning" rather than any other kind of reasoning (moral or political). But beyond that we are not told much. Nothing in this passage actually spells out in so many words the particular methods of legal reasoning Dixon is advocating.[117] Rather, legalism is presented as an approach to legal reasoning that *just does* enable the Court to steer clear of the forbidden practice of assessing "the merits or demerits" of legislative measures. It achieves this by providing the Court with the technical means to distinguish objectively between measures that fall on one side or the other of a clear "line" demarcating the constitutional from the unconstitutional. Finally, the speech cleverly suggests that staying on the right side of that line is what the Court has been doing all along – that if there is a reason to object to its past decisions it is that they have been "excessively legalistic." In this way, Dixon both reassures the public of the Court's commitment to staying out of politics and vindicates past decisions, however controversial, as having done just that.

American readers might be intrigued to see the Australian High Court defending its legitimacy on these grounds twenty years after the high point of legal realism in the US and three years before the decision in *Brown* v. *Board of Education*.[118] The explanation is not that Australians were ignorant of these developments. As we have seen, the pre-*Engineers* period was full of citations to US authorities and, even then, it was appreciated that the American style of reasoning appealed to a different conception of legal authority compared to the Australian. Though *Engineers* had discouraged reliance on US authorities, it was not as though Australians thereafter stopped following US legal developments.[119] Quite the contrary. It was rather precisely knowledge of

[116] Swearing in of Sir Owen Dixon as Chief Justice (1952) 85 CLR xi.
[117] Dixon was more forthcoming in some of the other speeches collected in *Jesting Pilate*.
[118] *Brown* v. *Board of Education of Topeka* 347 U.S. 483 (1954).
[119] Dixon himself had served as Australian Minister to the US from 1942 to 1944 and had kept in touch with Felix Frankfurter and Dean Acheson among others. See Fiona Wheeler, "Book Review: *Owen Dixon*, Philip Ayres, The Miegunyah Press, 2003" (2003) 31 *Federal Law Review* 416;

US legal developments and the controversy surrounding them that likely convinced Dixon to throw in his lot with legalism. US legal culture had long served as something of an anti-model for Australians, and the ructions over legal realism only served to fuel that feeling. If the US had turned to legal realism, Australia would go its own way, and do exactly the opposite.

Exactly what "doing the opposite" entailed, however, needs to be clearly understood. As we have seen, Dixon was studiously not committing himself to a precise set of legal reasoning methods – to bright-line conceptual tests over balancing, for example. Rather he was committing himself to a particular way of defending the High Court's institutional legitimacy.[120] What Dixon's speech is, in the end, is a credo, and a credo that takes a stance on a very particular issue – about whether it is better for the safeguarding of the Court's institutional legitimacy to level with the public and admit that political values inevitably come into decision-making, or whether it is better to strenuously maintain the fiction of apolitical and impartial adjudication. Having seen the US go the other route on that question – and the ructions that this had entailed for the legitimacy of the Supreme Court – the Australian High Court, with Dixon at his head, chose to go a different route – to publicly invoke the idea of law's autonomy from politics.

That choice, for reasons already intimated, proved to be fateful for the Australian JR regime, and secured its consolidation during Dixon's tenure as Chief Justice in a form approximating democratic legalism. Many of the reasons why this happened have already been canvassed. To state them in one place again, those reasons are: Dixon's stature as a judge and the credibility he brought to the claim that law was a technical discipline separate from politics through his own personal work ethic, intellectual brilliance, and dominance of the Court;[121] the calm uneventfulness of Dixon's leadership of the Court under Menzies' prime ministership, which made it seem that Dixon's swearing-in speech had not just been a credo but also an accurate prediction about how the Court might steer clear of political conflicts; the increasing association in the Australian legal-cultural imagination of Dixonian legalism with the methods the Court had invoked in *Engineers*,

---

Geoffrey Sawer, *Australian Federalism in the Courts* (Melbourne: Melbourne University Press, 1967) 73 (commenting on Dixon's knowledge of US case law); Tony Blackshield, "Legalism" in Tony Blackshield, Michael Coper, and George Williams (eds.), *Oxford Companion to High Court of Australia* (Melbourne: Oxford University Press, 2001) 429.

[120] See Sawer, *Australian Federal Politics and Law* 73.

[121] See David Ritter, "The Myth of Sir Owen Dixon" (2005) 9 *Australian Journal of Legal History* 249, 261: "The myth of Dixon functions by marrying the epic reputation of the 'greatest judge in Australian history' to certain hegemonic values associated with judicial technique and the role of law."

even though those methods were in fact quite different; the continuing political acceptance of *Engineers* as its inexorable doctrinal logic drove a series of decisions that expanded Commonwealth power at the expense of the states; and the fusing together of the political acceptance of *Engineers* with the rhetorical claims of legalism for which Dixon was such a powerful advocate.

The two chief justiceships after Dixon's, those of Sir Garfield Barwick and Sir Harry Gibbs, were less successful, for different reasons. Barwick, for his part, had been a stellar member of the Bar, but as Chief Justice lacked authority. In public speeches his understanding of legalism was less sophisticated than Dixon's and appeared to equate it with a narrow literalism that neither *Engineers* nor his predecessor as Chief Justice had advocated.[122] Barwick's decisions on income tax matters were notoriously pedantic – thwarting repeated Commonwealth attempts to clamp down on tax avoidance.[123] Worse, in 1975, Barwick became embroiled in Australia's most serious constitutional crisis, the dismissal of Gough Whitlam as Prime Minister.[124] By the time of Barwick's retirement in 1981, therefore, the reputation of the Court for studious political neutrality had been considerably weakened.

Gibbs was a more effective Chief Justice than Barwick had been from a purely managerial point of view, and his own reputation as a legalist in the Dixonian mold remained strong.[125] Nevertheless, his chief justiceship was plagued by the controversial presence on the Court of Lionel Murphy, a former Labor Party Attorney-General who had been a strong advocate of a bill of rights.[126] Though Murphy was by no means the first former politician to be appointed to the Court, he was a particularly divisive figure.[127] His judgments on the Court pushed the same progressive agenda that had inspired his political career, albeit this time without a democratic mandate. Murphy was thus initially alone among his fellow justices in discovering in the

[122] In Barwick's retirement speech, reported in (1981) 148 CLR v, Barwick said: "When we have a statute to interpret, we have a text. The legislature has expressed itself in words, and those words bind. They cannot be sidestepped and the Court's task is to say what the words mean and there are quite distinct and understandable rules by which courts interpret statutory provisions. In the case of a constitution, it is so, but even to a greater degree. There is no room for the Court to change the Constitution."

[123] See Brian Galligan, "The Barwick Court" in Dixon and Williams, *The High Court* 201, 216.

[124] See George Winterton, "Garfield Barwick" in Blackshield, Coper, and Williams, *The Oxford Companion* 56, 58.

[125] See Nicholas Aroney and Haig Patapan, "The Gibbs Court" in Dixon and Williams, *The High Court* 220, 222.

[126] Ibid 223–5.

[127] See John Williams, "Lionel Keith Murphy" in Blackshield, Coper, and Williams, *Oxford Companion to the High Court of Australia* 484, 484–6.

Constitution a series of implied freedoms – of movement and speech, and from slavery, serfdom, sexual discrimination, and cruel and unusual punishment.[128] In reasoning style, Murphy's judgments were openly realist. He had a fondness for citing American authorities and often wrote cursory and under-justified decisions.[129] If this were not enough, towards the end of his time on the Court, Murphy was the subject of media allegations of graft and a series of Senate select committee inquiries into accusations that he had attempted to influence the course of justice in a criminal trial.[130] The second accusation led to a criminal conviction that was quashed on appeal. Murphy died in office shortly after a Parliamentary Commission of inquiry into his conduct had been terminated in view of his terminal illness.[131]

On the one hand, Murphy J's tenure on the Court might not have been too damaging to the ideological appeal of legalism, given that his record both on and off the Bench would have provided ample evidence for many of the need for a clear separation between law and politics. On the other, Murphy J's open embrace of value-driven reasoning challenged the Court's methods in ways that had not happened before. By so obviously pursuing his progressive political agenda from the Bench, Murphy J raised the possibility that the other justices might have been similarly influenced by their political views, only better at hiding it. In any event, the Gibbs Court, with Murphy J as its most flamboyant member, is regarded as marking a transition between the less successfully defended legalism of the Barwick Court and the very deliberate assault on legalism that occurred under the next Chief Justice, Sir Anthony Mason.

3.4 THE MASON COURT'S CHALLENGE

At the time of his appointment to the High Court as an ordinary justice in 1972, there was little reason to suspect that Mason would go on to lead a concerted attempt to break legalism's hold on Australian legal culture. His practice at the Sydney Bar, where he had worked closely with Barwick, had mainly been in "equity and commercial law."[132] After taking on the role of Commonwealth Solicitor-General in 1964, Mason had perforce become more involved in constitutional law matters, but nothing in his performance of that role

---

[128]   Ibid.
[129]   Ibid.
[130]   Ibid.
[131]   Ibid.
[132]   Kristen Walker, "Anthony Mason" Blackshield, Coper, and Williams, *Oxford Companion* 459, 459.

suggested that he was an iconoclast in the making. Indeed, Mason's early judgments on the High Court as an ordinary justice were marked by an explicit rejection of judges' law-making role. In *Trigwell*, for example, Mason said that "[t]he court is neither a legislature nor a law reform agency. Its responsibility is to decide cases by applying the law to the facts as found."[133] After his appointment as Chief Justice in 1987, however, Mason became associated with the most determined effort in the High Court's history to transform societal conceptions of its legitimate role in national politics. With his fellow reform-minded justices, William Deane, John Toohey, and Mary Gaudron, Mason formed a majority bloc of four justices who challenged the legalist orthodoxy, both in their decision-making and in their extracurial statements.[134]

The reasons for Mason's personal judicial transformation and, more generally, for his Court's challenge to legalism have been considered in an extensive scholarly literature.[135] Broadly speaking, two sets of factors have been identified, the first personal-professional, and the second, institutional. On the personal-professional side, scholars have stressed the influence on Mason and the other reform-minded justices of Professor Julius Stone, chair of Jurisprudence and International Law at Sydney Law School and Mason's teacher during his time as a law student there after the end of World War II. On the institutional side, the factors stressed have been various changes to the appellate process in Australia, including the final termination of all routes of appeal to the Privy Council, and the global rise of rights-based constitutionalism.[136]

As noted in the introduction to this chapter, Stone was an immigrant to Australia who had worked with Roscoe Pound at Harvard Law School.[137] His work in jurisprudence may in many ways be understood as an attempt to develop aspects of Pound's thinking that Pound had left unfinished.[138]

---

[133] *State Government Insurance Commission* v. *Trigwell* (1979) 142 CLR 617. See also *Miller* v. *TCN Channel Nine Pty Ltd* (1986) 161 CLR 556, 581.

[134] See, for example, Anthony Mason, "The Role of a Constitutional Court in a Federation: A Comparison of the Australian and the United States Experience" (1986) 16 *Federal Law Review* 1; John Toohey, "A Government of Laws, and Not of Men?" (1993) 4 *Public Law Review* 158.

[135] For Stone's influence on Mason, see particularly, Michael Kirby, "A. F. Mason – From *Trigwell* to *Teoh*" (1996) 20 *University of Melbourne Law Review* 1087, 1098.

[136] See Patapan, *Judging Democracy* and Pierce, *Inside the Mason Court Revolution*.

[137] See Leonie Star, *Julius Stone: An Intellectual Life* (Melbourne: Oxford University Press, 1992) 29–32.

[138] Anthony R. Blackshield, "The Legacy of Julius Stone" (1997) 20 *University of New South Wales Law Journal* 215, 220.

Despite Pound's break with the legal realists, Stone saw himself as part of the broader reaction against formalism that Pound's intervention had triggered.[139] His scholarly output ranged across a number of areas, but in relation to legal reasoning focused on continuing the realist tradition of exposing the "leeways of choice" that appellate judges enjoy.[140] One of Stone's most influential jurisprudential ideas was thus the notion that appellate court decision-making may be analyzed in terms of "categories of illusory reference" – forms of reasoning that mask the discretionary choices being made.[141] When the answer to a case could not be reached by fitting the facts under a particular legal category (rule, principle, or standard), Stone argued, judges perforce had to make law. Judges who had been socialized in the declaratory theory of law, however, would be inclined to resist owning up to this fact, and instead try to do everything in their power (sincerely rather than disingenuously) to present their decisions as though they had merely applied preexisting law. These creativity-denying moves, Stone argued, could be detected in various types of logical breakdown, such as circular reasoning, unjustified choices of one competing legal norm over another, or resort to meaningless or indeterminate concepts.[142]

As a student at the University of Sydney in the late 1940s, Mason, along with a number of other future justices of the Court, had been exposed to these ideas in the year-long course in jurisprudence that he took with Stone. At the time, the University of Sydney Law School was the only law school in New South Wales, the state that, together with Victoria, produced the vast majority of Australia's leading barristers and High Court justices.[143] Stone's influence on an entire generation of lawyers was thus significant. The relatively small size of the Australian legal-professional community at the time meant that he, a single charismatic figure, was able to make a tremendous impact on settled understandings of the law/politics relation. Stone's influence on Australian legal culture was at the same time, however, also *not* the influence of a broader intellectual movement. That, as explained below, made a difference to the extent to which his realist ideas gained traction.

---

[139] Ibid.
[140] Julius Stone, *Precedent and Law: Dynamics of Common Law Growth* (Sydney: Butterworths, 1985) 97.
[141] Julius Stone, *The Province and Function of Law: Law as Logic, Justice, and Social Control* (Sydney: Maitland, 1946) 149–214; Julius Stone, *Legal System and Lawyers' Reasonings* (Stanford: Stanford University Press, 1964) 235–300.
[142] Julius Stone, *Precedent and Law: Dynamics of Common Law Growth* (Sydney: Butterworths, 1985) 62.
[143] See Blackshield, "The Legacy of Julius Stone" 218.

In addition to this personal-professional factor, Mason assumed the chief justiceship at a time when several changes to the Court's institutional environment were beginning to take effect. Those changes included the passage of the *Australia Acts* in 1986, which saw the final termination of appeals from Australian state courts to the Privy Council,[144] and a changed global setting in which charters of rights were increasingly being adopted and beginning to transform the way judges in other countries engaged their national political systems.[145] Both these developments, on the standard account of what happened, pushed the Mason Court to begin redefining its institutional role.

The final legal break with Britain, for its part, meant that the Australian Constitution was from 1986 effectively (if not formally) repatriated as the product of the sovereign will of the Australian people. Rather than an immutable Act of the Imperial Parliament, the Constitution could henceforth be treated as a living document whose meaning evolved as each new generation of Australians sought to make it fit for their purposes. The increasingly global discourse over the role of national high courts, in turn, prompted the reform-minded justices to begin thinking about what was specifically Australian about this newly repatriated Constitution. If its national character was to be drawn out, they reasoned, the values underpinning the Constitution needed to be explicitly stated. In the absence of a charter of rights, the best way of doing that was to offer a substantive account of the political system that the Constitution had established.

For Mason, the impulse to change was not just the need to identify the values underpinning the Constitution but also the need to be more candid about the way *extra-legal* values intruded into the justices' decision-making processes. In a paper published just before his appointment as Chief Justice, Mason thus wrote:

> The asserted advantage of a legalistic approach is that decisions proceed from the application of objective legal rules and principles of interpretation rather than from the subjective values of the justices who make the decisions. Unfortunately, it is impossible to interpret any instrument, let alone a constitution, divorced from values. To the extent they are taken into account, they should be acknowledged and should be accepted community values rather than mere personal values. The ever present danger is that

---

[144] Patapan, *Judging Democracy* 18.
[145] Ibid 19. The adoption of the Canadian Charter of Rights and Freedoms in 1982 was probably the most influential development in this respect, along with the repatriation of the Canadian Constitution at that time.

"strict and complete legalism" will be a cloak for undisclosed and unidenti-fied policy values.[146]

In this passage, Mason uses the accepted practice of referring to community values when developing the common law to argue that constitutional inter-pretation, too, should take community values into account – not just those values that the framers could be said to have held, but also *contemporary* community values. This "living constitutionalist" approach hardly seems novel now, but in the late 1980s in Australia it represented a profound chal-lenge to the Dixonian legalist orthodoxy. As malleable as the reasoning methods that the High Court had deployed until then were, they had all been premised on the assumption that there was a defined set of authoritative legal materials to which judges could legitimately refer, and that those materi-als generated answers without the need to resort to anything outside the law. Mason's questioning of this idea bears all the hallmarks of Stone's influence, including the latter's stress on the leeways of choice that appellate judges enjoy in resolving gaps in the law. What Mason emphasized in Stone's work in particular was the idea that these choices ought to be openly acknowledged, so that the values judges rely on when filling gaps in the law may be debated and appropriately grounded in shared conceptions of the principled commitments and purposes of Australian constitutionalism.[147]

One could hardly think of a more direct challenge to Dixon's 1952 swearing-in speech. Whereas Dixon, as we have seen, premised his public defense of the High Court's role on the need to sustain the public's faith in the impartiality of constitutional adjudication – a goal that he argued could best be pursued by presenting law as an autonomous system of reasoning – Mason thought that the requirement of judicial candor pressed in the opposite direction. While sustaining the public's faith in judicial impartiality was still the primary focus, that goal was better pursued by being frank about the fact that judges make legally unconstrained, value-laden choices.[148]

On assuming the Chief Justiceship, this judicial philosophy underpinned Mason's attempt to transform both the High Court's role in the Australian political system and the reasoning methods used to support its decisions.

[146]   Anthony Mason, "The Role of a Constitutional Court in a Federation: A Comparison of the Australian and the United States Experience" (1986) 16 *Federal Law Review* 1,5.

[147]   Ibid.

[148]   As Martin Krygier has pointed out, there is a third option, namely that judicial choice is controlled by law, not in the form of formally posited legal norms, but in the form of traditional habits of mind and thoughtways of the kind Karl Llewellyn stressed. See Martin Krygier, "Julius Stone: Leeways of Choice, Legal Tradition and the Declaratory Theory of Law" (1986) 9 *University of New South Wales Law Journal* 26.

Before that time, as we have seen, the Court's role had been restricted mostly to matters of federalism. The Mason Court tried to change this by identifying and rendering justiciable a number of additional structural limits on federal and state legislative power. In doing so, the Court developed a range of doctrines that depended, both for their initial derivation and for their ongoing application, on a new, more substantive style of reasoning.

The best known of these doctrines is the so-called "implied freedom of political communication," which was first identified in a pair of cases decided in 1992: *Nationwide News Pty Ltd v. Wills*[149] and *Australian Capital Television Pty Ltd v. Commonwealth*.[150] Interestingly, in the first of these cases, Mason CJ did not join the four justices who premised their decision on the implied freedom.[151] Rather, he reached the same result by holding that the legislative provision in question, a section in the *Industrial Relations Act 1988 (Cth)* that criminalized the act of bringing a member of the Industrial Relations Commission into disrepute, was not supported by the conciliation and arbitration power in s 51(xxxv). Mason's judgment is significant because it comes very close to suggesting that common-law freedoms function as a constitutional bill of rights. When a provision is not obviously within the primary scope of a head of power, Mason CJ held, the Court should consider whether it is reasonably necessary for the achievement of a legitimate objective. As part of that assessment, the extent to which the provision results "in any infringement of fundamental values traditionally protected by the common law" was relevant.[152] Had this idea been accepted by a majority of the justices, common-law freedoms would have been constitutionalized as implied restraints on Commonwealth laws not obviously in power.

In the event, Mason CJ's line of reasoning was not followed, and it never became part of the Court's standard approach to the characterization of Commonwealth laws.[153] Instead, the other reform-minded justices premised their decisions in *Nationwide News* on the existence of a freedom of political communication derived from the Constitution itself. Deane and Toohey JJ, for example, held in a joint judgment that, just as the Constitution contained "general doctrines" of divided Commonwealth and state powers and separated

---

[149] (1992) 177 CLR 1 ("*Nationwide News*").
[150] (1992) 177 CLR 106 ("the *ACTV* case").
[151] Those judges were Deane, Toohey, Brennan, and Gaudron JJ. In *ACTV*, McHugh J joined Mason CJ in upholding the freedom, but he and Brennan J were never as enthusiastic in their support for it as the four reform-minded justices.
[152] *Nationwide News* 31.
[153] The closest parallel is Deane and Toohey JJ's judgment in *Leeth v. Commonwealth* (1992) 174 CLR 455.

legislative, executive, and judicial powers, so too did it contain a "doctrine of representative government."[154] The genius of putting the point this way was that the first two doctrines had already generated implied limits on Commonwealth power – the first in the form of the *Melbourne Corporation* principle,[155] and the second in the form of the *Boilermakers* principle,[156] both of which had been Dixonian innovations. Having drawn that pedigreed parallel, Deane and Toohey JJ reasoned that the principle of representative government likewise could be seen to generate an implied freedom of political communication.

In the simultaneously decided *ACTV* case,[157] Mason CJ joined Deane and Toohey JJ and all the other justices (with the exception of Dawson J) in upholding the implied freedom, but gave a slightly different justification for it, one that explicitly linked it to Dixon's work in relegitimating the practice of implication-drawing.[158] In Mason CJ's view, the distinction between "unexpressed assumption[s]," reliance on which *Engineers* condemned, and implications, the drawing of which *Engineers* (as re-interpreted by Dixon) allowed, was that the former stood "outside" the Constitution, whereas the latter "inhere[d] in the instrument," either in the text itself or as a "logically or practically necessary" part of the constitutional structure.[159] The freedom of political communication, Mason CJ held, was implied in this second sense as being necessary to give effect to the principle of responsible government, which was in turn implied by those parts of the Constitution that established a bicameral Parliament with members "directly chosen by the people."[160]

As a justice less enamored of the implied freedom later noted, the unjustified conceptual leap in Mason CJ's judgment is the way it uses one implication, the principle of representative government, as a "premise" for another – the implied freedom of political communication.[161] Indeed, Mason CJ's entire judgment is quite conceptualist inasmuch as it uses the abstract and indeterminate notion of representative government to generate the implied freedom, which is then given justiciable content through a series of discretionary pronouncements about the nature of the freedom, the institution of government responsible for enforcing it, and the level of review required.

---

[154] *Nationwide News* 70.
[155] *Melbourne Corporation* v. *Commonwealth* (1947) 74 CLR 31.
[156] *R* v. *Kirby; Ex parte Boilermakers' Society of Australia* (1956) 94 CLR 254.
[157] (1992) 177 CLR 106.
[158] *ACTV* 134 (quoting *West* v. *Commissioner of Taxation (NSW)* (1937) 56 CLR 657, 681 and *Australian National Airways Pty Ltd* v. *Commonwealth* (1945) 71 CLR 29, 85).
[159] *ACTV* 135.
[160] *ACTV* 137 (referring to ss 7 and 24 of the Constitution).
[161] McHugh J in *McGinty* v. *Western Australia* (1996) 186 CLR 140, 234.

All of this is done on the basis that the freedom "inheres" in the instrument, as though it were a mere mechanical exercise for the justices to draw it out. That style of reasoning was precisely not what Mason had committed himself to in the paper he gave prior to his appointment as Chief Justice. Nor was it a style of reasoning of which Julius Stone would have approved.[162] The irony of *ACTV* is thus that, although the outcome of the case arguably served the goal of a more robust, open, and engaged democracy, the method of getting there was quite heavy-handed.

These and other criticisms of the degree of judicial creativity involved in the two implied-freedom-of-political-communication cases pitched the High Court into public controversy. The justices were accused in the press of making a "political statement" about how democratic rights should be protected.[163] The situation was not helped when Toohey J, shortly after the *Nationwide News* and *ACTV* decisions, gave a speech at a conference in Darwin in which he argued that the assumption on which the Australian Constitution had been based – that "regular popular elections were a sufficient safeguard against the possibility of legislative activity failing to conform to principles of generality, prospectivity, and sensitivity to basic human rights" – no longer held.[164] That being so, Toohey J said, the High Court ought to play a more prominent role in deriving implied limits on legislative power, either from the Constitution or the common law.[165] This speech provoked a flurry of attacks on the Court in Parliament. The most significant of these was by Michael Tate, the ALP Minister for Justice, who angrily dismissed the idea that the judiciary was the primary agent for protecting human rights, pointing out that representative government, the centerpiece of the two implied freedom judgments, had been achieved through political struggle.[166]

The two implied-freedom-of-political-communication decisions were not the only controversial Mason Court decisions. On June 30, 1992, three months before *Nationwide News* and *ACTV* were decided, the Court had held in

---

[162] See Nicholas Aroney, "Julius Stone and the End of Sociological Jurisprudence" (2008) 31 *UNSW Law Journal* 107.

[163] Stephen Loosely, "Beware the Danger of Politicizing the Courts" *Sunday Telegraph* (October 4, 1992) 50 (cited in Paul Kildea and George Williams, "The Mason Court" in Rosalind Dixon and George Williams (eds.), *The High Court, the Constitution, and Australian Politics* (Melbourne: Cambridge University Press, 2015) 244, 252).

[164] Toohey, "A Government of Laws" 163.

[165] Ibid 168–70.

[166] Commonwealth, Parliamentary Debates, Senate, October 7, 1992, 1280 (cited in H. P. Lee, "The Implied Freedom of Political Communication" in H. P. Lee and George Winterton (eds.), *Australian Constitutional Landmarks* (Melbourne: Cambridge University Press, 2003) 383, 392).

Mabo that the common law recognized a form of native title that secured to the indigenous inhabitants of Australia an entitlement to their traditional lands to the extent that these rights had not been extinguished by contrary Crown grants.[167] Although this decision did not go so far as to provide for the payment of compensation for past dispossession, it clearly had very far-reaching implications. The political opposition to *Mabo*, however, mostly came from the states, which had (as they still do) primary responsibility for land management.[168] At the federal level, the ALP government quickly moved to support the decision, partly out of conviction that it was right and partly in response to demands that the uncertainty over land ownership be speedily resolved.[169] *Mabo*'s role in the development of Australia's JR regime is thus hard to assess. Aside from the ambiguity of the political response, it was not a constitutional law decision, and thus the Court's creative development of the law was easier to justify as part of its ordinary function.

Another controversial decision along these lines was *Dietrich*, in which the Court held that, where the accused is charged with a serious offence, lack of legal representation may provide the basis, both for an order to stay the proceedings and also for a finding on appeal that a trial that proceeded without legal representation was unfair.[170] Although the Court explicitly dismissed the argument "that there was a right to counsel at public expense,"[171] the decision effectively meant that no trial of a serious offence could proceed unless counsel was provided. That result obviously had far-reaching budgetary implications. Like *Mabo*, however, the primary basis for *Dietrich* was the common law, in this case the criminal law right to a fair trial.[172] Once again, therefore, it was possible to defend the decision as the mere exercise of the Court's ordinary function.[173] Nevertheless, *Dietrich*, coming as it did in the same year as the two implied-freedom decisions and

---

[167]   *Mabo v. Queensland* (No 2) (1992) 175 CLR 1.

[168]   Kildea and Williams, "The Mason Court" 253.

[169]   See Peter H. Russell, "*Mabo*: Political Consequences" in Tony Blackshield, Michael Coper, and George Williams (eds.), *Oxford Companion to the High Court of Australia* (Melbourne: Oxford University Press, 2001) 450, 451.

[170]   *Dietrich v. R* (1992) 177 CLR 292.

[171]   Declan Roche, "Dietrich v The Queen" in Tony Blackshield, Michael Coper, and George Williams (eds.), *Oxford Companion to the High Court of Australia* (Melbourne: Oxford University Press, 2001) 207, 207.

[172]   Two of the justices, however, Deane and Gaudron JJ, held obiter that this common-law right was protected by Chapter III of the Constitution insofar as that Chapter conferred exclusive power on the federal judiciary to adjudicate and punish criminal offenders (ibid 326). See Kildea and Williams "The Mason Court" 249; Roche "Dietrich v The Queen" 207.

[173]   See Michael Kirby, *Judicial Activism: Authority, Principle, and Policy in the Judicial Method* (London: Sweet & Maxwell, 2004) 49 (defending the decision as "unsurprising").

Mabo, contributed to a generally hostile political atmosphere by the end of 1992.

The key point of interest from the perspective of this study is what happened from this moment on. In theoretical terms, the Mason Court's challenge to democratic legalism represented an attempt, not to transform that legitimating ideology altogether, but to put it on a more secure ideational footing. In essence, what the Mason Court was trying to do was to exploit the Court's accumulated legitimacy as the neutral umpire of Australian federalism to enter the terrain of substantive rights enforcement. That proposed change may be seen as an internal adjustment within democratic legalism, from a version of that ideal type in which respect for the separation of law and politics hinges on the courts' staying out of the business of rights adjudication to a version in which rights adjudication is justified as the apolitical enforcement of the conditions for free and fair democratic competition. Reasonable as it may now seem, this attempted change generated a great deal of resistance from traditionally minded justices and political actors with a vested interest in the existing regime. From their perspective, what they were witnessing was not a group of well-meaning justices trying to put democratic legalism on a more secure ideational footing, but a radical faction seeking to redraw the law/politics boundary in ways contrary to settled understandings. What transpired? And what can we learn from the Australian case about the politico-legal dynamics of judge-driven JR-regime change?

To make things simpler, the story from this point is restricted to the fate of the implied-freedom-of-political-communication line of cases. That line of cases was in any event the most prominent constitutional dimension of the Court's attempted transformation, and thus nothing much is lost by focusing on this aspect. The essential trajectory, which is representative of the transformation attempt as a whole, is one of containment and absorption rather than achieved transformation or complete retrenchment. The High Court, after Mason's retirement in 1995, ultimately endorsed the implied freedom, but did so by agreeing on a reasoning methodology that prevented the proliferation of the doctrine to other areas of constitutional law. In subsequent periods, the Court has returned to an ideology of legalism when defending its role publicly. This has not, however, prevented the incremental introduction of some of the ideas that the Mason Court promoted.

After *Nationwide News* and *ACTV*, the implied-freedom-of-political-communication line of cases turned to consider the common law, and in particular whether the implied freedom of political communication could be said to give rise to a new constitutional defense to an action for defamation.

In *Theophanous*[174] and *Stephens*,[175] a narrow majority consisting of just the
four reform-minded justices held that the implied freedom gave rise to what
they eventually said in the second case was a modified common-law defense of
qualified privilege. In the course of these two decisions, however,
a considerable gap opened up between the reform-minded justices and two
of the other justices, Brennan and McHugh JJ, who had initially supported the
implied freedom in *Nationwide News* and *ACTV*. McHugh J, in particular,
was scathing about the methodology that the reform-minded justices had used
to identify the freedom, developing what had seemed in *ACTV* like a small
difference of opinion into a full-scale assault on the legitimacy of the majority's reasoning methods. The nub of McHugh J's complaint was that the
reform-minded justices had used the concept of representative government
as a "free-standing principle"[176] or "premise"[177] from which the implied freedom could be derived. This way of reasoning, McHugh J argued, ran contrary
to the settled view since *Engineers* that "it is not legitimate to construe the
Constitution by reference to political principles or theories that find no
support in the text of the Constitution."[178]

McHugh J himself had supported the identification of the implied
freedom in *ACTV*, but had done so on the narrow basis that it was
a necessary implication of the text of ss 7 and 24, not of any free-floating
principle of representative government or worse, representative
democracy.[179] That made a difference to the scope of the freedom,
McHugh J held, inasmuch as ss 7 and 24 were directed specifically at
federal elections.[180] In particular, all that could be inferred was that the
Constitution guaranteed the freedom of the people and their political
representatives to communicate with each other in the immediate run-
up to the ballot. In *Theophanous* and *Stephens*, this line of reasoning led
McHugh J to conclude that the implied freedom had no impact on the
common law. Beyond this, it meant, on the one hand, that the scope of
the freedom was considerably narrower than the majority had held in
Nationwide News and *ACTV* and, on the other, that representative government could not be used to generate other implied freedoms. Thus, in

---

[174] *Theophanous v. Herald & Weekly Times Ltd* (1994) 182 CLR 104.
[175] *Stephens v. West Australian Newspapers Ltd* (1994) 182 CLR 211.
[176] Ibid 234.
[177] Ibid.
[178] Theophanous 198.
[179] ACTV 229–33. Section 7 and 24 provide for Senators and members of the lower house to be
       "directly chosen by the people."
[180] Ibid.

McGinty, McHugh J held that the concept could not be used to recognize an implied equality of voting power.[181]

In *Theophanous* and *Stephens*, McHugh J had been on the losing side of a 4:3 split, but by the time *McGinty* was decided in 1996, Mason CJ had retired and Deane J had left to become Governor General. Three justices of the Brennan Court, with Gummow J replacing Mason CJ and Deane's spot yet to be filled, joined McHugh J in a new majority. Shortly afterwards, in the initial hearing in *Levy*,[182] Dawson J, who had never signed up to the implied freedom, more or less invited the parties to challenge *Theophanous* and *Stephens*.

The resolution of the impasse eventually came in *Lange* v. *Australian Broadcasting Corporation*.[183] To the surprise of many, the justices wrote a *per curiam* judgment upholding the freedom. With hindsight, their reasons for doing that were straightforward: the Court needed to present a united front in the face of the many criticisms that had been made of it. From the perspective of McHugh J and Brennan CJ, it was more important that the Court survive this episode with its reputation for law-governed decision-making intact than that their view of the implied freedom be vindicated in every respect. This pragmatic striving for unanimity, however, produced a muddled decision in *Lange* in which McHugh J's views on method were combined with the Mason Court majority's views on the scope of the implied freedom. Since the whole point of McHugh J's insistence on using the correct *Engineers* methodology had been to narrow the scope of the freedom, the outcome in *Lange* was inadequately justified. While it resolved the doctrinal uncertainty over the freedom, the decision – like that in *ACTV* – was not a model of the transparent judicial reasoning methods that Mason CJ in his pre-appointment speech had undertaken to introduce.

The other important consequence of the compromise in *Lange*, and the goal that McHugh J and Brennan CJ had arguably been striving for, was that it put a stop to the proliferation of the implied-freedom line of cases. Of all the various implied freedoms that one or more justices at various times mooted, only one – the implied right to vote – has been vindicated.[184] Like the implied freedom of political communication, this right could be derived directly from ss 7 and 24 of the Constitution, and thus its existence was hard to deny once *Lange* had endorsed the legitimacy of the narrower text-based method. The Brennan Court, however, declined an invitation to recognize an implied

[181]   *McGinty* v. *Western Australia* (1996) 186 CLR 140.
[182]   *Levy* v. *Victoria* (1997) 189 CLR 579.
[183]   *Lange* v. *Australian Broadcasting Corporation* (1997) 189 CLR 520.
[184]   *Roach* v. *Electoral Commissioner* (2007) 233 CLR 162; *Rowe* v. *Electoral Commissioner* (2010) 243 CLR 1.

freedom of association,[185] and none of the other freedoms originally mentioned in Murphy J's various judgments ever made any headway.[186] While the Brennan Court thus did not radically deviate from the course begun in 1987, and introduced one novel constitutional doctrine of its own,[187] it is generally seen as a Court that contained rather than extended the Mason Court's reforms.[188]

After Brennan's retirement in 1998, Murray Gleeson was appointed as Chief Justice with the apparent aim of finally putting to rest the public controversy surrounding the Court. In his main public statement on judicial method, Gleeson CJ presented a fairly orthodox understanding of legalism as a contestable, but nevertheless specifically legal, set of reasoning techniques that had in common their ability to exclude judicial policy preferences.[189] On the surface of things, therefore, the Gleeson Court appeared to be headed towards a complete retrenchment of the Mason Court's reforms. As things turned out, however, the Court did not overrule the implied-freedom-of-political-communication decisions. Moreover, Gleeson CJ, despite the way he chose to present his judicial philosophy in public, was not a narrow technocrat when it came to the actual practice of constitutional law. Although he was part of the majority in *Wakim*,[190] a notoriously literalist decision that struck down a legislative scheme to which all the states and the Commonwealth had consented, his other decisions displayed a wider range of reasoning techniques, including policy reasoning.[191] The same was true of the other justices.[192] The Gleeson Court is thus best understood not as having rejected all of the methodological innovations that the Mason Court tried to

---

[185]   See *Kruger v. Commonwealth* (1997) 190 CLR 1.
[186]   See *R v. Director-General of Social Welfare (Vic); Ex parte Henry* (1975) 133 CLR 369, 388 (holding that the Australian Constitution guaranteed freedom from "slavery or serfdom"); *Ansett Transport Industries (Operations) Pty Ltd v. Wardley* (1980) 142 CLR 237, 267 (finding an implied constitutional guarantee against sex discrimination).
[187]   See *Kable v. Director of Public Prosecutions* (1996) 189 CLR 51 (holding that state courts exercising federal jurisdiction could not be used as instruments of the executive).
[188]   See David F. Jackson, "Brennan Court" in Tony Blackshield, Michael Coper, and George Williams (eds.), *Oxford Companion to the High Court of Australia* (Melbourne: Oxford University Press, 2001) 68; Patrick Emerton and Jeffrey Goldsworthy, "The Brennan Court" in Rosalind Dixon and George Williams (eds.), *The High Court, the Constitution, and Australian Politics* (Melbourne: Cambridge University Press, 2015) 261.
[189]   See Murray Gleeson, "Judicial Legitimacy" (2000) 20 *Australian Bar Review* 4, 9.
[190]   *Re Wakim; Ex parte McNally* (1999) 198 CLR 511.
[191]   See Leslie Zines, "Chief Justice Gleeson and the Constitution" in H. P. Lee and P. Gerangelos (eds.), *Constitutional Advancement in a Frozen Continent: Essays in Honour of George Winterton* (Sydney: Federation Press, 2009) 269.
[192]   Zines, *The High Court and the Constitution* 599–610.

introduce, but as being more circumspect about how to present its role publicly.

In summary, then, the following points may be made about the longer-term effects of the Mason Court's reforms. First, to the extent that those reforms were aimed at introducing greater candor about the role of extralegal values in the judicial reasoning process, they failed. In times of trouble, High Court justices' instinct is still to fall back on a conception of law as a technically exacting discipline capable of generating politically neutral answers to controversial questions. To that extent, a version of democratic legalism premised on the denial of law's politicality still holds sway. Secondly, however, the reform-minded justices' attempt to articulate some of the unwritten political values informing the operation of the Australian constitutional system was not entirely unsuccessful. The implied freedom of political communication has survived and, as noted in the next section, has been supplemented by several other doctrines that give the Court a role in enforcing underlying political values. To that extent, Australian democratic legalism has become more substantive, i.e., it is now a JR regime in which claims to political authority mutually legitimate claims to legal authority premised on the Court's apolitical enforcement of the conditions for free and fair political competition.

The reasons for this partially achieved transformation are complex.[193] For comparative purposes, the significant factors are the following. First, the attempt to transform the prevailing JR regime was principally judge-led. Unlike the situation in the US in the first part of the last century, there were few significant external pressures on the Australian JR regime in 1987. Both sets of factors that the literature stresses – the personal-professional and the institutional – are more in the nature of internal-legal rather than external-political factors. Further, unlike the situation in India after the 1975–7 State of Emergency,[194] legalism as a legitimating ideology had not been fundamentally discredited when Mason took up the chief justiceship. While Murphy J's criminal prosecution and Barwick CJ's involvement in the dismissal of Prime Minister Whitlam in 1975 had cast a shadow over the Court's claim to political neutrality, there was no reason in theory why the Court needed to deal with these crises by acknowledging the role of extralegal values in constitutional adjudication as opposed to retreating to the safe haven of legalism.

Second, the Mason Court did not make the most effective use of the opportunity it was given in *Nationwide News* and *ACTV* to launch its new methods. As we have seen, Mason CJ's judgment in the latter case is fairly conceptualist, as

---

[193] For a detailed examination, see Pierce, *Inside the Mason Court Revolution* 245–84.
[194] See Chapter 5.

though he was not yet certain of the best way to present the new reasoning style. Or perhaps it was just that it is one thing to espouse a new form of reasoning, another to put it into practice when so much of one's legal-professional training conspires against the new thought-ways. In any event, in justifying the implied freedom of political communication formalistically, as though it inhered in the Constitution, when plainly it did not, Mason CJ opened the implied-freedom line of cases to the sort of containment strategy that McHugh J deployed. It is a counterfactual to speculate what might have happened had the reform-minded justices simply presented the freedom as required for the effective modern-day operation of the constitutional system that the framers had adopted, but that at least would have been more consistent with the judicial philosophy that Mason CJ had espoused in his pre-appointment speech.

Finally, because the implied freedom of political communication was the lynchpin of the Mason Court's reforms, its vulnerability to containment rendered the entire enterprise vulnerable along with it. *Mabo* and *Dietrich*, as innovative decisions, were far more successful, but they could be subsumed into an orthodox understanding of the Court's role in developing the common law and thus the attempt to transform the Court's reasoning methods did not really benefit by their comparatively smoother passage.

3.5 THE CONTEMPORARY AUSTRALIAN JR REGIME

The containment of the full suite of reforms that the Mason Court sought to introduce means that the Dixonian epithet of "strict and complete legalism" still accurately describes the legitimating ideology underpinning the contemporary Australian JR regime. Law's authority is still premised on a strict conception of the separability of law and politics and on the assumed capacity of legal reasoning methods to constrain the influence of judicial policy preferences. At the same time, however, the High Court's constitutional jurisdiction has expanded to the enforcement of a range of structural guarantees that have less to do with federalism and more to do with the enforcement of the political values underlying the Australian democratic system. In addition to the implied freedom of political communication, which remains an active part of the Court's docket, the principle of the separation of judicial power has emerged as a fertile source of litigation with rights-protecting potential, particularly in the context of immigration detention.[195] The partial success of the

---

[195] The leading early statement of the principle is *Chu Kheng Lim* v. *Minister for Immigration, Local Government, and Ethnic Affairs* (1992) 176 CLR 1. After a period of seeming retrenchment (see, for example, *Al-Kateb* v. *Godwin* (2004) 219 CLR 562) the idea that the separation

Mason Court revolution, therefore, was to legitimate the High Court's involvement in the enforcement of some of the structural preconditions for the effective operation of the Australian democratic system.

Within this adjusted democratic legalist regime, many different forms of judicial reasoning now flourish. That is not surprising, since, as we have seen, the preeminence in Australia of legalism as an ideological claim about the law/politics relation has never been dependent on the consistent deployment of a particular set of reasoning methods. Rather, it has always been the strength of Australian democratic legalism that it has been able to sever legalism as ideological claim from legalism as method. In the modern era, this feature of the regime has allowed the High Court to develop, *sotto voce*, many of the more substantive, value-infused reasoning methods that the Mason Court sought to introduce. On occasion, those methods are still contested as not belonging – as being too political for Australian tastes – but the absence of any real orthodoxy around legal reasoning methods means that these objections have little purchase.

This section illustrates these points by discussing two relatively recent decisions in prominent areas of constitutional law: the development in *Clarke*[196] of a multi-factor test for assessing alleged violations of the *Melbourne Corporation* principle (the broad federal limit on Commonwealth power that Dixon J developed in the course of rehabilitating the legitimacy of implication-drawing); and the adoption in *McCloy*[197] of a structured proportionality test for violation of the implied freedom of political communication.

The *Melbourne Corporation* principle, it will be recalled, was the revised version of the implied immunity of instrumentalities doctrine that Dixon J had carefully labored to construct after his appointment as an ordinary justice in 1929. The doctrine was eventually vindicated in the 1947 decision that bears the principle's name.[198] Since then, the principle has not in fact proved to be much of a defense against the expansion of Commonwealth legislative power.[199] Part of the reason for this was that there was some ambiguity in the original statement of the principle. Dixon J in his judgment in the

---

of judicial power under the Australian Constitution limits the Commonwealth's capacity to deal with asylum seekers is enjoying a renaissance. See, for example, *Plaintiff S4/2014 v. Minister for Immigration and Border Protection* (2014) 253 CLR 219 and *Plaintiff M68/2015 v. Minister for Immigration and Border Protection* (2016) 257 CLR 42.

[196] *Clarke v. Federal Commissioner of Taxation* (2009) 240 CLR 272.

[197] *McCloy v. New South Wales* (2015) 257 CLR 178.

[198] *Melbourne Corporation v. Commonwealth* (1947) 74 CLR 31 (*Melbourne Corporation*).

[199] See *Queensland Electricity Commission v. Commonwealth* (1985) 159 CLR 192 and *Re Australian Education Union; Ex Parte Victoria* (1995) 184 CLR 188.

Melbourne Corporation case thus suggested two alternative triggers for it, one a finding that the Commonwealth had singled out the states for special discriminatory treatment in one of its laws,[200] and the other a finding that the impact of the law was such as to destroy the states' capacity to function as "independent entities" in the federation.[201] As some of the other justices in *Melbourne Corporation* pointed out,[202] it was possible for a Commonwealth law to do the former without producing the latter consequence, and to produce the latter consequence without doing the former. It was therefore unclear whether the test had separate formal and substantive dimensions or whether it was essentially a substantive test with some formal indicators.

In 1985, before he became Chief Justice, Mason J attempted to clarify the principle in his judgment in *Queensland Electricity Commission*,[203] but ironically ended up vindicating quite a formalistic understanding of it. The case involved an industrial dispute in Queensland over state legislation restricting workers' rights and banning strikes by electricity workers in particular. Thirty trade unions sought to resist the legislation by organizing "a 24-hour land, sea and air blockade" of the state with a view to forcing the Queensland government to withdraw the legislation.[204] With the state government in crisis and unable to cope, the Commonwealth intervened by enacting the *Conciliation and Arbitration (Electricity Industry) Act 1985* (Cth), which provided for the expedited settlement of the dispute through the Commonwealth Conciliation and Arbitration Commission. Section 6(1) of the Act named the particular dispute between the Electrical Trades Union and the state authorities as the object of the law. That constituted a clear singling out of Queensland for special treatment. But the law as a whole was attempting to do exactly the reverse of what the *Melbourne Corporation* principle had been designed to guard against. Rather than destroying Queensland's capacity to function, s 6(1) attempted to preserve it by providing a means for the expeditious resolution of a potentially crippling industrial dispute.

After a careful analysis of the history of the development of the principle, Mason J held that it consisted of two *independent* limbs – a formal, antidiscrimination limb protecting the states against Commonwealth legislation singling them out for special treatment, and a substantive limb protecting them from legislation undermining their capacity to function.

---

[200]   *Melbourne Corporation* 79.
[201]   Ibid 82.
[202]   See Starke J's judgment (ibid 70–5).
[203]   (1985) 159 CLR 192.
[204]   This summary is based on Williams, Brennan, and Lynch (eds.), *Australian Constitutional Law and Theory* 1092.

The contravention of either of these limbs, Mason J held, would justify a finding of invalidity.[205] Since s 6(1) had a clear discriminatory operation, it followed that it fell to be struck down.[206] This was a curious conclusion to reach for a judgment written by someone who was about to inveigh against the evils of formalism. As with his judgment in *ACTV*, Mason J here appears to be unable to put his judicial philosophy into practice. The clear purpose of the *Melbourne Corporation* principle was to provide a backstop defense against Commonwealth laws that undermine federalism by destroying states' capacity to assert and fulfil their constitutionally appointed roles. Section 6(1) was very far from being such a law. Its evident purpose was to assist Queensland in resolving a disruptive industrial dispute and thereby to restore orderly government – exactly the opposite of the evil that the principle was designed to counter.

Against this background, it is interesting to consider what the modern Court, and particularly former Chief Justice Robert French, has made of the principle. In *Clarke*,[207] decided in 2009, the Court was asked to consider a Commonwealth law that established a special scheme for taxing high-income-earning state employees' pension benefits.[208] Although targeted at state employees, the law was in fact merely extending to them a general taxation scheme that had been applied to all high-income earners.[209] The reasons for targeting state employees was that their pensions were drawn directly from the various state consolidated revenue funds, making it impossible to tax them in the same way as other high-income earners, i.e., incrementally as contributions to their superannuation funds were made.[210] As in *Queensland Electricity Commission*, therefore, the formal, antidiscrimination element of the principle was clearly satisfied, even though the substantive intent of the scheme was to create a uniform legislative framework that imposed the same taxation burden on all taxpayers falling into the same income category.

By the time *Clarke* was decided, Mason J's formalist understanding of the principle had already been politely reinterpreted.[211] The fact that the Commonwealth law singled out state employees was thus no longer

[205] *Queensland Electricity* 217.
[206] Ibid 219.
[207] *Clarke* v. *Federal Commissioner of Taxation* (2009) 240 CLR 272.
[208] *Superannuation Contributions Tax (Members of Constitutionally Protected Superannuation Funds) Assessment and Collection Act 1997* (Cth); *Superannuation Contributions Tax (Members of Constitutionally Protected Superannuation Funds) Imposition Act 1997* (Cth).
[209] Williams, Brennan, and Lynch (eds.), *Australian Constitutional Law and Theory* 1101.
[210] Ibid.
[211] *Austin* v. *Commonwealth* (2003) 215 CLR 185, 248–9.

conclusive: a majority of justices had already adopted a single-limb, substantive understanding of the principle. What is noteworthy about the decision in *Clarke*, rather, is the way French CJ articulated the new test for violation of the principle. After stating its substantive rationale,[212] French CJ listed six considerations that he said needed to be "weighed together" to ascertain whether the *Melbourne Corporation* principle applied to limit Commonwealth power.[213] Some of the considerations, such as "[w]hether the law in question singles out one or more of the States and imposes a special burden or disability on them which is not imposed on persons generally" were qualitative, while others, such as "[t]he effect of the law upon the capacity of the States to exercise their constitutional powers" went to the law's substantive impact.[214] In combination, they compromised a "multifactorial" test.[215]

Although appearing in a separate concurring judgment, French CJ's approach looks like becoming the standard methodology for assessing violations of the *Melbourne Corporation* principle.[216] *Clarke* thus illustrates the way in which the modern High Court has taken the Mason Court's injunction to develop more substantive reasoning methods to heart. It is a particularly striking example because it corrects a failure to introduce that change in one of Mason J's own judgments.

The second example concerns the modern understanding of the implied freedom of political communication. We saw in Section 3.4 how this freedom had been at the center of the Mason Court's reform agenda, and how the compromise in *Lange* restricted the full achievement of that agenda.[217] The modern High Court has remained faithful to this compromise and no new freedoms have been developed, apart from the implied right to vote, as previously mentioned.[218] At the same time, however, the implied freedom has become quite an active area of the Court's jurisprudence, with numerous cases decided over the last twenty years.[219] For the most part, those cases have applied the two-part understanding of the test for contravention of the freedom agreed to in *Lange*, with one slight adjustment in *Coleman v. Power*.[220] In the first part of the test, the Court considers whether the law burdens the implied

---

[212]   *Clarke* 298.
[213]   Ibid 299.
[214]   Ibid.
[215]   Ibid.
[216]   It was applied by three justices in the most recent case in this area, *Fortescue Metals Group Ltd* v. *Commonwealth* (2013) 300 ALR 26.
[217]   *Lange* (1997) 189 CLR 520.
[218]   See *Roach* and *Rowe*.
[219]   See Williams, Brennan, and Lynch (eds.), *Australian Constitutional Law and Theory* 1327–35.
[220]   *Coleman v. Power* (2004) 220 CLR 1.

freedom of political communication "in its terms, operation, or effect," and in the second the Court considers whether the law is "reasonably appropriate and adapted to serve a legitimate end in a manner which is compatible with the maintenance of the constitutionally prescribed system of representative and responsible government."[221] That methodology, though superficially resembling the standard two-stage test for rights violations, preserves the character of the freedom as a limit on legislative power rather than an individual right.[222]

In *McCloy*, which was decided in 2015, the Court surprised commentators by recasting the second stage of the test as a structured proportionality inquiry on the German and ECHR model.[223] As expressed by the four-judge joint judgment in *McCloy*, the test for contravention of the implied freedom is now divided into three stages – burden, compatibility, and proportionality – with the third stage further fleshed out into an assessment of the specificity, necessity, and adequacy of the balance achieved in the law.[224] The third component of the third stage corresponds very closely to strict proportionality in the German/European sense, i.e., a comparison of the importance of the legislative purpose being pursued against the severity of the restriction on the freedom.[225]

This example once again illustrates the freedom that the High Court enjoys under the broad rubric of legalism. The commitment at a legal-cultural level to a strict conception of the law/politics distinction has not prevented the Court from adopting tests that have been criticized in other jurisdictions as impermissibly prone to the influence of subjective political values. While some High Court justices have protested against the introduction of proportionality analysis along these lines,[226] the preponderant view on the Court is that this form of analysis is reconcilable with orthodox understandings of the judicial role. As happened in Germany in the 1950s and 1960s, the Australian High Court has been able to absorb proportionality analysis within its menu of legitimate methods without giving up on the idea of law as an autonomous

---

[221] Ibid 50.

[222] *Lange* (1997) 189 CLR 520, 560.

[223] See Anne Twomey, "McCloy v New South Wales: Out with US Corruption and in with German proportionality" on AUSPUBLAW (October 15, 2015). https://auspublaw.org/2015/10/mccloy-v-new-south-wales/.

[224] *McCloy* para 2 (per French CJ, Kiefel, Bell, and Keane JJ).

[225] On the development of proportionality analysis in Germany, see, for example, Michaela Hailbronner, *Traditions and Transformations: The Rise of German Constitutionalism* (Oxford: Oxford University Press, 2015) 117–18.

[226] See, for example, Heydon J's judgment in *Monis* v. *The Queen* (2013) 295 ALR 259, 321 ("How does the application of so amorphous a test avoid the dangers of judicial legislation?"). See also Gordon, Nettle, and Gageler JJ's judgments in *McCloy*.

system of reasoning.[227] Australian judges, of course, have no interest in doing the sort of abstract philosophizing of which the German Federal Constitutional Court is so fond. There is thus no talk in Australia of an "objective order of values."[228] But the High Court does present the key conceptual construct in its implied freedom test – the "constitutionally pre-scribed system of representative and responsible government" – as though it had an objectively ascertainable meaning. In this way, a faith in the determinacy of legal reasoning methods has been maintained.

3.6 CONCLUSION

One of the main "observable implications"[229] of the theory set out in Chapter 2 was that JR regimes evolve on the back of competing legal and political authority claims. Another was that such regimes stabilize around one of four possible JR-regime types that are defined by the ways that law and politics might conceivably accommodate each other's authority claims. A third implication was that, once stabilized, JR regimes are relatively resistant to change absent an exogenous shock. This section concludes the discussion of the Australian case by showing how the material presented in this chapter is both consistent with all those implications and adds to our understanding of them.

The centrality of the *Engineers* case in the scholarly literature suggests an initial periodization of the evolution of the Australian JR regime into its pre-1920 and post-1920 phases. Before 1920, no JR regime in the sense defined in this study could be said to have been consolidated. Rather, it was still an open question how law and politics would accommodate each other's authority claims under the new federal Constitution. Would the preexisting Westminster conception of the judiciary as clearly subordinate to democratic politics drive the development of a JR regime something along the lines of democratic legalism? Or would the new, more powerful role given to the High Court under the 1900 Constitution trigger the development of a different

---

[227] See Jacco Bomhoff, *Balancing Constitutional Rights: The Origins and Meanings of Postwar Legal Discourse* (Cambridge: Cambridge University Press, 2013) 72–121; Hailbronner, Traditions and Transformations 117–21.

[228] BVerfGE 7, 198 (*Lüth*).

[229] Gary King, Robert O. Keohane, and Sidney Verba, *Designing Social Inquiry: Scientific Inference in Qualitative Research* (Princeton, NJ: Princeton University Press, 1994). By citing "KKV" this study does not mean to align itself with the controversial propositions these authors make about the extent to which quantitative methods may be applied to qualitative case studies. See James Mahoney, "After KKV: The New Methodology of Qualitative Research" (2010) 62 *World Politics* 120.

understanding of the law/politics relation, one more akin to the American conception? Given the uncertainty over this issue, the period from 1900 to 1920 is best described as a critical juncture – a period during which two trajectories towards JR-regime consolidation opened up, neither of which was foreordained by the preexisting tradition.

What drove the eventual move to democratic legalism? And does the theory set out in Chapter 2 both help to explain what happened and fit with the facts?

The period immediately before the decision in *Engineers*, as noted in Section 3.1, was marked by a disjuncture between the strongly federalist Constitution that the framers had adopted and the *de facto* centralization of power within the Commonwealth brought about by war and economic integration. This disjuncture put the two implied doctrines that the original members of the Court had developed under increasing strain. Already contested on doctrinal grounds by the post-1906 appointees to the Court, external political developments placed additional pressure on a reading of the Constitution whose authority ultimately depended on the justices' public reputations – on their having participated in the Convention Debates and their consequent claimed personal knowledge of the purposes of federation. While that had been enough in the initial stages of the Constitution's development, the passage of time and changes to the country's circumstances progressively brought this conception of law's authority into conflict with the political authority to enact far-reaching Commonwealth legislation derived from national democratic mandates.

The first element of the theory – the existence of competing legal and political authority claims – is thus satisfied. That these competing claims should have driven the establishment of a JR regime along the lines of democratic legalism was not, however, foreordained. In the abstract, the easiest way of resolving the tension between the strongly federalist Constitution that the framers had adopted and the weakly federalist Constitution both major political groupings preferred would have been for law to be seen as a flexible tool – as an instrument that judges may adapt to changing circumstances. That line of resolution strongly favored an understanding of the judicial task in constitutional interpretation as being about the creative drawing out of the framers' founding vision – precisely the understanding that the early Court had stressed when first developing the two implied doctrines. How was it, then, that democratic legalism ultimately triumphed?

The explanation presented in this chapter started by pointing to certain features of the constitutional text that facilitated this form of law/politics accommodation. While the framers' intention to create a strong federal system was well known, they had not done a particularly good job of articulating that intention. Instead of specifying in so many words what the states' residual powers were, the framers had left those powers to be determined by default, after construction of the scope of the Commonwealth's powers. Many of those powers – such as the power over external affairs – were expressed in general terms, with no evident limit on their scope unless one read into the Constitution the framers' unspoken assumptions about the federal balance. This quality of the constitutional text left the two implied doctrines vulnerable to the legalist posture adopted in the main judgment in *Engineers*. All that the majority justices needed to do was to point to the fact that the two implied doctrines enjoyed very little textual support. They could then be dismissed as dependent on an impermissibly political interpretation of the Constitution in contrast to the textually grounded reading that the main judgment preferred. The fact that the text of the Constitution did not accurately represent the framers' intentions was no answer to this move when the only way of establishing those intentions was to refer to the Convention Debates, reference to which had been disallowed.[230]

While it is possible to see the main judgment in *Engineers* as a kind of confidence trick – as being all about the justices' deliberate obfuscation of what they were doing – the simpler explanation is that the Constitution was open to an expansive reading and that, for some of the justices at least, this is what orthodox methods of statutory interpretation required. To be sure, two of the justices, Higgins and Isaacs JJ, may have had strategic motives inasmuch as their embrace of legalism was driven by a preference for an expanded Commonwealth. But the main judgment as a whole cannot be said to be *politically* strategic. Rather, the Court embraced legalism because this was the most convenient device for challenging the legitimacy of the two implied doctrines, a goal on which both the centralizers by political conviction and centralizers by legal-professional socialization agreed. Legalism as legitimating ideology was in this sense a contingent choice – neither strategically motivated nor determined by the existing tradition but a function of a mix of these factors.

The process leading up to the *Engineers* decision in this way supports the conjecture in Chapter 2 about the factors driving the evolution of JR regimes. The Australian JR regime did discernibly evolve from 1900 through 1920, and that evolution was driven by competing legal and political authority claims.

---

[230] *Tasmania* v. *Commonwealth and Victoria* (1904) 1 CLR 329 and *Municipal Council of Sydney* v. *Commonwealth* (1904) 1 CLR 208.

Evolution, however, is not the same thing as consolidation. As noted in Section 3.1, the *Engineers* decision marked, not a transition from one settled JR regime to another, but the point at which a trajectory towards JR-regime consolidation opened up. The full consolidation of democratic legalism in Australia depended on the subsequent process in which the Court's expansionary reading of the Commonwealth's legislative powers won political acceptance and came to be associated with an ideology of law's separation from politics. That process was finally completed only in the 1950s, when Dixon CJ's explicit embrace of legalism brought together the three main factors driving it – the doctrinal centrality of *Engineers*, legalism as ideological claim, and the association of this claim with the political acceptance of the Commonwealth's expanded powers.

The delayed consolidation of the regime, Section 3.2 argued, had to do with the fact that, until the late 1940s, legalism had not really been tested. While *Engineers* had announced legalism as a method for publicly justifying the Court's function, and influential justices like Latham CJ had thereafter associated themselves with it, the delayed extrapolation of the doctrinal consequences of *Engineers* meant that, in the 1920s and 1930s, the evolution of the Australian JR regime went into a kind of developmental stasis. During this time, there was no process through which legalism's ideological claim about the separability of law and politics could fuse itself in the constitutional-cultural imagination with a matching democratic political authority claim. It was only after the great conflict between the Court and Australia's two major political groupings in the late 1940s and early 1950s that this fusion occurred. In that final stage, as Section 3.3 argued, Dixon's 1952 swearing-in speech was pivotal. It was this speech that first deployed legalism in a major public defense of judicial review. By explicitly tying the Court's authority to an ideology of law's separation from politics, Dixon's speech became the focal point for the consolidation of the regime.

To say that the Australian JR regime consolidated at *precisely* that point in 1952 would be to attribute to complex events and abstract constructs too great a degree of temporal specificity. As foreshadowed in Chapter 2, JR-regime consolidation is not a point-in-time event but a slow-moving, macrosocial process in which certain ways of understanding law's authority and its relationship to political authority gradually become ascendant in a constitutional culture.[231] Consolidation in this sense does not lead to the total eclipse of

---

[231] See Paul Pierson, "Big, Slow-Moving, and ... Invisible: Macrosocial Processes in the Study of Comparative Politics" in James Mahoney and Dietrich Rueschemeyer (eds.), *Comparative Historical Analysis in the Social Sciences* (Cambridge: Cambridge University Press, 2003) 177.

rival conceptions of the law/politics relation. They exist as alternative ideological constructs waiting for their turn to attach themselves to concrete events
and actions. Consistent with this view, Dixon's 1952 speech marks not so much
a causal trigger as a constitutional-cultural moment to which all subsequent
public statements about the law/politics relation have had to refer, whether
they are seeking to call Dixon's speech up in defense of a position or to disavow
allegiance it.

   After an extended period of relative stability, Section 3.4 continued, the
Mason Court challenged the Dixonian orthodoxy in the late 1980s. By all
accounts, the reform-minded justices on the Court were motivated by
a sincere concern for the deficiencies of the existing JR regime. They
genuinely thought that that it would be better for the Court's institutional
legitimacy and the rule of law more generally if judicial review could be
justified in a more open and transparent manner. There was considerable
merit in this view. The Court's existing reasoning style *was* overly formalistic and less than fully candid about the role of extralegal values in constitutional adjudication. Moreover, judicial review had been sufficiently
well institutionalized by this time that it should have been possible to
make progress towards a more sophisticated understanding of the law/
politics relation without harming public perceptions of the Court's
independence.

   Why was it, then, that for most commentators, the efforts of the reform-
minded justices failed? The chapter offered several reasons for its understanding of this phenomenon. The first was that the factors driving the attempted
internal adjustment of the regime, while real, were not in the nature of
forceful exogenous shocks. Rather, they were all contextual changes that had
been developing over several years. Thus, while the adoption of the various
Australia Acts in 1986 were significant, they were in truth the culmination of
a gradual process that had been going on since 1968 when appeals from the
High Court in federal matters were abolished.[232] The rise of rights-based
constitutionalism, too, was a gradual process, in which Australia's national
character could be said to have been defined precisely by its refusal to adopt
a constitutional statement of core political values. Finally, Stone's teachings
exposed the Mason Court judges to a different way of thinking but did not by
themselves justify any change to the existing regime. Rather, the justices
themselves had to do all the work of justification. That task, without a clear
and identifiable exogenous shock to which they could point, was a formidable

[232] See the Privy Council (Limitation of Appeals) Act 1968 (Cth).

one; institutional traditions, as Sir Anthony Mason himself acknowledged, "die hard."[233]

The earlier transformation of Australia's strongly federalist Constitution into a weakly federalist one, by contrast, had been shaped by the complex interaction of external political developments, judicial choices, and the tradition that had gone before. This transformation had thus been judge-driven in a qualitatively different way to the transformation the Mason Court judges sought to effect. Whereas the first transformation had been a side effect of the contingent choice of a legalist conception of the law/politics relation in *Engineers*, the second transformation relied on the justices convincing their fellow legal professionals and the community at large that that there was a societal challenge worth responding to. That was always going to be a difficult task because the legitimacy of the new reasoning methods and the revitalized understanding of law's authority towards which the reform-minded justices were trying to shift Australian constitutional culture were defined by the terms of an already consolidated JR regime.

The extent to which the Mason Court's reforms foundered should not be overstated. The implied freedom of political communication, as Section 3.5 noted, is now a settled doctrine and has become a very active part of the High Court's case law. The modern Court has also developed the separation of judicial power principle to protect the rights of detainees, particularly in the immigration context. That has allowed the Court to position itself, not just as the guarantor of the structural preconditions for democracy, but also as the backstop limit on what popularly elected majorities may do to unrepresented and vulnerable minorities. While all of this has been going on, the more substantive reasoning methods that the reform-minded justices on the Mason Court tried to introduce have been taken up by later justices under the cover of a continued public commitment to legalism. These developments, however, point to the severability of legalism as ideology and legalism as method rather than to delayed regime transformation. If there is one overarching lesson that the Australian case teaches, it is that democratic legalism's ideological ascendance may be maintained even as judicial reasoning methods evolve. In the absence of an exogenous shock, this style of JR regime adapts to new circumstances through incremental adjustments to legal-professional understandings of legitimate methods of legal reasoning.

---

[233] Mason, "The Role of a Constitutional Court in a Federation" 11 (referring to ongoing Australian attachment to "the notion of parliamentary supremacy").

4

From Democratic Legalism to Instrumentalism: India's Constitutional-Cultural Transformation

India is in many ways an obvious choice of country for this study. The institutional history of its Supreme Court, with its distinct, evolutionary phases and moments of both great strength and weakness, is well known. After the initial, hard-fought battle over the *zamindari* abolition laws, the Court famously failed to protect detainees' rights during the 1975–7 Emergency,[1] only to recover from that position to become "one of the most powerful constitutional courts in the world."[2] According to the now familiar story,[3] two justices in particular, P. N. Bhagwati and V. R. Krishna Iyer, exploited the perceived deficiencies of the Court's legalistic response to the Emergency to reassert its authority on a different basis. Motivated in part by sincere political convictions and in part by a desire to restore their personal judicial reputations, Bhagwati and Krishna Iyer fashioned a series of Public Interest Litigation (PIL) doctrines during the 1980s that transformed the Court's role in Indian politics. Having started as a conservative defender of property rights, the Court – under the cover of, and to a certain extent implementing, Indira

---

[1] See the discussion in Section 4.2 below.

[2] Manoj Mate, "Public Interest Litigation and the Transformation of the Supreme Court of India" in Diana Kapiszewski, Gordon Silverstein, and Robert A. Kagan (eds.), *Consequential Courts: Judicial Roles in Global Perspective* (New York: Cambridge University Press, 2013) 262, 262. See also Pratap Bhanu Mehta, "India's Judiciary: The Promise of Uncertainty" in Devesh Kapur and Pratap Bhanu Mehta (eds.), *Public Institutions in India: Performance and Design* (New Delhi: Oxford University Press, 2005) 158, 159 n2.

[3] The leading work on the first 35 years of the Court's life is Granville Austin, *Working a Democratic Constitution: A History of the Indian Experience* (New Delhi: Oxford University Press, 1999). Another important work focusing on the pre-1980 period is Upendra Baxi, *The Indian Supreme Court and Politics* (Lucknow: Eastern Book Co, 1980). On the Supreme Court's post-1977 trajectory, see Upendra Baxi, "Taking Suffering Seriously: Social Action Litigation in the Supreme Court of India" (1985) 4 *Third World Legal Studies* 107; S. P. Sathe, *Judicial Activism in India: Transgressing Borders and Enforcing Limits* (New Delhi: Oxford University Press, 2002).

Gandhi's pro-poor populism, became an effective institutional voice for socially marginalized groups.

After 1989, the Congress Party lost its stranglehold on power and public policy shifted to the right as successive coalition governments sought to open India's economy to foreign investment. In this changed political environment, the Court's authority came to be premised less on its reputation for pro-poor decision-making and more on its role in upholding good governance.[4] With the Court controlling the judicial appointments process, individual justices were as likely to be motivated by conservative views as they were by the progressive political commitments that had driven the Court's rehabilitation. But the constitutional-cultural acceptability of ideologically motivated decision-making became, if anything, more entrenched. Whether railing against the conditions of Delhi's slums or enforcing environmental rights, the modern Court draws on a legitimating ideology that is very different from the one that prevailed in 1950. In place of the studied legalism of the Court's early decisions, the modern Court's authority rests on the justices' claim to be articulating the best contemporary understanding of constitutional justice. In short, the Indian experience over the last seventy years appears to provide a textbook illustration of this study's main concern: the way in which judicial review is influenced by, but at the same time transforms, societal conceptions of the law/politics relation.

The downside of textbook examples, of course, is that they tend to be overdetermined. The Indian Supreme Court's institutional trajectory since 1977 has been so strong and enduring that there are likely several plausible explanations for it, each one of them compatible with a different theory of judicial empowerment.[5] Nevertheless, there is something to be said for low-hanging fruit: the sociological process this study investigates is complicated enough as it is without declining to exploit one of the most obvious examples on offer. Also, like the other countries studied, India was not the original inspiration for the theory presented in Chapter 2. While it may be an obvious choice, the Indian case thus still provides a good demonstration of the theory's explanatory reach. More than this, refracting the Indian story through the prism of the theory promises to serve two of the main aims of this study: (1) enriching scholarly debates about the constitutional politics of the countries

---

[4] Nick Robinson, "Expanding Judiciaries: India and the Rise of the Good Governance Court" (2009) 8 *Washington University Global Studies Law Review* 1.

[5] See, for example, Manoj Mate, "Elite Institutionalism and Judicial Assertiveness in the Supreme Court of India" (2014) 28 *Temple International & Comparative Law Journal* 360,363 (explaining the Supreme Court's "selective assertiveness" as a function of "values of national political, professional, and intellectual elites").

chosen for analysis; and (2) harnessing the intellectual energy of those debates to support generalizable insights into the politico-legal dynamics of judicial review.

There are two reasons in particular why this is so. First, reinterpreting the Indian story helps to focus attention on an issue that is present in the local literature but not emphasized as much as it should be: the way in which the transformation of the Supreme Court's role in national politics has been a transformation, not just of the functions it performs, but also of societal conceptions of the law/politics relation. When Bhagwati and Krishna Iyer joined the Court, its public reputation was that of an ideologically conservative institution whose legalistic doctrines had failed to check the Congress Party's descent into authoritarianism. By the time these two justices left the Bench, the Court's creative, politically progressive interpretation of its mandate was regarded as essential to the preservation of India's democracy. That way of seeing the transformation helps in turn to explain why the current situation, in which the Court has become a virtual "one-stop shop" for the resolution of all manner of social and economic problems, has proved to be so stable. In the conditions of Indian politics over the last forty years, law's "empire"[6] has expanded in line with declining public confidence in the capacity of representative institutions to drive meaningful social and economic change. By positioning itself, first as an institutional voice for the vulnerable and the marginalized, and then as a more middle-class-friendly enforcer of good governance standards, the Court has become the most trusted public institution in India. With each new corruption scandal it exposes, and each new governance failure it remedies, the Court entrenches its position as the guardian of India's democracy. The stability of this situation, however, is somewhat pathological, associated as it is with a self-reinforcing cycle of dependency in which the Court's interventions in support of the democratic system obviate the need for the democratic system to correct itself.[7]

The further advantage of refracting the Indian case through the prism of the typological theory is that it provides a new way of conceptualizing the evolution of Indian constitutional politics. The standard story thus distinguishes four main periods in the Supreme Court's institutional life: (1) the establishment period from 1950 to the controversial *Golaknath* decision in 1967;[8] (2) an ensuing period of instability from the time of that decision to the end of the

---

[6] Ronald Dworkin, *Law's Empire* (Cambridge, MA: Harvard University Press, 1986).

[7] Cf. Richard Bellamy, *Political Constitutionalism: A Republican Defense of the Constitutionality of Democracy* (Cambridge: Cambridge University Press, 2007) (arguing that it is the inevitable consequence of judicial review to undermine democracy).

[8] *I. C. Golaknath* v. *State of Punjab* AIR 1967 SC 1643.

Emergency; (3) the first part of the Court's rehabilitation from 1978 to 1989 when Bhagwati and Krishna Iyer's influence was at its height; and (4) the period after 1989 to date, during which the Court has cemented its position at the center of Indian politics.[9] In the interpretation offered here, those periods are reframed as: (1) the consolidation of a democratic legalist conception of the law/politics relation through adaptation of the received colonial conception to the institutional and political circumstances of postindependence India; (2) the exogenous shock of the Emergency; (3) a judicially led transformation of Indian constitutional culture to an understanding of judicial review as deeply immersed in politics; and (4) the consolidation of this democratic instrumentalist understanding through public and political acceptance of the Court's interventionist role.[10] The ease and intuitive logic of that re-description illustrates the theory's explanatory reach. For students of Indian constitutional politics, it also adds something to the local debate – an understanding of the politico-legal dynamics driving the Court's transformation after 1989 from a pro-poor institution into an all-purpose enforcer of good governance standards.

The rest of this chapter makes the detailed case for these claims. The subsections follow the standard periodization, with the discussion in each case translating the familiar Indian story into the terms of the typological theory. The chapter concludes with a summary of the general lessons learned, both from the perspective of the local Indian debate and from the broader, comparative perspective of this study.

4.1 THE ESTABLISHMENT PERIOD: 1950–1967

The literature on the Indian Supreme Court's establishment period emphasizes two issues of relevance to this study: (1) an inherited tradition of legalism; and (2) the role played by India's first Prime Minister, Jawaharlal Nehru, in promoting respect for judicial independence.

---

[9] Other periodizations are, of course, possible. See, for example, Gobind Das, "The Supreme Court: An Overview" in B. N. Kirpal et al. (eds.), *Supreme but not Infallible: Essays in Honor of the Supreme Court of India* (New Delhi: Oxford University Press, 2000) 16 (identifying seven periods from 1950 to 1998); Charles R. Epp, *The Rights Revolution: Lawyers, Activists and Supreme Courts in Comparative Perspective* (Chicago: University of Chicago Press, 1998) 83 (dividing the Court's institutional history "into two periods, one in which leading justices championed property rights but not due process and equality, and the second in which the reverse has been true").

[10] As explained below, the shift from the social-egalitarianism of Bhagwati and Iyer to the liberal-environmentalism of the current Court must be seen as an ideational shift within democratic instrumentalism rather than a wholesale regime transformation.

As to the first issue, several scholars have noted the formative influence on Indian constitutional culture of "the British legacy of Austinian positivism."[11] This was a matter both of elite public attitudes towards the role of the judiciary and of inherited legal reasoning methods. After nearly a century of British colonial rule,[12] the judiciary was viewed as an important but largely subordinate actor in the governmental system. Its place was to interpret rather than make law. Although the passage of the 1950 Constitution, with its American-style Supreme Court and list of fundamental rights, challenged these attitudes,[13] they died hard. Until the *Golaknath* decision in 1967,[14] the prevailing view was that Parliament was the ultimate custodian of the Constitution. It followed that if Parliament chose to amend the constitutional text, this was a legislative amendment like any other – one that the courts needed to implement faithfully. On this view of things, the role of the judiciary had not fundamentally changed in 1950. While the Constitution had given the Supreme Court the power of judicial review, that power was subject to Parliament's ultimate power of constitutional amendment under Article 368. Given the Congress Party's overwhelming majority in the Lok Sabha and the state parliaments, the procedural preconditions for the exercise of that power were easily met.[15] In functional terms, therefore, it was as though the pre-1950 relationship between the political branches and the judiciary had been retained in a different form, with Parliament's power to override judicial decisions by amending the Constitution taking the place of the Westminster doctrine of parliamentary sovereignty.[16]

---

[11] See Mate, "Public Interest Litigation" 263–4, quoting Mark Galanter, *Competing Equalities: Law and the Backward Classes in India* (Berkeley, CA: University of California Press, 1984) 484; Manoj Mate, "The Origins of Due Process in India: The Role of Borrowing in Personal Liberty and Preventive Detention Cases" (2010) 28 *Berkeley Journal of International Law* 216, 217; Burt Neuborne, "The Supreme Court of India" (2003) 1 *International Journal of Constitutional Law* 476, 479; Sathe, *Judicial Activism in India* 1–3, 42–3; Rajeev Dhavan, "Introduction" in Mark Galanter, *Law & Society in Modern India* (Oxford: Oxford University Press, 1998) xiii, xvii-xx.

[12] The British Crown took over the government of India from the East India Company in 1858, but a "system of courts" was set up in Bengal from 1772. See Galanter, *Law & Society in Modern India* 17–18.

[13] See Rajeev Dhavan, "Borrowed Ideas: On the Impact of American Scholarship on Indian Law" (1985) 33 *American Journal of Comparative Law* 505, 511–12 (discussing the American influence on the drafting of the Indian Constitution and on styles of reasoning).

[14] I. C. Golaknath v. State of Punjab AIR 1967 SC 1643.

[15] Article 368 of the Constitution provides for amendment by simple majority of each House and two thirds of those present. For amendments affecting the states, the agreement of a majority of the states is also required. The Congress Party won 364 of the 489 seats in the Lok Sabha in the 1952 general election, 371 of 494 in 1957, and 361 of 494 in 1962. Over the same period, it held comfortable majorities in the upper house and in most of the states.

[16] See Baxi, *Indian Supreme Court and Politics* 3 (referring to Mahajan J's view that if the legislature could amend an ordinary law in response to a judicial decision "it could also do the

Likewise, when it came to methods of legal reasoning, judges who had been trained in England or in the English tradition saw their duty as being to give effect to sovereign political commands.[17] In constitutional interpretation, that meant close adherence to the text and the intention of the legislature. In the best-known example of this approach, *A. K. Gopalan v. State of Madras*,[18] the Supreme Court held that Article 21's guarantee against deprivation of "life or personal liberty except according to procedure established by law" meant exactly that, but also no more than that: no one could be detained except on the authority of a duly enacted law, but beyond this there was no requirement that the law should conform to the principles of natural justice.[19] The main reason given in *Gopalan* for this position, apart from the text of Article 21 itself, was the history of the provision's enactment – in particular the fact that, while known to the Constituent Assembly, the wording of the American due process clause had been deliberately avoided.[20] For judges trained in the English positivist tradition, that was conclusive of the matter: the people's representatives had chosen their words carefully and their duty was to be faithful to that choice.

In isolation, it is possible to understand *Gopalan* in another way – as a function of the judges' ideological attitudes. The detainee (or "detenu" as it is put in India) was a member of the Communist Party and thus not the most sympathetic of litigants. *Gopalan* also fits a consistent pattern of executive-mindedness on the part of the Supreme Court in national security cases.[21] But the reasoning methods on display in *Gopalan* are evident in other early decisions, too. In *Romesh Thappar v. State of Madras*, for example, the Court interpreted the public-security qualification on free speech in Article 19(2) as applying only to legislation addressing "serious and aggravated forms of public disorder."[22] That decision severely restricted the scope of government intrusions on press freedom in the name of public security – the opposite outcome in ideological terms to the decision in *Gopalan*. In another case, *State of Madras v. Srimathi Champakam Dorairajan*, the Court struck down

---

same with regard to the Constitution"). In *A. K. Gopalan v. State of Madras* 1950 SCR 88, 320 Das J held that "our Constitution has accepted the supremacy of the legislative authority."

[17] See Rajeev Dhavan, *The Supreme Court of India: A Socio-Legal Critique of its Juristic Techniques* (Bombay: Triphathi, 1977) 26 (noting that 40 percent of Supreme Court judges at that point had been educated in England).

[18] 1950 SCR 88.

[19] Ibid.

[20] Ibid 111.

[21] See Dhavan, *The Supreme Court of India* 206–8; Epp, *The Rights Revolution*, 74; Neuborne, "The Supreme Court of India" 504–6.

[22] *Romesh Thappar v. State of Madras* (1950) SCR 594, 601.

a law reserving medical college places according to caste as an infringement of the right not to be discriminated against on this ground in Article 29(2). Here, the deciding factor was the provision in Article 37 that the Directive Principles of State Policy – on which the reservations policy had relied – were nonjusticiable, and thus, the Court held, subordinate to the fundamental rights.[23] As with the outcome in *Romesh Thappar*, this decision cannot easily be attributed to ideological bias or a general attitude of deference to executive authority. Rather, it was a case of the Court's seeking out a clear textual basis for its decision and then using traditional English statutory interpretation methods to justify the result.

So much for the inherited tradition of legalism. The second issue stressed by the literature is the role played by Nehru in moderating executive-judicial conflict. Granville Austin, the Indian Constitution's most celebrated historian, quotes India's first Prime Minister as saying "the independence of the judiciary has been emphasized in our Constitution and we must guard it as something precious."[24] Nehru, Austin continues, "rejected the idea of a packed court of individuals of the government's 'own liking for getting decisions in its own favor'." Instead, "[h]e wanted first-rate judges, not subservient courts."[25] While that attitude did not guarantee that there would be no conflict between the judiciary and the executive during Nehru's lifetime, it did mean that such conflict as occurred was mostly dealt with in a mutually respectful way. Thus, for example, after the Supreme Court in *Bela Banerjee* struck down the resettlement of refugees from East Pakistan for failure to pay the affected landholders adequate compensation,[26] there was no attack on the Court's independence. Rather, Parliament, as it had done in other cases, simply amended the Constitution.[27] The Court, in turn, respected Parliament's constitutional power to do that.

The story of the early Court's property rights decisions,[28] and the constitutional amendments they provoked, has been told on numerous occasions.[29]

---

[23]   *State of Madras v. Srimathi Champakam Dorairajan* (1951) SCR 525, 530.
[24]   Austin, *Working a Democratic Constitution* 124 (quoting a letter written by Nehru to his chief ministers on 18 December 1950).
[25]   Ibid.
[26]   *State of West Bengal v. Bela Bannerjee* AIR 1954 SC 170.
[27]   See Austin, *Working a Democratic Constitution* 101–10 (discussing the Fourth Amendment, which ousted judicial review of the adequacy of compensation where property was acquired for public purposes).
[28]   In addition to *Bela Bannerjee*, see *State of West Bengal v. Subodh Gopal* AIR 1954 SC 92; *Dwarkadas Srinivas v. Sholapur Spinning & Weaving Co* AIR 1954 SC 119 (1954).
[29]   See, for example, H. C. L. Merillat, "The Indian Constitution: Property Rights and Social Reform" (1960) 21 *Ohio State Law Journal* 616; Sathe, *Judicial Activism in India*, 46–60; Neuborne, "The Supreme Court of India" 487–9.

Here, the point is simply that, as bitter as this contest was, there was never any question, for as long as Nehru was Prime Minister, that the Supreme Court's power of judicial review would be removed altogether. Rather, each adverse decision was countermanded on its own terms, with the amendment generally going no further than was required to achieve the Congress Party's immediate policy goal. In this way, the tussle over property rights reinforced rather than undermined the dominant conception of the judiciary's place in the constitutional scheme. If it was the judiciary's appointed role to hold the executive to the terms of the written Constitution, it was equally the political branches' role to reexpress the people's will more clearly. Law and politics were in this sense, if not in harmonious balance, at least locked into a stable and mutually legitimating relationship.

As was the case with the *Gopalan* decision,[30] it is possible to think of the Supreme Court's property rights decisions as a function of the judges' ideological attitudes. Certainly, the Court in the establishment period did all it could to regulate the way in which the state governments went about abolishing the *zamindari* system, and it is reasonable to assume that their class position had a lot to do with this; legalist attitudes may have been sincerely held, but they were also convenient for judges seeking to soften the impact of social reform. That being the case, is it not best to think of the Court during this period as an ideologically motivated Court, with legalism acting as a rhetorical façade and the Court protected from political attack, not by a deep-seated constitutional-cultural faith in the constraining power of law, but by Nehru's pragmatic appreciation for the legitimating benefits of judicial review?

While not implausible, this understanding must overcome two significant hurdles. First, as we have seen, an inherited tradition of legalism held sway during the establishment period. Unless one adopts the skeptical view that a commitment to the separability of law and politics is always either perverse or self-delusional, this must have meant that the judges' class-based ideological attitudes were at least somewhat tempered by their fidelity to law. To the extent that the judges' decisions were influenced by ideology, in other words, it was a complex ideology in which their legal-professional socialization and class position would both have been prominent. From there, it is an open question which of these two influences played a greater role in particular decisions. Perhaps in property rights cases there was no great tension between these two aspects of the judges' ideological makeup. But a sweeping claim that the Supreme Court's case law as a whole gave expression to their class-based ideological attitudes requires more substantiation.

[30]   A. K. *Gopalan* v. *State of Madras* 1950 SCR 88.

The second hurdle that the alternative reading must overcome is the fact that the Supreme Court, until 1967, always did in the end defer to Parliament's power to amend the Constitution. This is a strong indication that the judges' legalist socialization was real and influential. As noted in Chapter 2,[31] judges who espouse this conception of their role cannot indefinitely resist a governing party that can plausibly lay claim to a fairly won democratic mandate. Unless democracy itself is compromised or threatened, the logic of legalism demands that judges live out their commitment to the separation of law and politics by giving effect to sovereign political commands. In the Indian case, the operation of this logic provides the best explanation for the Supreme Court's initial approach to the constitutionality of constitutional amendments. In both cases of this kind that came to the Court before 1967, a majority of the judges accepted that duly passed constitutional amendments were essentially unreviewable. In the first such case, *Sankari Prasad*,[32] the decision was unanimous, with the Court holding that constitutional amendments were not "law" for purposes of Article 13(2), and thus not subject to the fundamental rights. In the second case, *Sajjan Singh*,[33] the Court divided 3–2, upholding *Sankari Prasad* on the basis that it was correctly decided and that there were in any event insufficient grounds to overturn a decision of such long standing. The two dissenting judgments in this case have been attributed to Nehru's passing shortly before the matter came to the Court, with commentators suggesting that the judges concerned had some sort of prescient insight into the threats to democracy to come.[34] If so, the Court's vacillation in this case is not inconsistent with legalism but simply a function of disagreement on the Bench about the future legitimacy of the Congress Party's democratic mandate.

On this evidence, the law/politics relation in India during the establishment period is best understood as following the legitimation logic of democratic legalism. At a constitutional-cultural level, this period was characterized by a strong, inherited faith in the separability of law and politics. This broad set of public attitudes was complemented by a legal-professional ideology that equated sound decision-making with fidelity to the text of the Constitution and the history of its enactment. While there are some reasons to think that the judges' class interests played a role in the Court's property rights decisions, the judges were not free simply to write their ideological attitudes into law. Rather,

---

[31] See the discussion in Section 2.4.1.
[32] *Sri Sankari Prasad Singh Deo v. Union of India* AIR 1951 SC 458.
[33] *Sajjan Singh v. Rajasthan* AIR 1965 SC 845.
[34] See Sathe, *Judicial Activism in India* 257.

each decision the Court took had to be supported, and was thus to some extent constrained, by adherence to accepted reasoning methods. Nor could the Court be said to have been quiescent, since on numerous occasions it enforced the Constitution to strike down legislation.[35] The political branches, in turn, respected the Court's power to do that, provided that it was used sparingly and not in a way that permanently blocked the Congress Party's social reform agenda. As is characteristic of this style of regime, the stability of this arrangement lay in each side's capacity to legitimate the other: the political branches, by enforcing the Court's decisions, or at least counter-manding them only by way of constitutional amendment, and the judiciary, by maintaining a strict legalist stance that resulted in the striking down of some laws but, more importantly, lent legitimacy to the laws the Court left intact.

This seemingly stable equilibrium began to give way after the Supreme Court's decision in *Golaknath*.[36] The events surrounding that decision and its impact on the development of conceptions of the law/politics relation in India are the subject of the next section.

4.2 FROM *GOLAKNATH* TO *SHUKLA*: 1967–1977

The political backdrop to the *Golaknath* decision, in which the Court for the first time asserted the primacy of the fundamental rights over Parliament's constitutional amendment power, was complex and can only be roughly summarized here. One of the main precipitating events, certainly, was Nehru's death in May 1964. As we have seen, he had been the Court's most important backer. A lawyer by training, Nehru respected the value of judicial independence, if not always the value of lawyers.[37] His socialist faith in the power of the plan was thus tempered by an appreciation for the way controversial social reforms may be legitimated by judicial review. In contrast, his daughter, Indira Gandhi, who became Prime Minister in 1966 after Lal Nahdur Shastri's brief tenure,[38] had a more conventional socialist understanding of the judicial role. For her, judges were part of the executive arm of government – committed cadres who through their ideological identification with the cause of social reform could help to implement the government's policies more

---

[35] See Pratap Bhanu Mehta, "The Rise of Judicial Sovereignty" (2007) 18 *Journal of Democracy* 70, 74 (noting that 128 pieces of legislation were struck down during the establishment period).

[36] *I. C. Golaknath v. State of Punjab* AIR 1967 SC 1643.

[37] See Alice Jacob, "Nehru and the Judiciary" in Rajeev Dhavan and Thomas Paul (eds.), *Nehru and the Constitution* (Bombay: Triphathi, 1992) 63, 63–5.

[38] Shastri died in office on January 11, 1966.

effectively.[39] She was thus far more inclined than her father had been both to ascribe adverse judicial decisions to ideological bias and to seek to counteract those decisions by promoting judges who shared her political outlook.[40]

Gandhi's more instrumentalist understanding of the judicial role came to the fore later, in the controversy over the transfer and supersession of judges.[41] In the buildup to *Golaknath*, it was not so much her attitude to the judiciary that mattered as her determination to accelerate the pace of social reform. Whereas Nehru's socialism had been chastened towards the end of his life by recognition of the limiting effects of an inefficient bureaucracy,[42] Gandhi's socialism was impervious to such considerations. For her in any case it was never really about the effectiveness of the plan. Rather, it was the effectiveness of the *platform* that mattered – the rhetoric of social reform that would inspire and give hope to a nation while at the same time ensuring her reelection to office.[43] Gandhi's ascendancy to the leadership of the Congress Party thus radicalized its social reform agenda even as it reduced the possibility that meaningful social reform would be carried out.[44] The inevitable result of that, in turn, was heightened tension over the extent to which the stability of the existing social order would be sacrificed, not just to the cause of social reform, but to a social reform program that never had much chance of success.[45]

It was in this general atmosphere of uncertainty about the future that *Golaknath* was decided.[46] The heart of the case was a challenge to the 1953 Punjab Security of Land Tenures Act, which the Constitution (Seventeenth Amendment) Act of 1964 had placed in the Ninth Schedule to the Constitution, and thus ostensibly immunized from judicial review. In ruling by the narrowest of margins (6–5) that it could, after all, review constitutional amendments for conformance to the fundamental rights, the Court not only

---

[39]   See Austin, *Working a Democratic Constitution* 174, 328, 516–17.

[40]   Ibid.

[41]   See the discussion below.

[42]   See Rajeev Dhavan, "If I Contradict Myself, Well, Then I Contradict Myself . . . Nehru, Law and Social Change" in Rajeev Dhavan and Thomas Paul (eds.), *Nehru and the Constitution* (Bombay: Triphathi, 1992) 45.

[43]   Austin, *Working a Democratic Constitution* 175 (describing the Congress Party's turn to a more radical socialism as a response to its poor performance in the 1967 general elections).

[44]   Ibid 187–8 (describing the "radicalization of the Congress Party and of government policy" under Gandhi).

[45]   Ibid 291 (on Gandhi's failure to translate her power and popularity into "social revolutionary accomplishments").

[46]   Ibid 175, 198 (describing how the *Golaknath* case was decided just a few days before the results of the fourth general elections, in which the Congress Party's majority in the Lok Sabha was reduced to 25 seats and in which it lost control of eight states, were announced).

overturned its earlier decisions in *Sankari Prasad* and *Sajjan Singh*.[47] It also upset the modus vivendi that had prevailed under Nehru. Before this decision, as we have seen, the relatively cordial relationship between the Court and Parliament had depended on the former's respect for the latter's amendment power in exchange for the latter's respect for the former's independence. Now, for the first time, the Court insisted that its power to enforce the fundamental rights was superior to any view that Parliament took of the circumstances in which those rights could be sacrificed to the exigencies of social reform. The fact that the prime mover behind this decision, K. Subba Rao CJ, almost immediately resigned from the Court to become the liberal Swatantra Party's candidate for President, did not help matters.[48] That additional twist meant that the Court had not just broken the tacit agreement that had supported its independence. It had also spectacularly lifted the veil on legalism's claim to politically neutral decision-making.

Golaknath was in other respects quite a calculated decision since the Court did not in the end invalidate the constitutional amendments in question. Rather, citing the American doctrine of "prospective overruling,"[49] it postponed the exercise of its newly declared power to future cases. Within four years of *Golaknath*, however, the Court had handed down two further decisions that could not be described as calculated and which, in a compounding sequence of events, led to a further deterioration in judicial-executive relations. In the first of these, *R. C. Cooper* v. *Union of India*,[50] the Court struck down Gandhi's flagship bank nationalization law as a violation of the state's duty to pay adequate compensation in Article 31(2). In the second, *Madhav Rao Scindia* v. *Union of India*,[51] it was a presidential order depriving princes of their privy purses that was the object of the Court's attention. Depending on your view of the social contract embodied in the 1950 Constitution, these two decisions were either courageous acts of judicial resistance to profound threats facing India's democracy or flagrant acts of antidemocratic defiance. Either way, the significant point is that they both concerned the Congress Party's newly radicalized agenda. The deterioration in judicial-executive relations, in other words, was not just a function of a legalist court making itself vulnerable to charges of ideological bias, but also of a dominant, but

---

[47] *Sri Sankari Prasad Singh Deo* v. *Union of India* AIR 1951 SC 458; *Sajjan Singh* v. *Rajasthan* AIR 1965 SC 845.
[48] See Austin, *Working a Democratic Constitution* 202, Sathe, *Judicial Activism in India* 257–8.
[49] *Golaknath* 1967 (2) SCR 762, 808.
[50] AIR 1969 SC 1126.
[51] AIR 1971 SC 530.

increasingly threatened,[52] political party upping the social reform ante – all of this occurring in a context in which a charismatic figure (Nehru) was no longer available to keep the two sides in check.

The Gandhi-led Congress Party responded to the adverse decisions in *Golaknath*, *R. C. Cooper*, and *Madhav Rao* by introducing a series of constitutional amendments.[53] This had all happened before under Nehru. What was different on this occasion was the directness of the assault, not just on the legal and policy effect of the decisions, but on the Supreme Court's powers. The Twenty-Fourth Amendment thus explicitly excluded constitutional amendments from Article 13's prohibition on the making of laws that infringed the fundamental rights.[54] The Twenty-Fifth Amendment targeted both the Court's power to adjudicate the adequacy of compensation and the primacy of the fundamental rights over laws purporting to give effect to the Directive Principles of State Policy.[55] On the most generous interpretation, these measures constituted an attempt to return the balance of constitutional power to its pre-*Golaknath* position. Less generously, they were a determined move to permanently divest the Court of its capacity to oversee the constitutionality of social reform legislation.

The validity of the Twenty-Fourth and Twenty-Fifth Amendments was challenged in the 1973 *Kesavananda* case.[56] For some commentators, this is the real watershed moment in Indian constitutional politics because it was in this case that the Court for the first time upheld the "basic structure" doctrine – the reading of Parliament's amendment power that to this day underwrites its custodianship of the Constitution.[57] The legitimacy of *Kesavananda*, however, was only consolidated after 1977. When first decided, the case was inextricably bound up with the deterioration in judicial-executive relations that had begun with the decision in *Golaknath*. The history of Indian constitutional politics cannot therefore be neatly dichotomized into life before and after *Kesavananda*. Rather, there are three distinct chapters: the initial

---

[52]   In the 1967 general elections, the results of which were released within days of the *Golaknath* decision, the Congress Party's majority in the Lok Sabha was reduced to 25 seats. It also lost control of eight states. See Austin, *Working a Democratic Constitution* 175.

[53]   See the Twenty-Fourth, Twenty-Fifth, and Twenty-Sixth Amendments to the Indian Constitution respectively.

[54]   Austin, *Working a Democratic Constitution* 244.

[55]   Ibid.

[56]   *Kesavananda Bharati Sripadagalvaru v. State of Kerala* AIR 1973 SC 1461 (also involving a challenge to the Twenty-Ninth Amendment).

[57]   See Raju Ramachandran, "The Supreme Court and the Basic Structure Doctrine" in B. N. Kirpal et al. (eds.), *Supreme but not Infallible: Essays in Honour of the Supreme Court of India* (New Delhi: Oxford University Press, 2000) 107, 108.

accommodation between the Court and the Congress Party encapsulated in *Sankari Prasad*,[58] the transitional period between *Golaknath* and the end of the Emergency, and the new equilibrium that stabilized around *Kesavananda*, but which was in actual fact the product of later developments.

The exact holding in *Kesavananda* has proven notoriously hard to state.[59] In outline, the decision was to the effect that the term "law" in Article 13(2) did not include constitutional amendments and thus that *Golaknath* should be overruled, but that amendments should nevertheless conform to the Constitution's "basic structure."[60] The key passage in this respect was the Court's discussion of the meaning of the word "amend" in Article 368, which the majority argued could not possibly mean total abrogation or destruction of the Constitution.[61] Beyond this, however, the Court did not clearly say what the basic structure was or how it should be determined. For Sikri CJ, the basic structure included, but was not limited to, the "secular" and "federal" character of the Constitution, its "supremacy," the "separation of powers between the legislature, the executive, and the judiciary" and the "republican and democratic form of government."[62] For Shelat and Grover JJ, "the unity and integrity of the nation" and "the mandate given to the state in the Directive Principles of State Policy" were also important.[63] Hegde and Mukherjea JJ, for their part, suggested that the Preamble should be the guide.[64] Since all of these suggestions were said to be nonexhaustive, the end result was inconclusive. Far from undermining its contribution to the Court's post-1977 revival, however, the doctrinal fuzziness of *Kesavananda* has turned out to be a crucial part of its ideational power. By declining to provide clarity on the content of the basic structure, the decision allowed later judges to deploy the doctrine in a flexible and judicious way.[65]

Kesavananda's usefulness in this respect only came to light later. When delivered, its immediate significance was that it failed to appease the Court's political opponents. Ever since *Golaknath*, as we have seen, the Court's position had been deteriorating. This was a function not just of the controversial nature of that decision, but also of Gandhi's ability to take political advantage of it. When

---

[58] *Sri Sankari Prasad Singh Deo v. Union of India* AIR 1951 SC 458.
[59] See Mate, "Public Interest Litigation" 268; Austin, *Working a Democratic Constitution* 265–9; Zia Mody, *10 Judgements that Changed India* (Sobhaa Dé Books, 2013) 12–15.
[60] *Kesavananda* passim.
[61] See Austin, *Working a Democratic Constitution* 265.
[62] *Kesavananda* AIR 1973 SC 1461, 1535.
[63] *Kesavananda* AIR 1973 SC 1461, 1603.
[64] Ibid para 661 p. 484.
[65] Writing in 2002, Sathe, *Judicial Activism in India* 93, reported that the basic doctrine had been used only five times to that point to strike down constitutional amendments.

Golaknath was decided, the Congress Party was three days away from its worst ever (to that point) electoral result – the 1967 elections, in which its majority in the Lok Sabha fell to twenty-five seats.[66] Gandhi, however, skillfully used the outcry over *Golaknath* and Subba Rao CJ's resignation to rebuild her public support.[67] She then went on to exploit the *Bank Nationalization* and *Princely Purse* decisions in the same way.[68] So effective was this strategy (along with Gandhi's populist appeal more generally) that, at the next general elections in 1971, the Congress Party was able to win back nearly all the ground it had lost in 1967.[69] At the end of that year, the defeat of Pakistan in the liberation of Bangladesh saw Gandhi's personal star rise even higher.[70] Thus it was that, when *Kesavananda* was decided, Gandhi was in a confident and commanding position. Even before the outcome of the case was known, she had hatched a plan to supersede the three next most senior justices in the appointment of Sikri CJ's successor.[71] The plan was put into action the day after the *Kesavananda* decision,[72] making it seem like an immediate reprisal when it fact it was the culmination of a process that had begun in 1967.

From their shocked response,[73] the three superseded judges – Shelat, Hegde, and Grover JJ – seem to have been completely unaware of what was being planned. The entire Court, however, was acutely aware of the importance of the *Kesavananda* decision, having been put under intense pressure by the executive in the leadup to and hearing of the case.[74] That pressure, it is fair to surmise, was what lay behind the decision to overrule *Golaknath* and once again deploy the device of prospective overruling.[75] Neither of those measures proved sufficient, however. As Austin relates, "within minutes of arriving home from a retirement party for Chief Justice Sikri," Justice Hegde telephoned Justice Shelat to give him the shocking news that they and Justice Grover had been bypassed in favor of the more politically compliant Justice A. N. Ray.[76]

---

[66] Austin, *Working a Democratic Constitution* 198.
[67] Ibid.
[68] See text accompanying notes 55–56.
[69] Mate, "Public Interest Litigation" 269 (noting that the Congress Party won 350 out of 545 seats).
[70] See Ramachandra Guha, *India after Gandhi: The History of the World's Largest Democracy* (London: Macmillan, 2007) 461–3.
[71] Austin, *Working a Democratic Constitution* 278–80.
[72] Ibid 278.
[73] Ibid.
[74] Ibid 269–77.
[75] See *Kesavananda* order.
[76] Austin, *Working a Democratic Constitution* 278. Ray J had dissented in both the *Bank Nationalization* and the *Princely Purses* cases (ibid 282). The other three were all seen as oppositional. Hegde in particular was feared because of his decision in the *Gandhi Election*

Attacks on a judiciary do not necessarily lead, of course, to a decline in independence. It all depends on how weakened the Court already is at the time of the attack. Sometimes, too, the real effects of an attack may take time to become apparent. In the Indian case, the supersession of Hegde, Shelat, and Grover JJ had two significant consequences, one immediate and the other longer-term. First, the supersession contributed to the generally threatening atmosphere in which the Emergency cases were decided. By demonstrating how career-damaging defiance could be, or just how futile it was to defy Gandhi when the consequence of such defiance was simply loss of influence on the Court, the supersession must have affected the judges' assessment of the personal and institutional repercussions of resisting the Emergency. The second, longer-term significance of the supersession was that it led to the creation of the Bench that was eventually to rehabilitate the Court's reputation. Both Justices Bhagwati and Krishna Iyer were thus appointed in the immediate aftermath of *Kesavananda*.[77] In Bhagwati's case, his appointment came on the back of a career as a young and progressive Chief Justice of the Gujarat High Court with a particular interest in promoting legal aid for the poor.[78] Krishna Iyer, for his part, had been a member of the Law Commission appointed by Gandhi in 1971 to suggest ways in which the Constitution might be amended so as to implement the Directive Principles.[79] Like Bhagwati, he was a perfect example of the kind of committed judge Gandhi had in mind. Judges who share their political promoter's ideology, however, are often those most able to assert their Court's independence.[80] And so it proved in the Indian case. As explained in greater detail in the next section, Bhagwati and Krishna Iyer were key players in the Court's post-1977 revival. They were able to play this role, and continue playing it after Gandhi's return to office in 1980, precisely because they were her appointees – judges who could be understood to be implementing her pro-poor agenda. The great irony of the supersession is thus that it at once weakened the judges' resolve in resisting the Emergency and supplied the ingredients for the Court's later revival.

The sequence of events leading up to the Emergency was again quite convoluted. The key point was that, despite her resounding 1971 election

---

case (ibid). At the same time, numerous High Court judges were forcibly transferred away from their home jurisdictions (ibid 137; Mate, "Public Interest Litigation" 269).

[77] Both were sworn in on July 17, 1973, within three months of the supersession. See George H. Gadbois, Jr, *Judges of the Supreme Court of India: 1950–1989* (New Delhi: Oxford University Press, 2011) 194.

[78] Ibid 194–5.

[79] Austin, *Working a Democratic Constitution* 189.

[80] The same could be said, for example, of the members of the Chaskalson Court in South Africa.

victory and the strong performance of the Congress Party in the state elections that followed in 1972, widespread popular opposition to Gandhi's rule began to develop in 1974.[81] The reason for this rapid deterioration in Gandhi's fortunes had to do partly with a downturn in India's economy following the 1973 oil crisis, and partly with her failure to address corruption within the Congress Party, particularly at state level.[82] In January 1974, a student uprising began in Gujarat against the rule of the chief minister, Chimanbhai Patel.[83] This spread rapidly to Bihar and other northern states. In March 1974, the students asked Jayaprakash Narayan, an old Congress Party stalwart, but someone who had been out of active politics for a number of years, to head their movement. The protests rolled on for a further year under Narayan's leadership, culminating in a mass rally in Delhi on March 6 attended by 750,000 people.[84]

While all of this was going on, the Allahabad High Court had been hearing a challenge to Gandhi's 1971 election to the Lok Sabha that had been brought by her losing opponent, Raj Narain.[85] The alleged wrongdoing – the use of government vehicles and other state resources to assist her in her campaign – hardly seemed significant in light of the ease of Gandhi's victory. On June 12, 1975, however, Sinha J ruled in Narain's favor, thereby throwing the continuation of Gandhi's prime ministership into doubt.

As alarming as it was, the Allahabad High Court's decision was not immediately threatening to Gandhi since the Supreme Court (in the person of Krishna Iyer) quickly granted a stay of the order pending an appeal.[86] The situation in the country, too, though turbulent, was not in any sense out of control.[87] It therefore came as quite a shock when Gandhi, without consulting her cabinet,[88] moved to declare an internal state of emergency on June 25, 1975. The feeling that this was something of an overreaction was compounded when, rather than waiting for the Supreme Court's decision in her election case, Gandhi attempted to put the outcome beyond doubt by persuading the Lok Sabha to pass a retrospective constitutional amendment ousting judicial review of the election of a sitting Prime

---

[81] This discussion draws on Guha, *India after Gandhi* 477–88.
[82] Ibid 475.
[83] Ibid 477.
[84] Ibid.
[85] Austin, *Working a Democratic Constitution* 314–19.
[86] Ibid 318.
[87] This was the official finding of the Shah Commission of Inquiry held into the Emergency (ibid 309).
[88] Ibid 309.

Minister. The applicable election laws were also retrospectively amended at the same time.[89]

It is impossible to know how the Supreme Court would have decided Raj Narain's complaint in the absence of these amendments. The electoral fraud charges were, as noted, quite trivial and the Allahabad High Court's decision might have been overturned according to the law as it previously stood. In the event, the Court upheld Gandhi's election on the basis of the retrospectively amended election laws but struck down the retrospective constitutional amendment on the ground that it was contrary to the rule of law, equality, and free and fair elections – principles that were variously said to be part of the Constitution's basic structure.[90]

The Court's decision in the *Gandhi Election* case, as it became known, was not a clear-cut capitulation to political power. By confirming the basic structure doctrine in the most difficult of circumstances, the Court tried to hold on to its role as custodian of the Constitution. Significantly, too, the judges who joined the majority on this point had all dissented in *Kesavananda*.[91] This sent a strong signal that *Kesavananda* would henceforth be respected as binding precedent – a point that was to prove important shortly afterwards when an attempt was made to pressurize the Court into reconsidering that decision.[92] Against this, however, the Court's handling of the second part of the *Election* case – the challenge to the retrospective amendments to the election laws – is difficult to defend on legal grounds. Khanna J's decision to invalidate the constitutional amendment as a violation of fundamental democratic principles, but to allow the legislative amendment as somehow not a violation of these same principles, is particularly hard to fathom. As Upendra Baxi has argued, this part of the decision only makes sense if one assumes that Khanna J and the Court as a whole were attempting some sort of "statesmanlike" act of institutional self-preservation.[93] Rather than a capitulation, then, the *Election* case is probably best seen as a strategic compromise aimed at placating the Congress Party in the matter of Gandhi's election while preserving the Court's capacity to take a more robust stand against the Emergency at some later point.

---

[89] By the Thirty-Ninth Amendment. For details, see Austin, *Working a Democratic Constitution* 319–20.

[90] *Indira Nehru Gandhi* v. *Raj Narain* AIR 1975 SC 2299; 1976 (2) SCR 347. Discussed in Austin, *Working a Democratic Constitution* 323–4; Baxi, *Indian Supreme Court and Politics*, 56–66 (noting that the majority judges in the *Election* case had not supported the basic structure doctrine in *Kesavananda*).

[91] Baxi, *Indian Supreme Court and Politics* 56–7; Austin, *Working a Democratic Constitution* 324; Ramachandran, "The Supreme Court and the Basic Structure Doctrine" 116–17.

[92] Austin, *Working a Democratic Constitution* 328–33.

[93] Baxi, *Indian Supreme Court and Politics* 64.

The problem with *Shukla*,[94] and the reason it has become so notorious, is that this was the case in which the need to take a robust stand against the Emergency undoubtedly arose, only for the Court to fail to act. At its heart, the case concerned the constitutionality of a presidential order issued on June 27, 1975 – two days after the Emergency had been declared – suspending the right to approach a court for enforcement of the rights conferred by Article 14 (equal protection), Article 21 (no deprivation of life or liberty with due process), and Article 22 (right to be informed of grounds of detention) of the Constitution.[95] In the ten High Court cases collected in the appeal, seven had softened the impact of this provision by holding that it did not exclude the ordinary administrative law grounds for challenging a detention order.[96] Khanna J, in his famous dissent, took a different but equally convincing approach, arguing that Article 21 was not the sole repository of the right to personal liberty.[97] Rather, there were various statutory rights against arbitrary deprivation of liberty that had survived both the presidential order of June 27 and s 18 of the Maintenance of Internal Security Act (which purported to override all existing common law and natural rights). Since it did not apply to these rights, Khanna J concluded, the presidential order could not be said to have completely ousted the High Courts' power under Article 226 to issue writs of *habeas corpus*.[98]

While it is possible to find some holes in Khanna J's judgment,[99] the arguments he presented were at least as convincing as the majority's view that Article 21 subsumed all other rights to personal liberty. His decision therefore showed that there was a legally plausible argument through which the Emergency might have been resisted. There are also reasons to think that, had the majority joined in Khanna J's judgment, there might well have been a groundswell of public support for the Court, sufficient to dissuade the Congress Party from attacking it.[100] It is for this reason that *Shukla*, together with the subsequently decided *Bhanudas* case,[101] in which the Court declined to review the legality or conditions of preventive detention, have been so roundly condemned. As received and

---

94   A. D. M. *Jabalpur* v. *Shivkant Shukla* (1976) 2 SCC 521.
95   Baxi, *Indian Supreme Court and Politics* 80.
96   Ibid 79–80.
97   Section 18 of the Maintenance of Internal Security Act was made applicable notwithstanding contrary common law and natural rights – but not statutory rights. See Baxi, *Indian Supreme Court and Politics* 85.
98   Ibid.
99   Ibid 84–116.
100 Austin, *Working a Democratic Constitution* 343.
101 *Union of India* v. *Bhanudas Krishna Gawde* AIR 1977 SC 1027.

reinterpreted,[102] *Shukla* stands as the prime example of a case in which a threatened constitutional court failed to take a stand on principle in circumstances where the principled stand was not only legally available, but may also have been the best option from a strategic point of view. Even if the Court had been attacked, *Shukla* was the sort of case where the issue of principle was so fundamental that the institutional repercussions of a stand on principle would arguably have been less severe than the repercussions – in terms of lost reputation – of capitulation.[103]

All of this is true, and yet the significant point about the *Shukla* decision is that the Court did eventually recover from it. Not just that, but the Court's capacity to recover from it, as we shall see in the next section, was in part a function of the intense public reaction to the horror of the detentions that the Court's decision had allowed. As much as it deserves its reputation, therefore, *Shukla* is also testament to the fact that constitutional courts may recover from even very severe blows to their standing – indeed, that judicial capitulation to executive pressure, precisely by allowing the executive to overplay its hand, may provide the basis, not only for a court's resurgence but for institutional growth beyond anything that might have been imagined.

4.3 THE COURT'S REHABILITATION: 1977–1989

While the extent of its own responsibility for this process may be debated,[104] the Supreme Court's influence in national politics clearly declined between 1967 and 1977. Its decision in *Shukla* was symptomatic of this trend and a damaging blow to the Court's authority in its own right. The Court's pre-1967 property rights decisions had also been controversial, of course. But the Court had at least then plausibly been able to claim that its decisions were offered in good faith. This in turn had allowed it to influence the content of the *zamindari* abolition laws even as its decisions were being countermanded. During the Emergency, however, its capacity to influence policy in this way had been all but lost. Its professed legalism, far from enabling the Court to

---

[102] As with *Kesavananda*, discussions of the *Shukla* decision tend not to analyze the actual content of the different judgments. Baxi's close reading of Khanna J's judgment (*Indian Supreme Court and Politics* 84–116) is exceptional in this regard.

[103] "Arguably" because at the time *Shukla* was decided there was talk of the creation of a Superior Judicial Council with majority political membership and final powers of constitutional interpretation. See Austin, *Working a Democratic Constitution* 333, 342–3. Had that proposal been adopted in consequence of an adverse decision in *Shukla* decision, it is possible that independent judicial review would have been destroyed altogether.

[104] As noted earlier, it is best to think of the Court's decline as a compounding sequence of events.

resist the Congress Party's assault on democratic rights, had been used to mask the abdication of its constitutionally mandated role. Law and politics, it seemed, were indeed separate, but only in the perverse sense characteristic of authoritarian legalism, where a claimed commitment to that ideal under-pins a judicial reluctance to speak legal truth to political power.

In the course of the Court's institutional decline, the personal reputations of the judges had also been badly damaged. Bhagwati J, in particular, as a judge with social-egalitarian views who had been expected to defend the Constitution,[105] came in for a lot of criticism. In January 1978, a month before Beg was due to retire as Chief Justice, the *Times of India* published a statement on its front page by a group of concerned Bombay lawyers and public intellectuals claiming that neither Bhagwati nor Chandrachud, the judge next in line for the chief justiceship, was a fit and proper person for the job. Their decisions in *Shukla*, it was argued, had been "arrive[d] at ... in total [dis]-regard to precedent, by reasoning manifestly unsound, and [dressed up] by expressions that will testify only to a marked inclination to rule in favor of the State."[106] Such open and direct public criticisms of sitting judges had never before been heard.[107]

In the end, after receiving the support of his fellow judges, Chandrachud did succeed Beg as Chief Justice.[108] But the criticisms made of his and Bhagwati J's role in the *Shukla* decision lingered. In Baxi's influential assessment,[109] it was this experience that supplied the added judicial motiva-tion for the Court's post-1977 revival.[110] Determined to restore his reputation, Bhagwati set about proving that he was a better judge than his performance under the Emergency had indicated. He was joined in this initiative by Krishna Iyer, who had not been party to the *Shukla* decision, but who was on the Court at the time and who was the person most frequently cited as proof of Gandhi's preference for politically "committed" judges.[111] Together, Krishna Iyer and Bhagwati began fashioning a series of doctrines that broa-dened access to the Court and gave its case law a markedly pro-poor cast. In restoring their personal reputations in this way, Krishna Iyer and Bhagwati

---

[105]   Austin, *Working a Democratic Constitution* 338.
[106]   Ibid 438. See also Gadbois, *Judges of the Supreme Court of India* 254–5; Baxi, *Indian Supreme Court and Politics* 191–8.
[107]   Gadbois, *Judges of the Supreme Court of India* 254.
[108]   Ibid 255–6. See also Austin, *Working a Democratic Constitution* 438–9.
[109]   Baxi, "Taking Suffering Seriously" 113, 121 n 67. See also Sathe, *Judicial Activism in India* 106–7.
[110]   "Added" because the other part of the motivation was a sincere ideological commitment to pro-poor lawyering.
[111]   Austin, *Working a Democratic Constitution* 298.

also restored the Court's reputation, and more particularly, its public support.[112]

The Court's post-Emergency doctrines will be discussed in a moment. Before doing so, a few points about the political environment for judicial review after 1977 should be noted, for the Court's rehabilitation was not just about the expiation of judicial guilt. It was also a function of political factors that allowed the judges to influence the Supreme Court's trajectory in the way that they did. The first and most obvious of these was the persistence in India after 1977 of great inequalities in the distribution of wealth, discrimination along gender lines, and social marginalization according to caste and religion.[113] Neither Nehruvian socialism nor Gandhian populism had made much impact on these stubborn features of Indian society. If there was a constituency, then, whose support the Court needed to win, it was the huge underclass of people for whom the Constitution's promise of social and economic transformation had yet to be made real.

The second point is that, as much as the Court's reputation had been damaged by the Emergency, the executive's reputation had been damaged more. While unforgettably awful for those who had suffered its depredations, the Emergency had at least taught Indians an important lesson about the way political power may be abused and the consequent need for independent judges. The Court undoubtedly benefited from this "never again" feature of the political context as its post-1977 case law progressed.

The final contextual factor worth mentioning is that the restoration of constitutional democracy in India was first and foremost an act of popular self-government. The Indian people, not the Court, voted Gandhi and the Congress Party out of office in March 1977. Although the Janata Party coalition that came to power at this time did not last very long,[114] it fulfilled its central mission of overturning the worst excesses of Emergency rule.[115] In particular, through the Forty-Third and Forty-Fourth amendments to the Constitution (which the Congress Party supported), the Janata Party restored many of the key components of the Court's judicial review power.[116] It was this act of constitutional reconstruction that provided the initial impetus for the

---

[112] There has been extensive debate in the literature about whether Bhagwati and Krishna Iyer JJ's actions in this respect were sincere or strategic. See Mate, "Public Interest Litigation" 264; Mehta, "India's Judiciary" 167; Baxi, "Taking Suffering Seriously" 129. The consensus seems to be that it was a bit of both.

[113] See Guha, *India after Gandhi*, 605–32.

[114] Austin, *Working a Democratic Constitution* 393–481; Guha, *India after Gandhi* 522–45.

[115] See Mate, "Public Interest Litigation" 270; Mate, "Elite Institutionalism" 368–70.

[116] Lavanya Rajamani and Arghya Sengupta, "The Supreme Court" in N. G. Jaya (ed.), *The Oxford Companion to Politics in India* (New Delhi: Oxford University Press, 2010) 80, 86.

Court's rehabilitation. The doctrines the judges developed accelerated the Court's recovery, but they would have been useless without the political momentum provided by the people's clearly expressed desire to return to something like the constitutional status quo ante.

So much for the political environment in which the Court operated. How did Bhagwati, Krishna Iyer, and the other judges who shared their social-egalitarian vision navigate that environment to restore the Court's influence? This part of the story, too, has been told on many occasions.[117] In retelling it here, the aim of this section is to show that the Court's rehabilitation is best attributed, not to a conscious political strategy, but to the dynamic interaction of its developing doctrines and the political factors just mentioned.

The first steps were taken during the brief period of Janata Party rule from 1977 to 1979. In arguably the most significant case decided at this time, *Maneka Gandhi*,[118] the Court reoriented its approach to Article 21, reading that provision's guarantee against deprivation of "life or personal liberty except according to procedure established by law" as guaranteeing, not just any procedure, but a "fair, just and, reasonable" one.[119] The case came to the Court after the Janata Party government had seized Indira Gandhi's daughter-in-law's passport without affording her a hearing. In holding that a hearing was indeed required, the Court read the funda-mental rights for the first time as an "integrated scheme."[120] On its own, the Court reasoned, Article 21 provided only a procedural guarantee.[121] When read together with Article 14 (equality) and Article 19 (fundamental freedoms), however, it was clear that any procedure through which a person was deprived of an aspect of their liberty needed to conform to the principles of natural justice.[122]

Maneka Gandhi in this way marked a fundamental break from the inter-pretive methods that had dominated the establishment period. As noted ear-lier, Article 21 had been deliberately drafted so as to exclude the American doctrine of substantive due process. In downplaying this drafting history, and emphasizing instead the connection between Article 21 and Articles 14 and 19, the Court abandoned the textual originalism of *Gopalan* and nailed its colors to the mast of its own, ideologically motivated understanding of the Indian

---

[117]   See, for example, Baxi, "Taking Suffering Seriously"; Sathe, *Judicial Activism in India.*
[118]   *Maneka Gandhi v. Union of India* (1978) 1 SCC 248.
[119]   Ibid para 40.
[120]   Ibid para 3.
[121]   This was the holding in *A. C. Gopalan v. State of Madras* 1950 SCR 88 (discussed in Section 4.1).
[122]   See Bhagwati J's judgment in *Maneka Gandhi* in particular.

constitutional project.[123] From this time onwards it was clear the Court's authority would be tied, not to the plausibility of its claim to be faithfully implementing the written Constitution, but to the public's willingness to embrace its interventionist role in national politics.

The next step in this process was *Sunil Batra v. Delhi Administration.*[124] To students of Indian constitutional politics, this case is well known as the occasion on which Krishna Iyer responded to a letter sent by a prisoner alerting the Court to the appalling conditions of detention at Tihar Jail. In accepting this communication as equivalent to a writ proceeding under Article 32, the Court launched its "epistolary jurisdiction"[125] – one of the doctrinal innovations that later came to play a major part in encouraging public interest litigation. *Sunil Batra* is also significant, however, for extending *Maneka Gandhi's* expansive approach to Article 21 to a socially ostracized class of beneficiaries – prisoners facing capital punishment. Even after being sentenced, the Court held, prisoners on death row should not be kept in solitary confinement unless absolutely necessary.[126] The conditions of their detention, this meant, had to be proportionate to the threat that they posed to their fellow inmates. Furthermore, all prisoners, whatever the nature of their alleged crimes, should be seen to have forfeited only those fundamental rights as were incompatible with their incarceration.[127] With that, the Court announced its intention to use Article 21 as the lynchpin of its efforts to hold the executive to account for its treatment of ordinary Indians, even – especially – those who found themselves on the wrong side of the criminal law.

The final case of the Janata Party era worth noting, *Minerva Mills,*[128] was in fact decided shortly after the Congress Party had been returned to power in January 1980. Most of the arguments, however, were heard during the caretaker prime ministership of Charan Singh in the second half of 1979. That gave *Minerva Mills* the peculiar character of a case in which the

---

[123] See P. N. Bhagwati, "Judicial Activism and Public Interest Litigation" (1984) 23 *Columbia Journal of Transnational Law* 561, 566 (describing the Court's move away from formalism to "substantive justice"). See also Mate, "The Origins of Due Process in India" 246 (describing the rejection of legalism in the *Maneka Gandhi* case).

[124] *Sunil Batra v. Delhi Administration* AIR 1978 SC 1675; (1978) 4 SCC 494. See also *Sunil Batra v. Delhi Administration* AIR 1980 SC 1579; (1980) 3 SCC 448.

[125] See Baxi, "Taking Suffering Seriously" 118, 120. See also discussion in R. Sudarshan, "Courts and Social Transformation in India" in Roberto Gargarella et al. (eds.), *Courts and Social Transformation in New Democracies: An Institutional Voice for the Poor?* (Aldershot: Ashgate, 2006) 153, 156.

[126] *Sunil Batra* (note 124).

[127] Ibid.

[128] *Minerva Mills v. Union of India* AIR 1980 SC 1789.

government had to defend legislation that it had itself tried unsuccessfully to repeal.[129] The particular provisions at issue were sections 4 and 55 of the Forty-Second Amendment, which had sought to countermand the Court's ruling in *Kesavananda*.[130] In striking down both those provisions, the Court reclaimed the last of the powers it had lost under the Emergency. The significance of *Minerva Mills* is thus the way the Court was able to use the final stages of the post-Emergency political moment to reassert its custodianship of the Constitution.

With Gandhi back in office in January 1980,[131] the post-Emergency impetus behind the Court's rehabilitation fell away. Instead, Bhagwati and Krishna Iyer moved to position the Court as a partner in the implementation of the Congress Party's social transformation project. It is thus noteworthy that, in the first part of the 1980s, the Court rarely opposed the national government.[132] Rather, it expanded its role in ways that aligned with Gandhi's overarching policy goals. After her assassination in 1984, the Court became more assertive under Rajiv Gandhi's less ideologically strident, more inclined-to-appease prime ministership.[133] But in this instance, too, the Court's rehabilitation is best understood, not as a conscious political strategy but as a judge-led reworking of the Court's mission in the changing conditions of Indian politics.

There were three main facets to the Court's jurisprudence as it developed after 1980, each of them foreshadowed by the three Janata-era cases just discussed. The first consisted of a series of doctrinal innovations that facilitated new forms of Public Interest Litigation (PIL). The effect of the Court's decisions in this respect was indirect in as much as its doctrines invited certain types of case that progressively transformed its institutional role. The second

---

[129] During the Janata Party government, the Congress Party still controlled the upper house, thus preventing the repeal of all the Emergency amendments. See Austin, *Working a Democratic Constitution* 498; Ramachandran, "The Supreme Court and the Basic Structure Doctrine" 118–19.

[130] The former section had amended Article 31C to the effect that no law enacted to promote the Directive Principles could be held to violate Articles 14, 19, or 31, while the latter had provided that "there shall be no limitation whatever on the constituent power of Parliament."

[131] See Austin, *Working a Democratic Constitution* 485–97.

[132] See Mate, "Public Interest Litigation" 265 (citing *R. K. Garg* v. *Union of India* (1981) 4 SCC 675 in which the Court adopted a deferential standard for the review of economic policy).

[133] In *Mohammed Ahmed Khan* v. *Shah Bano Begum* AIR 1985 SC 945, for example, the Court held that s 125 of the Code of Criminal Procedure, 1973, entitled a Muslim woman to maintenance on divorce, thus overriding the position in Muslim personal law according to which maintenance is payable only during the three-month *iddat* period. Rajiv Gandhi's Congress Party government responded by enacting the Muslim Women (Protection of Rights on Divorce) Act, 1986 in what was widely seen as an attempt to placate aggrieved Muslim leaders and secure their vote. See Mody, *10 Judgements that Changed India* 49–73.

facet, the expansion of Article 21 to encompass a range of social and economic rights, complemented the first by collapsing the distinction between the Directive Principles in Part 3 and the fundamental rights in Part 4 of the Constitution. This doctrinal shift allowed the Court to resolve the tension between these two historically antagonistic parts of the Constitution while at the same time giving the fundamental rights a pro-poor tilt. The third and final facet was more direct in the sense that it consisted of a series of doctrines through which the Court explicitly redefined the limits of its powers vis-à-vis the political branches. Included in this facet were cases dealing with the judicial appointments process and the basic structure doctrine.

It is not possible here to survey all the cases in which these three facets were developed. The Court's post-1977 case law has in any case already been the subject of a number of in-depth studies.[134] Instead, what the remainder of this section does is to highlight a few cases that illustrate the principal point of interest – the way in which the Court's doctrines, in dynamic interaction with the changing political environment, transformed prevailing conceptions of the law/politics relation.

In the case of the Court's PIL case law, the main doctrinal innovations were the relaxation of the procedural rules governing access to the Court, a similar relaxation of the rules governing *locus standi*, and the development of a new remedy – continuing mandamus – that allowed the Court to retain supervisory control of cases. As to the first, we have seen already how the Court in *Sunil Batra* allowed a detainee to bring a case on behalf of a fellow prisoner by writing a simple letter. After 1980, this way of accessing the Court proliferated and became the main way in which human rights abuses were brought to the attention of the Court.[135] The function of this "epistolary jurisdiction" in the Court's case law was always somewhat symbolic, however. Even after its introduction, only a tiny percentage of the many human rights abuses that the poor in India suffered every day were litigated, let alone redressed through litigation.[136] From the point of view of the Court's public support, however, this did not matter provided that the Court was seen to be, metaphorically speaking, open to the poor.

The Court's epistolary jurisdiction was complemented by a reform to the rules of *locus standi*, which saw it dispense with the requirement that an

---

[134] See Baxi, "Taking Suffering Seriously"; Sathe, *Judicial Activism in India*.

[135] See *Veena Sethi v. State of Bihar* (1982) 2 SCC 583; *People's Union for Democratic Rights v. Union of India* AIR 1982 SC 1473, (1982) SCC 253; *Dr Upendra Baxi v. State of Uttar Pradesh* (1983) 2 SCC 308; *Ram Kumar Misra z State of Bihar* (1984) 2 SCC 451.

[136] See Mark Galanter and J. K. Krishnan, "'Bread for the Poor': Access to Justice and the Rights of the Needy in India" (2004) 55 *Hastings Law Journal* 789.

applicant be able to show that they had a personal interest in the case. The paradigm case of this sort was *Bandhua Mukti Morcha* v. *Union of India*,[137] in which the Court gave standing to a non-governmental organization seeking to end the practice of bonded labor. There was nothing in Article 32(1), Bhagwati held, to suggest that the person who moved the Court to enforce a fundamental right had to be the person whose right was allegedly being violated.[138] Earlier, in *S. P. Gupta* v. *President of India*,[139] the Court had given standing to a group of advocates to contest the transfer of High Court judges to other jurisdictions against their will. This case, too, had involved applicants who had not themselves suffered any harm. On this occasion, however, the fact that the advocates were "officers of the court" had appeared to restrict the grant of *locus standi* to instances where the applicants could show that they had at least an indirect interest in the case.[140] In *Bandhua Mukti Morcha* this qualification was dropped, or rather the point was made that all citizens had an indirect interest in the violation of fundamental rights.

The final doctrinal innovation driving the rise of PIL was the development of the continuing mandamus remedy. This device was first deployed in *Hussainara Khatoon* v. *State of Bihar*,[141] a case in which the Court was approached by an advocate who had read about the plight of undertrial prisoners in the newspaper. According to the report, some of the prisoners had been in prison for longer than the maximum penalty attached to the crime for which they had been charged.[142] In response, the Court, again in the person of Bhagwati, held that the prisoners' right to a speedy trial under Article 21 had been violated. It then issued a series of directions on how the system for holding prisoners awaiting trial could be improved. This was done in the form of a number of interim orders, thus ensuring that the Court remained seized of the case, with the ability to monitor the implementation of its orders over time.[143]

Even this brief survey illustrates how the Court's PIL doctrines transformed, not just its role in the political system, but also the way law and politics interacted at the constitutional level. Whereas the Court's role before *Golaknath* had been about enforcing the terms of the written Constitution –

[137] AIR 1984 SC 802; (1984) 3 SCC 161.
[138] AIR 1984 SC 802 at 813. The only qualification on this was that the person bringing the action should not be a "meddlesome interloper or busybody." Ibid.
[139] (1981) Supp (1) SCC 87.
[140] Mate, "Public Interest Litigation" 272.
[141] AIR 1979 SC 1360; 1980 1 SCC 81.
[142] Ibid.
[143] See Baxi, "Taking Suffering Seriously" 116ff; Sathe, *Judicial Activism in India* 204; Mate, "Public Interest Litigation" 273–4.

with its democratic legitimacy contingent on the plausibility of its claim to be doing that – its PIL jurisprudence turned it into a people's court, with its own unmediated access to the demos. In the process, the Court became the primary site for discussion of virtually every major policy issue facing the country.[144] From being an adversarial court in which it addressed only those issues put to it by counsel, it became an inquisitorial court with a brief to consider any matter it thought to be pertinent to the case.[145] Even this does not convey the full extent of the changes, since the Court's relaxed rules of access meant it could investigate matters more or less of its own volition. All that was required was a newspaper report and someone willing to act as the named litigant. To support it in its work, the Court began to appoint commissioners and experts whose task it was first to recommend solutions that could be included in the Court's orders and then to monitor them to ensure they were carried out.[146] Although careful always to say that its guidelines were issued pending legislation, the Court in effect took over several areas of public policy where the legislature, through lack of political will or inattentiveness, had failed to act.[147] With that, the distinction between politics, understood as the site of social contestation over material and ideological resources, and law, as the means through which political power is projected, weakened.

This transformation process was further accelerated by the second major facet of the Court's case law: its expansion of Article 21 to embrace a range of implied social and economic rights, including rights to livelihood,[148] fresh water and air,[149] and health.[150] We have seen how this aspect of its jurisprudence started in the *Maneka Gandhi* and *Sunil Batra* cases. Article 21 was also the source of the right to a speedy trial in *Hussainara Khatoon*.[151] In addition to these, one other case worth mentioning – because it so neatly encapsulates what went on – is *Olga Tellis*.[152] This was the case in which the Court held that pavement dwellers had the right not to be arbitrarily evicted from their

---

[144] Mehta, "The Rise of Judicial Sovereignty" 79 ("it is hard to think of a single [policy] issue … on which the courts of India have not left their mark").

[145] See Neuborne, "The Supreme Court of India" 503.

[146] P. N. Bhagwati, "Judicial Activism and Public Interest Litigation" (1984) 23 *Columbia Journal of Transnational Law* 561, 574–7.

[147] See Ashok H. Desai and S. Muralidhar, "Public Interest Litigation: Potential and Problems" in B. N. Kirpal et al, (eds.), *Supreme but not Infallible: Essays in Honour of the Supreme Court of India* (New Delhi: Oxford University Press, 2000) 159, 165 (giving a list of policy areas taken over by the Court).

[148] *Olga Tellis* v. *Bombay Municipal Corporation* (1985) 3 SCC 545; AIR 1986 SC 180.

[149] *M. C. Mehta* v. *India* AIR 1988 SC 1037.

[150] *Vincent* v. *India* AIR 1987 SC 990.

[151] 1979 AIR 1360 SC.

[152] *Olga Tellis* v. *Bombay Municipal Corporation* (1985) 3 SCC 545; AIR 1986 SC 180.

shelters. Although nowhere mentioned in the Constitution, the Court reasoned, the right to shelter was conceptually entailed by the right to life in Article 21 given that: (a) the right to life was meaningless without the right to livelihood;[153] and (b) the evidence showed that the pavement dwellers concerned were unable to support themselves anywhere else.[154] The doctrinal significance of *Olga Tellis* is thus the way it folds what was meant to be a nonjusticiable directive principle of state policy (the right in Article 39(a) to "an adequate means of livelihood") into Article 21. At the same time, *Olga Tellis* shows how this doctrinal shift was vitally dependent on the Court's preparedness to interpret the right to life in substantive political terms, with reference to the social and economic conditions in which it was being enforced.

The final facet of the Court's post-Emergency case law concerned cases in which the Court directly defined its powers vis-à-vis the political branches. The most significant example of this type was *S. P. Gupta*.[155] We have looked at the *locus standi* aspect of this case already. Its relevance now is the substantive issue raised: the respective roles of the executive and the Chief Justice in the appointment and transfer of High Court judges. During the Emergency, fifty-six High Court judges had been transferred without their consent to other jurisdictions in what was widely believed to be a form of punishment.[156] The transfers had stopped after being successfully challenged in the Gujarat High Court.[157] With Gandhi's return to power in 1980, however, a new version of the problem arose: the use of Article 224, which provides for the appointment of temporary "additional judges," as a routine way of testing whether prospective High Court judges were suitable for permanent appointment.[158] In the view of many, "suitability" in this context meant, not the judges' professional competence, but their demonstrated loyalty to the Congress Party. In March 1981, in the midst of the public outcry over this issue, the Law Minister, Shiv Shankar, caused an even greater stir by addressing a circular to the Governor of Punjab and the Chief Ministers of other states. In it, he requested them to ask the additional judges serving in their respective High Courts to indicate whether they consented to being transferred to another High Court on expiry of their two-year term. Apart from the impression this created that the judges were malleable instruments of Congress Party

[153]   Ibid.
[154]   Ibid.
[155]   *S. P. Gupta* v. *President of India* (1981) Supp (1) SCC 87.
[156]   Mody, *10 Judgements that Changed India* 166.
[157]   Ibid 167.
[158]   Ibid 167.

policy, the circular had not been sent to the Chief Justice, in apparent contradiction to Article 222.

Hearing various challenges to the circular together, the Supreme Court in S. P. *Gupta* handed down a complex judgment that appeared to trade the doctrinal advances made in respect of the *locus standi* aspect of the case for a more deferential approach to the appointments question.[159] While emphasizing that transfers could not be used to punish judges, a 4–3 majority of the Court stopped short of holding that a judge's consent was a necessary precondition for transfer.[160] The same majority held that, while the Chief Justice had to be consulted before a transfer was made, his opinion was simply one of several that needed to be sought and did not amount to a veto.[161] Finally, the Court held that additional judges did not have a right to be permanently appointed, although there was a "weightage" in favor of that happening.[162]

The decision in S. P. *Gupta* is significant for what it reveals about Bhagwati's influence on the Court and the extent to which the reorientation of the Court's role could be said to have been consciously directed. In the months preceding this decision, Bhagwati had been involved in a public falling out with Chandrachud over the latter's alleged failure, in his capacity as Chief Justice, to organize a judicial conference to discuss the issues raised by the *Minerva Mills* case.[163] Bhagwati had at the same time himself been heavily criticized for writing a letter to Gandhi congratulating her on her reappointment and bemoaning the slow progress made with her judicial transformation program.[164] In S. P. *Gupta*, Bhagwati was the senior judge, but "violate[d] his own strictures" by declining to hold a conference.[165] The end result of this was a sprawling, 600-page decision in which each of the seven judges wrote separately. If there was a trade-off in S. P. *Gupta*, then, it cannot be attributed to a coordinated strategy on the part of the judges, and certainly not to one that Bhagwati himself directed. Nevertheless, the unintended consequences of the decision were extremely advantageous for the Court. By ceding control of the judicial appointments process to the executive, S. P. *Gupta* bought the Court the time it needed for its PIL and Article 21 doctrines to take effect. When the judicial appointments question returned to

---

[159] Sathe, *Judicial Activism in India* 264. See also Mate, "Public Interest Litigation" 272–3.
[160] Mody, *10 Judgements that Changed India* 171; Austin, *Working a Democratic Constitution* 527.
[161] Mody, *10 Judgements that Changed India* 171.
[162] Austin, *Working a Democratic Constitution* 527.
[163] *Minerva Mills* v. *Union of India* (1981) 1 SCR 206; (1980) 2 SCC 591; AIR 1980 SC 1789.
[164] Austin, *Working a Democratic Constitution* 501.
[165] Ibid 505 and 527.

the Court in 1993,[166] it was accordingly in a much stronger position to assert a controlling role in the process.

A similar effect can be observed in relation to the Court's basic structure doctrine jurisprudence. After the major work done in restoring *Kesavananda* in *Minerva Mills*,[167] this part of the Court's case law fell into relative inactivity. The only other decisions in this area before 1989 were *S. P. Sampath Kumar v. Union of India*[168] and *P. Sambamurthy v. Andhra Pradesh*,[169] neither of which was particularly significant. *Kumar* concerned Article 323A of the Constitution, an Emergency-era amendment ousting the writ jurisdiction of the High Courts in respect of the decisions of administrative tribunals. The Court dealt with this challenge by protecting the independence of the tribunals themselves rather than insisting that the High Courts' writ jurisdiction be preserved. In *Sambamurthy*, the Court struck down a minor constitutional amendment allowing state governments to alter the orders of administrative tribunals. Like *S. P. Gupta*, therefore, these cases point to the way the Court's power grew on the back of the indirect effects of its PIL and Article 21 jurisprudence, rather than by direct assertion.

4.4 THE MODERN ERA: 1989–2015

The Indian Supreme Court's current phase, which began around 1989, has been marked by a distinct change in the ideological orientation of the Bench. In place of the social-egalitarian views that drove much of its case law in the post-Emergency period, Supreme Court judges today are far more likely to hold mainstream liberal or even conservative attitudes. This is evidenced both in the Court's approach to the constitutionality of economic reforms, where it has upheld a range of fairly harsh neoliberal measures, and in its increased concern for environmental rights.[170] The basic form of the law/politics interaction in India, however, has remained unchanged: the Court's legitimacy is still founded on its public support, and the Court still frequently intervenes in public policy to address alleged failures of the democratic system. Rather than signaling progress towards a new equilibrium, therefore, the changes witnessed since 1989 are

---

[166] See discussion of the *Second and Third Judges* cases in Section 4.4 below.

[167] See also the contemporaneously decided case of *Waman Rao* v. *Union of India* (1981) 2 SCC 362; AIR 1981 SC 271 (discussed in Ramachandran, "The Supreme Court and the Basic Structure Doctrine" 122–3).

[168] (1987) 1 SCC 124. See Mate, "Elite Institutionalism" 383.

[169] (1987) 1 SCC 362 discussed in Sathe, *Judicial Activism in India* 88–9.

[170] See discussion below.

best viewed as an incremental adjustment within democratic instrumentalism.

The primary purpose of this section is to substantiate this understanding of the current phase. In doing so, the section provides support for the conjecture in Chapter 2 that democratic instrumentalism, when associated with a deep-seated transformation in constitutional culture rather than short-term strategic or political factors, will likely be impervious to shifts in judicial ideology. The secondary purpose is to investigate the claim, now quite often heard in the local literature, that the Indian Supreme Court's role in national politics, however crucial it might have been in the 1980s in shoring up deficiencies in democratic politics, has today become dysfunctional. Here, the section will seek to show how the problems identified by Indian scholars may be attributed to certain inherent features of democratic instrumentalism.

That there has been some sort of change in the way the Supreme Court operates after 1989 is now generally accepted.[171] That date is said to be significant for two main reasons. First, it marks the advent of coalition politics – the last year in which the Congress Party (and indeed any party, until 2014) was able to govern India on its own. Second, 1989 is identified as the start of a major shift in economic policy, from the state socialism that characterized the period of Congress Party dominance to the free-market strategies that every national government since 1991 has pursued.

Until the Bharatiya Janata Party's victory in 2014, no political party in India had been able to win an overall majority in the Lok Sabha for some thirty years.[172] Instead, from the end of Rajiv Gandhi's prime ministership in 1989, India was governed by two main coalitions: the United Progressive Alliance, with the Congress Party at its center, and the National Democratic Alliance, headed by the BJP. Each of these coalitions consists of a range of regional and caste-based parties, with smaller parties sometimes shifting between the two. Though the BJP in 2014 was able to win an absolute majority in the Lok Sabha in its own right, it decided to keep the NDA coalition together. The main reason for this is that, with just 30 percent of the national vote, the BJP's capacity to hold on to its majority and win future elections is dependent on the

---

[171] See Mate, "Public Interest Litigation" 263; Prashant Bhushan, "Supreme Court and PIL: Changing Perspectives under Liberalization" (2004) 39 *Economic & Political Weekly* 1770; Robinson, "Expanding Judiciaries" 43; Surya Deva, "The Indian Constitution in the Twenty-First Century: The Continuing Quest for Empowerment, Good Governance and Sustainability" in Albert H. Y. Chen (ed.), *Constitutionalism in Asia in the Early Twenty-First Century* (Cambridge: Cambridge University Press, 2014) 343.

[172] The last time this occurred was in 1984, with Rajiv Gandhi's victory following his mother's assassination.

pre-election deals it strikes with its alliance partners. Likewise, the Congress Party's chances of returning to power are dependent on this kind of support.[173]

The shift to neoliberal economic strategies began in all earnest under Narasimha Rao's Congress Party prime ministership in 1991.[174] Before this, however, V. P. Singh, a former member of Rajiv Gandhi's cabinet who was elected as Janata Dal Prime Minister on an anti-corruption ticket in 1989,[175] had shown the electoral importance of sound economic credentials. No party has proposed centralized control of the economy since then. The underlying cause of this consensus, of course, was the triumph of free-market capitalism at the end of the Cold War. The endurance of free-market policies across all subsequent national governments, however, has been a function of the dynamics associated with the BJP's entrance into politics in 1980.[176] Unable to govern on its own without regional support,[177] the BJP has moderated its Hindu nationalism by stressing its economic record in the states it has governed. This was particularly true of the 2014 elections, but it has been part of the BJP's strategy all along.[178] While the Congress Party still emphasizes its commitment to economic intervention on behalf of marginalized groups, it has in practice been forced to compete on the BJP's terrain.

The impact of these two developments on constitutional politics in India was much as one would expect. The fragmentation of electoral politics meant that the Court's independence (at least until 2014) was not tied to its ability to manage its relationship with a single political party. Rather, the Court operated in the political space opened up by robust electoral competition.[179] In practical terms, this meant that the Court's judicial review power was

---

[173] On the dependence of central parties on regional and caste parties, see Deva, "The Indian Constitution in the Twenty-First Century" 345, 349.
[174] Mate, "Elite Institutionalism" 368.
[175] Guha, *India after Gandhi* 596–7.
[176] On the rise of the BJP and the Hindutva movement generally, see Martha Nussbaum, *The Clash Within: Democracy, Religious Violence, and India's Future* (Cambridge, MA: Harvard University Press, 2007).
[177] In the 2014 elections, the BJP won an absolute majority of seats in the Lok Sabha but only 31 percent of the popular vote. Its parliamentary majority was dependent on pre-election voting deals with minor parties. See Eswaran Sridharan, "Behind Modi's Victory" (2014) 25 *Journal of Democracy* 20; Ashutosh Varshney, "Hindu Nationalism in Power" (2014) 25 *Journal of Democracy* 34.
[178] Ibid. See also Alfred Stepan, "India, Sri Lanka, and the Majoritarian Danger" (2015) 26 *Journal of Democracy* 128, 137.
[179] See the discussion in Chapter 2 on the so-called political fragmentation thesis. Mehta, "The Rise of Judicial Sovereignty" 75 argues that the main reason the basic structure doctrine has not been challenged since 1980 is India's "fragmented political system." He suggests this might change in the event that a single party "gain[s] enough parliamentary heft to wield the amendment power."

protected, not by the difficulty of amending the Constitution (for that still occurs on a regular basis[180]), but by the difficulty of amending the Constitution in a way that would fundamentally undermine its independence. After the BJP's election victory in 2014, this part of the dynamic has been changing.[181] In the twenty-five years before that, however, the Court was able to exploit the fragmentation of electoral politics to expand its powers, most notably in the area of judicial appointments.

Likewise, the change in economic policy after 1989 has had the effect that the judges appointed to the Court after 1989 have tended to hold either mainstream liberal or conservative views. With both major coalitions occupying the center of the political spectrum, and elite opinion following the global trend to neoliberalism, the attitudes of the judges towards such issues as the role of the state in the economy, the relative importance of public- versus private-sector corruption, and the balance between environmentalism and economic development, have inevitably drifted rightwards, too. As demonstrated below, this shift is detectable both in the content of the Court's case law and in the sometimes very revealing remarks judges have made about the issues before them. This ideological reorientation, however, has not affected the Court's reasoning style or its interventionist approach to public policy. Rather, the Court has used the procedural rules, doctrines, and remedial powers it developed for purposes of its PIL jurisprudence to serve its new good governance agenda. While not entirely abandoning its commitment to the poor and the marginalized,[182] the Court has tended to favor the interests of the middle class over the interests of less privileged groups when the two conflict.[183]

This shift in the judges' ideological orientation is evident in two main areas: the review of economic policy decisions and environmental rights. Before 1989, the Court's deferential approach in the first area was driven by the judges' ideological identification with the Congress Party's social welfare objectives.[184] Today, the same doctrines that the Court developed to defer to those objectives are used to defer to neoliberal economic restructuring

---

[180] Deva, "The Indian Constitution in the Twenty-First Century" 352 reports that there were nineteen constitutional amendments from January 2000 to January 2012.

[181] See the discussion at the end of this section of the Constitution Ninety-Ninth Amendment Act and various other measures taken to improve judicial accountability mechanisms.

[182] See, for example, *Unni Krishnan* v. *State of AP* (1993) 1 SCC 645 (on the right to basic education).

[183] See Mate, "Elite Institutionalism"; Balakrishnan Rajagopal, "Pro-Human Rights but Anti-Poor? A Critical Evaluation of the Indian Supreme Court from a Social Movement Perspective" (2007) 18 *Human Rights Review* 157, 168.

[184] See for example, *R. K. Garg* v. *Union of India* (1981) 4 SCC 675.

programs. In *BALCO Employees Union v. Union of India*,[185] for example, the
Court applied the rational-basis review standard it had developed in the 1981
Garg case[186] to condone the procedure followed in the privatization of a state-
owned aluminum corporation. The case started when a union representing
employees at the corporation and the government of the state in which its
main business was situated challenged the sale of a 51 percent controlling
share in the corporation to a private party. The principal allegations were that
the business had not been properly valued, that the employees had not been
properly consulted, and that the corporation, given that its business was
situated on tribal land, ought to have been sold to the state government
concerned.[187] The Court dismissed all of these arguments on the grounds
that the decision to privatize the corporation, given its poor economic performance, was rational. While that approach was consistent with the Court's
approach in *Garg*, and with the review standard that many other constitutional
courts would have applied,[188] the Court was not being asked to second-guess
the decision to privatize BALCO itself, but rather to oversee the manner in
which the decision was carried out. The Court's failure to see that distinction,
together with some rather dismissive remarks it made about the intervener in
the case,[189] have been cited as proof of its underlying free-market bias.

    The second set of cases that illustrates the Court's rightwards drift concerns
its enforcement of environmental rights, and particularly its entrance into
such policy areas as pollution control and forest management. While the
Court decided some important environmental rights cases in the 1980s,[190]
this aspect of its case law became more prominent in the 1990s.[191] That on its
own does not signify anything, of course. The poor have as much interest in
clean air and water as anyone else, and the rising number of cases was
a function of the way environmentalist groups took advantage of the Court's

[185]   AIR 2001 SC 350; (2002) 2 SCC 343. See Bhushan, "Supreme Court and PIL" 1770–1; Mate,
       "Elite Institutionalism" 390–3.
[186]   (1981) 4 SCC 675.
[187]   Mate, "Elite Institutionalism."
[188]   The US Supreme Court and South African Constitutional Court, for example.
[189]   Dr B. L. Wadhera, a political scientist, who had often participated in PIL cases in the past,
       applied to join the case. The Court declined Dr Wadhera's application for lack of a sufficient
       connection to case. In the course of its judgment, the Court criticized the abuse of PIL
       procedures (Mate, "Elite Institutionalism" 377).
[190]   See, for example, the *Taj Trapezium Case* (*M. C. Mehta v. Union of India* Writ Petition 13381
       of 1984).
[191]   In addition to the cases discussed in the text, see *Tarun Bharat Sangh v. Union of India* AIR
       1992 SC 514; *Virender Gaur v. State of Haryana* (1995) 2 SCC 577; T. N. *Godavarman
       Thirumulkpad v. Union of India* (1997) 2 SCR 642; *Andhra Pradesh Pollution Control Board
       v. M. V. Nayudu* (1999) AIR SC 812.

PIL doctrines to prosecute their cause. Environmental rights, however, often come into conflict with the interests of the poor and the working class, and it is the way the Court has dealt with this tension that has led some to conclude that it is biased towards the middle class.

One prominent example of this was the *Delhi Vehicle Pollution* case,[192] which concerned the impact of the widespread use of diesel fuel on the quality of the air in New Delhi.[193] After calling for various reports on this issue in the 1980s, the Court started to ratchet up the intrusiveness of its orders in the early 1990s, until in 1998 it finally mandated the conversion of all public transport buses in New Delhi to Compressed Natural Gas (CNG) within a set time frame.[194] The order caused massive disruption to the public transport system, with 75 percent of the bus fleet stranded on pain of being found in contempt.[195] While it could be argued that the Court's firm stance was required to drive a necessary conversion to greener technologies, the time frame the Court set caused great hardship to poor commuters, while leaving middle-class car drivers (who accounted for the bulk of the pollution) largely unaffected. There is also evidence that the change to CNG led to increased public transportation costs, once again mostly affecting the poor.[196]

A similar lack of concern for the poor is evident in the *Almira Patel* slum clearance case.[197] The central issue in this case was the build-up of solid waste in New Delhi, which the Court attributed to the increasing number of slum settlements. Easily accessible data, however, showed, as one would expect, that low-income groups generate significantly less solid waste per capita than high-income groups.[198] The solid-waste buildup should thus properly have been seen as a function of inadequate municipal services and the harsh conditions in which slum-dwellers are forced to live. Apart from its insensitivity to this point, the Court's judgment revealed a lack of understanding for the plight of slum dwellers, likening the provision of alternative accommodation

---

[192] M. C. Mehta v. *Union of India* Writ Petition 13029 of 1985. Though launched in 1985, this case only really gained momentum in the 1990s and thus it is reflective of the Court's new approach.

[193] This discussion draws on Armin Rosencranz and Michael Jackson, "The Delhi Pollution Case: The Supreme Court of India and the Limits of Judicial Power" (2003) 28 *Columbia Journal of Environmental Law* 223 and Lavanya Rajamani, "Public Interest Environmental Litigation in India: Exploring Issues of Access, Participation Equity, Effectiveness, and Sustainability" (2007) 19 *Journal of Environmental Law* 293.

[194] M. C. Mehta v. *Union of India* (1998) 9 SCC 589.

[195] Rajamani, "Public Interest Environmental Litigation" 300.

[196] Ibid 308–9.

[197] *Almira Patel* v. *Union of India* (2000) 2 SCC 166 (discussed in Rajamani, "Public Interest Environmental Litigation" 302 and Mody, *10 Judgments that Changed India* 89).

[198] Rajamani, "Public Interest Environmental Litigation" 302.

to them to rewarding a "pickpocket."[199] While these remarks are the most egregious example of anti-poor bias on the Supreme Court, the fact that the judge who made them rose to such a prominent position says something about the attitudes prevalent on the Bench as a whole.[200]

Despite these evident changes in the social philosophy of the judges who staff the Supreme Court, there has been no major change in the way law and politics interact at the constitutional level. The Court remains a forceful player in national politics and it continues to combine legislative, executive, and judicial functions in a way that defies traditional categorization.[201] Its reasoning style, too, has not changed significantly. Indeed, as discussed in a moment, the Court's tendency to ignore precedent in favor of ad hoc decision-making has, if anything, become more entrenched. At the wider level of Indian constitutional culture, there appears to be no going back to the era when the Court's legitimacy was founded on a plausible claim to the political neutrality of its role. Rather, the idea that judges' social philosophy plays a part in their decisions is now widely discussed and accepted.[202] For all these reasons, it makes sense to think of the latest phase in Indian constitutional politics as amounting, not to a transition to a new regime type, but to an internal adjustment within the legitimation logic of democratic instrumentalism.

That understanding of the current phase provides support for the conceptual elaboration of this regime type in Chapter 2. As conjectured then, because democratic instrumentalism is the product, not of fortuitous political conditions, but of a drawn-out process of constitutional-cultural development, it is relatively impervious to shifts in judicial ideology. Indeed, the essential characteristic of this ideal type is political acceptance of the inevitability of ideologically driven judicial decision-making. The Indian case confirms that this characteristic holds even where the initial transformation to a more instrumentalist conception of law occurs at the instance of an identifiable political ideology. In just the same way that democratic instrumentalism in the US developed on the back of the Warren Court's liberal-progressivism,[203] so

[199] As quoted in Rajamani, "Public Interest Environmental Litigation" 302–3. See also Mody, 10 *Judgments that Changed India* 89.
[200] For a discussion of this issue, see Rajagopal, "Pro-Human Rights but Anti-Poor?" 167–8.
[201] See the discussion of the *Vishaka* case below.
[202] See, for example, Rajabopal, "Pro-Human Rights but Anti-Poor?" 167 ("The social philosophy of the individual judges often determines the outcomes of cases in India (as elsewhere)"); Rajamani, "Public Interest Environmental Litigation" 301–2.
[203] Of the many treatments of this topic, see in particular Mark V. Tushnet (ed.), *The Warren Court in Historical and Political Perspective* (Charlottesville, VA: University of Virginia Press, 1993); Morton J. Horwitz, *The Warren Court and the Pursuit of Justice* (New York: Hill and

too did the emergence of this style of JR regime in India depend on the pro-poor ideological commitments of the post-1977 generation of judges. Once these two ideologically driven transformations had achieved their effects, however, the JR regimes in both cases stabilized and adapted to further changes in judicial ideology without changing their fundamental form. In the American case, the Warren Court's liberal-progressivism gave way to the Burger, Rehnquist, and Roberts Courts' conservative counter-reaction. As a matter of constitutional culture, however, political acceptance of ideological decision-making became, if anything, more entrenched.[204] Much the same thing appears to have happened in India after 1989. The post-Emergency Court's social-egalitarianism has given way to the modern Court's middle-class, liberal-environmentalism without any fundamental change to the way law and politics interact at the constitutional level. Indeed, in both cases, rather than threatening its fundamental form, changes in judicial ideology have ended up reinforcing democratic instrumentalism's legitimation logic.

Stable as it is, the current JR regime has been subject to two interrelated lines of critique. One has to do with the quality of the Court's jurisprudence, the other with the impact of the Court's interventionist role on the quality of India's democracy. Lavanya Rajamani and Arghya Sengupta, for example, have described the Court's current case law as "marked by rhetoric, impreci-sion, and intellectual fuzziness."[205] Pratap Bhanu Mehta, for his part, has charged the judges with engaging in a "jurisprudence of exasperation,"[206] by which he means the substitution of expressions of judicial dissatisfaction with the general state of affairs in India for a coherent constitutional vision. For Mehta, it seems, the problem is not so much the proliferation of mainstream liberal views on the Bench as the absence of any kind of "coherent public philosophy."[207]

Mehta and others have pointed to the institutional origins of this problem in the operation of three-judge benches on a multi-member court.[208] This

Wang, 1998); Lucas A. Powe Jr., *The Warren Court and American Politics* (Cambridge, MA: Harvard University Press, 2000).

[204] There is a vast literature on this. See, for example, James L. Gibson and Gregory Caldeira, "Has Legal Realism Damaged the Legitimacy of the US Supreme Court?" (2011) 45 *Law & Society Review* 195 (arguing that ideological decision-making on the USSC is now legitimate in the eyes of the American public).

[205] See Rajamani and Sengupta, "The Supreme Court" 80.

[206] Pratap Bhanu Mehta, "Can a Jurisprudence of Exasperation Sustain the Court's Authority" *Telegraph*, October 17, 2005.

[207] See Mehta, "Rise of Judicial Sovereignty" 72.

[208] See Mehta, "India's Judiciary: The Promise of Uncertainty" 173; Mate, "Elite Institutionalism" 367; Nick Robinson, "Structure Matters: The Impact of Court Structure

compartmentalization of the Bench, together with the sheer number of cases decided,[209] means that it is virtually impossible for any single judge to keep track of what the others are doing. Freed from the strictures of precedent, judgments tend to focus on doing individualized justice in the case at hand. Under these conditions, it is not surprising that judicial decision-making has been driven by the judges' personal world views. That those views tend to be socially and economically conservative is, in turn, an almost inevitable side-effect of the fact that judges are drawn from the upper echelons of the legal profession. After the *Second and Third Judges* cases,[210] in which the Court took over control of the judicial appointments process from the executive, the Supreme Court has essentially had the power to reproduce itself. The predictable result of this has been the reorientation of the Court's case law in line with the ideological attitudes of the Supreme Court bar.

The second line of critique relates to the impact of the Court's intervention-ism on the overall health of the democratic system. The nub of this point is the way the Court has taken over legislative and executive functions – thus going beyond the ordinary separation of powers. The best-known example of this was the Court's decision in *Vishaka* v. *State of Rajasthan*,[211] in which it issued detailed guidelines on the prevention of sexual harassment based on the Convention on the Elimination of All Forms of Discrimination against Women. More than ten years later, the Lok Sabha passed the Protection of Women against Sexual Harassment at the Workplace Act.[212] This statute might very well not have been enacted without the Court's decision. But the question remains whether the Court should have taken on what amounted to a legislative function.

Beyond the standard normative objections to this practice, there are ques-tions about whether the Court has the capacity to sustain the kind of inter-ventions it has attempted, particularly where it has taken over whole areas of regulation, such as the management of forests.[213] These cases inevitably take up immense amounts of time and resources. The Court has sought to counter-act this by employing experts and commissions. But it is not merely a resources problem. It is also, as Balakrishnan Rajagopal has observed, the fact that the

on the Indian and US Supreme Courts" (2013) 61 *American Journal of Comparative Law* 173. The total number of judges on the Supreme Court at the time of writing was 31.

[209] At the end of 2011, there were 56,383 cases pending in the Supreme Court (Deva, "The Indian Constitution in the Twenty-First Century" 351).

[210] *Supreme Court Advocates-on-Record Association* v. *Union of India* (1993) 4 SCC 441; *In re Special Reference No. 1 of 1998* (1998) 7 SCC 739; AIR 1999 SC 1.

[211] AIR 1997 SC 3011; (1997) 6 SCC 241.

[212] Deva, "The Indian Constitution in the Twenty-First Century" 358.

[213] The leading case is *Tarun Bharat Sangh* v. *Union of India* AIR 1992 SC 514.

Court, in playing the role of "an instrument of governance," rather than an "institution of justice," inevitably gets drawn into "the logic of the state."[214] This tends to reduce the usefulness of the Court to social movements and facilitates its getting sucked into whatever ideological model of development is currently being pursued.[215]

Allied to this problem is the incapacitating effect on the political branches of the Court's interventions. One of the criticisms of the *Delhi Vehicle Pollution* case, for example, is that the Court "usurp[ed] the authority of the existing pollution control authorities to fulfil their duties independently."[216] The pretext for Court's intervention was that the legislature was prevented from moving away from diesel by its allegiance to certain interest groups. The Court's intervention in the matter, however, raised problems of its own – not the least of which was a classic Fullerian polycentricity problem of reconciling the many competing interests involved in the policy choice.[217] As much as the Court's decisions succeeded in getting around legislative inaction, its proposed solution was not necessarily better than the one the legislature would have arrived at. As Jackson and Rosencranz argue: "Some of the roadblocks to CNG implementation could have been avoided, or at least minimized, had the conversion been originally mandated through the normal legislative process ... [T]he Court's action seems likely to impede capacity building in the pollution control agencies, and thereby to compromise the development of sustained environmental management in India."[218]

Clearly, where the Court enters a policy area and exercises supervisory jurisdiction it runs the risk that it may prevent the democratic branches from performing their role properly. Although that kind of intervention could still qualify as a legitimate exercise of judicial power on Waldronian grounds,[219] from a more sociological perspective, it is doubtful whether it contributes in the long run to the overall health of the democratic system. Almost by definition, curial intervention of this sort *prevents* restoration of proper democratic functioning by becoming a kind of crutch on which the democratic system learns to depend. To a certain extent, this sort of dependency-effect can be addressed by wise decision-making – by judges choosing

---

[214] Rajagopal, "Pro-Human Rights but Anti-Poor?" 159.
[215] Ibid 166.
[216] Rosencranz and Jackson, "The Delhi Pollution Case" 225.
[217] Lon L. Fuller, "The Forms and Limits of Adjudication" (1978) 92 *Harvard Law Review* 353.
[218] Rosencranz and Jackson, "The Delhi Pollution Case" 254.
[219] Jeremy Waldron, "The Core of the Case against Judicial Review" (2006) 115 *Yale Law Journal* 1346 (arguing that judicial review is morally justified where democracy is dysfunctional in some way).

remedies that prompt rather than usurp democratic action.[220] In general, however, it is fair to say that this has not been the Indian Supreme Court's approach. Rather, the Court has tended to supplant the role of the democratic branches in those policy areas in which it has chosen to intervene.[221]

The Indian experience in this way provides support for the normative worry about democratic instrumentalism that was tentatively offered in Chapter 2. As argued then, the problem with this JR regime at a conceptual level is that the Court's detachment from the rhetoric of legal constraint is a detachment in the end from democratic accountability. The political conditions and constitutional-cultural adaptations that support the Court's forceful interventions in policy under this regime free it from the need to link its decisions to past democratic commitments. Rather, the Court's legitimacy is tied to popular satisfaction with the substantive outcomes of the cases it decides. While such a regime can prove very stable, it almost inevitably comes at the price of the proper functioning of democratic politics.

In the Indian case, the negative impacts of the Court's interventionism on the quality of democracy have until now gone largely unchecked because the Court's decisions have proven popular and the political branches have lacked the means to do anything about it. There are some signs, however, that this situation may be changing. At the level of elite public opinion, there is growing discontent with the Court's interventionist style. One sign of this has been the long-running attempt to improve judicial accountability mechanisms. The attempt started with the Judges (Declaration of Assets and Liabilities) Bill of 2009, which was tabled in the Rajya Sabha, but then withdrawn following "fiery debate."[222] The Court was sufficiently shaken, however, to decide of its own accord to put details of the judges' assets and liabilities on its website.[223]

Since then, the Assets and Liabilities Bill has been subsumed under the Judicial Standards and Accountability Bill 136 of 2010. In addition to the provision on declaration of assets, the Standards Bill proposes the establishment of a National Judicial Oversight Committee and a Complaints Scrutiny Panel for the Supreme Court and each High Court.[224] As of 2015, this Bill had

---

[220]   See Katharine G. Young, *Constituting Economic and Social Rights* (Oxford: Oxford University Press, 2012).

[221]   See, for example, the *Vishaka* case discussed above.

[222]   Rajamani and Sengupta, "The Supreme Court" 93.

[223]   *The Times of India*, "Supreme Court judges to disclose assets" August 27, 2009.

[224]   See Deva, "The Indian Constitution in the Twenty-First Century" 360–1; Nilesh Sinha, "Just Deserts or Honor at Stake? India's Pending Judicial Standards and Accountability Bill" (February 2, 2013) available at: www.iconnectblog.com/2013/02/just-deserts-or-honor-at-stake-indias-pending-judicial-standards-and-accountability-bill.

still not been passed, and it seems now to have been overtaken by the debate around judicial appointments. But it enjoys cross-party support (having been introduced by the UPA and further prosecuted by NDA) and it thus seems inevitable that it will eventually be passed.

The most recent development was the Constitution (Ninety-Ninth Amendment) Act of 2014, which provided for the establishment of a National Judicial Appointments Commission.[225] The Commission was set to replace the collegium system for judicial appointments established through the *Second and Third Judges Cases*.[226] It is that system that has come to symbolize the Court's power, but which also lies at the center of allegations that it has become too powerful. Under the proposed new regime, Supreme Court judges would have been appointed by a Commission consisting of the Chief Justice, two other Supreme Court judges, the Union Minister in charge of Law and Justice, and two eminent persons appointed by a cross-party committee, at least one of whom would have had to have been from a socially marginalized group.[227] Rather than an attack on the Court's independence, the establishment of the Commission could be seen as a legitimate attempt to rein the Court in and make it more accountable. Nothing in the amendment was particularly alarming from a comparative perspective. The Court, however, struck down the 99th Amendment as a violation of the basic structure doctrine, and particularly its guarantee of judicial independence.[228]

4.5 CONCLUSION

Developments in India after 1977 show that constitutional judges, with sustained political backing, may sometimes play a leading role in the transformation of societal conceptions of the law/politics relation. As such, the Indian case provides an interesting contrast to the Australian. As we saw in Chapter 3, the Australian High Court's attempt in the 1980s to take on a more robust role in enforcing implied political values was frustrated by the difficulty of abandoning the legalist posture on which the mid-century acceptance of its judicial

---

[225] Section 3 of the Act inserted a new article 124A in the Constitution to this effect.
[226] *Supreme Court Advocates-on-Record Association* v. *Union of India* (1993) 4 SCC 441 and *In re Special Reference No 1 of 1998* (1998) 7 SCC 739; AIR 1999 SC 1.
[227] See proposed Article 124A(1) as introduced by section 3 of the Amendment Act.
[228] *Supreme Court Advocates-on-Record-Association* v. *Union of India* (2016) 4 SCC 1. For a comprehensive discussion and critique of this decision, see Rehan Abeyratne, "Upholding Judicial Supremacy in India: The NJAC Judgment in Comparative Perspective" (2017) 49 *George Washington International Law Review* 569.

review function had been premised. The Indian story, however, suggests that JR regimes do not always exert this inertial force. Examining the reasons for the contrasting outcomes in these two cases might help to clarify the underlying causal mechanism.

The comparison between the two cases must begin with attention to the precise circumstances in which the Indian Supreme Court's new understanding of its mandate began – the immediate aftermath of the Emergency, when memories of the Court's legalism-driven refusal to resist the suspension of *habeas corpus* were still fresh. Seen in that context, cases like *Maneka Gandhi* presented the Court with a time-sensitive opportunity to refashion both its review function under Article 21 and the way it went about justifying its decisions. In strategic terms, one could say that the judges, realizing that the public mood was behind the Court's playing a more interventionist role, calculated that the legal legitimacy costs of a change in reasoning style would be offset by a concomitant rise in public support. But that way of putting things, as is often the case with the strategic approach, relies too much on a conscious awareness of these factors. Better, then, simply to say that *Maneka Gandhi* was decided at a time when the inherited tradition of legalism had been discredited, and when the Court had an opportunity to drive the development of a new conception of the law/politics relation.

That explanation still leaves the question of why the Court chose to adopt the particular conception that it did. There is some evidence that the judges who sat in *Maneka Gandhi*, including Bhagwati and Krishna Iyer, were more exposed than their predecessors had been to American influence.[229] That would account for the use of a more substantive reasoning style. It is also possible that this was better suited to reorienting the Court's doctrines in the social-egalitarian direction that Bhagwati and Krishna Iyer wanted them to go. By facilitating a contextual reading of the Constitution, the approach adopted in *Maneka Gandhi* supported the Court's later expansion of the right to life in Article 21.[230] That effect only came later, however, and it is thus again hard to say that Bhagwati and Krishna Iyer consciously intended it. The immediate doctrinal challenge in *Maneka Gandhi* was to get around the *Gopalan* decision. The simpler explanation is thus that the substantive style was chosen

---

[229] Dhavan, "Borrowed Ideas"; Manoj Mate, "The Origins of Due Process in India" 253ff.

[230] That change might equally well have been effected by endorsing the amendment to Article 31C in *Minerva Mills*, of course, but Bhagwati was there alone in upholding that provision. See Austin, *Working a Democratic Constitution* 503–4 (explaining how Bhagwati first declined to join the rest of the judges in issuing the order in *Minerva Mills*, and then wrote a separate opinion dissenting on the Article 31C point).

because it allowed the Court to distinguish that case and treat the fundamental rights as an "integrated scheme."[231]

Whatever prompted the change in reasoning style, the crucial point is that it quickly became authoritative. In case after case, the Court used the methods it had adopted in *Maneka Gandhi* to devise new doctrines. In the process, legalism gave way to its ideological opposite – a conception of constitutional adjudication as deeply immersed in politics. The interesting question in view of this experience is not why the Court switched to a more substantive style of reasoning, but why this style took hold so quickly and helped to trigger such a fundamental transformation in societal conceptions of the law/politics relation.

The answer to this question, this chapter has suggested, lies in the way the Court's doctrines interacted with the political environment in which they were developed. Of all the commentators on the Court's rehabilitation, Manoj Mate has gone the furthest towards explaining this process. Drawing on Alec Stone Sweet's work on the judicialization of politics in Europe, he has described the way in which the Indian Supreme Court's PIL doctrines enabled it to "accrete power in a cyclical, path-dependent 'chakra'."[232] By "strategically" developing its PIL jurisprudence, Mate argues, the Court was able to build its public support. This in turn allowed it to increase its participation in "governance" to the point where it became "indispensable to ruling elites." Whether indispensable or not, he concludes, the Court's public support made it "increasingly difficult to attack."[233]

Mate's analysis is convincing, save for his attribution to the judges of a conscious awareness of the cyclical process they were triggering.[234] While certainly sensitive to the Court's institutional situation, the judges who contributed to the construction of the Court's PIL doctrines could not have known exactly what the effect of these doctrines would be. Their primary motivation, in any event, was not to restore the Court's reputation for its own sake but to interpret the Constitution in a way that made it relevant to the poor. That motivation was a composite of their personal ideological convictions and their sincere beliefs as judges that the interpretation they were offering was

---

[231] *Maneka Gandhi* (note 124 above).
[232] See Mate, "Public Interest Litigation" 284, referring to Martin Shapiro and Alec Stone Sweet, *On Law Politics and Judicialization* (New York: Oxford University Press, 2002) 184–208. See also Alec Stone Sweet, *Governing with Judges: Constitutional Politics in Europe* (New York: Oxford University Press, 2000).
[233] Mate, "Public Interest Litigation" 286.
[234] Ibid 285 ("Judicialization allows courts to act strategically in expanding their role in governance and policy making through the gradual and incremental process of case-by-case dispute resolution").

a plausible understanding of the Indian constitutional project. The fact that their doctrines built the Court's public support was a side-effect of their determination to pursue this interpretation rather than its primary goal.[235]

In other circumstances, the power-accreting trajectory that the Court's PIL doctrines triggered might have triggered a political backlash. The Court was, after all, transparently taking over functions traditionally reserved for the political branches. Bhagwati and Krishna Iyer, however, were pursuing the agenda that Indira Gandhi in a sense had appointed them to pursue. She thus had no reason to rein them in. During the crucial period between 1981 and 1984, she was also preoccupied with various demands for greater regional autonomy, including the violent political uprising in the Punjab that eventually claimed her life.[236] The power-accreting trajectory the Court's PIL doctrines triggered accordingly met with little resistance. In an "iterative process,"[237] those doctrines increased its public support, which in turn emboldened the Court to expand them and intervene ever more assertively in public policy.

To Mate's observations on this point must be added the profound effect that the Court's new understanding of its mandate had on Indian constitutional culture. As the Court's new understanding became entrenched and worked its external effects, societal conceptions of the relationship between law and politics changed. What had seemed unthinkable before – the ideologically motivated intervention by the Court in matters of public policy – now seemed to be an essential part of its legitimate role in making the Constitution meaningful to ordinary Indians. In this way, the Court's new understanding triggered, not just a power-accreting trajectory, but also a fundamental transformation in the way law and politics interacted at the constitutional level. With the Court's independence safeguarded by the twin effects of its public support and the Congress Party's disinclination to attack it, the Court was free to pursue its own ideologically motivated understanding of constitutional justice. As the 1980s progressed, this approach became accepted as the natural order of things, making it independent of both short-term political factors and changes in the ideology that informed the Court's decisions.

---

[235] This is why it is somewhat misleading to describe the Court's PIL case law as amounting to a form of "judicial populism" (Upendra Baxi, *The Indian Supreme Court and Politics* 121–248; Baxi, "Taking Suffering Seriously" 107, 111–13). That may be an accurate description of Indira Gandhi's political style, but judges like Bhagwati and Krishna Iyer were committed to improving the situation of the poor as an end in itself.

[236] See Guha, *India after Gandhi* 552–70.

[237] Mate, "Public Interest Litigation" 285.

Kesavananda was the centerpiece of this new democratic instrumentalist regime. While *Minerva Mills* had affirmed the basic structure doctrine, *Kesavananda* was always the more important of the two cases. Its ideational power, as noted previously, was that it was vague about the exact content of the doctrine. This meant that it could serve as a kind of shorthand for the Court's wide-ranging role. With its legitimacy no longer tied to its strict adherence to the written Constitution, the Court was free to intervene in any public policy issue that could plausibly be said to implicate the Constitution's vision for a just society. Unlike the democratic legalist regime that had prevailed under Nehru, this was not a case of the Court's claim to neutrality legitimating the democratic legislation it left untouched. Rather, it was a case of the dysfunctionality of democratic politics giving the Court the space to operate, and the Court's interventions coming to serve both the judges' interest in influencing public policy and the public's interest in having a powerful Court that could make up for some of the failings of representative institutions.

While undoubtedly an improvement on the situation that had pre-vailed before the Emergency, the problem with this new JR regime was that its stability depended on the Court's decisions appealing directly to popular sentiment. That aspect undermined the mediating role of the people's representatives and more formal lines of democratic accountability.[238] With the ordinary restraints of the traditional separa-tion of powers gone, and the political branches unable to rein the Court in because of its public support, the Court's power grew essentially unchecked. Worse than this, the Court's interventions in public policy had a distorting effect in as much as they diverted attention away from the underlying causes of the democratic dysfunctions the Court was addressing.

These perverse side-effects of the new JR regime have only worsened with time. As the literature on the Court's post-1989 case law shows, its continued interventions in public policy have undermined the capacity of representative institutions to play their proper role in the constitu-tional system. This is particularly true of the Court's environmental rights decisions, where the Court has taken over whole areas of govern-ance, but it is also true of other areas of law as well. As vital as the Court's role appears to be in curing democratic deficiencies, the Court's interventions have also produced democratic pathologies of their own. The recent attempts to reform the judicial appointments process and to

---

[238] See Mehta, "The Rise of Judicial Sovereignty" 80.

institute better mechanisms for judicial accountability should be seen in that light. While there is always the possibility that such mechanisms might be used to curtail judicial independence, they are arguably a necessary correction aimed at returning the Indian constitutional system to a more appropriate balance between curial power and democratic politics.

5

The Postcolonial Adaptation of Authoritarian Legalism in Zimbabwe

On May 31, 2013, the newly established Zimbabwe Constitutional Court decided an application brought by a concerned voter alleging that the country's then long-serving President, Robert Mugabe, was in breach of his constitutional duties for failing to set an election date within the prescribed period.[1] The Court upheld the application in a split decision, with six of the nine judges signing on to Chief Justice Godfrey Chidyausiku's majority judgment. The two provisions at the heart of the case – ss 58 and 63 of the 1979 Zimbabwe Constitution – stipulated that, in the event that Parliament was automatically dissolved by reason of the expiry of its five-year term, the next election should be held within four months, on a date determined by the President by proclamation.[2] The majority judgment, trumpeting its commitment to modern, purposive methods of interpretation, dismissed as absurd the idea that the Constitution's drafters could have intended that Zimbabwe should function without a Parliament for so long. Instead, Chidyausiku CJ

---

[1] *Mawarire v. Mugabe NO & Others* (2013) ZWCC 1 (accessible at www.zimlii.org). The case was heard under the "former" Zimbabwe Constitution (i.e., the 1979 Lancaster House Constitution as it stood prior to the 2013 amendments). Although the effective date for the commencement of the new Constitution was May 22, 2013, a provision in a Schedule to the new Constitution provided for the suspension of the provisions relating to the timing of the first elections in favor of the former Constitution. For an illuminating discussion of the *Mawarire* case, see Gift Manyatera and Chengetai Hamadziripi, "Electoral Law, the Constitution, and Democracy in Zimbabwe: A Critique of *Jealousy Mbizvo Mawarire v. Robert Mugabe NO and 4 Others* CCZ 1/13" (2014) 1 *Midlands State University Law Review* 72.

[2] Section 58(1) of the 1980 Constitution provided (1) that "[a] general election shall be held on such day or days within a period not exceeding four months after the issue of a proclamation dissolving Parliament under section 63(7) or, as the case may be, the dissolution of Parliament under section 63(4) as the President may, by proclamation in the *Gazette*, fix." Section 63(4) provided for the automatic dissolution of Parliament after five years and s 63(2) for the dissolution of Parliament at any time by the President. In the latter event, s 63(7) provided that the dissolution should take effect on the day before the elections as determined by s 58(1).

held, ss 58 and 63 should be read as requiring the President to authorize the holding of the next election on the day immediately following the automatic dissolution of Parliament. This he could do by issuing a proclamation to that effect four months *in advance* of Parliament's automatic dissolution. Since performance of that constitutional obligation had become impossible, the election should be held as soon as possible after the end of Parliament's term on June 29, 2013, and in any event no later than July 31, 2013.[3]

Speaking through his lawyer, President Mugabe gracefully "accepted" the Constitutional Court's decision.[4] Any notion that this was a Mandela-like act of political statesmanship, however, needs to take account of the fact that Mugabe and his political party, ZANU-PF, had the most to gain from an early election. In the five years preceding the Court's decision, Zimbabwe had been ruled by an Inclusive Government consisting of the main opposition party, the MDC-T, a smaller breakaway opposition party, the MDC-M, and ZANU-PF. This arrangement followed the signing of a Global Political Agreement (GPA) in September 2008 in terms of which these three parties undertook to resolve the political deadlock resulting from the violence-marred elections of March-June that year. According to the GPA, the 2013 elections had to be held under conditions of equal competition between all political parties. Independent observers were of the view that this requirement could not be met within the expedited period mandated by the Constitutional Court's decision.[5] It was clear, therefore, that the decision, while appearing to reprimand the President for failing to fulfil his constitutional duties, in fact gave him precisely what he wanted – a watertight reason to override the GPA and have the polls held at a time when conditions for free and fair elections were not yet in place. Indeed, it was widely believed that the applicant in the case, Jealousy Mawarire, was not, as he claimed, a concerned voter, but in fact an agent of the ruling party who had brought the case on its behalf and for its benefit.[6]

[3] In their dissents, Malaba DCJ and Patel JA held that ss 58 and 63 plainly conferred on the President the discretion to fix an election date at any time within four months after the automatic dissolution of Parliament. This interpretation, they argued, did not lead to an absurd result given that there are several democratic countries in which elections are held well after the dissolution of Parliament. Ibid 27–45 and 45–51.
[4] "Polls by July 31, Mugabe ordered" *Daily News* (June 1, 2013).
[5] International Crisis Group, "Zimbabwe's Elections: Mugabe's Last Stand" *Africa Briefing* 95 (July 29, 2013).
[6] Brian Raftopoulos, "The 2013 Elections in Zimbabwe: The End of an Era" (2013) 39 *Journal of Southern African Studies* 971, 976; Jason Moyo, "Mugabe outwits Tsvangirai on election date" *Mail & Guardian* (June 7, 2013) available at http://mg.co.za/article/2013-06-07-00-mugabe-outwits-tsvangirai; "Expert rips into Chidyausiku judgment" *News Day* (June 6, 2013) (reporting on analysis of the *Mawarire* case by Derek Matyszak).

After initially insisting that the GPA's requirements for the holding of free and fair elections should be met, the Southern African Development Community (SADC), the regional body that had helped to broker the agreement, announced on June 15, 2015, that the Constitutional Court's decision should be treated as binding. While the parties might try to "engage" the Court to secure an extension of the election date, its Executive Secretary said, SADC "would respect the Court's decision if the appeal fails."[7] At the same time, the Chair of the African Union (AU) announced that the rule of law required adherence to the decision.[8] Those two statements by the regional organizations most closely involved in monitoring the Zimbabwe political conflict ended any real prospect that the elections would be delayed.[9]

In the ensuing "harmonized elections" of July 31, 2013, ZANU-PF was duly returned to government with two thirds of the parliamentary seats.[10] Mugabe at the same time retained the presidency with 61 percent of the vote.[11] Though the size of ZANU-PF's election victory was somewhat surprising, analysts agree that it was not solely the product of vote rigging or intimidation.[12] In the four years of Inclusive Government, much had changed. The MDC, already split at the time of the GPA between its Morgan Tsvangirai (MDC-T) and Arthur Mutambara (MDC-M) factions, had descended into further infighting.[13] Tsvangirai himself, following the death of his wife in 2009, had had a string of romantic relationships that had undermined his moral stature among socially conservative Zimbabweans.[14] At a structural level, the

---

7   Raftopoulos, "The 2013 Elections in Zimbabwe" 977.
8   Ibid.
9   ZANU-PF did bring a further application to the Court for an extension that was "designed to fail" (ibid).
10 ZANU-PF won 159 of the 210 contested House of Assembly seats and 37 of the 60 contested Senate seats.
11 The figures for Mugabe's main rivals were Tsvangirai on 34 percent and Ncube just under 3 percent.
12 In addition to the literature discussed in the main text, see Phillan Zamchiya, "The MDC-T's (Un)Seeing Eye in Zimbabwe's 2013 Harmonised Elections: A Technical Knockout" (2013) 39 *Journal of Southern African Studies* 955 (arguing that the MDC-T made several strategic errors in its election preparations, including ignoring technical advice and failing to resolve internal rifts); Blessing-Miles Tendi, "Robert Mugabe's 2013 Presidential Election Campaign" (2013) 39 *Journal of Southern African Studies* 963 (arguing that Mugabe ran a slick and authoritative 2013 presidential campaign); and Adrienne LeBas, "The Perils of Power Sharing" (2014) 25 *Journal of Democracy* 52 (arguing that participation in the GPA weakened the MDC-T).
13 Raftopoulos, "The 2013 Elections in Zimbabwe" 984.
14 Petina Gappah, "Morgan Tsvangirai's messy love life is a gift to his enemies" *The Guardian* (September 20, 2012); LeBas, "The Perils of Power Sharing" 63; Julia Gallagher, "The Battle for Zimbabwe in 2013: From Polarisation to Ambivalence" (2015) 53 *Journal of Modern African Studies* 27, 41.

economic shifts triggered by Zimbabwe's Fast-Track Land Reform Program and the opening up of the mining sector to informal participation had created a new, more loyal ZANU-PF constituency.[15] On another view, the prospect of further political violence should ZANU-PF again be threatened at the polls persuaded many voters to prioritize political stability over their true democratic preferences.[16] Whatever the real reason, Zimbabwe, after four years of Inclusive Government, returned to the post-independence status quo, albeit this time under a new Constitution that had been adopted in February 2013 as part of the political reconstruction process.

The events of June and July 2013 illustrate in microcosm the way in which ZANU-PF has been able to use a potent mixture of revolutionary nationalist ideology, democratic form, naked political violence, and selective respect for judicial independence to resist threats to its authoritarian rule since 1980. ZANU-PF's deployment of these four devices has for the most part been remarkably consistent. There has thus never been a period when political violence could be said to have been completely off the agenda. Starting in 1983–7, with the *Gukurahundi* massacres that targeted supporters of the main opposition party, PF-ZAPU,[17] violence has marked every election since then.[18] Violence was also used in the suppression of student protests in the late 1980s, the farm invasions of early 2000, and the urban-slum clearance operation known as *Murambatsvina* ("clear out the trash") in 2005. All this time ZANU-PF claimed to be acting as the rightful custodian of Zimbabwe's national liberation project, with opponents demonized as stooges of the white minority or Britain and as lacking in liberation war credentials.[19] And all this time ZANU-PF sought endorsement at the ballot box, preferring to rig elections and intimidate opposition party supporters over dispensing with the holding of elections altogether.

One element in the mix of strategies has shown more variation, however, and that is the way in which law has been used to serve authoritarian ends. Focusing just on that issue, there have been four distinct phases since independence. During the first and longest, from 1980 until a series of overt attacks

[15]   Raftopoulos, "The 2013 Elections in Zimbabwe."
[16]   Gallagher, "The Battle for Zimbabwe in 2013."
[17]   See the Legal Resources Foundation and the Catholic Commission for Justice and Peace in Zimbabwe, "Breaking the Silence, Building True Peace: A Report on the Disturbances in Matabeleland and the Midlands 1980 to 1988" (1997).
[18]   Daniel Compagnon, *A Predictable Tragedy: Robert Mugabe and the Collapse of Zimbabwe* (Philadelphia, PA: University of Pennsylvania Press, 2011) 47; Human Rights Watch, "'Bullets for Each of You': State-Sponsored Violence since Zimbabwe's March 29 Elections" (June 2008) 11–4.
[19]   Compagnon, *A Predictable Tragedy* 53.

on the judiciary in 2000, the judiciary enjoyed a measure of independence and played an occasionally effective role in upholding constitutional rights. So much so that a presidential amnesty had to be deployed in April 1988 to pardon the perpetrators of the *Gukurahundi* massacres, some of whom had been arraigned before the courts and convicted.[20] From February 2000, however, when a ZANU-PF-drafted Constitution was decisively rejected at a national referendum,[21] there was a concerted campaign of intimidation against the judiciary. On November 24, 2000, a group of liberation war veterans invaded the Supreme Court.[22] In February 2001, Chief Justice Gubbay was forced to resign and other Supreme Court judges were told that their safety could not be guaranteed.[23] It was at this time that Chidyausiku, a ZANU-PF loyalist, was appointed as Chief Justice of the Supreme Court with an apparent brief to reverse the most inconvenient of its decisions, particularly on land reform.[24] Any pretense that the judiciary was independent was dropped at this stage, with ZANU-PF ruling though a combination of electoral manipulation, nationalist rhetoric, and brute force. During this period, the country descended into economic and political chaos, with rampant inflation, corrupt government, and massive political violence eventually leading to the signing of the GPA in 2008.[25] After five years of Inclusive Government, ZANU-PF regained control of the political system through the means just explained. From this point, the judiciary again began to assert its independence, with Chidyausiku CJ himself handing several seemingly bold human rights decisions.[26]

   This chapter examines the reasons behind these fluctuations in the use of law as a legitimating device in Zimbabwe. Its starting assumption is that ZANU-PF, notwithstanding the holding of regular elections, has never been committed to multiparty democracy, and that Zimbabwe should accordingly be classified throughout the period in question as an authoritarian state. Indeed, Zimbabwe is a quintessential example of a state in which a legitimating ideology of revolutionary nationalism substitutes for a genuine commitment to free and fair elections. What has fluctuated instead in Zimbabwe has been ZANU-PF's willingness to deploy law in the overall

---

[20] Clemency Order 1 of April 18, 1988 (cited in Compagnon, *A Predictable Tragedy* 290 n 39).
[21] Compagnon, *A Predictable Tragedy* 47, 55 identifies February 2000 as the critical turning point.
[22] This episode is discussed in Section 5.3.2.
[23] The High Court was raided on November 24, 2000. See Section 5.3.2.
[24] Discussed in Section 5.3.2.
[25] See Section 5.4.
[26] These are discussed in Section 5.5.

process of legitimation. Before 2000, that willingness was driven in part by a desire for international recognition, in part by the difficulty of amending the independence Constitution, and in part by certain continuities between the way law was used as a legitimating device before independence and its deployment thereafter. On being threatened by a credible electoral alternative in 2000, however, ZANU-PF immediately moved to curtail judicial independence in its bid for survival. While this experience illustrates how quickly an authoritarian legalist regime can descend into pure instrumentalism, it also shows how unstable the latter type of regime may be. Without the legitimating cover of a nominally independent judiciary, ZANU-PF survived just eight years before being forced to the negotiating table. That the negotiations proved to be a route back to authoritarian legalism, rather than a stepping stone to democratic constitutional government, is attributable to the hold that this style of regime has had on Zimbabwean constitutional culture and to Mugabe's skill in exploiting the conditions for its restabilization.

The chapter starts with an introduction to constitutional politics in Zimbabwe, concentrating on aspects of the preindependence situation that have continued to exert an influence after 1980. It then analyzes each of the phases just mentioned, giving reasons in each case for concluding that a distinct conception of the law/politics relation could be said to have stabilized, and examining the reasons behind the collapse of the identified conception in each case. A concluding section summarizes the comparative lessons that the Zimbabwe case teaches and the contribution that it makes to the refinement of the typological theory in Chapter 2.

5.1 LAW AND POLITICS IN ZIMBABWE BEFORE INDEPENDENCE

British control of what was then known as Southern Rhodesia was secured in 1896–7 with the violent suppression of the *First Chimurenga* (resistance war). Between then and 1923, the territory was administered by the British South Africa Company under a royal charter. It was granted self-government by Britain in 1923.[27] White colonial settlement from the 1900s was accompanied by large-scale uncompensated expropriation of indigenous land rights, with two thirds of the African population forced into "reserves" by 1924.[28] The Land Apportionment Act of 1931 and its successor, the Land Tenure Act of 1970,

---

[27] Under the Southern Rhodesia (Annexation) Order in Council of 1923. See G. N. Barrie, "Rhodesian UDI – an Unruly Horse" (1968) 1 *Comparative and International Law Journal of Southern Africa* 110, 110.

[28] Roger Southall, *Liberation Movements in Power: Party & State in Southern Africa* (Pietermaritzburg: University of KwaZulu-Natal Press, 2013) 23.

allocated half of the land surface to whites, including nearly all of the viable agricultural land.[29] White settlement accelerated after World War II, but never reached the levels that it did in South Africa.[30] When the African decolonization process started in the 1950s, the settler regime in Southern Rhodesia was accordingly more vulnerable to calls for black majority rule than its larger neighbor to the south. In 1962, when Britain tried to force the issue,[31] the conservative Rhodesian Front, in an all-white election, defeated the United Federal Party, which had in turn ousted its relatively liberal leader, Garfield Todd, in 1958. In 1965, the Rhodesian Front government under Prime Minister Ian Smith issued a Unilateral Declaration of Independence from Britain, setting the country on the path to international isolation and guerrilla war.

ZANU-PF's political predecessor, the Zimbabwe African People's Union (ZAPU), was founded in 1961 with Joshua Nkomo as its first President. At this point, the first guerrilla recruits were sent abroad for military training.[32] Nkomo himself, however, distanced himself from their activities and was criticized for being too moderate and mainly interested in international diplomacy.[33] In 1963, the Zimbabwe African National Union (ZANU) was formed as a more radical and militant alternative to ZAPU.[34] Robert Mugabe became ZANU's first Secretary General, serving under Ndabaningi Sithole as President. Mugabe, Sithole, and Nkomo were all detained by the Rhodesian Front government for eleven years between 1964 and 1974. In 1974, while still in prison, Sithole was controversially deposed and Mugabe elected President of ZANU by fellow detainees.[35] Mugabe was shortly afterwards released from prison as part of a détente process initiated by South African Prime Minister B. J. Vorster and Zambian President Kenneth Kaunda.[36] In March 1975, Mugabe's main rival for the leadership of ZANU, Herbert Chitepo, was assassinated. No direct evidence of Mugabe's involvement in the assassination was ever produced, although a commission of inquiry established by Kaunda found that the assassination had been ordered by a group in ZANU high

[29] Ibid 24.
[30] Ibid 28 (stating that in 1975 the ratio was 1:20 white to black compared to 1:5 in South Africa); Norma J. Kriger, *Zimbabwe's Guerrilla War: Peasant Voices* (Cambridge: Cambridge University Press, 1992) 1 (giving figures of 275,000 whites and 5 million Africans in the early 1970s).
[31] Southall, *Liberation Movements in Power* 20.
[32] Ibid 37.
[33] Ibid 37–8.
[34] Ibid 38.
[35] Compagnon, *A Predictable Tragedy* 12; Southall, *Liberation Movements in Power* 46.
[36] Southall, *Liberation Movements in Power* 46.

command aligned to Mugabe.[37] Mugabe's leadership of ZANU was eventually confirmed in 1977 after an attempt to unify ZIPRA and ZANLA under a single command failed.[38]

The 1963 ZAPU-ZANU split was not just about Nkomo's allegedly too moderate leadership style. It also marked an ethnic division in the two liberation movements, with ZAPU predominantly consisting of isiNdebele speakers from the southwestern part of the country and ZANU of chiShona speakers from the midlands and the west.[39] (Nkomo himself was from the Kalanga group, chiShona-speaking but culturally more closely aligned with the Ndebele.[40]) From the very beginning, there were violent clashes between supporters of the two movements and the Organization of African Unity was eventually constrained to recognize both of them.[41] ZAPU and ZANU each had its own military wing and international backers: the Zimbabwe People's Revolutionary Army (ZIPRA), supported by the Soviet Union, and the Zimbabwe National Liberation Army (ZANLA), supported by China. The African National Congress of South Africa, then itself involved in training a guerrilla army, was seen to be closer to ZAPU, an association put down to linguistic and cultural ties. (The Ndebele are descendants of a Zulu breakaway group that fled South Africa in the nineteenth century.)

The first incursion by guerrilla fighters into Rhodesia across the Zambezi River occurred in 1966, but it was not until December 1972 that the first white settler was killed.[42] During the 1970s, the white minority government's position became increasingly precarious as the guerrilla campaign intensified and its geopolitical position weakened. The independence of Mozambique in 1975 exposed Rhodesia's eastern border to ZANLA guerrilla fighters and the tribal areas essentially became no-go zones for government troops, at least at night.[43] Academic opinion differs about how much physical coercion ZANLA used to gain control of the local population, but the most comprehensive study concludes that significant sincere support was supplemented by violent intimidation.[44]

[37] Compagnon, *A Predictable Tragedy* 13; Southall, *Liberation Movements in Power* 47.
[38] Martin Meredith, *Mugabe: Power, Plunder, and the Struggle for Zimbabwe's Future* (New York: Public Affairs, 2002) 37; Southall, *Liberation Movements in Power* 48.
[39] Southall, *Liberation Movements in Power* 38.
[40] Compagnon, *A Predictable Tragedy* 10.
[41] Southall, *Liberation Movements in Power* 38–9.
[42] Kriger, *Zimbabwe's Guerrilla War* 92.
[43] Southall, *Liberation Movements in Power* 46.
[44] See Kriger, *Zimbabwe's Guerrilla War* 116–69. See also Compagnon, *A Predictable Tragedy* 47–9; Southall, *Liberation Movements in Power* 57.

The National Party of South Africa's decision in the mid-1970s that apartheid's survival depended on the settlement of the Rhodesian question hastened the end of the guerrilla war.[45] An abortive attempt to negotiate a peace was held in Geneva in 1976. This was followed by a short-lived multiracial government consisting of moderate Africans led by Bishop Abel Muzorewa and the Ian Smith-led Rhodesian Front.[46] When that failed, Smith was forced to enter into peace negotiations with ZAPU and ZANU, unified for that purpose as the Patriotic Front (PF). Brokered by Britain at Lancaster House, the peace negotiations led to the adoption of an independence Constitution and the first democratic elections from February 27–29, 1980. Independence itself was achieved on April 18, 1980.

ZANU-PF decisively won the independence elections, with 63 percent of the vote and 57 of the 80 contested seats (with 20 seats reserved for the white minority). While reflective of its leading role in the guerilla war and of the Shona ethnic group's numerical dominance, there were also claims that ZANU-PF's victory was attributable to the fact that many of its best fighters had not reported at confinement camps as agreed at Lancaster House, but instead had remained in the reserves and villages to ensure that their inhabitants cast the "correct" vote.[47] There appears to have been some continuity here between the methods ZANLA used to ensure support for its fighters during the bush war and the methods it used to secure electoral support.[48] PF-ZAPU, with 20 seats, became the main opposition party, while the United African National Congress led by Muzorewa and Smith won just 3 seats. Nevertheless, the combined opposition seats (including the reserved seats) were sufficient to deny ZANU-PF the 70-percent majority it required to amend most parts of the Constitution.[49] The provisions securing the reserved white seats and the Bill of Rights were additionally insulated by a 100-percent majority requirement in the lower house for ten and seven years respectively.[50]

Mugabe assumed office as Prime Minister in April 1980 with Canaan Banana as ceremonial President. The new head of state was initially

---

[45]   Southall, *Liberation Movements in Power* 46.
[46]   Ibid 48.
[47]   The British Governor, Christopher Soames, came close to banning ZANU-PF because of intimidation (Meredith, *Mugabe* 10).
[48]   See Kriger, *Zimbabwe's Guerrilla War* 213, 217.
[49]   Paragraph E.28 "Summary of the Independence Constitution," Annex C to the Lancaster House Agreement (setting a 70 percent majority requirement in the House of Assembly and a two thirds majority in the Senate).
[50]   Paragraph E.29 and E.30 "Summary of the Independence Constitution," Annex C to the Lancaster House Agreement (setting a 100 percent majority requirement in the House of Assembly and two thirds majority in the Senate for seven and ten years respectively).

magnanimous in victory, and included both whites and Joshua Nkomo's PF-ZAPU in his first Cabinet.[51] In a famous speech on the evening of his victory, Mugabe committed his party to limited government under the independence Constitution.[52]

The new ZANU-PF government inherited a legal order that had been subordinated to the exigencies of white minority rule. In addition to the racially discriminatory Land Apportionment Act, successive governments after 1958 had enacted a network of security laws that effectively banned any nationalist opposition or other political dissent and provided for indefinite detention without trial.[53] These included the Law and Order (Maintenance) Act,[54] the Unlawful Organizations Act,[55] and the Emergency Powers Act.[56] Successive six-month states of emergency, allowing de facto executive rule, were declared from 1965 to 1979.[57] As the guerrilla war intensified, entire villages were placed under nocturnal curfew and prisoners detained and tortured.[58] In the most notorious incident, Rhodesian troops attacked a refugee camp in Mozambique killing nearly 1,000 unarmed civilians, ostensibly to prevent their being trained and returning to Rhodesia as guerrilla fighters.[59] No one was ever prosecuted for these crimes, and indeed leading Rhodesian security force personnel initially retained their positions after independence in 1980.[60]

Like South Africa, Rhodesia knew some courageous and independent judges. For example, Sir John Fieldsend (who was later to become the first Chief Justice of Zimbabwe) resigned his position as Acting Judge of Appeal in 1968 in protest at the Appellate Division's decision recognizing Ian Smith's

---

[51]   Meredith, *Mugabe* 39.

[52]   Ibid 13.

[53]   Welshman Ncube, "State Security, The Rule of Law and Politics of Repression in Zimbabwe" *U-landsseminarets Skriftserie Nr 51* (University of Oslo Third World Seminar Series No 51, 1990).

[54]   Chapter 65 (1960).

[55]   Chapter 91 (1971).

[56]   Chapter 33 (1965), under which the Emergency Powers (Maintenance of Law and Order) Regulations issued.

[57]   Ibid. Karekwaivanane 336–7 says Emergency Powers Act allowed executive to amend legislation.

[58]   Ncube, "State Security" 7–10. There were 3,000 political prisoners in 1976 (George H. Karekwaivanane, "'It Shall be the Duty of Every African to Obey and Comply Promptly': Negotiating State Authority in the Legal Arena, Rhodesia 1965–1980" (2011) 37 *Journal of Southern African Studies* 333, 337).

[59]   Richard Carver, "Zimbabwe: Drawing a Line Through the Past" (1998) 37 *Journal of African Law* 69, 71.

[60]   Ibid 70–1.

government.[61] Chief Justice Robert Tredgold had earlier resigned in protest at the Law and Order (Maintenance) Act, describing it as a "savage, evil, mean, and dirty" law that would turn Rhodesia into a "police state."[62] For the most part, however, the legal profession, like that in South Africa, was complicit in promoting the imperatives of white minority rule.

While Zimbabwe lacks the in-depth scholarship that has been conducted on the South African legal order under apartheid, it is reasonable to assume that the same kind of dualist legal order described by Jens Meierhenrich in his study of South Africa would have prevailed in Rhodesia, i.e., a rule-of-law state operating in respect of white subsociety and a repressive rule-by-law state operating in respect of the majority population.[63] As George Karekwaivanane has explained, African litigants, by appealing to rule-of-law values, had at least some capacity for agency within this dual state and were able to challenge the Rhodesian legal order's attempt to create two hermetically sealed worlds.[64] "The reliance on the law as a mode of rule by the Rhodesian state," he argues, "rendered it available for appropriation by Africans."[65] In particular, the Rhodesian state's reliance on the rule of law as a legitimating ideology meant that Africans were able to assert "alternative [non-subaltern] conceptions of citizenship" through the legal process.[66] The judiciary was generally responsive to these claims, seeking "to implement the liberal tradition of the rule of law in its minimalist form."[67]

The Rhodesian Front's reliance on a legitimating ideology of the rule of law was most powerfully illustrated in the litigation following the Unilateral Declaration of Independence in 1965.[68] As Dias argued at the time, it was important to the white minority government to be seen to be subjecting itself to independent review of its actions by the courts.[69] The Rhodesian Front

---

[61] *Madzimbamuto v. Lardner-Burke NO; Baron v. Ayre* 1968 (2) SA 284 (RAD). See Jeremy Gauntlett, "Zimbabwe: The War on Law" paper delivered at a seminar hosted by the Human Rights Lawyers Association and others (London, March 19, 2009) (published in December 2009, *Advocate* 44–7).

[62] Ncube, "State Security" 5. See also Meredith, *Mugabe* 26.

[63] See Jens Meierhenrich, *The Legacies of Law: Long-Run Consequences of Legal Development in South Africa, 1652–2000* (Cambridge: Cambridge University Press, 2008); Martin Chanock, *The Making of South African Legal Culture 1902–1936: Fear, Favour, and Prejudice* (Cambridge: Cambridge University Press, 2001).

[64] Karekwaivanane, "It Shall be the Duty of Every African to Obey and Comply Promptly."

[65] Ibid 348.

[66] Ibid.

[67] Ibid.

[68] *Madzimbamuto v. Lardner-Burke NO; Baron v. Ayre* 1968 (2) SA 284 (RAD).

[69] R. W. M. Dias, "Legal Politics: Norms behind the *Grundnorm*" (1968) 26 *Cambridge Law Journal* 233.

accordingly resisted the temptation to pack either the High Court or the Appellate Division. The judges responded by refusing to recognize the 1965 Constitution as lawful, but nevertheless suggested the practical means through which the Smith regime could continue and eventually win legal recognition.[70]

No African judges were appointed before independence in 1980. Indeed, there were very few trained African legal professionals at all.[71] This partly explains why ZANU-PF initially did not replace the white and Asian judges serving on the Bench: it simply had no other practical choice. The small number of African legal professionals at independence also suggests that the institutionalized values of the Rhodesian legal profession would have exerted a profound influence over Zimbabwe's legal culture as it developed after 1980. As they were absorbed into the profession, young African lawyers would inevitably have been exposed to the tradition of thinking about the role of judges in disciplining public power that had prevailed before independence. As happened in other British post-colonies,[72] the mere fact of transition to a rights-based, democratic constitutional order would not have transformed that tradition overnight.[73] Rather, its immanent values, unspoken assumptions, and received practices would have continued to inform conceptions of the legitimate scope of legal and political authority. The next section explores this and other likely continuities between Zimbabwe's pre- and postindependence JR regimes.

5.2 BUILDING ON THE COLONIAL LEGACY: 1980–1998

It is often said that the Zimbabwean judiciary was remarkably independent in the first twenty years after the end of white minority rule.[74] And, indeed, as discussed later in this section, both the Supreme Court and the High Court

---

[70]   Ibid 259.

[71]   Compagnon, *A Predictable Tragedy* 145–6.

[72]   See Terence C. Halliday, Lucien Karpik, and Malcolm Feeley (eds.), *Fates of Political Liberalism in the British Post-Colony: The Politics of the Legal Complex* (New York: Cambridge University Press, 2012).

[73]   Equally, comparative experience suggests that indigenous traditions of legal reasoning and conceptions of public power, being less formalized and (wrongly) condemned as premodern, struggle to exert an influence, at least initially.

[74]   See Jennifer Widner with Daniel Scher, "Building Judicial Independence in Semi-Democracies: Uganda and Zimbabwe" in Tom Ginsburg and Tamir Moustafa (eds.), *Rule by Law: The Politics of Courts in Authoritarian Regimes* (New York: Cambridge University Press, 2008) 235, 248; Southall, *Liberation Movements in Power* 148; Compagnon, *A Predictable Tragedy* 142.

took several decisions that inconvenienced – embarrassed even – the ZANU-PF government. There has been very little analysis, however, of why such a dominant and fundamentally illiberal political party should have tolerated such assertive decision-making for so long. Most commentators simply paint a picture of heroic judges courageously defying the odds until they were eventually contained.[75] In a more insightful piece, Jennifer Widner argues that the Zimbabwe judiciary before 2000 was somewhat blinkered and high-minded, writing "elegant" opinions but failing to see that their "hard-hitting" judgments were aggravating relationships with the executive.[76] While this takes the analysis further, it still leaves ZANU-PF's initial tolerance for forceful decision-making unexplained. To be sure, the judges might have behaved more prudently, but what were the structural reasons behind the freedom they seemingly enjoyed?

This section argues that the relative independence from political control that the Zimbabwe judiciary enjoyed from 1980 to 1999 was a product of two main factors: (1) the ideational legacy of the way the judiciary had been used before 1980 to legitimate white minority rule; and (2) ZANU-PF's ability to build on and extend this legacy as part of its own authoritarian legitimation strategy. Despite its willingness to compete in regular democratic elections, ZANU-PF was never genuinely committed to multiparty democracy. Elections were held and their results tolerated only to the extent that they served its power-accreting interests. Likewise, judicial independence was tolerated, not for sincere reasons, but as a convenient and familiar legitimating device. In the same way that

---

[75] See, for example, Anthony Gubbay, "The Progressive Erosion of the Rule of Law in Independent Zimbabwe" Bar of England and Wales Third International Rule of Law Lecture, Inner Temple Hall, London (December 2009) (available at www.barcouncil.org .uk/media/100365/rule_of_law_lecture__agubbay_091209.pdf) and Jeremy Gauntlett, "Zimbabwe: The War on Law." Apart from Jennifer Widner's analysis (discussed in the next footnote), Daniel Compagnon provides the most sustained scholarly account. (See Compagnon, *A Predictable Tragedy* 141–56.) Compagnon does not, however, convincingly explain the causes of the changes to ZANU-PF's approach to the judiciary. His principal point is that the seeds of ZANU-PF's assault on the judiciary were sown early on, and that the assault should therefore be seen as an intensification of, rather than a radical departure from, ZANU-PF's consistently illiberal approach towards judicial independence. This analysis is useful, but it fails to explain the causes of the intensification.

[76] Widner "Building Judicial Independence in Semi-Democracies" 258. Earlier in this paper (at 248), after noting the Zimbabwe judiciary's "especially strong reputation for independence on the African continent," Widner states that "[a] series of impressive judges had led the [Supreme] [C]ourt." She then refers to concerns that "chief justices in neighboring countries occasionally expressed . . . that their Zimbabwe counterparts were too public, too visible." The implication is that the judiciary's early forcefulness was a function of charismatic personalities rather than structural factors, and that the judiciary's lack of prudence was partly responsible for its decline.

ZANU-PF took over the Rhodesian Front regime's security apparatus, so too did it replicate its predecessor's use of a distorted conception of law's autonomy from politics. The resulting, specifically Zimbabwean version of authoritarian legalism proved to be highly stable, breaking up only when the underlying strategic rationale for it collapsed.

5.2.1 ZANU-PF's Illiberalism

There are two main reasons to doubt that ZANU-PF's commitment to multi-party democracy was ever sincere. First, as we have seen, even in the very first elections in 1980 there was evidence of voter intimidation, particularly in the countryside. While explicable as a continuation of its liberation war practices, the fact that ZANU-PF sought to deploy these tactics provided an early indication of its win-at-all-costs mentality. That impression was horribly confirmed three years later when ZANU-PF used the discovery of arms caches in Matabeleland as a pretext to launch operation *Gukurahundi* – a five-year campaign of political intimidation and mass murder that ended only when PF-ZAPU was absorbed into ZANU-PF in 1987.[77] Quite apart from the shocking violence deployed, the campaign was unnecessary from a purely power-retention point of view.[78] With the PF-ZAPU's electoral threat restricted to the two Matabeleland provinces and, to a lesser extent, the Midlands, the only plausible explanation for the violence is that ZANU-PF's goal from the very outset was the creation of a one-party state.[79]

The second reason to doubt the sincerity of ZANU-PF's commitment to multiparty democracy relates to its internal political tradition and the revolutionary basis of its claim to legitimacy. After ZANU-PF's formation in 1963, as we have seen, there were bitter factional and leadership struggles within the organization, many of them settled violently rather than through democratic processes.[80] Mugabe's own ascension to the leadership occurred on the back of a prison coup, and was followed by the elimination of political rivals in suspicious circumstances.[81] Some of this violence may be explained as a function of exile and the guerrilla struggle in which ZANU-PF was engaged,

---

[77] See the Catholic Commission for Justice and Peace in Zimbabwe, *Crisis of Governance: A Report on Political Violence in Zimbabwe* (Harare, 2000).

[78] Later in Zimbabwe's electoral politics, with the rise of the MDC from 1999, violence did become "necessary" in this narrower sense. See Section 5.3.1.

[79] Indeed, the establishment of a one-party state later became an explicit part of ZANU-PF's political program, abandoned only when it became clear that it would not have the majority required to amend the Constitution.

[80] Kriger, *Zimbabwe's Guerrilla War* 152.

[81] Compagnon, *A Predictable Tragedy* 12–3.

but the overarching impression is of a political movement in which a culture of violence was tolerated and in which power was pursued at any cost.[82]

ZANU-PF's acceptance of the principle of multiparty democracy in the 1980 Constitution does nothing to contradict this impression. In stark contrast to the later South African constitution-making process, the 1980 Constitution was drafted by the former colonial power, and imposed on the parties at Lancaster House as a condition of Britain's support for independence. There was no process of popular participation in the design of the Constitution and ZANU-PF itself never took ownership of it. The Constitution was simply the price that had to be paid for the transition to black majority rule and something that could be changed as soon as political circumstances allowed. Thus, in 1987, on attaining the 70-percent majority required to amend the Constitution, ZANU-PF immediately moved to alter it.[83] In a series of sweeping changes, the positions of ceremonial President and Prime Minister were combined into a single presidential office, and the new executive President's powers expanded.[84] While the fact that ZANU-PF took the trouble to pass a carefully worded amendment demonstrates a significant ongoing concern for legal form, the substantive content of the amendments shows a determination to exert centralized political control at the earliest opportunity.

In pursuing this goal, ZANU-PF acted in the manner of a classic national liberation movement. Its struggle, as Roger Southall has argued, "was more one for majority rule than it was for political democracy."[85] The guerrilla war, despite its origins in the denial of political rights, had never been about the furtherance of liberal-democratic freedoms, but about freedom from colonial oppression. While there was some correspondence between that goal and the achievement of democratic government, ZANU-PF's conception of democracy was of the thin, majoritarian kind and moreover one that did not countenance the peaceful rotation of political power.[86] Rather, democracy was about the ascension to power of the national liberation movement, which, by dint of its leadership of the

---

[82] Southall, *Liberation Movements in Power* 57.
[83] As noted already, the Lancaster House agreement stipulated that, for the first ten years, an amendment to the Bill of Rights required 100 percent consensus in the lower house. A similar provision insulated the reservation of 20 seats for whites for seven years. In 1987, Mugabe first "enlisted the support of five white 'independents'" to pass an amendment abolishing the reserved seats. The absorption of PF-ZAPU allowed the passage of Constitutional Amendment 7 of 1987. See Compagnon, *A Predictable Tragedy* 34.
[84] Ibid.
[85] Roger Southall, *Liberation Movements in Power* 69.
[86] Ibid.

anti-colonial struggle, would thereafter enjoy a permanent right to govern.

It was crucial in this respect that ZANLA, ZANU-PF's military wing, should be seen to have been more active in the prosecution of the guerrilla war than its rival ZIPRA. While ZIPRA had had better trained forces, ZANU-PF leaders could truthfully claim, ZANLA had committed more fighters on the ground and had generally been more effective.[87] The political moderation of the PF-ZAPU leader, Joshua Nkomo, was exploited in the same way, and his role in the liberation struggle downplayed from the very outset. Despite being in many ways the father of Zimbabwe's liberation struggle, Nkomo was given no role in the independence celebrations, and treated instead as the mere head of a losing political party.[88] Through these and other ideological narratives, ZANU-PF moved to establish itself as the natural party of government – the true embodiment of the national liberation project and its only authentic spokesman.

While there are similarities between ZANU-PF and the African National Congress (ANC) of South Africa in this respect, there are also important differences, particularly in relation to their attitude to constitutionalism and human rights. The ANC's discourse on national liberation was always more inclusive than ZANU-PF's, and tempered by a genuinely liberal strand that dated back to its origins in the South African nonracial movement. The 1955 Freedom Charter, for example, is capable of being read in two ways, as both a revolutionary demand for indigenous control of natural resources and as a charter for individual human rights.[89] In addition, prominent ANC members like Albie Sachs and Kader Asmal were committed constitutionalists who exerted significant influence within the organization.[90] ZANU-PF had no equivalent of this – no internal tradition of constitutionalism and few prominent constitutionalist voices.[91]

Another significant difference between Zimbabwe and South Africa is the starker ethnic division in the former case. As noted earlier, Zimbabwe is split between two main ethnic groups – the Shona and the Ndebele – whose mutual antipathy dates to the nineteenth century. This division manifested

---

[87] See Kriger, *Zimbabwe's Guerrilla War* 3 (reporting that, at the end of the war, 19,300 guerrillas out of a total of 28,000 inside Zimbabwe were allied to ZANU-PF).

[88] Meredith, *Mugabe* 39.

[89] See Theunis Roux, *The Politics of Principle: The First South African Constitutional Court, 1995–2005* (Cambridge: Cambridge University Press, 2013) 153.

[90] Ibid 157.

[91] One exception was Herbert Chitepo, Rhodesia's first black barrister and ZANU leader assassinated in 1975.

itself early in the liberation struggle, with ZAPU and ZANU and their respective military wings roughly dividing along ethnic lines.[92] Though coming together in form of the Patriotic Front for purposes of the signing of the Lancaster House agreement, the two parties and their armies were never properly unified.[93] In consequence, the first democratic elections saw a high degree of ethnic bloc voting. This pattern has been repeated in subsequent elections, with the Ndebele switching their allegiance to whichever party seems best placed to safeguard their interests.[94] ZANU-PF, in turn, while nominally governing on behalf of all Zimbabweans, has been able to use Shona ethnic (and subethnic) loyalties to maintain its hold on power. In this sense, the transition to democracy in 1980 was not just about black majority rule, but also about which ethnic group would come to stand in for the black majority. With ZANU-PF's victory, the trajectory was set and its control of government thereafter used to turn all state apparatuses, including the army, against its political opponents.

5.2.2 *Continuities between the Pre- and Postindependence Regimes*

In acting thus, ZANU-PF was continuing a tradition of authoritarianism that had begun with colonization and the establishment of white minority rule. The democratic elections in 1980 marked in this sense, not a transition from authoritarianism to multiparty democracy, but a transition between two distinct authoritarian orders.[95]

Given their respective origins in colonial occupation and the anti-colonial struggle, there were some obvious differences between the two orders. In the case of the Rhodesian Front regime, the purported rationale for the denial of political rights to the black majority was the furtherance of colonialism's modernizing mission. To compensate for the absence of a genuine democratic mandate, the Rhodesian Front regime relied on a legitimating ideology of civilization versus disorder: whites were entitled to govern because they ostensibly brought with them more advanced forms of social organization and technological progress.[96] Against this, ZANU-PF's authoritarianism, as we

[92] Kriger *Zimbabwe's Guerrilla War* 47 (noting that there were many Shona officers in ZIPRA, but that most of the guerrilla fighters were Ndebele).

[93] See Compagnon, *A Predictable Tragedy* 297 n 6 (commenting on failed ZIPA unification).

[94] After initially supporting PF-ZAPU, the Ndebele switched their allegiance to the MDC in 2000, but that party itself later split along ethnic lines. See Philip Barclay, *Zimbabwe: Years of Hope and Despair* (London: Bloomsbury, 2010) 39–40.

[95] See David Coltart, *The Struggle Continues: 50 years of Tyranny in Zimbabwe* (Johannesburg: Jacana, 2016).

[96] Karekwaivanane, "It Shall be the Duty of Every African to Obey and Comply Promptly" 334.

have seen, is based on a discourse of revolutionary nationalism. Its right to govern without according full political rights to its opponents flows from its leading role in the guerrilla war of independence.

There were, however, also some points of continuity between the two authoritarian orders. These had to do, first, with the way ZANU-PF took over and exploited the Rhodesian Front's security apparatus and, second, with its use of qualified respect for judicial independence as a legitimating device. It is thus significant that ZANU-PF, on assuming power, chose not to dismiss senior members of the Rhodesian Front's military and central intelligence forces. The most dramatic demonstration of this was Ken Flower's continuation as head of the Central Intelligence Organization. Called into Mugabe's office after the independence elections, he was expecting to be harangued for previously plotting the new Prime Minister's assassination. Instead he was praised for his skills and asked to continue in his post.[97] General Peter Walls, the head of the Rhodesian armed forces, was similarly asked to continue, and did so until resigning in protest against the violent intimidation tactics that ZANU-PF used in the first democratic elections.[98]

These high-level appointments signaled ZANU-PF's intention to continue, at a more concrete level, the Rhodesian Front's use of violence and torture as tools of political coercion. Here, there was an apparently seamless integration of ZANU-PF's internal tradition of violent political succession and the Rhodesian security forces' use of violence and torture during the guerrilla war. As Richard Carver has shown, "specific methods of human rights abuses were passed on from the Rhodesian to the Zimbabwean forces, often practiced by the very same individuals."[99] Thus, in the first two years of independence, ZANU-PF deployed the old-order security forces against its political opponents. In November 1980 and February 1981, the Rhodesian African Rifles were used to put down an uprising by former ZIPRA combatants at their demobilization camp in Entumbane outside Bulawayo.[100]

In addition to its security personnel and methods, ZANU-PF retained the Rhodesian Front's authoritarian legal apparatus. All the security legislation previously mentioned was kept on the statute book, including the Law and Order (Maintenance) Act and the Emergency Powers (Maintenance of Law and Order) Regulations.[101] The latter were used to continue the Rhodesian

---

[97]   Meredith *Mugabe* 46; Carver, "Zimbabwe: Drawing a Line Through the Past" 70–1.
[98]   Meredith, *Mugabe* 12, 49 (commenting that Walls may also have resigned because he was refused promotion to full General).
[99]   Carver, "Zimbabwe: Drawing a Line Through the Past" 73.
[100]   Ibid 74.
[101]   Ibid 72; Ncube, "State Security" 73.

Front's practice of automatically renewing the state of emergency every six months.[102] In the view of Welshman Ncube, a former legal academic and later leader of one of the MDC factions, much of the repression meted out by the ZANU-PF regime can be traced to the pre-1980 repressive legal framework and the culture of state-sanctioned violence that grew up around it.[103]

The second major point of continuity between the pre- and postindependence authoritarian governments, and the more significant point for present purposes, was the strategic use of the judiciary. As we have seen, the Rhodesian Front tolerated a measure of judicial independence as part of its civilizing mission and quest for international legitimacy. In the crucial *UDI* case, the government submitted its actions to independent judicial review, trusting that the judges' sense of self-preservation and pragmatism would lead them to do the "right" thing. In the same way, ZANU-PF did not initially interfere with the courts, calculating that the benefits of independent judicial decision-making would outweigh their costs and that any truly inconvenient decisions could be bypassed or overturned.

There was thus no immediate purging of the old-order judiciary. The only major initial change was the replacement of Hector MacDonald by John Fieldsend as Chief Justice in July 1980. MacDonald had a reputation as a "hanging judge" and was intensely disliked by the national liberation movements, several of whose members he had sentenced to death.[104] His replacement, Fieldsend, as noted earlier, had resigned his position as Acting Judge of Appeal in protest at the Appellate Division's decision in the *UDI* case. While signaling a desire to remove actual political opponents from the bench, the substitution of MacDonald with Fieldsend, a white liberal, was hardly indicative of an attempt to subordinate the judiciary to political control. Rather, it sent a signal that ZANU-PF was committed to restoring the best traditions of the Bench and Bar.

No other changes were made to the composition of the Supreme Court and the High Court, which remained exclusively white and Asian apart from Enoch Dumbutshena, who was appointed to the High Court in May 1980. As noted, this reliance on old-order judges was partly a function of the absence of trained African lawyers; even the appointment of political lackeys requires some minimal legal-professional cover. It was also partly a function, however, of the same logic that undergirded ZANU-PF's retention of the Rhodesian Front's security force personnel: a desire to convey an impression of stability,

[102]   Ibid.
[103]   Carver, "Zimbabwe: Drawing a Line Through the Past" 73; Ncube, "State Security" 73.
[104]   See "Hector MacDonald" www.thetimes.co.uk/article/hector-macdonald-9tp36wvmzx3.

while at the same time benefitting from the continuation of a legitimation strategy that had proved successful in the past. It is thus significant that the 1980 Constitution gave Mugabe the power to increase the size of the Supreme Court from the very outset, but that he did not use it until 2001.[105] Instead, he waited for credible candidates to come through the ranks and appointed them as and when positions became available.[106]

On one view, this was just a clever long-term strategy: Mugabe was all the while building a constituency in the judiciary and was simply biding his time.[107] This interpretation, however, is not borne out by the facts. As we shall see in the next section, the main reason ZANU-PF moved against the judiciary in 2000 was that it was seen to be politically disloyal. That is hardly suggestive of a strategy up to that point of constituency-building. Rather, it confirms that the strategy had been the exact opposite of this: merit appointments designed to maximize the judiciary's legitimating potential. This interpretation is further supported by the record of high-level appointments. First, in 1984, when Fieldsend retired as Chief Justice, Mugabe appointed Dumbutshena to replace him. Dumbutshena, as noted, had been the first African judge on the High Court. In that capacity, he had handed down several uncompromising judgments.[108] Politically, too, he was hardly a ZANU-PF loyalist, having initially been a member of ZAPU and then a legal adviser to Muzorewa's UANC.[109] Second, when Dumbutshena in turn retired in 1990, Mugabe appointed Anthony Gubbay as his successor. Like Dumbutshena, Gubbay was a fiercely independent judge with mainstream liberal views, something that Mugabe must have known when appointing him. More than any other factor, these two appointments speak to a deliberate strategy of promoting judicial independence as a legitimating device through the 1980s and 1990s.

To be sure, from 1987, there was a subtle shift in ZANU-PF's approach to the judiciary. Along with the constitutional amendments centralizing power in the executive presidency, there were some amendments to the judicial appointments process for Supreme and High Court judges.[110] Whereas the initial constitutional position had been that these judges would be appointed

---

[105]   Compagnon, *A Predictable Tragedy* 142.
[106]   By 1999, 17 of 25 High Court and Supreme Court judges were black (ibid 151).
[107]   Ibid 143–4.
[108]   These are discussed in the next section.
[109]   See Compagnon, *A Predictable Tragedy* 146–7 for a brief biography of Dumbutshena. Dumbutshena was the High Court judge in the *York Brothers* and sabotage cases discussed in the next section.
[110]   Constitutional Amendment 7 (Act 23 of 1987).

on the "recommendation" of the Judicial Service Commission, the amendments changed that to a "prior consultation" requirement.[111] At the same time, Parliament's role was downgraded from a right to be informed of any disagreement between the President and the JSC before the appointment was made to a right be informed "as soon as possible" after the appointment.[112] Those two amendments undoubtedly tightened the President's grip on the judiciary, but they had more to do with the general move to centralization of control in the Presidency from 1987 than a change in ZANU-PF's strategy towards judicial independence. The fact that Mugabe did not actually use the judicial appointments process to appoint politically loyal judges prior to 2001 is the significant point.

5.2.3 *ZANU-PF's Response to Assertive Judicial Decisions*

Further evidence of the strategic deployment of judicial independence comes from the way ZANU-PF responded to the judiciary's decisions. As mentioned at the outset, between 1980 and 2000 the Supreme Court and the High Court handed down several bold decisions that enforced the Constitution in difficult circumstances. ZANU-PF's response to those decisions gives some clue to the strategic calculations it was making. In particular, the pattern that emerges is one where most decisions were accepted, but truly inconvenient decisions countermanded – either by way of constitutional amendment or another form of political override (for example, pardons to perpetrators of election violence[113]). All of this seems to have been well judged, with ZANU-PF apparently engaging in a continual cost-benefit analysis of the value to it of judicial independence.

In one of the first cases to come before Dumbutshena CJ, for example, the Supreme Court upheld an application by PF-ZAPU that it had not been given sufficient time to peruse the voters' roll before the finalization of electoral districts.[114] The decision was significant, not just because it concerned an opposition party, but also because it concerned the reviewability of executive

[111] Compagnon, *A Predictable Tragedy* 144.
[112] Ibid.
[113] In April 1988, virtually all the security personnel found guilty of murder and other crimes relating to Fifth Brigade activities were released, alongside 75 other members of the security forces under a special Amnesty granted by the President as part of a "reconciliation" gesture following the achievement of political unity between ZANU-PF and PF-ZAPU.
[114] *PF-ZAPU* v. *Minister of Justice* (cited in Anthony Gubbay, "The Light of Successive Chief Justices of Zimbabwe in Seeking to Protect Human Rights and the Rule of Law" 2001 Rothschild Foster Human Rights Trust Lecture available at www.rothschildfostertrust.com /trust/lectures/).

prerogatives.[115] Despite those two contentious aspects, the Court's decision was accepted without protest. In another decision, in 1987, the Supreme Court under Dumbutshena CJ held a law permitting adult whipping unconstitutional against the right to be free from cruel and inhuman punishment.[116] That decision, too, was accepted. Two years later, however, when the Supreme Court extended the ban on whipping to juveniles by a bare majority of 3 to 2,[117] there was an immediate reprisal in the form of a constitutional amendment.[118] In 1993, the Constitution was again amended to countermand a Supreme Court decision holding that undue delay in the execution of the death penalty constituted cruel and inhuman punishment.[119] The latter two examples are indicative of a ruling party that was prepared to use its strong majority in Parliament to override judicial decisions on human rights. Neither of the amendments was particularly worrying from a rule of law point of view, however, since they both concerned controversial moral questions over which the judges of the Supreme Court itself, in the first instance, had disagreed.

A different story emerges in cases that directly concerned ZANU-PF's security interests and members of the old-order regime. Three cases are illustrative here: the so-called *York Brothers* case; a case involving the sabotage of Zimbabwean air force planes by South African agents; and a case involving former Prime Minister Ian Smith. In the first case, heard in 1982 in the High Court before Dumbutshena, the two accused brothers had been arrested and charged with illegal possession of firearms. The trial against them collapsed, however, when a key witness left the country. It also emerged in court that a confession by one of the brothers had been extracted under duress.[120] On their release, the brothers were immediately redetained. The High Court invalidated this detention and a second redetention on procedural grounds. Finally, after the brothers were detained a third time, the High Court ruled that, as the detention was "investigative" rather than "preventive," it did not contravene the relevant constitutional

---

[115]   Ibid.
[116]   S v. *Ncube* 1988 (2) SA 702 (ZSC); (1988) LRG (Const) 442.
[117]   A *Juvenile* v. *The State* SC 64/89 (1989).
[118]   Section 5 of the Constitution of Zimbabwe Amendment No 11 Act 30 of 1990 (inserting s 15(3)).
[119]   Constitution of Zimbabwe Amendment No 13 Act 9 of 1993 (inserting s 15(5)) in response to *Catholic Commission for Justice and Peace in Zimbabwe* v. *Attorney-General, Zimbabwe* 1993 (1) ZLR 242 (S). Section 15 had earlier been amended to pre-empt consideration of the question whether hanging per se constituted cruel and inhuman punishment. See Constitution of Zimbabwe Amendment No 11 Act 30 of 1990 (inserting s 15(4)).
[120]   Gubbay, "The Light of Successive Chief Justices."

provision.[121] After the second detention order had been invalidated, the Minister of Home Affairs commented in Parliament that the government was "aware that certain legal practitioners are in receipt of moneys as paid hirelings, from governments hostile to our own order, in the process of seeking to destabilize us, to create a state of anarchy through the inherited legal apparatus." He continued: "We promise to handle such lawyers using the appropriate technology that exists in our law and order section."[122] Various other threatening statements were also made at the same time. In a speech in Parliament on July 29, 1982, for example, Mugabe said that "the Government cannot allow the technicalities of the law to fetter its hands in … [preserving] law and order in the country."[123]

In August 1983, the High Court, again in the person of Dumbutshena, dismissed a case against Air Vice-Marshall Hugh Slatter and five other senior air force officers who had been accused of involvement in the destruction of thirteen aircraft at Thornhill air force base near Gweru. The raid had been carried out by saboteurs under the direction of South African military intelligence and with the assistance of a junior air force officer.[124] Slatter and the other senior air force officers, Dumbutshena held, had confessed their involvement in the destruction of the planes only after being detained without legal representation and tortured. Their confessions were accordingly not admissible. As before, the accused were immediately rearrested on their release and kept in detention in the face of strong international criticism.[125] Mugabe even went so far as to argue that torture was an acceptable method of interrogation, and that the rule that confessions made under torture were inadmissible was "one of those principles born out of the stupidity of some of the procedures of colonial times."[126] Slatter and his fellow senior air force officers were nevertheless eventually released.

The final case worth mentioning is a 1989 case involving former Prime Minister Ian Smith. While visiting South Africa, then still under white minority rule, Smith had spoken out in favor of apartheid and against economic sanctions. The Zimbabwe House of Assembly responded by holding him in contempt of Parliament, suspending him for a year, and terminating

---

[121] Ibid.
[122] Quoted in Karla Saller, *The Judicial Institution in Zimbabwe* 2 (Cape Town: SiberInk, 2004) 2; Gubbay, "The Light of Successive Chief Justices."
[123] Quoted in Saller, *The Judicial Institution in Zimbabwe* 2.
[124] Meredith, *Mugabe* 53–4.
[125] Ibid 54.
[126] Ibid.

his salary and benefits for that period.[127] When the case reached the Supreme Court, again before Dumbutshena – this time as Chief Justice – the Speaker of Parliament produced a certificate stating that the matter fell within parliamentary privilege and that the Court was accordingly prevented from hearing it. Dumbutshena dismissed this argument and struck down the termination of Smith's pay and benefits (but not his suspension).[128] The Speaker initially refused to enforce the decision, saying that Parliament should "liberate itself from the Supreme Court Judges."[129] The Court responded by issuing a strongly worded defense of the rule of law. "We are satisfied," the statement read, "that our decision was correct, but that is not the point. The decision was ours to make."[130] After the Bar Council, the Law Society, the Faculty of Law at the University of Zimbabwe, and the Catholic Commission for Justice and Peace all supported the Court's stance, the Parliament relented.

The three cases involving security threats and members of the previous white minority government reveal a different approach to the value of judicial independence when compared to the Bill of Rights cases discussed earlier. In its responses to these decisions, ZANU-PF was clearly prepared to risk the appearance of defying the rule of law. Mugabe's statement on torture is particularly revealing, made as it was at the center of an international outcry when Zimbabwe was in the political spotlight. The statement undoubtedly damaged ZANU-PF's international standing (at least in the West) and yet, Mugabe was prepared to make it. The possibility that he was simply acting irrationally – in a fit of temper when cornered in an unfamiliar environment – cannot be ruled out, but there are some considerations that suggest that Mugabe's outburst might have been strategically well judged.

For one thing, the statement would undoubtedly have "played" much better at home than it did overseas. Mugabe's core political skill was always his ability to garner domestic political support by thumbing his nose at the West, and this was a prime example of that. By writing off the rule against the admission of coerced confessions as Western liberal claptrap, Mugabe was shoring up his anti-colonial credentials. Second, the three security cases represented real threats to the regime's core political interests in the way that the Bill of Rights decisions did not. It needs to be recalled here that when the *York Brothers* and air force sabotage cases were decided, South Africa was still under white minority rule. It was also common knowledge that South Africa

[127]   Gubbay, "The Light of Successive Chief Justices."
[128]   Ibid.
[129]   Ibid.
[130]   Ibid.

was using agents actively to destabilize Zimbabwe.[131] The threats to Zimbabwe's security at the heart of these cases were thus not figments of Mugabe's imagination. They were real and substantial. Considered in that light, Mugabe's statement on torture looks less like an irrational outburst and more like a calculated decision to dispense with rule-of-law niceties in favor of the security gains to be had from the coerced confessions and arbitrary detention.

One last case that is worth mentioning is a case involving a challenge to the result in the Harare South constituency in the April 1995 elections. ZANU-PF had won 118 of the 120 seats contested in that election, and thus the potential overturning of this one result did not represent a threat to it at the time. Nevertheless, the case became significant later for what it revealed about the potential role that an independent judiciary might play in enforcing political rights. The applicant, Margaret Dongo, had been a medical assistant in the guerrilla war and later a ZANU-PF MP and member of its central committee.[132] She had, however, become disillusioned with the party's involvement in corruption and in 1995 decided to run as an independent. After being narrowly defeated in the Harare South seat, she challenged the result in the High Court. Finding evidence of extensive vote rigging (there were 1,025 more votes cast than registered voters), Smith J set the result aside and ordered a rerun, which Dongo duly won.[133] ZANU-PF did not protest the decision at the time. Nevertheless, the case triggered other similar challenges and was later to become a symbol of the way the courts could be used to challenge electoral manipulation. As we shall see in the next section, the judiciary's role in this respect was a crucial reason for the move against it after 1998.

In summary: From 1980 to 1998 the conception of the law/politics relation that had prevailed in colonial times restabilized around a perpetuation of some factors and the introduction of others. The essential element of the colonial conception – the strategic deployment of selective respect for judicial independence – was taken over. However, whereas the white minority government had justified this bifurcation of the legal order by claiming to be the agent of civilization, ZANU-PF relied on an ideology of revolutionary nationalism. In the key *York Brothers*, *Air Force Officers*, and *Ian Smith* cases, that ideology was used to justify the violation of white settler rights; to extend the rule of law in those settings, the ideological rationale went, would be to weaken ZANU-PF's ability to protect the Zimbabwean people against

---

[131]   Meredith, *Mugabe* 50.
[132]   Ibid 104–5.
[133]   Ibid. See also Compagnon, *A Predictable Tragedy* 148.

neocolonial exploitation. In the absence of any credible electoral threat after the 1987 Unity Accord, further repression of political rights was unnecessary. As the *Dongo* case showed, ZANU-PF was prepared to tolerate the judiciary's power to overturn electoral results in a situation where it held 98 percent of the contestable seats. Equally, however, as the next section argues, when ZANU-PF's hold on power came under electoral threat, the strategic rationale for its selective respect for judicial independence collapsed.

5.3 THE INSTRUMENTALIST INTERLUDE: 1999–2008

All commentators identify a significant shift in ZANU-PF's treatment of the judiciary around 1999–2000.[134] From this point onwards, attacks on judicial independence, which had always occurred, became more sustained and destructive. Verbal threats turned into physical assaults, senior judges were intimidated into resigning, and Mugabe began to use his power over judicial appointments to stock the bench with political lackeys. Whereas ZANU-PF's authoritarian rule had initially been subject to legal constraints in defined areas, no one by the mid-2000s thought that the government was subject to meaningful judicial control. A shift in the official ideology of law's relationship to politics had occurred, from a situation in which law had been accorded some autonomy to one in which law no longer formed part of the package of legitimating devices through which ZANU-PF sought to maintain its hold on power. In typological terms, the Zimbabwean JR regime had transitioned from something approximating authoritarian legalism to authoritarian instrumentalism.

Drawing on existing accounts of this period, this section considers four main questions: (1) What caused this change in Zimbabwe's JR regime? (2) What can we learn from the Zimbabwean case about authoritarian legalism's susceptibility to this kind of transformation? (3) What was the character of the authoritarian instrumentalist regime that arose after 2000? (4) What does Zimbabwe's experience suggest about the stability of such regimes?

5.3.1 *The Causes of the Transition*

According to the standard account,[135] the immediate trigger for ZANU-PF's changed approach to the judiciary was the citizenry's unexpected rejection, in

---

[134] See, for example, Compagnon, *A Predictable Tragedy* 150–6; Widner, "Building Judicial Independence in Semi-Democracies" 249; Gubbay, "The Progressive Erosion of the Rule of Law in Independent Zimbabwe" 13.

[135] See, for example, Widner, "Building Judicial Independence in Semi-Democracies" 249; International Bar Association, *Report of IBA Zimbabwe Mission 2001* (London: IBA, 2001)

a February 2000 referendum, of a proposed new Constitution.[136] Though not existentially threatening in itself, the referendum result occurred in the context of growing political opposition to ZANU-PF's rule that had been building from the mid-1990s. As the first occasion on which ZANU-PF had lost any kind of national plebiscite on its performance, the referendum provided concrete evidence of the opposition's support. When the extent of that support was confirmed at the June 2000 general elections, ZANU-PF moved to clamp down on the judiciary as part of its attempt to regain political control.

This account is instructive as far as it goes. What it lacks, however, is a sense of the specific threat that the judiciary posed to ZANU-PF's rule, and why it was that the assault on the judiciary from 2000 onwards, given the useful legitimating function it had been performing, was so vitally necessary. To get a sense of that, the story needs to be rewound a little, first, to the beginnings of the opposition movement in the 1990s, and then to the actions that the courts took in the immediate buildup to the assault that convinced ZANU-PF's leadership that the judiciary needed to be neutralized.

If it had a distinct starting point, opposition to ZANU-PF's rule may be said to have begun in 1990, the year in which Zimbabwe embarked on an economically and socially disastrous Economic Structural Adjustment Program (ESAP).[137] The main achievement of the program, apart from the mandatory reduction in welfare spending, was to spawn a politically mobilized trade union movement. Centered on the Zimbabwe Congress of Trade Unions (ZCTU), the movement rapidly became an alternative voice on the challenges facing the country – not initially represented in Parliament, but providing the first real counter to ZANU-PF's political hegemony nevertheless.

In May 1997, the ZCTU joined a broad cross section of civic organizations to form the National Constitutional Assembly (NCA). Though its activities later came to embody its name, the NCA at first did not propose an alternative Constitution, but rather lobbied for the establishment of a participatory constitutional reform process.[138] The primary concern was the centralization of power in the presidency, and the need to impose some limit on the number of times Mugabe could stand for reelection.[139] Morgan Tsvangirai, the

---

33. According to Compagnon, *A Predictable Tragedy* 150, the significant "turning point" occurred a little earlier, in January 1999, "because this was the first time Mugabe directly attacked the judiciary as an institution and hinted at the need for a purge." See also, Gubbay, "The Light of Successive Chief Justices" 18 and Meredith, *Mugabe* 159–66.

[136] The circumstances leading up to the holding of this referendum are explained below.
[137] Compagnon, *A Predictable Tragedy* 199.
[138] Ibid 90.
[139] Ibid.

charismatic head of the ZCTU, at first chaired the NCA before resigning in September 1999 to lead a new political party, the Movement for Democratic Change (MDC).[140]

Despite its origins in the ZCTU, the MDC is not a classic workers' party. It has no equivalent, for example, of the British Labour Party's now-discarded Clause IV.[141] Rather, the MDC grew out of the ZCTU to become a broad-based party that included many representatives of the civic organizations that had joined the NCA but also, crucially, former supporters of PF-ZAPU, who had had no proper political home from the time of the Unity Accord in 1987. The MDC also drew on significant white minority and international donor support. Though never as extensive as ZANU-PF would later try to make out, the fact that there was at least some basis to the claim that the MDC was a "neocolonial" party proved to be an important factor in ZANU-PF's capacity to contain it.

While all this mobilization of the political opposition was going on, it was becoming increasingly clear that the ESAP had failed to bring Zimbabwe's balance of payments problem under control. Never properly implemented, the Program had always been more about "clientelistic capitalism"[142] than genuine public-sector reform. When evidence emerged in 1997 of massive corruption in claims against the War Victims Compensation Fund, the Zimbabwe National Liberation War Veterans Association (ZNLWVA) took to the streets and pressured Mugabe into authorizing a massive, unbudgeted payout to its members. The Zimbabwe dollar immediately lost 75 percent of its value against the US dollar and prices of basic goods soared.[143] In January 1998, there were food riots in Harare and the general economic outlook looked bleak.

Rather than focusing its efforts on dealing with the crisis, or perhaps in a misguided attempt to generate economic growth, ZANU-PF sent troops to the Democratic Republic of Congo (the DRC) where a civil war had been raging. The ostensible purpose of the August 1998 troop deployment was to support the newly established government of Laurent Kabila. The ulterior and only very thinly disguised motive, however, was to use Zimbabwe's

---

[140]   Ibid 99.

[141]   On origins of the labor movement in society, see Brian Raftopoulos, "The Labour Movement and the Emergence of Opposition Politics in Zimbabwe" (2000) 33 *Labour, Capital, & Society* 256.

[142]   Volker Wild, *Profit Not for Profit's Sake: History and Business Culture of African Entrepreneurs in Zimbabwe* (Harare: Baobab Books, 1997) 262 (cited in Compagnon, A Predictable Tragedy 201).

[143]   Raftopoulos, "The Labour Movement" 270.

engagement in the conflict as a vehicle to secure lucrative business deals for senior army officers and ZANU-PF officials.[144] Predictably, this ill-considered and clearly self-serving military foray led to a redoubling of the NCA's demands. At the same time, internal dissent within ZANU-PF grew,[145] forcing Mugabe at the party's December 1998 annual conference to agree to initiate at least a limited constitutional reform process.[146]

When initial attempts to broker a compromise with the NCA broke down,[147] Mugabe appointed his own 400-member Constitutional Review Commission in April 1999. The Commission's official brief was to consult widely with the public to solicit their views on the constitutional reforms. In reality, however, it was responsible to Mugabe, who retained complete discretion to adopt, reject, or amend its recommendations.[148] The chairman of the Commission was none other than Chidyausiku, not yet Chief Justice, but a High Court judge and already by then a known Mugabe loyalist. After a carefully managed public consultation process, the Commission delivered its draft to Mugabe in November 1999. The President duly altered it in January 2000 to insert a controversial clause on uncompensated land expropriation that had not been part of the Commission's deliberations. It was this patently inadequate and politically partisan draft that was rejected at the February 2000 referendum, with 54.7 percent of voters supporting a joint NCA-MDC "no" campaign.[149]

Following closely on this defeat, the June 2000 general elections, in which the MDC won 57 of the 120 contested seats, delivered another telling blow to ZANU-PF's seeming air of invincibility. Though formed less than a year before the elections, the MDC had been able to draw on the ZCTU's organizational support to make inroads into ZANU-PF's traditional Shona support base, particularly in the capital, Harare, and other major urban areas.[150] At the same time, it had taken over the mantle of PF-ZAPU in rural Matabeleland, with Ndebele voters shifting their allegiance to the MDC in large numbers.[151] That shift was triggered by two events: first, the release in

---

[144] Meredith, *Mugabe* 148.
[145] Compagnon, *A Predictable Tragedy* 91–2.
[146] Ibid 92.
[147] Ibid 93.
[148] The Commission was formed under the Commissions of Inquiry Act. This gave Mugabe power to amend its report (Compagnon, *A Predictable Tragedy* 93, 95).
[149] See, for example, Human Rights Watch, *"Our Hands Are Tied": Erosion of the Rule of Law in Zimbabwe* (November 2008) (at page 1, Summary); Bar Human Rights Committee of England and Wales, *A Place in the Sun: A Report on the State of the Rule of Law in Zimbabwe after the Global Political Agreement of September 2008* (June 2010) 24.
[150] Compagnon, *A Predictable Tragedy* 97–100.
[151] Ibid 101.

1997 of the Catholic Commission for Justice and Peace's report into the 1983–7 *Gukuranhadi* massacres, which rekindled memories of ZANU-PF oppression,[152] and, second, Joshua Nkomo's death on July 1, 1999, which absolved PF-ZAPU supporters from any bonds of obligation they might have felt to respect the 1987 Unity Accord.[153]

The MDC's achievement in winning 57 of the 120 contested seats was both less and more threatening to ZANU-PF than the raw numbers suggest. Less threatening because the constitutional amendments introduced in 1987 had given Mugabe the power to appoint 20 MPs, in addition to the 120 who were directly elected. With another 10 seats reserved for tribal leaders, the MDC would have needed 76 or more seats to form a majority government. Despite its remarkable performance, the MDC was therefore well short of actual victory. On the other hand, the MDC immediately brought High Court challenges to the results in 39 of the seats it had lost to ZANU-PF, enough to make a difference to the outcome if just more than half of the challenges went its way. In light of the outcome in the 1995 *Dongo* case,[154] this was more than just a hypothetical possibility.

If confirmation of the threat the judiciary posed was required, another series of events in the year leading up to the assault on the judiciary in February 2000 supplied it.[155] In January 1999, the Zimbabwe Defense Force had detained two journalists – Mark Chavunduka and Ray Choto – for breaking a story about an attempted military coup. The coup, the story ran, had been organized by officers disillusioned with Zimbabwe's involvement in the DRC. Determined to discover the story's source, military intelligence officers and CIO agents detained Chavunduka in an army barracks in Harare, where he was interrogated and tortured for seven days.[156] Over the course of that week, three separate habeas corpus orders were ignored. Only after Smith J threatened to have the Minister of Defense arrested was Chavunduka briefly released.[157] He was then redetained along with Choto and further tortured before the Supreme Court eventually declared the statutory provision under which they were being held unconstitutional.[158]

[152]   Ibid.
[153]   Ibid.
[154]   Discussed in Section 5.2.3.
[155]   This account is drawn from Compagnon, *A Predictable Tragedy* 150 and Meredith, *Mugabe* 149–56.
[156]   Meredith, *Mugabe* 149.
[157]   Compagnon, *A Predictable Tragedy* 150; Meredith, *Mugabe* 149.
[158]   Meredith, *Mugabe* 155.

While the journalists' case appears to show the helplessness of the judiciary in the face of ZANU-PF's determined repression, it was what followed that proved their real strength. In an open letter to Mugabe, three Supreme Court judges condemned the journalists' arrest and torture as a serious breach of the rule of law.[159] Mugabe responded by launching a full-scale attack on the judiciary, the independent press, and the white minority on national television. "If judges assume both a judicial and quasi-political role," he said, "what suffers is in effect their judicial function. In those circumstances the one and only honorable course open to them is that of quitting the bench and joining the political forum."[160] All twenty-five High Court and Supreme Court judges, only eight of whom by that stage were white, responded by issuing a statement condemning the President's attack on the rule of law and refusing to resign.[161] It was this show of unity more than anything else that convinced ZANU-PF that the judiciary needed to be subordinated. In effect, Mugabe's previous strategy, of appointing judges with strong legal-professional credentials to bolster the judiciary's legitimating potential, had proven too successful. ZANU-PF now clearly faced a defiant judicial branch that was unlikely to bow to political pressure in the resolution of the electoral disputes still outstanding.

Mugabe's initial solution to this threat was to issue an executive order under s 158(1) of the Electoral Act putting an end to all judicial proceedings relating to the June 2000 elections.[162] On January 30, 2001, however, the Supreme Court invalidated the order, once again exposing all 39 disputed seats to possible reversal. The MDC then proceeded to win the first seven of its cases in the High Court, with more pending.[163] This run of decisions, together with the *Dongo* case, marked the judiciary out as a distinct threat to ZANU-PF's survival. What had been a strategic strength before the rise of a credible political opposition – an independent judiciary with the capacity to legitimate ZANU-PF's authoritarian rule – had turned into a major weakness.

On this account of things, then, it was not just the rise of a credible political opposition that triggered the shift in Zimbabwe's JR regime. It was the combination of that development with the judiciary's demonstrated independence that mattered. As Daniel Compagnon puts the point:

---

[159] Meredith, *Mugabe* 151–2; Compagnon, *A Predictable Tragedy* 150.
[160] Quoted in Meredith, *Mugabe* 153.
[161] Compagnon, *A Predictable Tragedy* 151; Meredith, *Mugabe* 155.
[162] Compagnon, *A Predictable Tragedy* 153.
[163] Ibid.

Mugabe's political survival required that in the future the judiciary should not be a recourse for his numerous opponents . . . As long as a token respect for the independence of the judiciary and the rule of law brought more benefits (including a positive image in the West) than costs, Mugabe had complied with most court rulings and therefore accepted some temporary setbacks.[164]

What had changed, in other words, was the strategic rationale underpinning Zimbabwe's authoritarian legalist regime. As we have seen, ZANU-PF's support for judicial independence was never sincere but rather based on an ongoing cost-benefit analysis of the contribution independent judicial review could make to its political survival. Even before 1999, judicial independence was flouted whenever ZANU-PF's fundamental interests were at stake. What happened from 2000 was the emergence of a more or less permanent threat to its hold on power. That development pushed ZANU-PF to dispense with its policy of selective toleration in favor of the wholesale subordination of the judiciary.

Authoritarian legalist regimes, this analysis suggests, may be particularly vulnerable to sudden shifts in the level of support for the political opposition, especially where the regime has arisen in circumstances of one-party dominance. By definition, such regimes are premised on a less-than-fully-democratic claim to political authority. For the denial of political rights to be sustained, a complex legitimating ideology needs to be constructed that divides social life into rule-of-law-respecting and disrespecting spheres.[165] The problem in Zimbabwe, and the reason why authoritarian legalism might have collapsed so quickly there, was that, in the absence of a credible opposition until the late 1990s, the legitimating ideology that had been constructed justified the repression of white-settler civil and political rights rather than political rights more generally.

---

[164]   Compagnon, *A Predictable Tragedy* 151. Compare this explanation to Widner's: "Although the initial focal point was a decision about land reform, political contestation was the underlying concern" (Widner, "Building Judicial Independence in Semi-Democracies" 249). On this view, ZANU-PF used land reform to win back the war veterans' political support. The courts got in the way of that strategy by overturning the Fast-Track Land Reform Program. The courts also showed up the extent of electoral fraud in the 2000 elections. They consequently needed to be subdued (ibid 250).

[165]   This has been achieved in Singapore, for example, where the People's Action Party has over many years constructed an elaborate legitimating ideology that justifies the nonenforcement of political rights. See Jothie Rajah, *Authoritarian Rule of Law: Legislation, Discourse, and Legitimacy in Singapore* (New York: Cambridge University Press, 2012).

To the extent that there had been threats to the ZANU-PF regime, as we have seen,[166] those threats had taken the form of South Africa's destabilization efforts in the 1980s. At the time, it had been a simple enough matter for ZANU-PF to justify the denial of political rights as being necessary to maintain Zimbabwe's newly won independence from white-settler control. The threat posed by the MDC after 2000, by contrast, was (as much as ZANU-PF tried to portray it otherwise) a domestic political threat. This deprived the regime of what had been until then the usual ideological rationale for its suppression of its political opponents. Complicating matters further was the fact that, in abiding by the High Court's decision in the *Dongo* case,[167] ZANU-PF had effectively accepted the judiciary's authority to enforce political rights in cases involving indigenous African candidates unconnected to the white minority government.[168] It followed that, when the Supreme Court struck down Mugabe's executive order ousting the courts' jurisdiction to adjudicate the June 2000 electoral disputes, ZANU-PF had little room to maneuver. While it might have countermanded that decision by passing a constitutional amendment, that course of conduct would still have left the judiciary to enforce the amendment in circumstances where it could not be trusted. To be completely sure of staving off the MDC threat, ZANU-PF needed to subordinate the judiciary – in effect, to give up on the strategy of selective respect for judicial independence in favor of direct political control.

5.3.2 *The Assault on the Judiciary*

An undisguised assault on judicial independence of the kind launched by ZANU-PF after February 2000 poses obvious risks to an authoritarian power holder that has relied on a measure of rule-of-law legitimation. However much the assault might be necessitated by political threats to its survival, the subordination of the judiciary increases the burden on the remaining legitimation devices to fill the gap. In theoretical terms, the power holder needs to manage the transition to authoritarian instrumentalism by transforming the ideological basis for its authority claim.

In Zimbabwe's case, such a transformation did occur and temporarily succeeded in sustaining ZANU-PF's authoritarian rule. The key move was its ability to use the land reform issue – which had been simmering since

---

[166] Section 5.2.3.
[167] See discussion in Section 5.2.3.
[168] It had done so, of course, because in 1995 ZANU-PF held over 98 percent of the seats, meaning that a single overturned election result posed no threat to it.

independence, but whose legitimating potential had not been fully exploited – to disguise the motivation for its assault on the judiciary. By linking the judiciary's enforcement of indigenous African political rights to its enforcement of white-settler property rights, ZANU-PF was able to portray the judiciary as the enemy of the national liberation project and in this way justify its wholesale subordination.

To see how this ideational shift occurred it is necessary briefly to recount some of the main events following the February 2000 referendum loss. Within a few days of the results being announced,[169] armed gangs styling themselves "war veterans" began invading commercial farms – intimidating, physically assaulting, and in some cases murdering their white owners and African farmworkers. While some invasions of white commercial farms had occurred before then, they had generally been disowned by ZANU-PF and effectively policed.[170] What changed after February 2000 was the degree to which the invasions were not only tolerated by law enforcement agencies, but actively supported by the police and army.[171] The attacks were in fact coordinated from the President's office, and government vehicles were used to transport the invaders to the farms and supply them with food.[172] Far from disowning the invasions, ZANU-PF cabinet ministers voiced their active support for them, with Mugabe at one point saying that "[t]hose who try to cause disunity among our people must watch out because death will befall them."[173] It is clear, then, that the attacks were not some sort of spontaneous popular uprising but part of a deliberate attempt on the part of ZANU-PF to regain its revolutionary credentials.

The Zimbabwe Commercial Farmers Union responded to the invasions by challenging them in the High Court, winning what it must have thought was a decisive victory on March 17, 2000, when the Court declared the invasions illegal and ordered the police to remove the invaders within seventy-two hours.[174] This order was simply ignored, however, with the Commissioner of Police initially claiming lack of manpower and then describing the invasions as a political matter.[175] A further order from the

---

[169]   The referendum was held on February 12–13, and the results announced on February 15. The invasions began on February 26. See Meredith, *Mugabe* 165, 167.

[170]   Saller, *The Judicial Institution in Zimbabwe* 27.

[171]   Compagnon, *A Predictable Tragedy* 172; Meredith, *Mugabe* 167; Raftopoulos, "The Labour Movement" 277.

[172]   Compagnon, *A Predictable Tragedy* 172.

[173]   Quoted in Meredith, *Mugabe* 169.

[174]   *Commercial Farmers' Union* v. *Commissioner of Police and Others* HH-3544–2000 (cited in Compagnon, *A Predictable Tragedy* 173).

[175]   Compagnon, *A Predictable Tragedy* 173–4.

High Court on April 13[176] and a Supreme Court order to the same effect[177] were also ignored. At the same time, ZANU-PF sought to retrospectively validate what it now referred to as its Fast-Track Land Reform Program by amending the Constitution so as to insert the controversial provision on land reform that had been rejected at the February 2000 referendum.[178] In a legally bizarre but ideologically effective formulation, the amendment purported to impose an obligation on "the former colonial power . . . to pay compensation for agricultural land compulsorily acquired for resettlement, through an adequate fund established for the purpose."[179] It then absolved the Government of Zimbabwe from any obligation "to pay compensation for agricultural land compulsorily acquired" in the event that "the former colonial power fails to pay compensation through such a fund."[180]

From July 2000, the ongoing series of court cases arising from the farm invasions became intermingled with the thirty-nine High Court challenges to the June 2000 election results.[181] Instead of exposing ZANU-PF's violation of the rule of law to further scrutiny, however, the confluence of these two sets of cases played into its hands. In particular, by using its monopoly on public media,[182] ZANU-PF was able to portray the judiciary as the privileged, white-minority-friendly opponent of the *Third Chimurenga* (armed uprising to regain possession of the land). ZANU-PF was in this way able to rationalize what was in reality a clampdown on the judiciary's capacity to enforce political rights as the fulfilment of Zimbabwe's national revolutionary project.

The close nexus between the two sets of cases became even closer at the end of 2000. On November 24 that year, war veterans invaded the Supreme Court building in the middle of the hearing of a major constitutional challenge to the land reform program. They threatened to kill the judges and succeeded in disrupting the session.[183] This was followed shortly afterwards (on December 8) by the issuing of a presidential executive order ousting the courts' jurisdiction to hear electoral disputes. Two weeks later, on December 21, the Supreme Court invalidated the process followed by the

---

[176] *Commercial Farmers' Union* v. *Commissioner of Police and Others* HH-84-2000 (cited in Compagnon, *A Predictable Tragedy* 174).

[177] *Commercial Farmers' Union* 2001 (2) SA 925 (ZS).

[178] Amendment 16 in Act 5 of 2000 inserting a new s 16A purporting to cast obligation on Britain to compensate farmers. This was followed by the 17th amendment in August 2000 authorizing uncompensated acquisition of farmland. See Compagnon, *A Predictable Tragedy* 174.

[179] Section 16A(1)(c)(i).

[180] Section 16A(1)(c)(ii).

[181] As explained above.

[182] See Compagnon, *A Predictable Tragedy* 118–40.

[183] Bar Human Rights Committee, *A Place in the Sun*, 16.

Fast-Track Land Reform Program. On January 8, 2001, Chidyausiku gave a speech at the opening of the legal year in Bulawayo condemning Gubbay for his handling of the land reform cases and accusing him of political bias in favor of white farmers and against poor people.[184] Unbowed, Gubbay led the Supreme Court in overturning the presidential executive order on January 30, 2001. This turned out, however, to be his last official act. On February 2, 2001, Gubbay was informed that an earlier, tentative offer he had made to resign in late January had been accepted. He was immediately put on leave and took early retirement from March 1, 2001. Two other Supreme Court judges, Nick McNally and Ahmed Ebrahim, were also threatened. They initially refused to resign, but within a year both had left the Bench.[185]

In their stead, Mugabe began appointing political loyalists. First, Chidyausiku was made acting Chief Justice in March 2001, with the appointment confirmed in August of that year.[186] The new head of the judiciary's qualifications for the position were either woeful or perfect depending on your perspective. In addition to his work as chair of the Constitutional Reform Commission, Chidyausiku had served as Deputy Minister of Justice and Attorney General before being appointed to the High Court in 1987.[187] As a judge of the High Court, he had one of the worst records of being overturned on appeal and was not the most senior judge of that Court at the time of his appointment in 2001, let alone the most senior Supreme Court judge.[188] When his acting appointment as Chief Justice was announced in February 2000, the Zimbabwe Law Society, by then a predominantly black organization, collected thousands of signatures for a petition objecting to his appointment.[189] That ZANU-PF was prepared to ignore these objections is a strong indication both of the political nature of the appointment, and also of ZANU-PF's abandonment from this point of its previous strategy of rule-of-law legitimation.

The rest of the new judges appointed to the Supreme Court were little better. At the end of July 2001, Mugabe used the power he had always possessed under the Lancaster House Constitution to expand the size of the Supreme Court Bench from five to eight judges. The new judges appointed were all

[184] Compagnon, *A Predictable Tragedy* 154; Bar Human Rights Committee, *A Place in the Sun* 16; American Bar Association, *The State of Justice in Zimbabwe* 46.
[185] In McNally's case, through retirement. See Compagnon, *A Predictable Tragedy* 155; Bar Human Rights Committee, *A Place in the Sun* 17.
[186] Bar Human Rights Committee, *A Place in the Sun* 17.
[187] Compagnon, *A Predictable Tragedy* 144.
[188] Saller, *The Judicial Institution in Zimbabwe* 25.
[189] Ibid.

tainted by their strong political connections to ZANU-PF and less-than-convincing legal-professional credentials: Misheck Cheda was a former permanent secretary in the Ministry of Justice, Vernanda Ziyambi a known ZANU PF supporter, and Luke Malaba a former war veteran.[190] Both Cheda and Malaba's independence was further compromised by their appearance on a list of names, compiled by Margaret Dongo, of high-ranking officials who had personally received commercial farms.[191] Chidyausiku's name was also on this list.[192]

In light of these events, there is no escaping the conclusion that, from the beginning of 2001, ZANU-PF dispensed with any pretense that the senior judiciary was to remain independent. The manner of the sitting Supreme Court judges' forced resignation, Chidyausiku's appointment, and the effective bribery of three of the new Supreme Court justices by awarding them farms through the very land reform program whose constitutionality they would be called upon to adjudicate, destroyed any residual faith there might have been in ZANU-PF's respect for the rule of law. As blatant and desperate as this assault on judicial independence had been, however, ZANU-PF was able skillfully to manipulate the situation to its advantage. In particular, by eliding the judiciary's enforcement of indigenous African political rights with its enforcement of white-settler property rights, ZANU-PF was able to portray the courts as an opponent of Zimbabwe's national revolutionary project, and in this way to justify their wholesale subordination. The judiciary needed to be contained, the official rhetoric went, because it stood in the way of the achievement of what had always been the principal objective of the liberation war: the return of the land to the African masses.

Rather than the product of a deliberate strategy, this transformation in the ideological basis for ZANU-PF's claim to authority emerged step by step as it reacted to unfolding events. What started as an emergency containment measure – the use of land invasions after February 2000 to reestablish ZANU-PF's revolutionary credentials – changed over time into a relatively effective tool for depicting the judiciary as part of the neocolonial threat to Zimbabwe's continued independence. As the next section argues, this repackaging of ZANU-PF's claim to legitimacy grew more sophisticated as the first decade of the twenty-first century progressed.

[190] Compagnon, *A Predictable Tragedy* 155.
[191] Ibid.
[192] Ibid 155; Bar Human Rights Committee, *A Place in the Sun* 17.

5.3.3 *Assessing the Character of the Post-2000 Regime*

The immediate effect of the assault on the judiciary was to pack the Supreme Court with judges who were prepared to halt the challenges to the 2000 election results. After the initial run of seven High Court decisions, none of the thirty-nine electoral cases was finally resolved by the Supreme Court.[193] Instead, Chidyausiku, on being appointed as Chief Justice in March 2001, "shelved the appeals indefinitely."[194] In the result, all the ZANU-PF MPs whose election results were under challenge served their full term until 2005.[195]

In the longer term, the assault necessitated a change to the ideological framing of ZANU-PF's claim to political authority. Deprived of the legitimating benefits of independent judicial review, the party began constructing a new legitimating ideology based on (1) the complete subordination of the Supreme Court to the needs of the national revolutionary project; (2) the demonization of the MDC opposition as an urban, historically unaware tool of neocolonial interests; and (3) the securing of fresh electoral mandates through extreme violence and intimidation.

Following the pattern of his suspension of the election case appeals, Chidyausiku CJ began doing President Mugabe's bidding in land reform cases as well. On July 2, 2001, before the appointment of the three loyalist judges, the Supreme Court upheld its decision of December 2000 invalidating the Fast-Track Land Reform Program, with Chidyausiku CJ in dissent.[196] This decision, however, was reversed in December 2001 by a majority consisting of Chidyausiku CJ and Cheda, Malaba and Ziyambi JJ, the three loyalists.[197] The longer-serving and more liberal judges, Sandura, Muchechetere, and McNally JJ, were not asked to sit, even though it had been the practice until then to appoint a Full Bench to decide significant constitutional cases.[198]

In what has been described as a deliberate attempt to hollow out the country's rich tradition of "nationalist historiography," ZANU-PF supplemented its subordination of the judiciary by propagating a new form of "patriotic

---

[193]   Solidarity Peace Trust, *Subverting Justice: The Role of the Judiciary in Denying the Will of the Zimbabwe Electorate since 2000* (March 2005) 5–6 (reporting that, of the 39 petitions, 16 were heard by the High Court, with 7 decided in favor of the MDC and 9 in favor of ZANU-PF).

[194]   Compagnon, *A Predictable Tragedy* 153.

[195]   Solidarity Peace Trust, *Subverting Justice*.

[196]   See Compagnon, *A Predictable Tragedy* 155.

[197]   Ibid.

[198]   Ibid.

history."[199] According to this official narrative, which was promoted on national television, in state-owned newspapers and in "youth militia camps,"[200] ZANU-PF remained the chief custodian of Zimbabwe's national revolutionary project, save that the project was now extended to include former ZIPRA fighters loyal to the government.[201] The opposition MDC, by contrast, was depicted as a party ignorant of Zimbabwe's history of revolutionary struggle and committed instead to universalist liberal values that served a pro-Western agenda.[202] To vote for the MDC was thus to vote for a neocolonial party that would turn back the gains of the guerrilla war.

The third component of the new legitimating ideology consisted in a continued commitment to democratic elections (in 2002 and 2005), although this time accompanied by such extreme violence and blatant vote rigging that they were barely credible.[203]

These three devices succeeded for a while in constructing a new and relatively stable official understanding of the law/politics relationship. In place of the legitimating role played by independent judicial review, Zimbabwe's post-2000 JR regime was undergirded by a more elaborate and consciously maintained ideology of revolutionary nationalism. ZANU-PF's claim to political authority, on this understanding of things, was premised on its leading role in the revolutionary struggle, coupled with its ongoing commitment to taking back the land from white settlers, as evidenced by its promotion of the Fast-Track Land Reform Program. The Supreme Court's role in this new complex of legitimating ideas was to facilitate the implementation of the land reform program (as opposed to overseeing its procedural fairness and conformance to respect for individual rights).

The post-2000 period in Zimbabwe may in this sense be understood as a state-driven attempt to construct an authoritarian instrumentalist regime. What is particularly instructive about the Zimbabwean case is that, even in this less well-developed country, the new regime required a fair amount of sustained ideational work. In addition, the transformation occurred only after an exogenous shock to the preexisting regime that needed to be managed for reasons of political survival. Just as the late-nineteenth-century American industrialization and urbanization processes had challenged the premises of

---

[199] Terence Ranger, "Nationalist Historiography, Patriotic History and the History of the Nation: The Struggle over the past in Zimbabwe" (2004) 30 *Journal of Southern African Studies* 215.

[200] Ibid 219.

[201] Ibid 220.

[202] Ibid 223–4.

[203] Compagnon, *A Predictable Tragedy* 61–2 (noting reduced but still significant violence in 2005).

Classical Legal Thought, so too in Zimbabwe the rise of the MDC unsettled the legitimation logic of the pre-2000 regime. In the American case, JR-regime transformation was the product of legal-cultural actors exploiting the exogenous shock to promote a new understanding of the law/politics relation. In Zimbabwe, the transformation was driven by an authoritarian power holder's interest in political survival. But the causal mechanism of regime transformation – exogenous shock followed by ideological reconstruction work – was broadly similar.

Zimbabwe's authoritarian instrumentalist regime, though clearly consolidated by 2005, did not last very long. Again, the reasons for this are instructive for comparative purposes. For all ZANU-PF's sustained ideological work, the assault on the judiciary was associated with a series of other problems that undermined the stability of the regime by 2008. First, the Fast-Track Land Reform Program destroyed the commercial agricultural sector, particularly tobacco farming, Zimbabwe's highest export earner.[204] Second, money printed to pay the military and war veterans to sustain the revolutionary nationalist part of the new legitimating ideology contributed to a massive devaluation of Zimbabwe's currency.[205] And third, ZANU-PF's treatment of the judiciary and apparent encouragement of violence against white farmers and opposition supporters meant that the international donor community was reluctant to come to Zimbabwe's aid.[206] Together, these factors pushed the Zimbabwean economy to the brink of collapse.

In the chaotic first round of the March 2008 presidential elections, which were held for the first time simultaneously with parliamentary elections, Tsvangirai was announced as the narrow winner after a five-week delay. With MDC-T also winning the parliamentary elections,[207] ZANU-PF resorted to extreme violence to intimidate voters.[208] Tsvangirai was forced to withdraw his candidacy in the second round of the presidential election to protect his supporters, leaving Mugabe the victor with power now divided between the presidency and parliament. At this point, the Southern African Development Community (SADC) intervened to orchestrate a political solution. South Africa's then President, Thabo Mbeki, was appointed to conduct shuttle diplomacy between ZANU-PF and the MDC. With tremendous

---

[204]   Ibid 181.

[205]   Ibid 261.

[206]   Ibid 263.

[207]   The official ZEC tally gave the MDC-T 100 of the 210 seats, ZANU-PF 99, and the MDC-M 10.

[208]   The violence is documented in Peter Godwin, *The Fear: Robert Mugabe and the Martyrdom of Zimbabwe* (New York: Little Brown, 2011).

regional pressure on ZANU-PF to enter a coalition government it signed the Global Political Agreement (GPA) discussed in the introduction to this chapter.

In many ways, the GPA was an admission of defeat, but ZANU-PF still had sufficient de facto control to insist on getting all the major security portfolios and to include its key policies on land reform in the GPA. Like the National Party in South Africa, it strategically chose to negotiate the agreement from a position of political strength, backed by its ongoing control of the army. Nevertheless, the GPA marked the end of ZANU-PF's monopoly on power and the beginning of a period of coalition government.

What do these events tell us about the stability of authoritarian instrumentalism? In a society whose economy has come to depend on secure property rights and international trade, even a relatively secure authoritarian power holder like ZANU-PF cannot survive without some semblance of the rule of law for long. In typological terms, where an authoritarian legalist regime has existed, the economy adjusts to expect independent judicial review in those aspects of social life not immediately connected to the authoritarian power holder's political survival interests. Where respect for property rights, in particular, is impacted by a switch to authoritarian instrumentalism, as the Egyptian example also illustrates,[209] the power holder driving such a transition is vulnerable to the political consequences of any resultant economic collapse. We may think of authoritarian legalism, in this sense, as a more multifaceted and therefore durable JR regime than authoritarian instrumentalism, at least in the absence of a comprehensive legitimating ideology of law's subordination to politics.[210] In Zimbabwe's case, authoritarian legalism also had deep roots in colonial conceptions of the law/politics relation. It therefore promised a greater measure of stability were ZANU-PF somehow to engineer a return to it. The story of how that happened was briefly related in the introduction to this chapter, but is explained more fully in the next section.

5.4 RECOVERY AND RETURN: 2009–2013

With the collapse of the economy in 2008, ZANU-PF lost exclusive control of the country for the first time since independence. Regional organizations, like the AU and the SADC, began playing an increasing role in Zimbabwe's

---

[209] See Tamir Moustafa, *The Struggle for Constitutional Power: Law, Politics, and Economic Development in Egypt* (New York: Cambridge University Press, 2007).

[210] As, for example, occurred in Myanmar after 1962. See Chapter 6 for a discussion of this example and the distinction between the two subtypes.

internal affairs and brokered the signing of the GPA. Even as it entered the Inclusive Government, however, ZANU-PF retained the most important levers of power – the army, the police, and the support of the war veterans. The MDC, for its part, was not as strong as its performance in the 2008 elections might have suggested. Exhausted by a decade of political struggle and by the extreme violence meted out against its supporters, its two factions (MDC-T and MDC-M) agreed to join the Inclusive Government in circumstances where they risked reestablishing ZANU-PF's authoritarian rule. And that is indeed what happened. By helping to stabilize the economy and restore basic governmental services, the MDCs' participation in the Inclusive Government paved the way for Mugabe's return to power.

ZANU-PF's outmaneuvering of the two MDC parties in the Inclusive Government is explained in detail in the literature.[211] In outline, the MDC-T's responsibility under the GPA for health care and education meant that it could make a real contribution in those areas of governance. The successes it achieved, however, worked against its own political interests by alleviating the social and economic problems that had forced ZANU-PF to the negotiating table. The MDC-T's involvement in the Inclusive Government also neutered it as an opposition voice while exposing its internal divisions to the glare of public attention.[212] One dimension of this was the MDC-T/MDC-M split, which their participation as separate parties in the Inclusive Government entrenched.[213] The other was Tsvangirai's leadership style. Worn down by years of beatings and sham treason trials, he made several questionable decisions that the state-controlled media were able to use to portray him as an all-too-ordinary politician seduced by the material benefits of office.[214]

At the same time, the more informal nature of the Zimbabwean economy following its collapse in 2008 gave ZANU-PF the opportunity to grow its support among several new constituencies. The Fast-Track Land Reform Program, chaotic at the start, began to pay dividends as the beneficiaries adjusted to modern farming methods and agricultural markets. While the exact figures are contested, the production of tobacco and maize started to recover.[215] In another stroke of good fortune, rich diamond deposits were

---

[211]   See especially, LeBas, "The Perils of Power Sharing"; Brian Raftopoulos, "The Global Political Agreement as a 'Passive Revolution': Notes on Contemporary Politics in Zimbabwe" (2010) 99 *The Round Table* 705.

[212]   Raftopoulos, "The Global Political Agreement" 714–5.

[213]   Ibid 713.

[214]   LeBas, "The Perils of Power Sharing" 63.

[215]   Prosper B. Matondi, *Zimbabwe's Fast Track Land Reform* (London: Zed Books, 2012).

discovered in the south-east of the country.[216] ZANU-PF shrewdly permitted the unemployed young men who flocked to the area from the cities to engage in informal mining, thus winning it their support. Finally, ZANU-PF's policy of indigenizing ownership of major corporations added to its middle- and upper-class base.[217]

While re-growing its political support in this way, ZANU-PF began manipulating the constitution-making process. In contrast to 2000, when the constitutional reform process was driven by a Mugabe-appointed commission, the process under Article VI of the GPA was overseen by a Constitutional Parliamentary Select Committee, on which the MDC in fact had a majority.[218] The preamble to Article VI expressed the parties' determination "to create conditions for [the Zimbabwean] people to write a constitution for themselves." It went on to spell out a process for popular participation, with civil society representation on parliamentary committees, public hearings, public consultations, and two All Stakeholder conferences.[219] These provisions were in tension with the so-called Kariba draft Constitution of September 30, 2007. That document had been adopted as part of an earlier SADC process that had ended in a trilateral agreement between ZANU-PF and the two MDC factions. The Kariba draft retained the highly presidentialized system introduced by the 1987 amendments.[220] It was included as Annex B to the GPA but its actual relationship to the constitution to be drafted under Article VI was not made clear.[221] The GPA simply "acknowledge[d]" the Kariba draft while contemplating a new, more inclusive process. Thus, from the very beginning, a competition was set up between a more open, bottom-up, and participatory constitution-making process and a top-down political bargaining model.

Tilting the balance in favor of the latter was the fact that both the NCA, which had been behind the 2000 constitutional reform drive, and the ZCTU, chose not to participate in the Article VI process. Instead, the NCA launched a "Take Charge" campaign in July 2010 claiming to "expose the fraudulent process currently underway and led by politicians from ZANU PF and MDC."

---

[216] Raftopoulos, "The 2013 Elections in Zimbabwe" 981.
[217] Ibid 983.
[218] COPAC consisted of 17 men and 8 women, 11 members of MDC-T, 10 ZANU-PF members, 3 MDC-N members, and 1 representative of the traditional chiefs.
[219] Art. VI.
[220] Lia Nijzink, "The Relative Powers of Parliaments and Presidents in Africa: Lessons for Zimbabwe?" in Norbert Kersting (ed.), *Constitution in Transition: Academic Inputs for a New Constitution in Zimbabwe* (Friedrich Ebert Stiftung, 2009) 160, 181.
[221] Sokwanele, "Reflecting on Zimbabwe's Constitution-Making Process" (unpublished manuscript, August 2012) 18–9 available at www.sokwanele.com.

In particular, the NCA claimed that "the current COPAC/Kariba process (which is worse than the rejected Chidyausiku make-believe of 1999/2000), will be rejected by the people of Zimbabwe."[222] The reason for this stance may have been that the NCA's leaders felt excluded. In any event, the absence of the NCA – the main driver of the previous constitutional reform movement – weakened the participatory character of the Article VI process.

The impression that the constitution-making process was more about coopting the two MDC parties than soliciting a broad spread of views is borne out by assessments of the way the process unfolded. The public meetings scheduled in the GPA were delayed by more than a year until October 2010 by the formation of the Inclusive Government, the timing of which the GPA did not regulate.[223] Thereafter, the process more or less stuck to the GPA timetable, apart from one late-stage delay. In total, 4,943 meetings were held in all 1,957 wards. There were also two All Stakeholder conferences, one at the Harare International Conference Center (HICC) on July 13, 2009, and another to discuss the second draft Constitution on October 21, 2012. Judged by these numbers alone, therefore, the degree of participation was impressive. In reality, however, the process was marked by significant violence and intimidation. In a sign of things to come, the first All Stakeholder conference was disrupted by ZANU-PF activists.[224] Thereafter, public meetings were attended by war veterans and youth activists who directed discussion in ZANU-PF areas and disrupted meetings in areas where the two MDCs were strong.[225]

Given these problems with the public consultation process, the 2013 Constitution is more accurately described as a political agreement between ZANU-PF and the two MDC parties than a broad-based document.[226] That form of constitution is not necessarily fatal to democracy, as the South African

---

[222]   NCA Press Release, July 23, 2010 (quoted in Sokwanele, "Reflecting on Zimbabwe's Constitution-Making Process" 23).

[223]   Gwinyani A. Dzineza, *Zimbabwe's Constitutional Reform Process: Challenges and Prospects* (Institute for Justice and Reconciliation, 2012) 5.

[224]   LeBas, "The Perils of Power Sharing" 57.

[225]   Ibid. See also Dzinesa, *Zimbabwe's Constitutional Reform Process* 6 (citing Civil Society Monitoring Mechanism, *Annual Review of the Performance of the Inclusive Government of Zimbabwe: February 2010–February 2011* (Harare, 2011) and commenting on extensive "coaching" of participants) and Sokwanele, "Reflecting on Zimbabwe's Constitution-Making Process" 27 (documenting extensive "violence, intimidation, and harassment").

[226]   Dzineza, *Zimbabwe's Constitutional Reform Process* 6 argues that "ZANU –PF used the consultation process to ensure that the draft constitution reflected its preference for a powerful executive president, the removal of the office of the prime minister and the preservation of the current security structures." Anneke Meerkotter similarly concludes that the second COPAC draft of July 2012 was "something that can best be described as

example indicates.[227] The difference in Zimbabwe's case, however, was that the constitution-making process under the GPA bought ZANU-PF time to regroup. Unlike the National Party in South Africa, ZANU-PF was not negotiating the inevitable transfer of power, but the drafting of a new constitution in circumstances where it hoped eventually to win back exclusive control of the government.

The Constitution as enacted reflects the considerable bargaining power that ZANU-PF enjoyed under the Inclusive Government.[228] Despite consistent demands that the 1987 amendments to the independence Constitution should be overhauled, the 2013 Constitution still provides for a relatively strong presidency. Though not as centralized as the Kariba draft, it leaves significant powers in the hands of the President, including the power to declare war and states of emergency, and the power to issue pardons and appoint office bearers.[229] The 2013 Constitution also does not make its limit on presidential terms retrospective, meaning that Mugabe would in theory have been entitled to two further terms should he have remained in office.[230] Section 98 further provides for presidential immunity in office but not immunity for past presidents,[231] suggesting that Mugabe's strategy to avoid accountability for the *Gukurahundi* massacres and other crimes was to serve as President until he died.

One of the notional strengths of the 2013 Constitution, apart from the Bill of Rights, is that it establishes a range of new institutions, including a Constitutional Court and an independent National Prosecutions Authority separate from the Attorney General's office.[232] Chapter 12, following the South African model,[233] also provides for the establishment of independent institutions supporting constitutional democracy, including a Human Rights

a negotiated settlement between the key parties after a politically motivated community consultation process" (Anneke Meerkotter, "Trouble brewing in Zimbabwe – constitution-making in crisis" (August 31, 2012) available at www.polity.org.za/article/trouble-brewing-in-zimbabwe-constitution-making-in-crisis-2012-08-31).

[227] The 1993 South African Constitution was the product of the CODESA talks, in which agreement between the ANC and the National Party was treated as "sufficient consensus" to drive the process forward.

[228] Constitution of Zimbabwe 2013.

[229] Sections 111(1), 113(1), 112(1)(a), and 114(1) (power to appoint Attorney General) respectively.

[230] Section 91(2).

[231] Section 98(2). Section 98(4) does, however, extend a "good faith" defense to past presidents.

[232] The Constitution separates the office of the Attorney General from the National Prosecuting Authority. Section 114 makes the Attorney General the adviser to government on legal affairs. Sections 258–63 separately provide for a National Prosecuting Authority with guaranteed independence.

[233] Chapter 9 of the Constitution of South Africa, 1996.

Commission and the Zimbabwe Electoral Commission (ZEC). All these institutions have the potential on paper to support the development of a genuinely open and democratic society. The crucial strategic error on the part of pro-democracy groups, however, was their failure to insist on cross-party involvement in the staffing of these institutions. The Constitution provides, for example, for the President to appoint the chair of the ZEC after consultation with the Judicial Service Commission and the Parliamentary Committee on Standing Rules and Orders, with the other eight members of the ZEC appointed from a list supplied by the Committee.[234] The Constitutional Court is headed by a Chief Justice and Deputy Chief Justice, with the Constitution providing that these posts, together with the other seven positions on the Constitutional Court, are to be filled for the first seven years by the equivalent office bearers of the Supreme Court.[235] Accordingly, until 2020, the Constitutional Court will be staffed by Mugabe appointees.

Despite these flaws, the 2013 Constitution received 94.49 percent support at a referendum held on March 16, 2013. It was duly signed into law in May of that year. At this point, the transition to democracy in Zimbabwe might have gone one of two ways. On the one hand, democratic forces were pushing for a genuine shift to constitutional government with full liberal political rights. On the other, ZANU-PF stood poised to deploy the new Constitution as the centerpiece of a restored authoritarian regime. What factors influenced the outcome? Certainly, the pro-democracy movement's failure to insist that the members of the Constitutional Court be freshly appointed was a mistake, although whether activists could have foreseen exactly how Mugabe would manipulate this situation is another matter. Mugabe's tactic of using the Constitutional Court in the *Mawarire* case to give a rule-of-law imprimatur to his wish for an early election – overcoming the misgivings of SADC and the AU – was a masterstroke. It allowed him to draw on Zimbabwe's long-standing legalist tradition – indeed, on citizens' desire for the restoration of that tradition – to resume authoritarian control.

As noted in the introduction to this chapter, however, the 2013 election result cannot be ascribed entirely to the Constitutional Court's decision that the election should be held as early as possible. To judge by the local literature, the election was not completely rigged – there was genuine support for ZANU-PF and a definite turn against the MDC.[236] On another view, the

---

[234] Section 238.
[235] Section 166(1) read with para 18(2) of the Sixth Schedule of the Zimbabwe Constitution.
[236] Raftopoulos, "The 2013 Elections in Zimbabwe"; Gallagher, "The Battle for Zimbabwe in 2013."

memory of the violence that accompanied the 2008 elections fed into a fatalistic conviction that ZANU-PF would not tolerate defeat and thus that it would be better to vote for some measure of stability.[237]

5.5 RECONSOLIDATION: 2013 TO DATE

Since the adoption of the 2013 Constitution, the Zimbabwean JR regime has once again stabilized around a version of authoritarian legalism, with the new Constitutional Court providing an important source of legitimacy for ZANU-PF's ongoing rule. There does appear, however, to be greater fluidity in the party-political system. The general disarray within the ranks of MDC-T and MDC-M following their 2013 electoral defeat has created space for other political groupings to emerge. The NCA, untainted by what it depicts as the top-down constitution-making process, is now a formal political party. Margaret Dongo, the dissident ZANU-PF politician who successfully challenged her 1995 election loss, has formed her own political grouping. There are also various other ZANU-PF splinter parties.[238] ZANU-PF itself, until Mugabe's forced departure in 2017, was riven by internal fighting as factional leaders jockeyed for position.

In this new, more fragmented, political setting, the new Constitutional Court, headed by Chidyausiku, handed down several seemingly bold decisions from 2013 to 2017. One of the most significant of these was a decision striking down s 121 of the Criminal Procedure and Evidence Act, which had been used in prosecutions of opposition politicians to delay grants of bail for up to seven days.[239] In another case, the Court sentenced Prosecutor General, Johannes Tomana, to 30 days imprisonment for contempt of court after he failed to issue a certificate to allow a private prosecution.[240]

In purely political terms, the Constitutional Court's assertiveness from 2013 to 2017 is explicable either as strategic maneuvering in anticipation of Mugabe's impending departure,[241] as a function of the more fragmented

---

[237] Gallagher, "The Battle for Zimbabwe in 2013" 28.

[238] Joice Mujuru, for example, the widow of Solomon Mujuru, one of the few leaders capable of standing up to Mugabe before he died in suspicious circumstances, formed a political party after her ousting at ZANU-PF's December 2014 Congress.

[239] Chapter 9:07. See Bar Human Rights Committee, *A Place in the Sun* 18.

[240] See "Tomana jailed 30 dys [sic] for contempt of court over Kereke case" (New Zimbabwe, October 28, 2015) www.newzimbabwe.com/news-25717-Tomana+jailed+30+dys+for+con tempt+of+court/news.aspx.

[241] See Gretchen Helmke, *Courts under Constraints: Judges, Generals, and Presidents in Argentina* (New York: Cambridge University Press, 2012) (showing how judges in Argentina

political setting in which the Court was operating,[242] or simply as an attempt on Chidyausiku's part to establish some kind of reputation for independence on the eve of his retirement.[243] Viewed against the longer-term development of conceptions of the law/politics relation in Zimbabwe, however, the space that the Court was given to assert is role is not all that surprising. The crucial point from the perspective of this study is that the Court's resurgent independence did not fundamentally threaten ZANU-PF's hold on power. Indeed, it provided it with vital legitimating cover. In that sense, the Court's post-2013 activism may be explained as a function of ZANU-PF's interest in the restoration of Zimbabwe's authoritarian legalist regime.

5.6 CONCLUSION

The central theme of this chapter has been ZANU-PF's ability to combine qualified respect for judicial independence with an ideology of revolutionary nationalism. The only real exception to this package of legitimating devices was the period from 1999 to 2008 when ZANU-PF subordinated the Supreme Court in a desperate bid to prevent it from overturning the June 2000 election results. From that point, judicial review was instrumentalized in service to a comprehensive legitimating ideology centered on ZANU-PF's alleged exclusive right to implement Zimbabwe's anti-colonial project. While temporarily successful in staving off the immediate threat posed by the MDC, the political costs of dispensing with the legitimating cover of a relatively independent judiciary were high. By 2008, ZANU-PF had been forced to the negotiating table. That the constitution-making process that followed led to the restoration of authoritarian legalism rather than the hoped-for liberal constitutional state, was partly attributable to ZANU-PF's shrewd use of the political space that the Inclusive Government provided it to regroup, but also partly to the enduring hold that this type of JR regime exerts on Zimbabwe's constitutional-cultural imagination. Some societies, it would seem, may have a default JR regime to which they habitually return – a JR regime, that is, which structures legal and political action in ways that make it difficult to envisage any alternative.

The empirical material unearthed in this chapter also suggests several other generalizable insights. First, JR regimes may be able to survive both significant

---

have defected from political power-holders in anticipation of a change in the balance of political power).

[242] See Rebecca Bill Chavez, *The Rule of Law in Nascent Democracies: Judicial Politics in Argentina* (Stanford: Stanford University Press, 2004) (showing the effect of political fragmentation on judicial independence in Argentina).

[243] Chidyausiku retired on March 2, 2017 and died a few months later.

political transitions and their associated formal constitutional changes (in Zimbabwe's case, the transition to black majority rule in 1980 and the adoption of a new liberal-democratic constitution in 2013). Second, JR-regime consolidation in postcolonial settings may be less about contingent choices structuring path-dependent outcomes and more about post-colonial power holders' ability to adapt colonial conceptions of the law/politics relation to serve their political purposes. And, finally, the fact that the process of JR-regime transformation in Zimbabwe after 2000 fits the causal mechanism at work in the Indian and Australian cases, with some slight adjustments (to the nature of the exogenous shock and the actors driving the transformation), provides tentative empirical support for the generalizability of that mechanism. These insights, together with those from the previous two chapters, are further developed in the next chapter.

6

Testing the Typological Theory: A Medium-N Comparative Study of JR-Regime Change

Chapters 3–5 used this study's typological theory of JR-regime change to "order the evidence"[1] in the local literature on three societies. At the same time, these chapters helped to refine the theory by giving real-world examples of the processes through which JR regimes consolidate, transform, and incrementally change. The conclusion to each of the case study chapters summarized these refinements, progressively developing the theory along the way. This chapter seeks to build on this platform, both by testing the theory against a wider range of cases and by further demonstrating its usefulness as a comparative framework for understanding the politico-legal dynamics of judicial review.

"Testing" is a loaded word in the social sciences and thus it is worth briefly explaining what is meant by it here. Clearly, the typological theory is not predictive in the sense of proposing independent variables that are the hypothesized cause of defined outcomes. The theory does, however, generate certain "observable implications"[2] that may be tested in a qualitative social science sense. As a threshold matter, it should be possible to classify actually existing JR regimes in a reasonably representative group of societies under the four ideal types. In addition to that, the processes posited by the theory should fit what we already know about the long-run evolution of these actually existing JR regimes. Does the process of JR-regime consolidation, for example,

---

[1]   See Theda Skocpol and Margaret Somers, "The Uses of Comparative History in Macrosocial Inquiry" (1980) 22 *Comparative Studies in Society and History* 174, 176.

[2]   See Gary King, Robert O. Keohane, and Sidney Verba, *Designing Social Inquiry: Scientific Inference in Qualitative Research* (Princeton, NJ: Princeton University Press, 1994). "KKV"'s attempt to frame qualitative social science research in quantitative terms has met with some resistance (see, for example, James Mahoney, "After KKV: The New Methodology of Qualitative Research" (2010) 62 *World Politics* 120). However, the idea that even qualitative social science theories should be expressed so as to be empirically testable is not controversial.

correspond to well-known periods of ideational stability in the JR regimes chosen for analysis? If so, what more can we learn about the factors commonly driving this process? And is JR-regime transformation necessarily triggered by an exogenous shock, as the Indian and Australian case studies seemed to suggest? Or is it possible for JR regimes to transform through an endogenous process of internal contestation and challenge? Related to this, does the distinction between JR-regime transformation and within-regime incremental change hold up when exposed to the evidence emerging from a wider range of cases?

Aside from testing the typological theory in this way, this chapter also seeks to illustrate its usefulness in *understanding* the politico-legal dynamics of judicial review in a wider range of cases. As Skocpol and Somers have argued,[3] merely demonstrating the coverage of a theory is a worthy goal of comparative research, even where no causal propositions are being tested. Populating the typology with a wider range of cases at the same time helps to sharpen our understanding of the differences between actually existing JR regimes, particularly those that are classified as conforming to the same ideal type. Thus, for example, both the Australian and the German JR regimes are classified in this chapter as conforming to the democratic legalist type. At first blush, that might appear odd since there are so many well-known differences between conceptions of the law/politics relation in these two societies. Most obviously, German constitutional culture is premised on a deep-seated faith in judges' ability to construct a philosophically well-ordered system in which rights conflicts may be objectively resolved. Australian constitutional culture, on the other hand, is characterized by extreme skepticism about this possibility, and judges have restricted the adjudication of political values to a narrow set of freedoms that may be said to support the operation of the democratic system. And yet both the German and the Australian JR regimes are founded on a strong attachment to the separability of law and politics. It is just that the German regime assumes that rights adjudication does not necessarily threaten this ideal, whereas the Australian regime assumes that attachment to this ideal requires limiting the scope of judicial review. By drawing attention to this kind of difference, the ideal types function as "sensitizing devices – benchmarks against which to establish the particular features of each case."[4]

This chapter pursues these various aims through analysis of ten additional cases: Germany, Colombia, Hungary, Indonesia, South Africa, Chile, Singapore, Egypt, the Occupied Palestinian Territories, and Myanmar. This

---

[3] Skocpol and Somers, "The Uses of Comparative History" 178.
[4] Ibid.

list of cases is still not exhaustive, of course, but it does cast the net wider in two significant ways. First, it is not restricted to Commonwealth countries. While that restriction was a strength in the case study chapters inasmuch as it eliminated British colonial heritage as an explanatory factor, here we need to show that the typological theory has broader application – that the four ideal types and the processes of consolidation, transformation, and incremental change may be used to explain the long-run evolution of conceptions of the law/politics relation in a larger group of societies. Second, by increasing the N from 3 to 14 (including the US case considered in Chapter 2) this chapter makes possible the use of within-case process tracing and cross-case comparison to deepen understanding of the three social processes at the heart of the theory. As noted in Chapter 2, advances in the methods of comparative historical analysis over the last twenty years mean that a sample of this size may generate a range of insights into complex causal mechanisms that are not amenable to statistical analysis.

With those two general points in mind, the criteria used to choose the ten additional cases were as follows: (1) the availability of a rich, peer-reviewed secondary literature in English on the case that could be used to map it onto the typology;[5] (2) the prominence of the case in comparative constitutional studies (so that the limited space for discussion could be devoted to comparative analysis rather than supplying background empirical detail);[6] (3) the need to choose cases that were representative of the four ideal types and the processes of consolidation, transformation, and incremental change; (4) the need to choose cases where the ideational character of the JR regime had had time to develop; and (5) the requirement that each case should add something distinctive to the discussion.

The next section populates the typology by classifying the ten additional cases under the four ideal types. This exercise demonstrates the coverage of the theory as a basic threshold matter. At the same time, it lays an empirical

---

[5] See Theda Skocpol, *States and Social Revolutions: A Comparative Analysis of France, Russia and China* (New York: Cambridge University Press, 1979) xiv (arguing that comparativists must perforce rely on secondary literature because it is impossible for a single scholar to understand multiple cases in depth). See also Ruth Berins Collier and David Collier, *Shaping the Political Arena: Critical Junctures, the Labor Movement, and Regime Dynamics in Latin America* (Princeton, NJ: Princeton University Press, 1991) 13 (listing the availability of "secondary sources" as a criterion for case selection in a comparative study of eight Latin American countries).

[6] Cf. Ran Hirschl, *Comparative Matters: The Renaissance of Comparative Constitutional Law* (Oxford: Oxford University Press, 2014) 211 (complaining of reliance on "usual suspect" countries – an argument that does not apply in this instance where the goal is not to explore new phenomena but to use a new theoretical framework to reinterpret well-known phenomena).

foundation for the comparative analysis of the processes of JR-regime consolidation, transformation, and incremental change that follows in the rest of the chapter. Sections 6.3–6.5 focus on each of these processes in turn, first restating what has been learned from the case studies and then using within-case process tracing and Millian methods of agreement and difference to test the typological theory in its refined form. Section 6.6 presents a summing up and conclusion.

6.1 POPULATING THE TYPOLOGY

6.1.1 Democratic Legalism

Democratic legalism was defined in Chapter 2 as a JR regime in which a hegemonic conception of law as an autonomous social system locks into a conception of legitimate political authority as dependent on an open and competitive democratic mandate. Even at a very preliminary level, it was apparent that there might be as many as three subtypes of this style of regime: subtype (1), in which the adjudication of fundamental rights is thought to be unavoidably political and in which judicial review is therefore restricted to matters of legislative competence and other structural questions (*"rights exclusion"*); subtype (2), in which the adjudication of fundamental rights is thought to be essential to ensuring the openness and competitiveness of the democratic system and in which judges and the rest of the legal profession accordingly work hard to develop purportedly objective methods through which this task may be performed (*"substantive legalism"*); and subtype (3), in which the constitution provides for judicial review of fundamental rights, but in which assertive rights enforcement is frowned upon as threatening the necessary distinction between law and politics (*"deferential rights review"*).

The Australian case study in Chapter 3 illustrated how the first of these subtypes may develop and endure. In that country, a deep-seated suspicion of judges' ability to impartially adjudicate fundamental rights informed the design of the 1900 Constitution. Judicial review, it was decided, should be limited to matters of federalism and a few structural guarantees. That democratic legalism should have emerged from those beginnings, Chapter 3 noted, might appear to have been culturally and institutionally determined. Things were more complicated than this, however, because the Constitution, in providing for federalist judicial review, exposed the Australian JR regime to American influence. Drawing on US Supreme Court precedents, the early High Court developed a pair of doctrines that limited the scope of the federal Parliament's legislative powers. It was not until 1920 that legalist reasoning methods were conclusively vindicated and, even then, it took a further thirty years for the Court's preferred reasoning methods, its publicly articulated ideology of legalism, and the political acceptance of the Court's decisions to coalesce into a stable JR regime. Since then, the Australian JR regime has undergone one minor adjustment in the direction of a more substantive version of legalism: an increasing acceptance of the legitimacy of enforcing implied political values where these may be said to support the democratic system.

The post-1960 German JR regime provides the paradigmatic example of democratic legalism subtype (2) (*substantive legalism*). The stand-out feature of contemporary German constitutionalism is thus its conception of the 1949 Basic Law as an "objective order of values,"[7] the enforcement of which is thought to be essential to the liberal-democratic order. The reasons behind the emergence of this understanding have been explained in a series of recent studies.[8] In brief, while the role of legal positivism in facilitating the rise of National Socialism in theory called into question Germany's long-standing tradition of legalism,[9] there was little support for abandoning that conception of law's authority after 1945.[10] Rather, both the Federal Constitutional Court (FCC) and the legal-academic profession worked hard to reconcile judicial enforcement of fundamental rights with a continued commitment to the ideal of law's autonomy from politics. The key development was the emergence in the 1960s of proportionality as a structured method for reviewing fundamental rights violations. Rather than extralegal moral principles, fundamental rights were treated in *Lüth*[11] and subsequent cases as legally immanent values whose meaning could be objectively determined. This development was supported by the comparatively high degree of interparty consensus about the Basic Law's underlying political philosophy at the time of its adoption.[12] The idea that Germany should be a welfare state, for example, was a unifying concept to which both the left and right sides of politics were able to commit themselves.

---

[7] *Lüth* case BVerfGE 7, 198.

[8] Moshe Cohen-Eliya and Iddo Porat, *Proportionality and Constitutional Culture* (Cambridge: Cambridge University Press, 2013); Jacco Bomhoff, *Balancing Constitutional Rights: The Origins and Meanings of Postwar Legal Discourse* (Cambridge: Cambridge University Press, 2013); Michaela Hailbronner, *Traditions and Transformations: The Rise of German Constitutionalism* (Oxford: Oxford University Press, 2015).

[9] Gustav Radbruch, "Statutory Lawlessness and Supra-Statutory Law" (2006) 26 *Oxford Journal of Legal Studies* 1 (first published in 1946); David Dyzenhaus, *Legality and Legitimacy: Carl Schmitt, Hans Kelsen, and Hermann Heller in Weimar* (Oxford: Oxford University Press, 1997).

[10] Hailbronner, *Traditions and Transformations* 76 (explaining German legal professionals' reluctance to challenge legal positivism as a function of their unwillingness to accept moral blame for their part in the rise of National Socialism).

[11] BVerfGE 7, 198.

[12] Michaela Hailbronner, *Traditions and Transformations* 77.

In this way, Germany has avoided the American path of rival, ideologically inflected understandings of the Constitution. Assisted by a Basic Law that is founded on a relatively coherent political philosophy and by a legal-academic profession highly invested in rationalizing the FCC's case law,[13] Germany's JR regime has stabilized around a shared understanding of the purpose of judicial review as being the impartial enforcement of the preconditions for genuine multiparty democracy.

The contemporary Colombian JR regime is like Germany's in several respects. As happened in Germany, Colombia's longstanding tradition of legalism undergirded the strong powers given to its Constitutional Court in the 1991 Constitution.[14] And, as was the case in Germany, the Colombian Court and legal scholars worked hard to harmonize the judicial enforcement of fundamental rights with an ongoing commitment to the ideal of law's autonomy from politics. Recognizing that one of the problems with the Supreme Court's reading of the 1886 Constitution had been its excessive formalism, Colombian judges and legal scholars successfully called for a new, more "substantialist" approach to constitutional interpretation.[15] The result has been the flowering of one of the most creative constitutional jurisprudences in the world, with a consistently left-progressive approach to rights combining with innovative remedies.[16] As in Germany, the shift from formal to substantive legal reasoning occurred without abandonment of Colombian constitutional culture's traditionally strong commitment to the separability of law and politics.[17] Indeed, it is precisely this commitment that has allowed the Colombian Constitutional Court to continue to assert its powers in the face of political opposition to the impact of its decisions on public policy.

Where the Colombian JR regime differs from Germany's is in relation to the exclusion of the conservative side of politics from the Court's left-progressive understanding of the Constitution. As David Landau has observed,

[13] The most famous example of this, of course, is Robert Alexy's highly influential theory of judicial review (Robert Alexy, *A Theory of Constitutional Rights* trans. Julian Rivers (Oxford: Oxford University Press, 2002)).

[14] See Manuel José Cepeda Espinosa, "The Judicialization of Politics in Colombia: The Old and the New" in Rachel Sieder, Line Schjolden, and Alan Angell (eds.), *The Judicialization of Politics in Latin America* (New York: Palgrave Macmillan, 2005) 67, 92.

[15] Manuel José Cepeda-Espinosa, "Judicial Review in a Violent Context: The Origin, Role, and Impact of the Colombian Constitutional Court" (2004) 3 *Washington University Global Studies Law Review* 529, 650–4.

[16] See Manuel José Cepeda Espinosa and David Landau (eds.), *Colombian Constitutional Law: Leading Cases* (New York: Oxford University Press, 2017).

[17] David Evan Landau, *Beyond Judicial Independence: The Construction of Judicial Power in Colombia* (doctoral dissertation, Harvard University, 2015) 132–3.

that makes the Court more reliant on the popularity of the easily accessible and expeditious *tutela* action.[18] Through its expansive social rights jurisprudence, the Court has built a strong constituency among the middle class, which has allowed it in turn to extend concrete benefits to the poor.[19] The continued dysfunctionality of Colombia's democratic politics meanwhile ensures that the Court's intrusions into public policy are seen as being necessary to make up for shortcomings in the capacity of the other branches to attend to urgent social needs.[20] Finally, rather than by an influential community of legal scholars operating outside the Court, the coherence of the Court's jurisprudence is ensured by a judicial clerkship system that sees legal scholars directly involved in writing the Court's judgments.[21] This last feature is particularly significant in explaining why Colombia has avoided the Indian trajectory from politically committed, pro-poor decision-making to freewheeling ideological decision-making contingent on the composition of the Bench.

Twenty years ago, if one had been listing forceful constitutional courts, the Constitutional Court of Hungary would have been near the top of the list. Its first President, László Sólyom, was well known for assertively promoting liberal-constitutionalist values, even when this meant striking down politically significant legislation.[22] In one famous case, for example, the Court upheld the principle of nonretroactivity against a statute that sought to punish those responsible for suppressing the 1956 anti-communist uprising.[23] In another, the Court struck down parts of an austerity package aimed at reducing social security benefits on the grounds that the constitutional claimants had acquired vested rights in

---

[18] Ibid 31.
[19] Ibid 360.
[20] Ibid 31, 257, 284, 353.
[21] Ibid 173.
[22] Gábor Halmai, "The Hungarian Approach to Constitutional Review: The End of Activism? The First Decade of the Hungarian Constitutional Court" in Wojciech Sadurski (ed.), *Constitutional Justice, East and West: Democratic Legitimacy and Courts in Post-Communist Europe in a Comparative Perspective* (The Hague: Kluwer Law International, 2002) 189; Kim Lane Scheppelle, "Guardians of the Constitution: Constitutional Court Presidents and the Struggle for the Rule of Law in Post-Soviet Europe" (2006) 154 *University of Pennsylvania Law Review* 1757; Christian Boulanger, "Europeanization through Judicial Activism? The Hungarian Constitutional Court's Legitimacy and the 'Return to Europe'" in Wojciech Sadurski, Adam Czarnota, and Martin Krygier (eds.), *Spreading Democracy and the Rule of Law? The Impact of EU Enlargement on the Rule of Law, Democracy and Constitutionalism in Post-Communist Legal Orders* (Dordrecht: Springer, 2006) 263.
[23] Decision 11/1992 extracted and translated in László Sólyom and Georg Brunner, *Constitutional Judiciary in a New Democracy: The Hungarian Constitutional Court* (Ann Arbor, MI: University of Michigan Press, 2000) 214–28.

their entitlements.[24] These decisions might have suggested at the time that the Hungarian JR regime was consolidating around a version of democratic legalism subtype (2) (*substantive legalism*). Certainly, the Court's rights jurisprudence, based as it was on the centrality of human dignity and the doctrine of proportionality, appeared to be a deliberate imitation of the German approach. It is now clear, however, that this was merely the surface appearance of things. While the Sólyom Court behaved as though it were operating in a democratic legalist regime – or, rather, as though the judges thought that they could somehow will this type of regime into existence – its ideational support structures never properly developed.

One of the main reasons for this, the literature suggests, was Hungary's weak rule-of-law tradition. Like most of the Eastern European countries, with the possible exception of the Czech Republic,[25] a political culture of respect for judicial independence and individual rights had never really developed in Hungary. Rather, its dominant political tradition before the advent of communism had been a species of ethnic nationalism, which was hostile to minority rights, particularly of the Roma, Jews, and homosexuals.[26] When Hungary emerged from communism in 1989, there were accordingly two rival traditions on offer – this older, backward-looking tradition that still enjoyed considerable public support, and the newer, forward-looking tradition of liberal constitutionalism, which was associated with the return to Europe, but which in truth had never set down deep roots in Hungary's constitutional culture.[27]

Viewed against this background, Hungary's transition to liberal-democratic constitutionalism was always somewhat fragile. In the euphoria over the collapse of communism, the main concern was to facilitate Hungary's planned accession to the EU. In consequence, the 1989 amendments to the 1949 Constitution were driven by instrumental considerations rather than deep-seated constitutional-cultural values.[28] Making matters worse, the Sólyom Court relied on what it called the "invisible Constitution," a supposedly coherent set of liberal-democratic principles underlying, and

---

[24] Decision 43/1995 (extracted and translated in ibid 322–32).
[25] See Milos Calda, "Constitution-Making in Post-Communist Countries: A Case of the Czech Republic" paper presented at the American Political Science Association Convention, Atlanta, Georgia, September 2, 1999.
[26] Bojan Bugarič, "A Crisis of Constitutional Democracy in Post-Communist Europe: 'Lands in-between' Democracy and Authoritarianism" (2015) 13 *International Journal of Constitutional Law* 219, 236.
[27] Ibid 233–5.
[28] Ibid 234.

in certain respects superior to, the formal Constitution.[29] Without clear textual support, however, the legitimacy of this approach was questionable.[30] Though initially popular with the public,[31] the Court's activism irked legislators on all sides of the political spectrum. During Sólyom's tenure as President, the instability of this situation was masked by the fragmentation of Hungary's electoral politics, which prevented any one grouping from unilaterally amending the Constitution.[32] As the end of Sólyom's initial nine-year term approached, however, it became increasingly clear that a change was in the offing. In 1998, Sólyom, along with the other remaining liberal judges, was not reappointed. The Court thereafter lapsed into relative passivity.[33]

Hungary's JR regime might have continued down this path towards democratic legalism subtype (3) (*deferential rights review*) had it not been for certain developments in its electoral politics which, coupled with the relative ease of the constitutional amendment procedure, saw the resurgence of the older ethnonationalist tradition. In 2010, Fidesz, a center-right populist party,[34] was elected with a narrow majority of the votes but two thirds of the parliamentary seats. That gave it the power to amend the Constitution unilaterally, which it quickly utilized, first in a series of amendments in 2010 and then through a complete constitutional overhaul the next year. Fidesz's 2011 Constitution retained the Bill of Rights but dispensed with the *actio popularis*, which had been central to the Sólyom Court's activism. The new Constitution also amended the judicial appointments process to give Fidesz effective control.[35] The Constitutional Court was not completely passive during this process. After the first set of

---

[29] Sólyom first mentioned this idea in his opinion in the death penalty case (23/1990 (X.31)). See András Sajó, "Reading the Invisible Constitution: Judicial Review in Hungary" (1995) 15 *Oxford Journal of Legal Studies* 253, 258.

[30] Ibid 266–7.

[31] Oliver W. Lembcke and Christian Boulanger, "Between Revolution and Constitution: The Roles of the Hungarian Constitutional Court" in Gábor Attila Tóth (ed.), *Constitution for a Disunited Nation: On Hungary's 2011 Fundamental Law* (Budapest: Central European University Press, 2012) 269, 275.

[32] Sajó, "Invisible Constitution" 257. See also Kriszta Kovács and Gábor Attila Tóth, "Hungary's Constitutional Transformation" (2011) 7 *European Constitutional Law Review* 183, 187.

[33] See Kim Lane Scheppele, "The New Hungarian Constitutional Court" (1999) 8 *Eastern European Constitutional Review* 81, 82 (noting a turn to formalism under the Németh Court).

[34] Fidesz began life as a libertarian youth party, before shifting to the center-right. It is not the most radical ethno-nationalist party in Hungary. That dubious honor goes to Jobbik, which is enjoying increasing support.

[35] Kriszta Kovács and Gabor Attila Tóth, "Hungary's Constitutional Transformation" (2011) 7 *European Constitutional Law Review* 183; András Jakab and Pál Sonnevend, "Continuity with Deficiencies: The New Basic Law of Hungary" (2013) 9 *European Constitutional Law Review* 102.

amendments, it struck down a law retroactively taxing civil service bonuses. Fidesz, however, retaliated by stripping the Court's jurisdiction to review budgetary laws except in terms of a narrow set of rights.[36] In 2013, it went even further, enacting a constitutional amendment that annulled all the Court's pre-2012 decisions.[37] Today, the Court, with a Fidesz-appointed majority, has effectively been captured. While it is probably too early to say that the Hungarian JR regime has *stabilized* around a version of authoritarian legalism,[38] Fidesz's abuse of the constitutional amendment procedure, its subordination of the judiciary, and its ethno-nationalistic rhetoric are all indicative of a move towards that type of regime.[39]

As in Hungary, Indonesia's transition to liberal constitutionalism was closely connected to the emergence of a strong Constitutional Court. The major difference in the Indonesian case was that judicial review was never intended to play as significant a role as it did. Established as part of the staged constitutional amendment process from 1998 to 2002,[40] the Constitutional Court was originally imagined as a Kelsenian "negative legislator," with a limited mandate to oversee the presidential impeachment process and the compatibility of legislative and executive conduct with the Bill of Rights.[41] However, under the charismatic leadership of Jimly Asshiddiqie, its first Chief Justice, the Indonesian Constitutional Court rapidly grew into a forceful actor in national politics. A former constitutional law professor, Jimly set about cultivating a tradition of carefully reasoned opinion writing that departed from the perfunctory style associated with Indonesia's civil law tradition.[42] At the same time, Jimly had to contend with a rule-of-law tradition badly weakened by former President Suharto's subversion of the Supreme Court's independence.[43] His solution to that challenge was to insist on the Constitutional Court's acquiring

[36] David Landau, "Abusive Constitutionalism" (2013) 47 *University California Davis Law Review* 189, 208.

[37] Wojciech Sadurski, *Rights before Courts: A Study of Constitutional Courts in Postcommunist States of Central and Eastern Europe* 2nd ed (Dordrecht: Springer, 2014) 11–12.

[38] See Bojan Bugarič and Tom Ginsburg, "The Assault on Postcommunist Courts" (2016) 27 *Journal of Democracy* 69, 70 (describing the Hungarian political regime as "semi-authoritarian").

[39] See Miklós Bánkuti, Gábor Halmai, and Kim Lane Scheppele, "Hungary's Illiberal Turn: Disabling the Constitution" (2012) 23 *Journal of Democracy* 138.

[40] Donald L. Horowitz, *Constitutional Change and Democracy in Indonesia* (New York: Cambridge University Press, 2013).

[41] See Simon Butt and Tim Lindsey, *The Indonesian Constitution: A Contextual Analysis* (Oxford: Hart Publishing, 2012).

[42] Fritz Edward Siregar, *Indonesian Constitutional Politics: 2003–2013* (doctoral dissertation, UNSW Sydney, 2016) 123 (available at www.unsworks.unsw.edu.au).

[43] Sebastian Pompe, *The Indonesian Supreme Court: A Study of Institutional Collapse* (Ithaca, NY: Cornell Southeast Asia Program Publications, 2005).

a prestigious building in the center of Jakarta to affirm its status.[44] He also quickly established a media center for the Court, and worked tirelessly to explain the Court's rulings and its role in the political system to the Indonesian public.[45]

In many ways, Jimly's approach represented a textbook strategy for building the ideational support structures required for the consolidation of democratic legalism. Assisted by the fragmentation of Indonesia's electoral politics and the decisive popular break with Suharto's authoritarian rule,[46] the Constitutional Court rapidly became an important symbol of Indonesia's newfound commitment to democracy.[47] Jimly was unable, however, to secure his own position on the Court as the end of his second three-year term approached.[48] Having become associated with the Court's forceful role, he was defeated in an intracurial vote for the chief justiceship by Mohammad Mahfud, a newly appointed judge who had promised at his nomination hearing to return the Court to its original negative-legislator mandate.[49] Mahfud's accession to the chief justiceship interrupted the consolidation of Indonesia's JR regime. The main reason for this was that, far from keeping his nomination promise, Mahfud ramped up the Court's positive legislator role under the guise of a less technical, more outcomes-oriented "substantive justice" approach.[50] By abruptly changing the Court's reasoning style in this way, Mahfud exposed the Court to charges of judicial overreach. In 2011,[51] and again in 2013,[52] the Indonesian Parliament amended the Court's governing statute to return it to its original jurisdiction. While the Court struck down these amendments with seeming ease, its depiction of the legislation as an attack on its independence,

---

[44] Siregar, *Indonesian Constitutional Politics* 101.

[45] Ibid 117; Stefanus Hendrianto, From Humble Beginnings to a Functioning Court: The Indonesian Constitutional Court, 2003–2008 (doctoral dissertation, University of Washington, 2008) 213–6.

[46] See Marcus Mietzner, "Political Conflict Resolution and Democratic Consolidation in Indonesia: The Role of the Constitutional Court" (2010) 10 *Journal of East Asian Studies* 397.

[47] Ibid.

[48] Jimly's second term as Chief Justice was due to expire in 2009, but the vote was brought forward by one year because of the high turnover on the Court. See Siregar, *Indonesian Constitutional Politics* 104–8.

[49] Although the chief justiceship was decided by internal judicial vote, there were some suggestions of political influence. See Theunis Roux and Fritz Siregar, "Trajectories of Curial Power: The Rise, Fall, and Partial Rehabilitation of the Indonesian Constitutional Court" (2016) 16 *Australian Journal of Asian Law* 1, 10.

[50] Ibid 11. See also Siregar, *Indonesian Constitutional Politics* 115. In his academic writing, Mahfud characterized his approach as an attempt to embody Phillippe Nonet and Philip Selznick's concept of "responsive law" (ibid 163).

[51] Law No 8 of 2011. See discussion in Butt and Lindsey, *The Constitution of Indonesia* 144–6.

[52] In presidential emergency interim order (PERPU) No 1 of 2013 confirmed by Law No 4 of 2014.

notwithstanding legitimate concerns about the personal integrity of some of the justices,[53] was somewhat shortsighted. Instead of adjusting its understanding of judicial independence to the changing quality of Indonesia's democracy,[54] the Court has adopted a dogmatic conception more appropriate to the Suharto era. While the health of Indonesia's constitutional democracy depends on numerous other factors,[55] the Court's overzealous striking down of well-intentioned judicial accountability legislation has not helped to promote a stable understanding of law's legitimate claim to authority.

The final example of democratic legalism among the additional cases chosen for analysis is the post-1994 South African JR regime. Under apartheid, South African lawyers had embraced the idea of law's separateness from politics as a way of justifying their role in the denial of political rights to the black majority. South African legal culture had accordingly developed a strongly formalist conception of law's authority that gave primacy to textualist reasoning methods.[56] As in Germany, the transition to constitutional democracy threatened but did not in the end undermine this legitimating ideology. In South Africa's case, this was because a vigorous tradition of anti-apartheid human rights lawyering had shown that there was a nobler vision of law's separation from politics: not the distorted conception characteristic of authoritarian legalism, but a view of law as anti-politics – as a source of autonomous norms and values that could be used to check the worst abuses of authoritarian rule.[57]

---

[53] Stefanus Hendrianto, The Indonesian Constitutional Court at a Tipping Point, Blog of the International Journal of Constitutional Law, October 3, 2013, www.iconnectblog.com/2013/10/the-indonesian-constitutional-court-at-a=tipping-point.

[54] Owen M. Fiss, "The Right Degree of Independence" in Irwin P. Stotzky (ed.), *Transition to Democracy in Latin America: The Role of the Judiciary* (Boulder, CO: Westview Press, 1992) 55; Stephen Holmes, "Judicial Independence as Ambiguous Reality and Insidious Illusion" in Ronald Dworkin (ed.), *From Liberal Values to Democratic Transition: Essays in Honour of János Kis* (Budapest: Central European University Press, 2004) 3, 9.

[55] See Edward Aspinall and Marcus Mietzner, "Indonesian Politics in 2014: Democracy's Close Call" (2014) 50 *Bulletin of Indonesian Economic Studies* 347.

[56] Martin Chanock, *The Making of South African Legal Culture 1902–1936: Fear, Favour, and Prejudice* (Cambridge: Cambridge University Press, 2001); Jens Meierhenrich, *The Legacies of Law: Long-Run Consequences of Legal Development in South Africa, 1652–2000* (Cambridge: Cambridge University Press, 2008).

[57] Rather than presenting human rights as extralegal constraints on political power, anti-apartheid lawyers like Arthur Chaskalson sought to uncover the liberal principles within Roman-Dutch law. See Stephen Ellmann, *In a Time of Trouble: Law and Liberty in South Africa's State of Emergency* (Oxford: Clarendon Press, 1992); David Dyzenhaus, *Hard Cases in Wicked Legal Systems: South African Law in the Perspective of Legal Philosophy* (Oxford: Clarendon Press, 1991).

During the transition to democracy, this nobler vision of law's autonomy from politics became a vital resource for negotiators as they sought to
reassure each other that their constituencies' interests would be respected.
In contrast, say, to current-day Myanmar, negotiators in South Africa were
able to rely on a well-institutionalized tradition of legal reasoning that
gave reasonably precise content to political bargains. The transition to
democracy was in this way imagined as the extension of South Africa's
rule-of-law tradition to the population as a whole.[58] More than this, law
was envisioned as the vehicle through which South African society would
be reconstructed along more egalitarian lines. The 1996 Constitution, in
particular, was conceived as elaborating a coherent, left-progressive political philosophy that could be used as a programmatic guide to legislators
and judges alike.

For some commentators, this commitment to law-driven social transformation meant that the Constitutional Court should have openly declared
the politicized nature of its role. On this view, the progressiveness of the
Constitution's underlying political philosophy logically entailed the adoption of an American understanding of judicial review as the pursuit of
"ideological projects."[59] This view was obviously mistaken, however.[60]
Precisely because the 1996 Constitution elaborated a coherent left-
progressive political philosophy, it was perfectly feasible for the
Constitutional Court to portray its task as the impartial enforcement of
determinate legal prescriptions. That approach was at the same time both
strategically wise, given the fragility of South Africa's transition to democracy, and sincerely motivated, given the socialization of the judiciary in
a view of law as anti-politics.[61]

For all these reasons, the South African JR regime quickly stabilized around
something approximating democratic legalism subtype (2). As in Germany,
constitutional rights are seen in South Africa as objectively enforceable legal
norms rather than invitations for judges to engage in a free-ranging political
analysis of the problems facing the country. This ongoing commitment to
legalism has undoubtedly had some drawbacks. In the *United Democratic*

---

[58] See Meierhenrich, *The Legacies of Law.*
[59] See Karl E. Klare, "Legal Culture and Transformative Constitutionalism" (1998) 12 *South African Journal on Human Rights* 146, 159 (quoting Duncan Kennedy, *A Critique of Adjudication (Fin de Siècle)* (Cambridge, MA: Harvard University Press, 1997) 19).
[60] See Theunis Roux, "Transformative Constitutionalism and the Best Interpretation of the South African Constitution: Distinction without a Difference?" (2009) 20 *Stellenbosch Law Review* 258.
[61] See Theunis Roux, *The Politics of Principle: The First South African Constitutional Court, 1995–2005* (Cambridge: Cambridge University Press, 2013) 219–31.

Movement case,[62] for example, the Court declined to offer a substantive political analysis of the threat posed to South Africa's democracy by the ANC's electoral dominance. This arguably prevented the Court from creatively developing doctrines that might have addressed this problem [63] In other cases, however, the Court's presentation of law as a sphere of authority distinct from politics had its advantages. In the *Treatment Action Campaign* case,[64] for example, the Court explicitly relied on that conception in a decision challenging then-President Thabo Mbeki's denialist views on HIV/AIDS. Less spectacularly, but just as significantly, some of the formalist reasoning techniques that human rights lawyers had used to exploit loopholes in apartheid statutes reappeared in judgments enforcing constitutional rights.[65] In this way, the South African Constitutional Court has generally resisted the call to own up to the political nature of its function. Armed with a Constitution that does most of the substantive political theorizing for it, the Court has presented fundamental rights as legal rights whose meaning may be objectively determined.

6.1.2 *Democratic Instrumentalism*

Democratic instrumentalism, Chapter 2 theorized, emerges when a constitutional-cultural faith in law's autonomy weakens to be replaced by a conception of law as a tool for the pursuit of political goals. This type of regime consolidates when the influence of judicial ideology on constitutional decision-making is for some reason politically accepted. The distinction between democratic legalism subtype (2) (*substantive legalism*) and this form of JR regime is that the Constitution is not presented as embodying a coherent political philosophy but rather as being amenable to a coherent reading from two or more ideological perspectives. This understanding allows for the development of rival moral readings of the Constitution, each supported by its own line of precedents and interpretive methods, but neither of which permanently gains ascendancy.[66]

---

[62] *United Democratic Movement* v. *President of the Republic of South Africa* 2003 (1) SA 488 (CC).

[63] Sujit Choudhry, "'He had a Mandate': The South African Constitutional Court and the African National Congress in a Dominant Party Democracy" (2010) 2 *Constitutional Court Review* 1; Samuel Issacharoff, "Constitutional Courts and Democratic Hedging" (2011) 99 *Georgetown Law Journal* 961.

[64] *Minister of Health* v. *Treatment Action Campaign (No 2)* 2002 (5) SA 721 (CC) paras 20–2.

[65] See, for example, *Minister of Public Works* v. *Kyalami Ridge Environmental Association (Mukhwevho Intervening)* 2001 (3) SA 1151 (CC) paras 59, 64–5, 83, 89, 117.

[66] Cf. Landau, *Beyond Judicial Independence* 358 (distinguishing the US from Colombia and Germany on the basis of its "politicized" constitutional culture).

The paradigmatic example of this style of JR regime is the post-Warren-Court regime in the US. As explained in Chapter 2, the legal realist movement in the 1920s and 1930s successfully challenged law's claim to determinacy and with it the idea that law was an autonomous social system separate from politics. The American JR regime might thereafter have stabilized around a version of democratic legalism subtype (3) in which the justices, chastened by the near universal condemnation of *Lochner,* deferred to democratic determinations of constitutional rights. But this did not happen. Instead, the Warren Court's liberal activism set the American JR regime on a different trajectory. By invoking the idea of the Constitution as a repository of liberal political values, the Warren Court opened the door to understanding judicial review as a vehicle for the pursuit of comprehensive visions of constitutional justice. When the Republican party responded to this development by appointing its own ideologically motivated judges, the regime began to consolidate through a self-reinforcing process of bipartisan acceptance of this form of judicial decision-making.

In the case studies, the post-1990 Indian JR regime provided a further example of this ideal type. Although India's path towards democratic instrumentalism was very different from that followed in the US, there are sufficient similarities between the two JR regimes to warrant classifying them together. The crucial development in the Indian case was the weakening after 1989 of Bhagwati and Krishna Iyer's left-progressive reading of the Constitution.[67] From this point, the idea that constitutional decision-making in India, though underdetermined by the text, was nevertheless guided by a coherent political philosophy, began to weaken. Instead, the Court's decisions started to reflect a range of different ideological influences, with the outcome depending more on the composition of the bench than on binding precedent. While smaller benches and the nature of the judicial appointments process mean that these left-right swings in the Indian Supreme Court's case law are less structured than they are in the US, the crucial similarity is the institutionalization of ideologically motivated decision-making.

There are no further examples of democratic instrumentalism among the additional cases chosen for analysis. This conforms to expectations. As noted in Chapter 2, democratic instrumentalism depends on the political acceptance of, or at least, inability to resist, ideologically motivated decision-making. This style of regime is likely to be quite rare in practice. Where law is not wholly subordinated to politics, as is the case under authoritarian instrumentalism, its claim to authority is typically justified by distinguishing its methods, values, and

---

[67]   See the discussion in Chapter 4.

practices from those of politics. Situations in which judicial decision-making in a democracy is both clearly ideologically motivated and politically tolerated depend on an unusual combination of factors – though not necessarily always the same combination of factors, as the contrast between the US and India indicates.

6.1.3 *Authoritarian Legalism*

Authoritarian legalism, as conceived in Chapter 2, is a JR regime in which political authority is in part legitimated by the autonomy given to judges in defined areas of social life. Judges have final decision-making power in these areas and may rule on such matters as contractual disputes or inheritance rights without fear of political interference. In areas more sensitive to the power holder's interests, however, judges routinely defer to political prerogatives. The system as a whole is undergirded by a distorted ideology of law's separation from politics. "Distorted" because, instead of providing the basis on which law speaks truth to political power, legalism in such regimes functions to legitimate the distinction between the sphere of private relations, in which law reigns, and the no-go area of politics. Insofar as political rights, such as freedom of speech and security from arbitrary detention, are unreliably enforced in such constitutional systems, authoritarian legalism holds that this is necessitated by the political power holder's indispensable role in promoting some or other overarching societal interest, such as national security, ethnic harmony, or economic growth.

Chapter 5 showed how authoritarian legalism in postindependence Zimbabwe was essentially a continuation of the hegemonic conception of the law/politics relation that had developed during colonial times, with some adjustments. The denial of full political rights to the black majority, which had been justified by the white settlers' "civilizing" mission, switched at independence to the qualified protection of political rights in ostensible pursuit of Zimbabwe's anti-colonial project. The resulting JR regime was relatively stable until the rise of the Movement for Democratic Change (MDC) forced ZANU-PF to choose between the legitimating benefits of legalism and the political subordination of the judiciary. After a brief period of authoritarian instrumentalism, ZANU-PF was able in 2013 to exploit the opening created by the hoped-for transition to liberal constitutionalism to return the Zimbabwean JR regime to its historically dominant form.

The adaptation of colonial conceptions of the law/politics relation to post-colonial imperatives is an important phenomenon that warrants separate investigation.[68] Here, there is space only to note that this process is obviously influenced by the politico-legal dynamics of the postcolonial transition in each case. For example, the contemporary Singaporean JR regime, like the Zimbabwean JR regime, developed out of the peculiarly British variant of the colonial dual state. In both societies, political rights were suppressed after independence in the name of the governing party's claim to be uniquely qualified to promote the national interest. In Singapore's case, however, instead of exposing the contradictions in the colonial rule of law as an essential building block of its new legitimating ideology, the People's Action Party (PAP) sought to present itself as the natural custodian of the British rule-of-law tradition. The contrasting presentations of the colonial rule-of-law ideal in these two cases may be attributed to differences in Zimbabwe and Singapore's transition to independence. Unlike ZANU-PF, PAP could not point to its leadership of a glorious anti-colonial struggle. Nor, given Singapore's ethnic makeup, could it claim to represent an historically oppressed *indigenous* majority.[69] Thus, the Zimbabwean path of anti-colonial revolutionary legitimation was not open to it. Instead, PAP sought to present its rule as the continuation of a venerable – though, in truth, never actually instantiated – metropolitan rule-of-law tradition.

As in Zimbabwe, the adaptation of colonial conceptions of the law/politics relation in Singapore has given rise to a remarkably durable JR regime. At the time of writing, 52 years after independence, social and economic life in Singapore is still bifurcated into areas where the rule of law prevails and areas where it does not.[70] The latter include such matters as preventive detention under the Internal Security Act,[71] the use of defamation laws to harass the ruling party's political opponents,[72] the deployment of contempt of

---

[68] For an examination of the particular role played by the "legal complex" in this process, see Terence C. Halliday, Lucien Karpik, and Malcolm Feeley (eds.), *Fates of Political Liberalism in the British Post-Colony: The Politics of the Legal Complex* (New York: Cambridge University Press, 2012).

[69] This point, insofar as it pertains to Singapore, is drawn from Jothie Rajah, *Authoritarian Rule of Law: Legislation, Discourse, and Legitimacy in Singapore* (New York: Cambridge University Press, 2012).

[70] See Li-ann Thio, "Between Apology and Apogee, Autochthony: The Rule of Law Beyond the Rules of Law in Singapore" (2012) *Singapore Journal of Legal Studies* 269, 269; Rajah, *Authoritarian Rule of Law* 23.

[71] See Rajah, *Authoritarian Rule of Law* 16 for the literature on this topic.

[72] Ibid 17ff; Gordon Silverstein, "Singapore: The Exception that Proves Rules Matter" in Tom Ginsburg and Tamir Moustafa (eds.), *Rule by Law: The Politics of Courts in Authoritarian Regimes* (New York: Cambridge University Press, 2008) 73, 86–92; Thio, "Between Apology and Apogee" 287–94.

court proceedings to similar effect,[73] and the denial of rights to peaceful assembly.[74] On the other hand, not only are regular elections held, but elaborate attempts have been made to include minority groups in the political process through the introduction of Group Representative Constituencics.[75] The system as a whole is sustained by what has been called "performance legitimacy,"[76] i.e., the regime's success in fostering economic growth and national stability.[77]

These features make the Singaporean JR regime an intriguing example of the authoritarian legalist type. Not only is Singapore a very high-performing society in economic terms.[78] PAP's ability to exploit autonomous law's legitimating potential is extremely sophisticated. Singapore thus notoriously registers very highly on some rule-of-law indicators.[79] It is decidedly not a society in which authoritarian legalism is a function of weak legal institutionalization, economic underdevelopment, or persistent political violence. Rather, it is the paradigmatic example of a very deliberate and well-maintained bifurcation of the state into rule-of-law-respecting and disrespecting spheres. This makes it an important case to study, both from the point of view of understanding the sustained ideational work required to maintain this style of JR regime and its practical operation.

Unusually for a Latin American country, Chile had a well-established rule-of-law tradition prior to its infamous military coup in 1973. Starting in the 1920s with an attempt to reduce executive influence over the judiciary, the Supreme Court was given considerable autonomy over judicial promotions and appointments.[80] This institutional innovation helped to strengthen the Court's reputation for technical-legal proficiency, which in turn fed into a powerful legitimating ideology of law's separation from politics.[81] This

---

[73] Mark Tushnet, "Authoritarian Constitutionalism" (2015) 100 *Cornell Law Review* 391, 402–3.

[74] Ibid 404 (discussing the Public Order Act of 2009).

[75] Po Jen Yap, *Constitutional Dialogue in Common Law Asia* (Oxford: Oxford University Press, 2015) 50–1.

[76] Thio, "Between Apology and Apogee" 277.

[77] Rajah, *Authoritarian Rule of Law* 21ff.

[78] See Thio, "Between Apology and Apogee" 277 n 58 for GDP figures for Singapore from 1965 to 2009.

[79] See the assessments listed in Thio, "Between Apology and Apogee" 270 n 6; Silverstein, "Singapore: The Exception that Proves Rules Matter" 74 n 2.

[80] See Lisa Hilbink, *Judges Beyond Politics in Democracy and Dictatorship: Lessons from Chile* (New York: Cambridge University Press, 2007) 6, 41–72. See also the succinct version of this argument in Lisa Hilbink, "Agents of Anti-Politics: Courts in Pinochet's Chile" in Tom Ginsburg and Tamir Moustafa (eds.), *Rule by Law: The Politics of Courts in Authoritarian Regimes* (New York: Cambridge University Press, 2008) 102.

[81] Hilbink, *Judges Beyond Politics* 6.

historical experience influenced both the trajectory of the military coup and the process of recovery from it. As Lisa Hilbink explains, when General Augusto Pinochet took control of the country in September 1973, he dismantled every constitutional institution apart from the judiciary.[82] The courts rewarded the confidence shown in them by steadfastly declining to interrogate the human rights abuses that thereafter occurred. In its *amparo* (habeas corpus) docket, the Supreme Court intervened in only a tiny fraction of cases.[83] At the same time, it entirely "abdicate[d]" its power to review the decisions of military tribunals.[84] In specifically constitutional cases, it accepted the junta's position that military decrees in contravention of Chile's 1925 Constitution should be treated as constitutional amendments.[85] Even after the military introduced a new constitutional review mechanism in 1976 – the *recurso de protección* – the Supreme Court continued to show extreme deference to executive prerogatives. Without significant intimidation or threats, the courts effectively declined to review politically sensitive cases. On Hilbink's account, this was not a question of the judiciary's partisan support for the military junta, but of its socialization in an ideology of law's separation from politics.[86] The military junta, on this view of things, did not so much co-opt the judiciary as exploit an already existing legitimating ideology to support its rule. Even after the return to democracy in 1990, the Chilean judiciary stuck to its self-presentation as a politically impartial actor, thereby inhibiting the development of the more robust, judicially led style of constitutionalism seen in Colombia and Costa Rica.[87]

Finally, consider the emergence of authoritarian legalism in Egypt. As Tamir Moustafa relates the story,[88] Gamal Abdel Nasser's assault on the courts from 1952

---

[82]   Ibid 1.
[83]   Ibid 141.
[84]   Ibid 120.
[85]   Hilbink, "Agents of Anti-Politics" 108.
[86]   Hilbink, *Judges Beyond Politics* passim.
[87]   Ibid 189–207. See also Javier Couso, "The Judicialization of Chilean Politics: The Rights Revolution That Never Was" in Rachel Sieder, Line Schjolden, and Alan Angell (eds.), *The Judicialization of Politics in Latin America* (New York: Palgrave Macmillan, 2005) 105; Javier Couso and Lisa Hilbink, "From Quietism to Incipient Activism: The Institutional and Ideological Roots of Rights Adjudication in Chile" in Gretchen Helmke and Julio Ríos-Figueroa (eds.), *Courts in Latin America* (New York: Cambridge University Press, 2011) 99.
[88]   Tamir Moustafa, *The Struggle for Constitutional Power: Law, Politics, and Economic Development in Egypt* (New York: Cambridge University Press, 2007). For a more succinct version of the argument, see Tamir Moustafa, "Law and Resistance in Authoritarian States: The Judicialization of Politics in Egypt" in Tom Ginsburg and Tamir Moustafa (eds.), *Rule by Law: The Politics of Courts in Authoritarian Regimes* (New York: Cambridge University Press, 2008) 132.

was initially sustained by the "revolutionary legitimacy" emanating from his "populist agenda."[89] Public support for that agenda succeeded for a while in compensating for the decline in judicial independence. As the economy began to weaken, however, and as the concentration of power in the hands of a small elite began to undermine its capacity to govern, Nasser's successor, President Anwar Sadat, looked to attract foreign investment as the basis for renewed economic growth. When his initial suite of reforms failed, Sadat established the Supreme Constitutional Court (SCC) in 1979 with an explicit mandate to enforce the right to private property in the 1971 Egyptian Constitution.[90] The SCC's members were appointed by the President from lists prepared by the Court and the Chief Justice, with considerable weight given to legal-professional expertise.[91] At the same time, Sadat expanded the powers of the administrative courts in an effort to regain control of the bureaucracy.[92] After Sadat's assassination in 1981, these reforms were initially continued by President Hosni Mubarak, who abided by the SCC's rulings requiring compensation to be paid to the victims of property rights violations and excessive taxation.[93] In the late 1990s, however, after the SCC began to change into a forum for the enforcement, not just of economic rights, but also of political rights, Mubarak moved against the Court and the civil society support network that had grown up around it.[94] With the appointment of former Ministry of Justice official Fathi Nagab as Chief Justice in 2001, the executive's intention to contain the Court through exerting greater control over the judicial appointments process was clear.[95] In the Egyptian case, therefore, the development of authoritarian legalism was a deliberate strategy of political power holders in search of legitimation and social-control benefits. When the SCC attempted to expand the sphere of authority it had been given into areas of social life that posed a direct challenge to Mubarak's hold on power, however, its wings were clipped, and judicial review was returned to previous limits.[96]

6.1.4 Authoritarian Instrumentalism

Under authoritarian instrumentalism, law's subordination to politics is complete. Rather than serving as an instrument of democratically *competing*

---

[89] Moustafa, "Law and Resistance" 12.
[90] Ibid 135.
[91] Ibid 138–9.
[92] Ibid 145.
[93] Moustafa, *The Struggle for Constitutional Power* 134–6.
[94] Ibid Chapter 6.
[95] Ibid 198–9.
[96] Ibid 178–218.

visions of constitutional justice, law is instrumentalized in service to a single, overarching conception of the just society that brooks no alternatives. In such a JR regime, there is no conception of law as an autonomous source of authority that is capable of constraining political power. Law is rather a projection of political authority, and its role is to define the just society, promote its achievement and discipline citizens into conforming to its prescriptions.

Why would a system of judicial review ever be introduced in such a society, it might be asked? Does the very notion of judicial review not assume at least some commitment to law's autonomy and, if so, why would political power holders with little interest in that idea bother with this institution? The answer, the Zimbabwean case study in Chapter 5 and the further examples discussed in this section suggest, is twofold. First, authoritarian instrumentalism might arise as a managerial response to *insubordinate* judicial review – to judicial review under authoritarian legalism, that is, which disrespects the boundaries of law's legitimate sphere of authority as these have come to be defined. In those circumstances, political power holders may choose, not to disestablish judicial review, but to control it more effectively by staffing the judiciary with political loyalists. To the extent that the subordination of the judiciary in this way undermines public confidence in law's autonomy, *in any area of social life, even those formerly recognized as falling within law's legitimate sphere*, authoritarian legalism transforms into authoritarian instrumentalism.

In the nature of things, this first subtype tends to be a relatively transient phenomenon – more of a crisis management tool than a durable JR regime. That is because in authoritarian societies where law has traditionally served some legitimating function, the subordination of the judiciary leads to social and economic problems that the society's established institutions are ill-equipped to manage. An all-out assault on judicial independence may trigger the collapse of productive economic activities that have grown dependent on the enforceability of private property rights. Similarly, a civil service that has previously been held to account by independent courts might become unruly and difficult to manage. For all these reasons, the first subtype of authoritarian instrumentalism tends to revert relatively quickly to authoritarian legalism as political power holders either engineer a return to qualified rule of law or give in to pressure for such a return for reasons of political survival.

There is a second conceivable subtype of authoritarian instrumentalism, however, which may be more enduring. In JR regimes belonging to this subtype, the political subordination of the judiciary flows from an idea of law as a vehicle for the promotion of a comprehensive vision of the just society. Drawing either on a well-established political tradition or on a purpose-built legitimating ideology, political power holders in this style of regime succeed in constructing a sophisticated account of law's necessary subordination to politics. The function of judicial review in this subtype is to give concrete expression to the comprehensive vision of the just society that is being propagated and, where necessary, to resolve conflicts between different factions within the ruling elite. The Constitution in such JR regimes is conceived as a framework for effective governance rather than a source of individual rights, and judges who evince any inclination towards asserting law's autonomous authority over a defined area of social life are quickly brought into line.

The Zimbabwean JR regime from 2000 to 2006 is a clear example of the first subtype. ZANU-PF's assault on the judiciary from 2000 and the staffing of the Supreme Court and the High Courts with political lackeys quickly destroyed any faith in the judiciary's independence and consequently any capacity for judicial review to fulfil a legitimating function. As noted in Chapter 5, ZANU-PF attempted to make up for this legitimation gap by burnishing its revolutionary credentials. At the same time, there was a significant increase in physical violence and oppression. ZANU-PF's ability to use the Supreme Court's stand on the land rights issue to justify these changes, when the real threat the Court posed was that it would overturn unfavorable election results, was somewhat effective. For a while, it seemed that ZANU-PF might succeed in constructing a new legitimating ideology based purely on its allegedly indispensable role in resolving the land issue. But the disintegration of the Zimbabwean economy and the levels of political violence required weakened ZANU-PF's hold on power to the point where it was forced into a coalition government with the MDC in 2007. The economic and political stability generated by this new arrangement played into ZANU-PF's hands, giving it the opportunity in 2013 to exploit the hoped-for transition to liberal constitutionalism to engineer a move back to authoritarian legalism, Zimbabwe's historically dominant JR-regime type.

The emergence of judicial review as an instrument of political control in the Occupied Palestinian Territories (OPT) after 2005 provides a further example of this subtype. As was the case in much of the Arab world,[97] there had been no experience of judicially enforced constitutionalism prior to this date. The internationally recognized (but not democratically elected) voice of the Palestinian people in exile, the Palestinian Liberation Organization (PLO), had developed a top-down governance structure that provided for the settlement of disputes according to political prerogatives rather than

---

[97] With the notable exception of Egypt, as discussed in Section 6.1.3.

independently enforced general norms.[98] The OPT's legal system, for its part, was a complicated product of Ottoman, British, Egyptian, Jordanian, and Israeli influences.[99] The administration of justice in these circumstances had been severely compromised. The ongoing Israeli occupation of the West Bank and Israel's opposition to the establishment of an independent Palestinian state further hampered the development of independent legal institutions.[100] For all these reasons, conditions for the successful establishment of autonomous judicial review in the OPT could hardly be said to have been propitious. Nevertheless, such a system was incrementally introduced.

After the signing of the Declaration of Principles,[101] the Palestinian Legislative Council passed a Basic Law for a future sovereign Palestinian state in 1997.[102] This constitution-like document eventually entered into force in 2002. Article 103 provided for the establishment of a High Constitutional Court (HCC) with powers *inter alia* to enforce fundamental rights. Article 104 in turn provided that the Palestinian High Court should perform the functions of the HCC pending its establishment. A Law on the HCC was subsequently passed by presidential decree in December 2005.[103]

Given the chaotic nature of the governance arrangements in the OPT it is perhaps surprising that judicial review was introduced at all. The decision to provide for this institution becomes more understandable, however, when one considers the OPT's dependence on Western donor support and its ongoing struggle for independence.[104] From that perspective, the establishment of judicial review is best seen as part of a package of governance reforms whose purpose was to assist the OPT to achieve a degree of political stability even in the absence of recognition as a sovereign state. That purpose, however, has not been fulfilled. Instead, judicial review has mutated into a tool of authoritarian governance within the Fatah-controlled West Bank.

After Hamas won the 2006 parliamentary elections, the OPT split into two parts, with Fatah seizing control of the West Bank and Hamas ousting Fatah

[98] This section is heavily indebted to the work of one of my PhD students. See Mohammad Hussein Abualrob, *The Role of Constitutional Courts in Democratic Consolidation and State Formation in Palestine* (draft doctoral dissertation, UNSW Sydney).
[99] Ibid.
[100] Ibid.
[101] The Principles were agreed to in Oslo on August 20 and signed in Washington on September 13, 1993.
[102] The full history behind the enactment of the Basic Law is recounted in Nathan J. Brown, "Constituting Palestine: The Effort to Write a Basic Law for the Palestinian Authority" (2000) 54 *Middle East Journal* 25.
[103] Abualrob, *The Role of Constitutional Courts.*
[104] Ibid.

from the Gaza Strip in June 2007. Although there is occasional cooperation between the two factions and periodic talk of reconciliation, Fatah and Hamas effectively govern the West Bank and Gaza as two separate political units, each claiming legitimacy on a different basis. In the case of the West Bank, Fatah presents itself as the nonextremist alternative to Hamas that remains committed to the liberal values contained in the Basic Law. As part of this self-presentation, Fatah has submitted its actions to judicial review by the Palestinian High Court, which assumed the functions of the High Constitutional Court under Article 104. In reality, however, all three of the High Court's decisions in that capacity have been marked by political partisanship, not just towards Fatah but also towards particular factions within the party.[105] The same pattern has been repeated in the one decision taken by the High Constitutional Court after its establishment in April 2016.[106]

Hamas, for its part, claims the legitimacy of its 2006 election mandate. It simultaneously denies the legitimacy of the Palestinian High Court and, from April 2016, the HCC. In addition to Fatah's refusal to accept the outcome of the 2006 elections, Hamas's objection to the Court relates to the procedures governing the judges' appointment. After Hamas won the elections in January 2006, Fatah-aligned President Mahmoud Abbas withdrew his support for the Law on the HCC as enacted in December 2005 and proposed certain amendments, which the PLC passed one day before its dissolution in preparation for the incoming Hamas legislature. The amendments to the Law on the HCC provided for an executive-dominated appointments process, with the President appointing the judges after consultation with the Minister of Justice and the High Judicial Council, both institutions controlled by him. Hamas rejected the legitimacy of these amendments, claiming that they were contrary to the Basic Law and that they had been passed without the requisite quorum. It accordingly rescinded the amendments on assuming control of the PLC in March 2006.

The first of the Palestinian High Court's decisions handed down in its capacity as HCC under Article 104 dealt with the validity of this rescission

---

[105]   In CO1/2006, the Court held that legislation passed by Hamas rescinding the decision of the previous, Fatah-controlled legislature, was unconstitutional because it was enacted in one package, notwithstanding the absence of any requirement to this effect in the Basic Law. In CO1/2012, the PHC declined jurisdiction to decide the matter on the grounds that the merger of the Presidency and Prime Ministership was the subject of a political agreement between Hamas and Fatah, again without any clear constitutional basis. The Court's third decision in CO6/2012 upheld the President's power to abolish parliamentary immunity notwithstanding the lack of clear constitutional authority.

[106]   The High Constitutional Court established in April 2016 reheard CO6/2012 after a corruption court had dismissed the action against the parliamentarian concerned.

legislation.[107] In a decision that is hard to understand in purely legal terms, the Court held that the Hamas-dominated PLC's rescission of all the legislation hastily enacted by the outgoing PLC after Hamas's election victory in January 2006 was unconstitutional for having been enacted in a single legislative package. The Basic Law, however, does not explicitly prohibit omnibus repeal legislation, nor would legislation of this type likely be found unconstitutional in other jurisdictions. The decision accordingly smacks of political bias, an impression strengthened by the known partisan loyalties of the judges.[108]

President Abbas's willful flouting of the Basic Law's requirements regarding the judicial appointments process and the High Court and HCC's subsequent record suggest that judicial review in the OPT is currently performing a purely instrumental function. These two Courts' transparent lack of independence means that their decisions have almost no legitimation value. Rather, the purpose of judicial review is to entrench Fatah's ongoing political control of the West Bank. Like the political subordination of the judiciary in Zimbabwe after 2000, this arrangement amounts to a temporary crisis management strategy rather than the development of a comprehensive legitimating ideology capable of sustaining Fatah's rule over the long run.

Myanmar's JR regime, by contrast, appears to be a much more durable form of authoritarian instrumentalism, which conforms more closely to the second subtype alluded to earlier. Burma, as Myanmar was formerly known, was governed as part of the British Raj from 1885 to 1942.[109] After the lifting of the Japanese occupation in 1945, the country achieved its independence in 1948.[110] For the first fifteen years there was a brief flowering of democracy under the 1947 Constitution.[111] From 1962, however, General Ne Win's military regime systematically set about dismantling democratic institutions and replacing them with "the Burmese way to socialism."[112] As explained by Nick Cheesman, the conception of the law/politics relation that developed from this point cannot be understood simply as the absence of the rule of law. Rather, it must be understood as an "asymmetrically opposite" ideology with

---

[107] Constitutional Objection 1/2006.
[108] See Abualrob, *The Role of Constitutional Courts.*
[109] Melissa Crouch, "The Layers of Legal Development in Myanmar" in Melissa Crouch and Tim Lindsey (eds.), *Law, Society, and Transition in Myanmar* (Oxford: Hart Publishing, 2014) 33, 34–6. Note that British influence was exerted before 1885 as parts of Burma were progressively ceded to Britain (ibid 36).
[110] Ibid 39.
[111] Ibid 39–41.
[112] Robert H. Taylor, *General Ne Win: A Political Biography* (Singapore: ISEAS Publishing, 2015) 255ff.

its own organizing logic.[113] In particular, law was conceived, not as a counterweight to political power, but as the means through which power holders would ensure an orderly society founded on the traditional values of "stillness" and "calmness."[114]

Judicial review was introduced in the 2008 Myanmar Constitution and came into effect in 2011 as part of a political reform process aimed at opening up Myanmar's economy to the outside world.[115] These origins are reminiscent of Egypt's turn to judicial review under President Sadat.[116] Even a cursory reading of the 2008 Constitution, however, reveals that its purpose is not the protection of individual rights.[117] Rather, the 2008 Constitution is an elaborate scheme for the maintenance of military control of the most important political institutions while allowing for the development of a carefully controlled democratic element, or "discipline-flourishing" democracy.[118] The function of judicial review on this understanding is to provide a peaceful means for resolving high-level political disputes.[119] This is reflected particularly in the rules governing access to the Constitutional Tribunal, which limit direct standing to high-ranking political office bearers.[120] While the Constitution contains individual rights,[121] and provides for the referral of constitutional questions from other courts to the Tribunal,[122] no such referrals have been made to date. There is also no provision for making individual constitutional complaints directly to the Tribunal.[123]

---

[113] Nick Cheesman, *Opposing the Rule of Law: How Myanmar's Courts Make Law and Order* (Cambridge: Cambridge University Press, 2015) 19, 79–86. "By taking up a socialist banner, the new government could situate itself in an historical narrative of anti-imperial and anticapitalist struggle while creating opportunities to target adversaries through new legal and administrative measures couched in ideological terms" (ibid 80).

[114] Ibid 30.

[115] The 2008 Myanmar Constitution is available at www.burmalibrary.org/docs5/Myanmar_Co nstitution-2008-en.pdf.

[116] See the discussion in Section 6.1.3.

[117] See David C. Williams, "What's So Bad about Burma's 2008 Constitution? A Guide for the Perplexed" in Melissa Crouch and Tim Lindsey (eds.), *Law, Society, and Transition in Myanmar* (Oxford: Hart Publishing, 2014) 117.

[118] 2008 Myanmar Constitution, ss 6(d) and 405.

[119] Dominic Jerry Nardi, Jr., "How the Constitutional Tribunal's Jurisprudence Sparked a Crisis" in Andrew Harding (ed.), Constitutionalism and Legal Change in Myanmar (Oxford: Hart Publishing, 2017) 173, 184.

[120] 2008 Myanmar Constitution, s 325 limiting direct standing to the President, the Speakers of the two houses of Parliament, the Chief Justice of the Supreme Court, and the Chairperson of the Electoral Commission.

[121] 2008 Myanmar Constitution, Chapters I and VIII.

[122] Ibid s 323.

[123] See further Dominic Nardi, "Discipline-Flourishing Constitutional Review: A Legal and Political Analysis of Myanmar's New Constitutional Tribunal" (2010) 12 *Australian Journal of*

The practical functioning of judicial review in Myanmar may be gleaned from the small handful of cases decided to date. Before the first full round of democratic elections in 2015, the Constitutional Tribunal decided five cases.[124] It is apparent from the English translations and summaries of these decisions that the Tribunal members attempted to assert some measure of independence. However, after the Tribunal decided, in *President of the Union v. Pyidaungsu Hluttaw*,[125] that legislative committees were not "Union-level organizations," and thus not entitled to review executive decisions, impeachment proceedings were brought against all the Tribunal members, forcing their resignation.[126] Significantly, Myanmar's celebrated democracy icon, Daw Aung San Suu Kyi, who was at that time serving as a member of the lower house, supported these proceedings as being necessary to protect Parliament's capacity to control the executive.[127] Faced with a choice between respect for judicial independence and Parliament's supervisory powers, Daw Suu and her party, the National League for Democracy (NLD), prioritized the latter.

The NLD's approach to the Constitutional Tribunal's role has not significantly changed since it assumed office in November 2015. After appointing a majority of the Tribunal's members in March 2016,[128] the NLD has paid little attention to it. With the NLD now controlling all the offices required to make referrals to the Tribunal, this attitude has rendered it a virtual dead letter.[129] The NLD's position appears to be based on a deep suspicion of the Tribunal's capacity, despite its now politically progressive composition, to interpret the 2008 Constitution in a way that would promote the rule of law and a culture of democratic constitutionalism. While understandable to a degree, given the

Asian Law 1; Kevin Y. L. Tan, "Constitutionalism in Burma, Cambodia and Thailand: Developments in the First Decade of the Twenty-first Century" in Albert Chen (ed.), *Constitutionalism in Asia in the Early Twenty-First Century* (Cambridge: Cambridge University Press, 2014) 219.

[124] *Chief Justice of the Union v. Ministry of Home Affairs* (on the meaning of judicial independence in s 11 of the 2008 Constitution); *Dr. Aye Maung, et al v. Republic of the Union of Myanmar* (on whether state/region Ministers for National Races Affairs are equivalent to other Ministers); *President v. Dr. Aye Maung* (request to rescind the previous decision); *President v. Pyidaungsu Hluttaw* (on whether legislative committees are union-level organizations); and *Speaker of Mon State Hluttaw v. Myanmar* (challenge to municipal governance law).

[125] (2012) No. 2/2012 (C.T.) 4 (Myan).

[126] See Dominic J. Nardi, "Finding Justice Scalia in Burma: Constitutional Interpretation and the Impeachment of the Myanmar Constitutional Tribunal" (2014) 23 *Pacific Rim Law & Policy Journal* 631.

[127] Ibid.

[128] www.president-office.gov.mm/en/?q=briefing-room/orders/2016/03/31/id-6165.

[129] Since the NLD came to power, the Tribunal has decided only a handful of cases.

TABLE 6.1: *Populated typology of JR regimes*

Democratic Legalism	Authoritarian Legalism
Subtype (1): Australia (1920-present)	Soft: Hungary (2010-present); Singapore (1965-
Subtype (2): Germany (1950-present);	present)
Colombia (1991-present); Hungary	Hard: Chile (1973–90); Egypt (1979–90);
(1989–2009); India (1950–77);	Zimbabwe (1980–2000; 2007-present)
Indonesia (2002-present); South	
Africa (1995-present)	
Subtype (3): Hungary (1998–2010);	
Chile (1990-present)	
Democratic Instrumentalism	**Authoritarian Instrumentalism**
Structured two-party: United States	Subtype (1): Zimbabwe (2000–6); Egypt
(post-1970)	(1952–79); Occupied Palestinian Territories
Unstructured: India (post-1977)	(2006-present)
	Subtype (2): Myanmar (2011-present)

authoritarian character of that Constitution, the NLD's stance has tended to perpetuate the prevailing conception of judicial review in Myanmar as an institution that is entirely beholden to political prerogatives.[130]

6.1.5 *Summary*

In summary of the discussion in this section, Table 6.1 populates the typology as set out above.

The remaining sections of this chapter use the cases included in the populated typology to search for common patterns in the processes of JR-regime consolidation, transformation and incremental change across the societies studied.

6.2 CONSOLIDATION

The case studies in Chapters 3–5 provided several different examples of JR-regime consolidation, both following the initial establishment of judicial

---

[130] In 2014, before it took office, the NLD floated the idea of abolishing the Tribunal and transferring its powers to the Supreme Court. This suggests that its real concern may be with the idea of a separate Tribunal rather than judicial review itself. See Nardi, "How the Constitutional Tribunal's Jurisprudence Sparked a Crisis" 187. Given that it has appointed a majority of the Tribunal's members, however, the NLD's failure to utilize the Tribunal remains indicative of a generalized suspicion of the role of judicial review in promoting democracy, at least where judicial review is targeted at interpreting an authoritarian Constitution not of its own making.

review and after some or other process of regime destabilization. In further investigating this phenomenon, this section first briefly restates the case study examples and then suggests a provisional list of four pathways to consolidation and their associated causal mechanisms. The rest of the section examines whether the additional instances of JR-regime consolidation encountered in the ten shorter case studies conform to these pathways or whether the list needs to be modified to accommodate them.

Chapter 3 showed how the consolidation of the Australian JR regime followed a classic, increasing-returns path. The adoption of the 1900 Constitution, it was argued, brought together two rival understandings of law's claim to authority: the English tradition of statutory interpretation, in which law was conceived as the command of a sovereign that could be semantically deduced and implemented, and the more expansive American tradition of purposive, value-oriented constitutional interpretation. The confluence of these two traditions produced a critical juncture in which the High Court's presentation of the legitimate basis for its authority was underdetermined by past understandings. In the crucial *Engineers* case, the Court, for a combination of sincere and strategic reasons, adopted a legalist posture in rejecting two doctrines that had been premised on the more purposive, American style. That choice, producing as it did a generous under-standing of the Commonwealth's powers, triggered a self-reinforcing process of mutual law/politics legitimation that by the middle of the last century had given rise to a highly stable, democratic legalist regime.

The second major chapter in the Australian story – the partially achieved "Mason Court revolution" – provided a different example of JR-regime con-solidation, or rather, reconsolidation. In this instance, after many years of stability, an internal judicial challenge to the prevailing democratic legalist regime triggered a rearguard action from more traditionally minded judges. After the compromise reached in the *Lange* case,[131] the Australian JR regime reconsolidated around a slightly adjusted understanding of the legitimate basis for the Court's authority, one that allowed greater attention to be paid to the political values underpinning the workings of the democratic system. This change fell short of the decisive shift that Sir Anthony Mason and his like-minded justices had favored. Rather, it was a case of regime reconsolidation through accommodation of the internal challenge.

The Indian case study offered yet another example of JR-regime consolida-tion. The period immediately following the adoption of the 1950 Constitution, Chapter 4 argued, saw the Indian JR regime consolidate around a version of

---

[131]   *Lange v. Australian Broadcasting Corporation* (1997) 189 CLR 520.

democratic legalism in which the Supreme Court enforced property rights as restraints on majoritarian democracy. The conception of the law/politics relation underlying this regime was a logical extension of the colonial tradition of Austinian legal positivism. In place of the doctrine of parliamentary sovereignty, the Supreme Court developed a robust rights jurisprudence. Its assertion of this power, however, was subject to the Lok Sabha's easily and frequently exercised power of constitutional amendment, thus reproducing at one stage removed the relationship between the judiciary and Parliament that had prevailed under the Westminster system.

Finally, the Zimbabwean case study showed how a postcolonial political elite, even after a major constitutional rupture, may quickly drive the consolidation of a new JR regime by adapting a tried and tested legitimating ideology to new purposes. The story in this instance was one of continuity in the face of major institutional change – of ZANU-PF's ability to substitute the democracy-limiting logic of an anti-colonial, revolutionary tradition for the democracy-limiting logic of the colonial dual state. After the rise of the Movement for Democratic Change (MDC) in the 1990s, ZANU-PF was forced to take complete control of the judiciary and the Zimbabwean JR regime took on a more instrumentalist cast. In 2013, however, President Mugabe exploited the opening created by the adoption of a new Constitution to return the regime to its historically dominant form. In this way, the Zimbabwean case study suggested that certain societies may have a default regime to which they habitually return. Regime consolidation in these cases is not a slow, self-reinforcing process but rather a rapid collapsing back into familiar thought-ways – the legitimating complex of ideas that has tended historically to produce some measure of stability.

Taken together, the three case studies suggest that there are at least four different pathways to JR-regime consolidation, one of which is characterized by a self-reinforcing process of mutual law/politics legitimation and three of which have to do with the continuation of an existing regime in an amended form, either through the adaptation of the regime to new institutional circumstances, the accommodation of an internal challenge, or the reversion of the regime to an historically dominant type, as set out in Table 6.2.

As indicated in the third row of the table, each pathway to consolidation is associated with a different causal mechanism. *New regime formation* occurs when judicial review is established for the first time and a contingent choice between two or more rival interpretive traditions becomes entrenched through a cyclical process of judicial decision and political acceptance. *Adaptive continuity* is characterized by the retooling of elements of an existing legitimating ideology to serve new purposes. *Counterreaction* involves the accommodation of an endogenous challenge by incorporating aspects of the proposed new conception of the law/politics relation within the existing regime. *Reversion to dominant type* occurs when the regime returns to the society's historically dominant regime type after a brief interlude.

JR regimes are never completely "new," of course. Even JR regimes that come into existence after the adoption of a new constitution draw on existing understandings of the law/politics relation. Those understandings may condition the "new" JR regime in two ways: culturally – by shaping the legitimating ideology that undergirds the regime, and institutionally, by informing the design of constitutional institutions that reproduce that ideology as the constitution begins to function. This certainly seems to be true of the Australian case, where the self-reinforcing trajectory after *Engineers* was in part conditioned by past cultural assumptions and the institutional design of the 1900 Constitution. It is also true of the Indian and Zimbabwean cases insofar as colonial conceptions of the law/politics relation influenced the choices made by postcolonial rulers and judges as they sought to establish their respective claims to authority in the new institutional setting in which they found themselves.

In some cases, a constitution may be deliberately intended to drive a transition away from a discredited past, as happens most obviously when a democratic constitution replaces an authoritarian one. In those circumstances, the new constitution may seek to draw on an idealized conception of the law/politics relation that has not been part of the society's past traditions. Even in this situation, however, existing conceptions of the law/politics relation may continue to exert an influence and, in some instances, as happened in Zimbabwe after 1980, form the basis for a reconsolidated regime substantially like the one from which the society sought to depart. Where that happens, the de facto operation of the "new" JR regime may conform more closely to past conceptions of the law/politics relation than to the conception seemingly entailed by the new constitution.

JR-regime consolidation that occurs through increasing returns (*new regime formation*) is a slow-moving process in which the new conception of the law/politics relation is gradually entrenched. By contrast, the other three causal mechanisms identified in Table 6.2 all produce their effects quite rapidly. *Adaptation* is thus a relatively fast-acting mechanism in which an existing legitimating ideology is recalibrated to fit the new constitution. *Counterreaction* is likewise a fast-acting mechanism in which legal and political elites reassert the historically dominant understanding of the law/politics relation by incorporating aspects of a proposed rival understanding. Finally, *reversion to dominant type* occurs where the inherent instability of a newly

TABLE 6.2: *Provisional list of four pathways to JR-regime consolidation*

Path	1: *New regime formation*	2: *Adaptive continuity*	3: *Counterreaction*	4: *Reversion to dominant type*
Elaboration	Judicial review newly established – contingent choice between rival traditions – JR regime consolidates through increasing returns	Judicial review newly established – judges and/or political elites adapt old-order legitimating ideology to serve new purposes	Internal judicial challenge to JR regime causes some instability – counterreaction from regime supporters sees reconsolidation of JR regime with some new features	Recently established JR regime inherently unstable and/or weakened by external crisis – political elites drive transformation back to historically dominant regime
Causal mechanism	Increasing returns	Adaptation	Accommodation	Reversion
Duration	Slow	Fast	Fast	Fast
Examples	Australia after 1901	India after 1950; Zimbabwe after 1980	Australia in early 1990s	Zimbabwe after 2013

established JR regime coupled with an external crisis triggers a sudden reversion to an historically dominant regime type.

That is as far as the process of JR-regime consolidation may be elaborated on the strength of the three in-depth case studies. The discussion now turns to the ten shorter case studies to see whether consolidation in these instances conforms to the provisional list of pathways and, if not, what adjustments need to be made.

Both *new regime formation* and *adaptive continuity* are processes of consolidation that follow the establishment of judicial review for the first time. The key difference is that under the first pathway the new regime develops slowly as rival traditions vie for ascendancy, whereas the second involves the relatively rapid adaptation of past conceptions of the law/politics relation to a new institutional setting. In the ten additional case studies, the development of Hungary's JR regime after 1989 and Indonesia's JR regime after 2002 provide further examples of the first of these pathways. In the Hungarian case, the attempted constitutional construction of a democratic legalist regime triggered a counterreaction that saw the consolidation of an authoritarian legalist regime based on an older, ethno-nationalist tradition. In the Indonesian case, it is not yet clear which of the two contending traditions will win out, meaning that the consolidation process is not yet complete.

As noted in Section 6.2, the Hungarian Constitutional Court's reputation for forceful decision-making after 1989 was not a true reflection of the level of public support for liberal constitutionalism in that country. Instead of carefully winning political acceptance for its role, the Sólyom Court modelled itself on the German Federal Constitutional Court, as though it could exercise that Court's powers without the ideational support structures on which they depended. The Sólyom Court's failure to win political acceptance for its role meant that democratic legalism never properly consolidated. That ideational opening allowed populist political parties to present an alternative conception of the law/politics relation, one that drew on Hungary's older, ethno-nationalist tradition. After Fidesz's accession to power in 2010, a design flaw in the constitutional amendment procedure enabled it to impose its center-right political vision on the Constitution while at the same time locking out other political parties from effectively competing for power. As things stand at present, Hungary is on a path towards authoritarian legalism in which the formal trappings of constitutional democracy will be used to mask the concentration of power in a single political party.

The Hungarian case in this way supports the provisional understanding of the causal mechanism for *new regime formation* set out in Table 6.2, while at the same time adding something to it. As posited earlier, the presence of two or more rival traditions of thinking about the law/politics relation delays JR-regime consolidation until one of the traditions becomes associated with an understanding of the Court's mandate that wins political acceptance. Where a liberal constitutional reform process pits a new democratic legalist understanding of the law/politics relation against an older, ethno-nationalist tradition, the Hungarian case adds, overzealous judicial enforcement of the new understanding may strengthen the position of center-right political parties. Depending on the constitutional amendment procedure and the precise balance of political power, these parties may be able to use the disjuncture between the Constitution's aspirational promises and the lived experience of their constituents to drive the consolidation of an authoritarian legalist regime.

The Indonesian case, too, may be understood as an example of thus far failed democratic legalist *new regime formation*, although in this instance it is less clear which of the two contending traditions will eventually win out. As noted in Section 6.2, the 1998–2002 constitutional reform process in Indonesia signaled a decisive break with Suharto-era authoritarianism. That gave Jimly Asshiddiqie, the Constitutional Court's first Chief Justice, a relatively free hand to build public support for the Court's role. In his media appearances, his personal opinion-writing style, and the way he encouraged respectful disagreement among his colleagues, Jimly premised law's claim to authority on its tendency to promote the reasoned justification of decisions. Together with the contextual factors supporting the Court's independence, this approach did much to put Indonesia's JR regime on a path towards democratic legalism and, in particular, towards a version of that regime in which the legitimate basis for the Court's authority would have been its commitment to enforcing the constitutional ground rules for sound democratic governance.

Other traditions and ways of thinking about the Court's relationship to democratic politics were not completely marginalized, however. For one, there was the idea that the Court had been given a negative-legislator mandate and that the Jimly Court's forceful assertion of its role deviated from this original understanding. That view, held by a broad spectrum of Indonesia's political elite, hindered acceptance of the Court's decisions and fueled growing opposition to it. Second, there was also the more perfunctory judicial reasoning style and preference for unanimous decision-making that had been part of Indonesia's civil-law tradition. In many ways, this was the tradition against which the Jimly Court reacted, but it remained a forceful one insofar as it conditioned the way judges not under Jimly's direct influence thought about the Court's role.

After the appointment of Mohammad Mahfud as Chief Justice, the trajectory towards JR-regime consolidation that Jimly had mapped out became less straightforward. Rejecting his predecessor's more deliberative reasoning style, Mahfud emphasized the substantive justice of case outcomes. From this point, the pace of JR regime consolidation in Indonesia slowed. What had been a relatively straightforward process of building support for law's claim to authority on the conception of that claim that Jimly had favored was undermined by Mahfud's abrupt replacement of that conception with his own view, a move that was moreover associated with an upsurge in the Court's positive-legislator decisions – the very problem Mahfud had promised to resolve. While the Court might have been attacked in 2011 even if Jimly had not been ousted, Mahfud's approach did nothing to placate the Court's opponents. The Court survived, not because it enjoyed the support of a consolidated JR regime, but because of favorable contextual factors – the fragmentation of Indonesia's electoral politics and the consequent difficulty of amending the Constitution to restrict the Court's jurisdiction.

Like the Hungarian example, therefore, the Indonesian case provides support for the understanding of *new regime formation* set out earlier, while also adding something to it. Taking the form as that pathway does of a slow-moving, self-reinforcing process, any abrupt changes in judicial philosophy may retard regime consolidation. In effect, such changes disrupt the causal chain witnessed in the Australian case in terms of which a consistently maintained conception of law's claim to authority is progressively legitimated as judicial decisions premised on that conception win political acceptance. That is not to say that Indonesia's JR regime will not consolidate around a version of democratic legalism at some point in the future; given the factors already mentioned, this outcome still seems the most likely one. It is just that the path to this outcome has become less certain.

The additional examples of *adaptive continuity* in the shorter case studies are Germany after 1950, Singapore after 1965, Colombia after 1991, Myanmar after 2011, and the OPT after 2005. All these examples roughly conform to the pathway followed in India after 1950 and Zimbabwe after 1980. They are all thus instances in which judicial review was newly established and in which legal and political elites drove the consolidation of a new JR regime by adapting existing conceptions of the law/politics relation to the new institutional setting. In addition to providing empirical support for the understanding of this causal mechanism set out earlier, the ubiquity of these examples suggests that adaptive continuity might be the most common pathway to consolidation, which in turn has implications for the transformative potential of judicial review.

In Germany's case, as we have seen, the adoption of the 1949 Basic Law did not trigger a wholesale transformation to a more politicized conception of law. Rather, the Federal Constitutional Court drew on Germany's long-standing tradition of legalism to portray its task as being akin to the legal-technical elaboration of an "objective order of values."[132] As explained by Hailbronner, the legal profession – facing allegations of having aided and abetted the rise of National Socialism – had a self-interested motive for preserving a conception of law as autonomous from politics.[133] There was also a comparatively high degree of consensus between the main political parties over the political values informing the new constitutional order.[134] The adoption of a US-style understanding of judicial review as an institution through which the major political parties could seek to entrench their competing, ideologically inflected visions of constitutional justice was thus never really on the cards. Rather, the central question was how to accommodate rights-based judicial review within a legalist understanding of the law/politics relation. The solution to this problem was suggested by the Court in *Lüth* and then assiduously taken up by legal academics as they rationalized the Court's proportionality jurisprudence. With time, these doctrinal innovations drove a new understanding of the legitimate basis for law's claim to authority, one that was still compatible with legalism but which accorded greater weight to the Court's capacity objectively to weigh the competing political values on which German democracy was premised.

The consolidation of Colombia's JR regime after 1991 followed a similar pathway to Germany's in many respects, although in this instance popular support for the Constitutional Court and the judicial clerkship system played a greater role than legal-academic rationalization.[135] As noted in Section 6.1.1, Colombia's 1991 Constitution introduced a new institutional mechanism for the enforcement of human rights in the form of the *tutela* action. This created an opening for judges and legal scholars to challenge the formalist reasoning methods that had long prevented the Supreme Court from playing a meaningful role in rights enforcement. As explained by Manuel Cepeda and others,[136] the Constitutional Court sought to bring law closer to social reality. In so doing, the judges exploited the high degree of faith that had long existed in Colombia in the autonomy of law from politics to position the Court as the

---

[132] BVerfGE 7, 198 (*Lüth*).
[133] Hailbronner, *Traditions and Transformations* 76.
[134] Ibid.
[135] Landau, *Beyond Judicial Independence* 173.
[136] Cepeda Espinosa, "The Judicialization of Politics in Colombia"; Cepeda-Espinosa, "Judicial Review in a Violent Context"; Landau, *Beyond Judicial Independence*.

enforcer of the substantive ground rules of democracy. As in Germany, this way of presenting law's claim to authority was not so much a departure from the existing tradition as a question of adapting it to new circumstances. In effect, the legal and political establishment drove a transition from democratic legalism subtype (3) (*deferential rights review*) to democratic legalism subtype (2) (*substantive legalism*). That process, as further explained in Section 6.3, may be viewed either as the adaptation of Colombian democratic legalism to the institutional innovation of the *tutela* action or as a process of constitutionally engineered and judicially led transformation between two variants of democratic legalism.

South Africa provides a third example of JR-regime consolidation through adaptive continuity. The apparent choice in this instance was between presenting the 1996 Constitution as an objectively determinable framework for social reform or as an inherently contestable, emancipatory political project. In truth, however, the second option never really emerged as a serious rival. From the very beginning, the Chaskalson Court adopted the first approach as one more in keeping with the conception of law as a bulwark against the abuse of political power that had developed during the struggle against apartheid.[137] President Nelson Mandela, steeped as he himself was in this conception, readily accepted law's claim to authority on this basis.[138] There was thus considerable continuity in the South African case between the nature of law's claim to authority before and after the transition to democracy. What changed was the expansion of autonomous law's domain to include all South Africa's people and the formal specification *qua* constitutional rights of what had previously been common-law presumptions of statutory interpretation. This helps to explain the rapidity with which the South African JR regime consolidated after 1994. Rather than requiring the development of an entirely new conception of law's authority, democratic legalism was imagined as the fulfilment of a long-standing quest for judicially enforced political equality.

Likewise, the literature on Singapore stresses how PAP claimed to be building on an existing rule-of-law tradition.[139] The difference in Singapore's case was that this claim was partly false and partly true. False because the British rule of law had only ever existed in Singapore in the bifurcated version characteristic of the colonial dual state.[140] But at the same time true because PAP was in a sense continuing that tradition by retooling it

[137] Theunis Roux, *The Politics of Principle* 219–31.
[138] Ibid 173.
[139] Rajah, *Authoritarian Rule of Law*.
[140] Ibid.

for new authoritarian purposes. In place of the colonizer's civilizing mission, as we have seen, PAP justified restrictions on political rights as a function of its historic role in promoting ethnic harmony, national security, and economic prosperity.

In Myanmar, the 2008 Constitution introduced judicial review for the first time, but restricted access to the Constitutional Tribunal in ways that perpetuated long-held understandings of the role of law as being to maintain peace and stability.[141] Even after the NLD began playing a formal role in parliamentary politics, this view of law survived, perpetuated by the NLD's reluctance to give any role to the 2008 Constitution in the promotion of democracy, but also by a culturally conditioned preference for centralized political control of the judiciary. Judicial review in the OPT, by contrast, has not yet given rise to a legitimating ideology that adds anything to Fatah's de facto political control of the West Bank. Nevertheless, to the extent that any kind of JR regime has been consolidated, that regime is a continuation of instrumental conceptions of law that developed in response to the PLO's top-down governance methods in exile.

There are no further examples of *counterreaction* in the additional cases. This suggests that this form of consolidation may be a relatively rare phenomenon restricted to well-established JR regimes.

The two additional examples of the fourth and last pathway, *reversion to dominant type*, are Egypt after 1990 and Chile after 1990. In Egypt, the expansion of the Supreme Constitutional Court's mandate beyond the limits set in 1979 prompted a reversion back to authoritarian instrumentalism.[142] In contrast to the pattern witnessed in Zimbabwe, there was no opportunistic exploitation of a political opening. Rather, the authoritarian power holder simply pulled the plug on an experiment of its own devising.[143] In Chile, the path back towards democratic legalism after 1990 has been arduous and disappointing to some.[144] But its initial trajectory, towards democratic legalism subtype (3) (*deferential rights review*), rather than subtype (2) (*substantive legalism*), may be understood as a return to Chile's historically dominant JR-regime type.

Summarizing the above discussion, the additional examples may all be classified under the four provisional pathways, as set out in Table 6.3.

---

[141]   See the discussion in Section 6.1.4.
[142]   Moustafa, *The Struggle for Constitutional Power* 178–218.
[143]   Ibid.
[144]   Javier Couso, "The Judicialization of Chilean Politics: The Rights Revolution That Never Was" in Rachel Sieder, Line Schjolden, and Alan Angell (eds.), *The Judicialization of Politics in Latin America* (New York: Palgrave Macmillan, 2005) 105.

TABLE 6.3: *Four pathways to JR-regime consolidation – additional cases*

Path	1: *New regime formation*	2: *Adaptive continuity*	3: *Counterreaction*	4: *Reversion to dominant type*
Elaboration	Judicial review newly established – contingent choice between rival traditions – JR regime consolidates through increasing returns	Judicial review newly established – judges and/or political elites adapt old-order legitimating ideology to serve new purposes	Internal judicial challenge to JR regime causes some instability – counterreaction from regime supporters sees reconsolidation of JR regime with some new features	Recently established JR regime inherently unstable and/or weakened by external crisis – political elites drive transformation back to historically dominant regime
Examples	Australia after 1901; Hungary after 1989; Indonesia after 2002	India after 1950; Zimbabwe after 1980; Germany after 1949; Singapore after 1965; Colombia after 1991; South Africa after 1994; OPT after 2005; Myanmar after 2011	Australia in early 1990s	Zimbabwe after 2013; Egypt after 1990; Chile after 1990

6.3 TRANSFORMATION

Consider again Chapter 2's account of the transformation of the American JR regime over the course of the last century. Drawing on Horwitz's study of the transformation of American law more generally, the chapter noted the destabilizing impact of nineteenth-century industrialization and urbanization processes on prevailing conceptions of the law/politics relation.[145] Those external developments, it was argued, opened the way for the legal realist movement to promote a more pragmatic, value-oriented conception of law.[146] As a matter of constitutional culture, however, the transition to democratic instrumentalism took a little while longer. In effect, two pathways to regime consolidation opened up: the first would have seen the American regime restabilizing around a Frankfurterian conception of the judicial function as requiring deference to scientifically informed democratic choices, the second around the institutionalization of ideological decision-making through bipartisan political acceptance. It was the second of these pathways that eventually gained traction. With the Burger and Rehnquist Courts perpetuating the Warren Court's liberal-progressivism in a different ideological register, judicial review is today seen as an inescapably political institution through which liberals and conservatives promote their competing visions of the American constitutional project.

The US case in this way suggests that JR-regime transformation is contingent on the satisfaction of two main conditions, each of which is necessary but neither of which is on its own sufficient: (1) an exogenous shock to the prevailing JR regime; and (2) a more gradual process of ideational reconstruction in which legal and political elites with an interest in exploiting the crisis successfully promote a new understanding of the law/politics relation. The transformation need not be accompanied by any formal constitutional change, but does need to be institutionalized in key practices such as the judicial appointments process and the political acceptance of decisions.

Chapter 4 provided further support for this understanding of the causal mechanism by showing how the transformation of India's JR regime during the 1980s was also triggered by an exogenous shock, in this instance the 1975–7

---

[145]   Morton J. Horwitz, *The Transformation of American Law, 1870–1960: The Crisis of Legal Orthodoxy* (New York: Oxford University Press, 1992) 9–31. See also Howard Gillman, *The Constitution Besieged: The Rise and Demise of Lochner Era Police Powers Jurisprudence* (Durham, NC: Duke University Press, 1993).

[146]   Robert S. Summers, "Pragmatic Instrumentalism in Twentieth Century American Legal Thought – A Synthesis and Critique of our Dominant General Theory about Law and its Use" (1981) 66 *Cornell Law Review* 861.

Emergency. By exposing certain weaknesses in democratic legalism's capacity to deal with a determined assault on individual rights, the Emergency opened the way for Justices Bhagwati, Krishna Iyer and others to promote a new conception of the Supreme Court as the interventionist, pro-poor guardian of India's democracy. After 1989, the Court's commitment to a left-progressive reading of the Constitution weakened, but its decisions continued to reflect the influence of judicial ideology in a setting in which the Court controlled the appointment of judges and in which fragmented benches undermined the constraining role of legal doctrine. The Indian case therefore differs from the American in the nature of the exogenous shock that drove the transformation, the human agents behind the change, and the political and institutional setting in which the new JR regime took hold. Nevertheless, at a higher level of abstraction, there are sufficient similarities between the two cases to suggest that the same causal mechanism may have been at work.

The Australian case study in Chapter 3 provided further, negative support for this understanding of JR-regime transformation by showing how the *absence* of an exogenous shock to that country's democratic legalist regime hindered the full realization of "the Mason Court revolution."[147] In the 1980s, when Sir Anthony and his colleagues called for greater recognition of the role of shared community values in constitutional adjudication, extant understandings of the legitimate basis for the Court's claim to authority were stable and unthreatened. While there had been some changes to the Court's external environment, none of these were on the scale of the developments in the US or India. The reform-minded members of the Mason Court thus fell back on arguing that democratic legalism's denial of the influence of shared community values was an intrinsic problem to do with the way the Court related to the Australian public. That argument had some merit. As soon as the Court's decisions began to attract public controversy, however, more traditionally minded justices were able to halt the progress of the revolution. After the decision in *Lange*, the Australian regime reconsolidated around a modified version of democratic legalism that gave the Court a carefully defined role in enforcing the political values underpinning Australia's system of representative and responsible government. In this way, the Australian case supports the idea that an exogenous shock is a necessary condition for JR-regime transformation. Absent such a shock, calls for reform, even when they are made by elite judicial actors, may at most drive the modification of an existing regime.

---

[147]   Jason L. Pierce, *Inside the Mason Court Revolution: The High Court of Australia Transformed* (Durham, NC: Carolina Academic Press, 2006).

TABLE 6.4: *Preliminary assessment of conditions for JR-regime transformation*

	US	Australia	India	Zimbabwe
Exogenous shock to prevailing JR regime?	Yes	No	Yes	Yes
Elite political actors driving transformation?	Yes	No	Yes	Yes
Broad-based legal-cultural movement?	Yes	No	No	No
Judges able and willing to drive transformation?	Yes	Yes	Yes	Yes
Transformation in fact occurred?	Yes	No	Yes	Yes

Finally, the Zimbabwean case study explained how the political rise of the MDC in the 1990s unsettled one of the foundational premises of that country's authoritarian legalist regime. By challenging ZANU-PF's assumed right to govern in a series of closely fought elections, the MDC forced the ruling party to take more effective control of the courts. That in turn required ZANU-PF to find a substitute for the legitimating benefits of its initial commitment to judicial independence. It succeeded in part and for a limited time in doing this by manipulating the land rights issue to present itself as the sole legitimate heir to Zimbabwe's revolutionary nationalist tradition. In this instance, therefore, the ideational work required to construct the new regime was carried out by political power holders and co-opted judges. Once again, however, the essential elements of the causal mechanism seen in the American case – an exogenous shock followed by interested-actor regime reconstruction – were present.

Table 6.4 above summarizes the conditions for JR-regime transformation apparent from the American case and the three in-depth case studies.

That JR-regime transformation should depend on a destabilizing exogenous shock followed by ideational reconstruction work is a significant preliminary finding. While JR regimes obviously do not change character without at least some prompting, there is nothing in theory that precludes the possibility of transformation through internal ideational challenge or some other form of gradual, endogenous change. Indeed, in the sociological and political science literature on institutional transformation, both of those possibilities are given significant attention. In their seminal work on legal development, for example, Phillippe Nonet and Philip Selznick assume that the transition from repressive to autonomous law and then on to responsive law is an endogenous process driven by the developmental logic of each of those stages.[148] Kathleen Thelen's work on formal institutional change, in turn, has challenged the assumption that exogenous shocks are a necessary condition for significant transformation.[149] Formal institutions, she has shown, often evolve gradually and yet may be fundamentally transformed over time.[150] While neither Nonet and Selznick nor Thelen specifically address the institution of judicial review, the fact that they all stress the role of endogenous factors suggests that the finding emerging from the in-depth case studies requires further examination. Is it really the case that an exogenous shock is a necessary condition for JR-regime transformation? And, if so, is there something about JR regimes as legitimating complexes of ideas that might explain this fact?

The rest of this section investigates these questions by looking at four further instances of achieved or failed JR-regime transformation in Germany, Colombia, Chile, and Egypt. The analysis proceeds in two steps – first, tracing the process followed in these four instances, and then using congruence testing and Millian methods of agreement and difference to determine whether the causal mechanism apparent in the in-depth case studies also explains this larger group of cases. In all instances, the focus falls on the following variables: (1) the presence or absence of an exogenous shock to the prevailing JR regime; and (2) the presence or absence of one or more of the following change agents: political elites, pioneering judges, or a broad-based legal-cultural movement able and willing to drive the transformation forward.

The postwar German process is examined here as an instance of possible JR-regime transformation on the assumption that a JR regime of some kind, albeit a weak one, had developed before the Nazi Party came to power in 1933. Under the 1919 Weimar Constitution, the State High Court (*Staatsgerichtshof*) had limited judicial review powers, primarily overly federalist questions, but also in theory over individual rights

[148] Phillippe Nonet and Philip Selznick, *Law and Society in Transition: Towards Responsive Law* (Harper Torch, 1978).
[149] Thelen explicitly restricts her claims to formal institutions, defined as institutions that "are the products of conscious design and redesign" (Kathleen Thelen, "How Institutions Evolve: Insights from Comparative Historical Analysis" in James Mahoney and Dietrich Rueschemeyer (eds.), Comparative Historical Analysis in the Social Sciences (Cambridge: Cambridge University Press, 2003) 208, 208 n 1).
[150] Ibid. See also James Mahoney and Kathleen Thelen (eds.), "A Theory of Gradual Institutional Change" in James Mahoney and Kathleen Thelen, *Explaining Institutional Change: Ambiguity, Agency, and Power* (Cambridge: Cambridge University Press, 2010) 1; Martin B. Carstensen, "Ideas are Not as Stable as Political Scientists Want them to Be: A Theory of Incremental Ideational Change" (2011) 59 *Political Studies* 596 (drawing on discourse theory and "the interpretive approach" to identify two types of incremental ideational change).

violations.[151] The former was a more certain part of its mandate, with a long history in previous constitutions. The latter was more contested given that the Weimar Constitution, though it contained a list of fundamental rights, failed to specify whether they were justiciable or not.[152] This ambiguity was the subject of a lively discussion in the Association of German Scholars of State Law, with opinion divided between an anti-positivist school that favored judicial review and a positivist school that mostly did not.[153] In 1921, in the midst of this controversy, the State High Court announced that it had the power to review "the formal and material legality of laws."[154] A similar statement was made in 1925,[155] and thereafter the power of judicial review was exercised, albeit "only moderately, and with little impact."[156] It is fair to say, then, that before 1933 a version of democratic legalism subtype (3) (*deferential rights review*) had begun to develop under the Weimar Constitution.

After the end of World War II, there was intense debate in Germany about whether legalism, and in particular the positivist mindset that had come to be identified with that view of law's appropriate relationship to politics, had facilitated the rise of National Socialism. In the best-known version of this critique, Gustav Radbruch argued that "positivism, with its principle that 'a law is a law,' [had] ... rendered the German legal profession defenseless against statutes that are arbitrary and criminal."[157] This was more than just a failure of intellectual resources in Radbruch's view. It was that the positivist mindset had made it easier for the legal profession to separate out the obvious injustice of Nazi law from the question of its validity. In this way, legal positivism had not just failed to prevent, it had also in some sense aided and abetted the collapse of the Weimar Republic.

For a time, Radbruch's argument held sway, and there was a strong anti-positivist movement in Germany that proposed the adoption of a bill of rights

---

[151] Kommers and Miller, *The Constitutional Jurisprudence of the Federal Republic of Germany* 6; Hailbronner, *Traditions and Transformations* 42.

[152] Kommers and Miller, *The Constitutional Jurisprudence of the Federal Republic of Germany* 6.

[153] Bernd J. Hartmann, "The Arrival of Judicial Review in Germany Under the Weimar Constitution of 1919" (2004) 18 *Brigham Young University Journal of Public Law* 107, 119–23.

[154] Michael Stolleis, "Judicial Review, Administrative Review, and Constitutional Review in the Weimar Republic" (2003) 16 *Ratio Juris* 266, 272 (citing 102 RGZ 161–6 (1921)). See also Kommers and Miller, *The Constitutional Jurisprudence of the Federal Republic of Germany* 6 (making the same point but citing 107 RGZ 377–81 (1924)).

[155] Hartmann, "The Arrival of Judicial Review in Germany" 124.

[156] Stolleis, "Judicial Review" 272.

[157] Gustav Radbruch, "Statutory Lawlessness and Supra-Statutory Law" (2006) 26 *Oxford Journal of Legal Studies* 1, 6 (first published in 1946).

as an extralegal constraint on political power.[158] In the discussions over the design of the 1949 Basic Law, however, the horrors of Nazi Germany were mostly treated as a negative example of what happens when law is subordinated to politics.[159] The solution, therefore, was not to give up on the idea of law's autonomy, but to try to harmonize that idea with the adoption of a supreme-law constitution that mandated judicial consideration of fundamental rights. Ironically, as Hailbronner has pointed out, the intellectual resources for this task were provided by the proponents of Interest Jurisprudence (*Interressenjurisprudenz*), which was a more moderate version of the anti-positivist Free Law School (*Freirechtsschule*) that had flourished under the Weimar Republic.[160] Like the Free Law School, Interest Jurisprudence had developed as a reaction to legal formalism, but it had not gone as far in dislodging legal norms as the central focus of legal analysis.[161] It thus provided the means through which the FCC in *Lüth* was able to understand the bill of rights as an "objective order of values" while yet treating those values as legal principles that could be elaborated using impartial, apolitical reasoning methods.[162]

The German case in this way supports the understanding of the causal mechanism of JR-regime transformation emerging from the in-depth case studies. The horrors of the Second World War undoubtedly triggered a process of public reexamination of prevailing conceptions of the law/politics relation. The exogenous shock condition is thus clearly satisfied. In the end, however, the challenge to legalism was absorbed and used to refashion, rather than fundamentally overhaul, the existing regime. This occurred principally because German legal and political elites had little interest in promoting a more politicized conception of law. Rather, the process followed in Germany after the end of World War II is best viewed as the adaptation of Germany's long-standing commitment to the separation of law and politics to the requirements of the new constitutional order. Alternatively, if the focus falls on the precise form that democratic legalism took, then one might say that the exogenous shock of the Nazi era opened the way for legal and political elites to drive a successful process of transformation between democratic legalism subtype (3) (*deferential rights review*) and subtype (2) (*substantive legalism*).

[158] Hailbronner, *Traditions and Transformations* 76.
[159] Ibid 76–7.
[160] Ibid 73–4.
[161] Ibid.
[162] Ibid 78, 84–5.

The Colombian case may likewise be read as an instance either of failed wholesale transformation away from democratic legalism or as successful subtype transformation. During the period of liberal-conservative power-sharing from 1958 to 1986, the Supreme Court's record on constitutional rights was extremely poor, with few cases making it to the Court and even fewer successful.[163] The Court's performance contributed to a general feeling in Colombia that political institutions were far removed from the concerns of ordinary people.[164] As in Germany, however, this problem was not conceived as a crisis of legalism per se. Rather, it was seen as a crisis of interpretive method, and in particular of the Supreme Court's overly formalist approach.[165] When the new Constitution came to be drafted in 1991, the solution to the problem was therefore seen as being to create a new, more powerful institution, the Constitutional Court, and to extend new avenues for expeditious redress of rights violations through the *tutela* action. Under its visionary first justices, the Constitutional Court took up this invitation and creatively designed a range of new doctrines and remedies.[166] There was a significant constitutional-cultural transformation in that sense from an understanding of law as aloof to ordinary people's concerns to an understanding of law as central to them. All of this occurred, however, without impacting Colombians' profound faith in the autonomy of law from politics. Indeed, it was precisely that faith that drove the creation of the Constitutional Court and shored up its institutional legitimacy as it intruded ever further into the legislative process. The change that occurred in Colombia after 1991 is thus best understood, not as a transformation away from democratic legalism, but as an adjustment between two subtypes of that style of regime – from democratic legalism subtype (3) (*deferential rights review*) to democratic legalism subtype (2) (*substantive legalism*).

The JR-regime transformation processes in Egypt and Chile likewise both conform to the posited causal mechanism. In Egypt, as we have seen,[167] President Sadat established the Supreme Constitutional Court in 1979 as part of a deliberate attempt to reverse the exodus of local and foreign capital triggered by his predecessor, President Nasser's socialist reforms. That act may be understood as a deliberate attempt to construct an authoritarian legalist regime as a solution to an economic crisis. The new regime was successfully established insofar as the Supreme Constitutional Court's power to assert final

---

[163] Cepeda and Landau.
[164] Ibid.
[165] Ibid.
[166] Ibid.
[167] See Section 6.1.3.

decision-making power over property rights was politically accepted and institutionalized. The new regime did not last all that long, however, owing to the Supreme Constitutional Court's expansion of its mandate to include political rights enforcement, which forced President's Sadat's successor, President Mubarak, to rein it in.

In Chile in 1973, a long-standing democratic legalist tradition was upended by a military coup. Without much prompting from General Pinochet, the Supreme Court adjusted to the new arrangements by studiously deferring to the military regime's assessment of national security needs. The shift to authoritarian legalism in Chile was thus primarily a function of judicial socialization that inhibited judges from resisting the new authoritarian political order.[168] Even when the Pinochet regime invited the judges to play a more active role in enforcing constitutional rights through the *recurso de protección*, they declined. In Chile, after political actors drove the initial break from democracy, judges became active agents of the transformation to authoritarian legalism.

The Chilean case illustrates the susceptibility of the third subtype of democratic legalism (*deferential rights review*) to transformation at the instance of an authoritarian coup. Legalism, by definition, is constructed around a bifurcation of social life into the legitimate domains of law and politics. Where, in addition, judges routinely defer to political determinations of rights, national security threats may trigger a slide into authoritarian legalism. All that is required is judicial acquiescence in the repression of political rights as being necessary to the defense of the nation. Without a robust tradition of safeguarding rights through the democratic process (subtype (1)) or a tradition of substantive rights review (subtype (2)), democratic legalism subtype (3) has few defenses against a would-be authoritarian power holder that claims to have a privileged role in protecting the nation against real or imagined aggressors.

As indicated in Table 6.5, there are no instances in which a broad-based legal-cultural movement has been able to drive JR-regime transformation without the assistance of judicial and political elites. The causal mechanism for JR-regime transformation emerging from the in-depth case studies accordingly needs to be restated as follows: In societies that have adopted a system of strong-form judicial review, the wholesale transformation of a JR regime (or transformation between two subtypes of the same regime) occurs when: (1) the existing regime is destabilized by an exogenous shock; and (2) political and

---

[168]   Hilbink, *Judges Beyond Politics.*

TABLE 6.5: *Conditions for JR-regime transformation (with additional examples)*

	US	Aus.	India	Zim.	Germ.	Germ. subtype	Colom.	Colom. subtype	Egypt	Chile
Exogenous shock to prevailing JR regime?	Yes	No	Yes	Yes	Yes	Yes	Yes	Yes	Yes	Yes
Political actors driving transformation?	Yes	No	Yes	Yes	No	Yes	No	Yes	Yes	Yes
Broad-based legal-cultural movement?	Yes	No	No	No	No	Yes	No	Yes	No	No
Judges able and willing to drive transformation?	Yes	Yes	Yes	Yes	No	Yes	No	Yes	Yes	Yes
Transformation in fact occurred?	Yes	No	Yes	Yes	No	Yes	No	Yes	Yes	Yes

judicial actors with an interest in the transformation are willing and able to drive it forward.

6.4 WITHIN-REGIME INCREMENTAL CHANGE

In addition to the wholesale transformations just discussed, JR regimes clearly also develop incrementally over time. In the case studies, the main example of this process was the gradual evolution of the Australian JR regime after the failure of the Mason Court revolution. As we saw in Chapter 3, after the per curiam opinion in the *Lange* case halted the dramatic shift that Sir Anthony Mason had called for, conceptions of the law/politics relation continued to evolve in a more understated way. In public speeches, successive chief justices suggested subtle variations to longstanding cultural tropes.[169] At a formal doctrinal level, the High Court endorsed the use of a structured test for proportionality in implied freedom of political communication cases.[170] None of these changes suggest that the Australian JR regime is moving whole-sale towards a more politicized conception of law. High Court judgments and public commentary still invoke a hegemonic idea of law's necessary separation from politics. But the Australian JR regime clearly is evolving towards a more substantive version of democratic legalism in which the High Court's role in enforcing the political values underpinning Australia's system of representative and responsible government is increasingly accepted.

In South Africa, too, the Constitutional Court's disinclination to respond to Karl Klare's call openly to declare the political nature of its function does not mean that conceptions of the law/politics relation have remained static. One incremental development, for example, has been the Court's growing role in policing the quality of democracy *within* political parties. As South Africa's democratic transition has progressed, it has become increasingly apparent that the African National Congress's ongoing electoral dominance has facilitated serious problems of patronage politics and corruption.[171] While South African lawyers' aversion to substantive political theorizing inhibits the Constitutional Court from articulating the structural causes of this problem directly, it has worked in subtler ways to build legitimacy for decisions that hold political

---

[169]   Robert French, "Judicial Activist – Mythical Monsters?" (2008) 12 *Southern Cross University Law Review* 59, 61.

[170]   *McCloy v. New South Wales* (2015) HCA 34.

[171]   Sujit Choudhry, "'He had a Mandate': The South African Constitutional Court and the African National Congress in a Dominant Party Democracy" (2010) 2 *Constitutional Court Review* 1; Samuel Issacharoff, "Constitutional Courts and Democratic Hedging" (2011) 99 *Georgetown Law Journal* 961.

parties to standards of democratic accountability in their internal organizational processes.[172] In the *Treatment Action Campaign* case, for example, the Court was able to use its explicit social rights mandate to get around what was essentially a problem of internal party-political authoritarianism – President Thabo Mbeki's denialist views on HIV/AIDS that were hindering the rollout of antiretroviral medicines.[173] In another case, *Ramakatsa*,[174] the Court required the ANC to abide by its own procedural rules for the selection of delegates to a provincial party conference. In this way, the Court has expanded the Constitution's reach into areas of politics previously thought to be off-limits. To the extent that these decisions have been accepted and enforced, conceptions of law's legitimate sphere of authority have evolved.

Similar incremental changes to dominant conceptions of the law/politics relation have occurred in Germany. There, the accession to power of the Social Democratic Party (SDP) and the rise of the radical student movement in the 1960s triggered a series of challenges to "hierarchical authority."[175] The FCC, after striking down several of Chancellor Willie Brandt's social reforms, became a target of some of these attacks.[176] Its reasoning methods were critiqued in scholarly journals and there were calls for greater judicial candor in opinion writing.[177] The Court responded, first by publishing the names of the individual judicial authors of opinions and then by permitting dissenting opinions in 1971.[178] These institutional reforms reflect a slight weakening in the previously dominant conception of law as an objective science. Dissents remain comparatively rare on the FCC, however,[179] and German constitutionalism is still characterized by a strong faith in law's autonomy.

In Singapore, the 1988 decision in *Chng Suan Tze* v. *Minister for Home Affairs* was associated with a shift in the prevailing ideational structure from latent to explicit dualism.[180] In that case, the Court of Appeal ordered the release of political prisoners detained under the Internal Security Act (ISA) on

---

[172] See Theunis Roux, "Constitutional Courts as Democratic Consolidators: Insights from South Africa after Twenty Years" (2016) 42 *Journal of Southern African Studies* 5; Theunis Roux, "The South African Constitutional Court's Democratic Rights Jurisprudence: A Response to Samuel Issacharoff" (2014) 5 *Constitutional Court Review* 33.

[173] Anthony Butler, "The Negative and Positive Impacts of HIV/AIDS on Democracy in South Africa" (2005) 23 *Journal of Contemporary African Studies* 3, 13.

[174] *Ramakatsa* v. *Magashule* 2013 (2) BCLR 202 (CC).

[175] See Hailbronner, *Traditions and Transformations* 86–90.

[176] Ibid 86.

[177] Ibid 87.

[178] Ibid.

[179] Ibid.

[180] *Chng Suan Tze* v. *Minister for Home Affairs* (1988) 2 S.L.R.(R.) 525 (C.A.) at 86; (1989) 1 MLJ 69 (Sing.).

the grounds that their detention had been procedurally improper. At the same time, the Court asserted (without exercising) its power to decide whether grounds for detention objectively existed. That uncharacteristically bold move forced the People's Action Party to declare its hand more explicitly. After correcting the procedural irregularity and rearresting the detainees,[181] PAP brought a constitutional amendment ousting the courts' power to "invalidate any anti-subversion law." It also amended the ISA to oust the courts' jurisdiction to review the substantive grounds for detention.[182] In this way, the implicit understanding that had always existed in Singapore that there were areas of social life beyond the courts' remit was forced to the surface.

These and other examples confirm the dynamic quality of JR regimes as continually evolving ideational complexes. None of the in-depth case studies or the additional capsule studies, however, suggests that such changes lead over time to wholesale JR-regime transformation. Instead, they point to the capacity of JR regimes, absent an exogenous shock, to adjust to environmental changes. This, as noted earlier, is a significant finding. While the fourteen societies considered in this chapter are not exhaustive of all instances of JR-regime transformation, the fact that there are no instances of transformational change through incremental development points to a significant difference between the sorts of processes considered in this study and the institutional changes considered in other work.[183]

The main reason for this difference, it may be speculated, is that JR regimes are not formal institutions in Thelen's sense – "the products of conscious design and redesign."[184] Rather, they are complexes of legitimating ideas – features of a society's constitutional culture whose norms and values exist in public discourse. The sorts of incremental change that Thelen observes, therefore, are precluded. Without the possibility of a disjuncture opening up between formal rules and their actual social function, phenomena such as "displacement," "layering," "drift," and "conversion"[185] cannot really occur. Rather, the sorts of incremental change that we see occurring within JR regimes are subtle adjustments in conceptions of the law/politics relation.

---

[181]   Silverstein, "Singapore: The Exception that Proves Rules Matter" 80.
[182]   Adding Article 149(3). See Po Jen Jap, *Constitutional Dialogue in Common Law Asia* 73–7; Rajah, *Authoritarian Legalism* 15–20 (on ISA); Tushnet, "Authoritarian Constitutionalism" 419–20.
[183]   Mahoney and Thelen, "A Theory of Gradual Institutional Change" 1, 1–2.
[184]   Kathleen Thelen, "How Institutions Evolve: Insights from Comparative Historical Analysis" in James Mahoney and Dietrich Rueschemeyer (eds.), *Comparative Historical Analysis in the Social Sciences* (Cambridge: Cambridge University Press, 2003) 208, 208 n 1.
[185]   Ibid.

Absent an exogenous shock, these changes do not appear to affect the fundamental nature of the regime, even over time.

6.5 CONCLUSION

This chapter has sought to test some of the main "observable implications"[186] flowing from the typological theory of JR-regime change presented in Chapter 2. Those implications include some very general propositions, such as the contention that actually existing JR regimes evolve on the back of competing legal and political authority claims, and some more specific claims, such as the claim that JR regimes tend to resemble one of four ideal types and that, once stabilized, these regimes are relatively resistant to change absent an exogenous shock.

Section 6.1 began by populating the typology, showing how ten additional cases drawn from distinct parts of the world with different legal systems and political traditions could all plausibly be located under one of the ideal types. At the same time, the exercise of classifying these societies' JR regimes helped to clarify certain well-known differences between them. Myanmar and the OPT's JR regimes, for example, were both classified as conforming to the authoritarian instrumentalist type. Comparing those societies' JR regimes within that type in turn helped to contrast the way in which Fatah's support for judicial review in the OPT is a temporary political survival strategy whereas in Myanmar the provision for judicial review in the 2008 Constitution is the product of a longer-term process of ideational development. In some instances, these differences were significant enough to support the identification of subtypes with their own internal dynamics and reasons for stability.

Sections 6.2–6.4 proceeded to use the populated typology to develop generalizable insights into the processes of JR-regime consolidation, transformation, and incremental change. Section 6.2 showed that the process of consolidation could be broken down into a relatively small number of pathways that accounted for all the instances of regime stabilization in the ten additional case studies. One of these pathways, *adaptive continuity*, was found to fit eight of the fifteen examples of consolidation discussed, suggesting that JR regimes have an inertial quality that often works against the ambitions of formal constitutional amendment. This finding was further supported by the identification of the *reversion to dominant type* causal mechanism, which accounted for another three examples of JR-regime consolidation. Together,

---

[186] Gary King, Robert O. Keohane, and Sidney Verba, *Designing Social Inquiry: Scientific Inference in Qualitative Research* (Princeton, NJ: Princeton University Press, 1994).

these two findings suggest that JR regimes often possess considerable ideational power, in the first case facilitating the perpetuation of long-held conceptions of the law/politics relation even in the face of major constitutional
change, and in the second case functioning like a vortex pulling the society
back to familiar thought-ways despite sustained efforts to transform them.

A similar insight emerged from the discussion of the process of JR-regime
transformation in Section 6.4. JR regimes, that subsection suggested, are
relatively difficult to dismantle once consolidated. Wholesale transformation
would appear to require an exogenous shock – a significant external event
challenging existing views of the law/politics relation. But even that is not
sufficient to drive fundamental regime change. Wholesale transformation,
Section 6.4 found, also needs to be assisted by influential legal or political
actors willing and able to drive it forward. Absent that, traditional conceptions
of the law/politics relation provide a powerful ideational resource for legal and
political actors with an interest in preserving them. Notice, too, that the five
instances of successful JR-regime transformation identified in the chapter (the
US, India, Zimbabwe, Egypt, and Chile) all involved either a change in the
basis for law's claim to authority or a change in the basis for legitimate political
authority, but not both at the same time. In two-dimensional, typological
terms, horizontal or vertical transformation appears possible, but not diagonal
transformation.

Finally, Section 6.5 showed that within-regime incremental change is
a common phenomenon. JR regimes in this sense are constantly evolving.
Significantly, however, there were no instances where such incremental
change led to wholesale transformation over time.

These findings invite both normative reflection on the merits and demerits
of each regime type and consideration of their practical implications – the
subject of the concluding chapter.

7

Findings and Implications

The idea of JR-regime change, the previous chapters have shown, helps to explain the development of conceptions of the law/politics relation in a range of societies. This study's real-world application has been established to that extent. But why does it all matter? What are this study's normative and practical implications?

This chapter offers two main answers to that question. First, it argues that paying attention to the ideational dimension of judicial review reveals a sociologically important aspect of this institution, which in turn facilitates a more realistic assessment of its moral worth. Contrary to the view expressed in the leading treatments of this topic, the moral justifiability of judicial review cannot be assessed in purely abstract, philosophical terms, but only in all its empirical complexity. That is obviously true of democratic societies, where the impact of judicial review on the quality of democracy is constantly changing as both the functioning of democratic institutions and judicial practices change. But it is no less true of authoritarian societies where the provision of judicial review as part of a package of legitimating devices has some emancipatory potential under certain conditions.

The second reason why attention to the ideational dimension of judicial review matters is that this perspective provides practical guidance on how judicial review might be used to achieve desired ends. A range of actors – constitutional drafters, judges, public impact litigators, and pro-democracy groups, but also (would-be) authoritarian rulers – look to judicial review to promote their interests. The character of a society's JR regime structures these engagements. Along with formal constitutional rules, societal conceptions of the law/politics relation constitute preferences and constrain what these actors are able to achieve. Understanding the nature of this structuring influence has practical implications for constitutional design, judicial decision-making, and democratic activism.

Before setting out these two sets of implications in more detail, this chapter first summarizes this study's main findings. While Chapter 6 has done some of this work already, that chapter was principally about the causal mechanisms of JR-regime change. Beyond that, this study has generated several more general insights about the politico-legal dynamics of judicial review. Summarizing these provides a convenient way into its normative and practical implications.

7.1 MAIN FINDINGS

Judicial review, this study has shown, forces the always-present tension between law and politics to a head in a distinctive way. In giving judges the power to strike down legislation and executive conduct, the adoption of a judicially enforced constitution both draws on and influences prevailing conceptions of the law/politics relation – the society's JR regime. This process of ideational development is distinct from the everyday business of constitutional politics, on the one hand, and changes to the formal constitution, on the other.

As to the first issue, this study's opening gambit was to propose, as a provisional, empirically verifiable matter, that the mere fact of constitutional disagreement does not necessarily threaten the stability of a JR regime. That is because, to the extent that the regime defines the legitimate scope of the arguments made, each successfully resolved dispute in theory reenforces it. On this understanding, the everyday business of constitutional politics is one thing, the ideational development of a society's JR regime another.

This distinction has significant implications for comparative research on constitutionalism and judicial review. Whereas almost all the attention in the literature to date has been paid to the surface level of constitutional politics, understanding the impact of judicial review on governance, and on the improvement of democracy in particular, requires us to have regard to the slower-moving process through which judicial review influences constitutional-cultural norms and values. Our interest in judicial review as an institution, after all, stems from its potential, not just to constrain political action, but to constrain it in a way that promotes liberal political values. While that is a question of the interests that judicial review affects, those interests cannot be understood in purely material terms. They must be understood as interests that are enmeshed in a web of ideas about the legitimate scope of legal and political authority. Judicial review influences political action, on this understanding, not just by keeping self-interested political actors to the rules of the game, but also by constituting preferences about what the game is about and how it should be played.

With the nature of the problem redefined in that way, this study has asked a series of new research questions. The key issue explored was how JR regimes change. Granted, in some societies at certain times, there might be such a thing as an identifiable legitimating ideology through which the law/politics relation is understood. But JR regimes clearly are not static. Rather, they are constantly evolving as actors draw on the ideational resources of the existing regime in the cut-and-thrust of constitutional politics. What is the nature of this evolutionary process, this study asked? Is it purely an incremental one, in which each new constitutional dispute progressively changes extant under-standings of the law/politics relation, or might there be periods of more profound change, as the example of the *Lochner* era discussed in Chapter 2 suggests? If so, what drives these periods of more profound change? Is the process largely an endogenous one, of internal contestation and challenge, or is it driven by exogenous factors? If the latter, what is the role of human agents?

This study's main finding on these questions was that JR regimes do develop incrementally, but that incremental development in practice never leads to wholesale regime transformation. For that to occur, there must be an exogen-ous shock that destabilizes the regime by undermining its economic or political premises. In addition, JR-regime transformation requires the inter-vention of legal and political actors with an interest in driving the change to a new conception of the law/politics relation. Just as crises in economic institu-tions are not self-identifying,[1] so too must the problems with extant concep-tions of the law/politics relation be identified, and alternative conceptions proposed, if change is to occur. Transformation in this sense is a function of exogenous and endogenous factors. While an exogenous shock is a necessary condition for regime transformation, it is not sufficient. Transformation also requires the work of human agents able and willing to exploit the exogenously triggered opportunity.

This study also found empirical support for the proposition that conceptions of the law/politics relation in different societies tend to approximate one or the other of four ideal types. In total, fourteen societies were discussed covering all the major areas of the world, legal traditions, and political systems. In each case, it proved possible to use the secondary literature on the society con-cerned to classify its JR regime under one of the ideal types and to trace its historical development. While different in their specifics, recurrent patterns in the consolidation of the studied JR regimes were found and expressed in the form of four causal mechanisms: new regime formation, adaptive continuity, counter-reaction, and reversion to dominant type.

---

[1] See Mark Blyth, *Great Transformations* (New York: Cambridge University Press, 2002).

These findings have implications both for the comparative literature on constitutionalism and judicial review, and for the broader political science literature on institutional change. As to the first, the importance of these findings is that they show how theorizations of the judicialization of politics need to be premised on a proper understanding of the contrasting environments in which constitutional courts operate. To date, comparative research on the judicialization of politics has been about understanding how it has come about that so much policy-making power has been accorded to constitutional courts across the globe. Why have rational political actors, scholars have asked, adopted and maintained systems of judicial review when those systems give judges the power to write their personal policy preferences into law? And how have constitutional courts been able to assert and build their policy-making power given that they do not control the purse or the sword?

That understanding of the circumstances of constitutional politics, this study shows, is just one culturally determined understanding among many. In effect, it amounts to the scientization of the American conception of judicial review. As soon as that conception is seen to be just one of many possibilities, the need for different theorizations of the judicialization of politics depending on the constitutional-cultural setting becomes clear. For constitutional courts in democratic legalist regimes, for example, it makes little sense to model judges as rational policy maximizers. Both judges' legal-professional socialization and understandings of law's legitimate claim to authority in such regimes make that an implausible motivation. Likewise, in authoritarian instrumentalist regimes, talk of strategically maximizing policy preferences makes no sense when law has little autonomous authority of any kind.

The need for different assumptions and theoretical models depending on the JR regime in which a constitutional court is operating is perhaps why a general theorization of the judicialization of politics has thus far proved so elusive.[2] If all the world was America, then theoretical models derived from the American conception of judicial review would have a good chance of explaining the judicialization of politics in other societies. But all the world is not America. Indeed, the American JR regime, this study shows, is quite exceptional. Almost every starting assumption about the political dynamics of judicial review accordingly needs to be rethought, from whether judges are accurately described as policy maximizers to whether the context for judicial

---

[2] See Martin Shapiro, "The Mighty Problem Continues" in Diana Kapiszewski, Gordon Silverstein, and Robert A. Kagan (eds.), *Consequential Courts: Judicial Roles in Global Perspective* (New York: Cambridge University Press, 2013) 380, 382.

review is best modelled as a constraining institutional and political environment as opposed to a constitutive one. Indeed, if the insights of this study are taken seriously, we need to stop talking about the political dynamics of judicial review and start talking instead about the politico-*legal* dynamics of this institution.

This study's distinction between everyday constitutional politics and the ideational dimension of judicial review also has implications for the more general political science literature on institutional change. As noted in Chapter 1, one of the main issues in dispute in that literature is whether institutions change through largely exogenous or endogenous processes. Standard historical institutionalist accounts use a "punctuated equilibrium" model in which institutions consolidate through path-dependent processes and then only change at the instance of an exogenous shock. For Kathleen Thelen and others, this approach ignores instances of incremental, yet over time transformational, change.[3] There is also a troubling structuralism about such theorizations in as much as they struggle to explain the role of human agents in the transformational change in question.[4] The causal sequence is some version of *equilibrium – exogenous shock – destabilization – institutional reconstruction*, but exactly how the last stage of this process works is unclear.

In the case of JR regimes, this study shows, the punctuated equilibrium model works well to explain periods of ideational stability followed by more dramatic, exogenously driven change. That is perhaps because JR regimes are in their nature legitimating ideologies that over time develop a deep-structural logic that is relatively robust against the everyday business of constitutional politics. This is not to say that JR regimes do not incrementally develop, but absent an exogenous shock, this study has found, the deep-structural logic of a JR regime remains intact. Even the two instances of subtype transformation considered in Chapter 6 – Germany and Colombia – required an exogenous shock as an initial trigger.

To that extent, this study does not support Thelen's findings on incremental institutional change. The likely explanation for that, Chapter 6 speculated, was that Thelen's thesis is restricted to what she calls "formal institutions," i.e.,

---

[3] Wolfgang Streeck and Kathleen Thelen, "Introduction: Institutional Change in Advanced Political Economies" in Wolfgang Streeck and Kathleen Thelen (eds.), *Beyond Continuity: Institutional Change in Advanced Political Economies* (New York: Oxford University Press, 2005) 1.

[4] Mark Blyth, Oddný Helgadóttir, and William Kring, "Ideas and Historical Institutionalism" in Orfeo Fioretos, Tulia G. Falleti, and Adam Sheingate (eds.), *The Oxford Handbook of Historical Institutionalism* (New York: Oxford University Press, 2016) 142.

institutions with explicit rules.[5] JR regimes, by contrast, are ideational constructs – complexes of legitimating ideas that have no explicit form, but exist as
an aspect of constitutional culture. That makes them different, too, from just
any set of ideas or even "policy paradigms" in Peter Hall's sense.[6] Their
legitimation logic, once consolidated, gives them a tight structure that this
study has found may be broken only through an exogenous shock. Equally,
however, as complexes of legitimating ideas, JR regimes, once destabilized, do
not just reformulate themselves, but require the intervention of actors with an
interest in exploiting their instability. In this sense, JR-regime transformation is
a function of an exogenous trigger and endogenous agency.

That finding lends support to Blyth, Helgadottir, and Kring's call to bridge
the divide between "pure" historical institutionalist scholars, for whom institutions are formal institutions and interests are material interests, and idea-
tionally oriented historical institutionalists, for whom ideas always matter to
institutional change, may in fact in certain circumstances themselves be
thought of as institutions, and for whom interests are never wholly material
but always caught up in a web of meaning.[7] What this study shows is that
ideational institutions might be just as durable, if not more so, than formal
institutions. The assumption that ideas tend to develop incrementally while
formal institutions evince a pattern of long periods of stability and then
exogenously driven change, does not hold. Both of these processes may
accurately describe change in either formal or ideational institutions under
different circumstances. In the case of ideational institutions, the explanatory
power of the punctuated equilibrium model likely correlates to the extent to
which actors with theoretically opposed interests are in fact invested in the
same legitimation structure.

One further implication of this study for the more general political science
literature on institutional change has to do with the differences between JR
regimes in democratic and authoritarian societies. In specifying the sources of
interpretive information about JR regimes, Chapter 2 noted that official state
ideology was likely to be a more useful guide to the character of a JR regime in
authoritarian societies than judicial decisions or public attitudes. JR regimes
in democratic societies, by contrast, tend to be more bottom-up and pluralis-
tic. The case studies and comparative chapter confirmed that intuition. On
one view, that means that this study's dependent variable wrongly conflates

---

[5] For most lawyers, familiar as they are with the incremental development of the common law,
    that idea makes perfect sense.
[6] Peter A. Hall, "Policy Paradigms, Social Learning, and the State: The Case of Economic
    Policymaking in Britain" (1993) 25 *Comparative Politics* 275.
[7] Blyth, Helgadottir, and Kring, "Ideas and Historical Institutionalism."

two quite distinct phenomena. A JR regime in a democratic society is not the same thing as a JR regime in an authoritarian society: the first is a contested, ever-evolving tradition and the second a matter of propaganda. On another view, the fact that we need to draw on distinct sources of information to characterize JR regimes in democratic as opposed to authoritarian societies is a research finding of sorts, and moreover one that tracks recent claims in the political science literature on ideational power. Martin Carstensen and Vivien Schmidt, for example, distinguish between the power "through" ideas and the power "over" ideas.[8] The first of these forms of power has to do with the "capacity of actors to persuade others to accept and adopt their views of what to do and think through the use of ideational elements,"[9] whereas the second has to do with the "capacity of actors to control and dominate the meaning of ideas."[10] That distinction maps onto the distinction found here between the more persuasive character of JR regimes in democratic societies and the more coercive character of such regimes in authoritarian societies. The fact that we need to draw on distinct sources of information to capture that difference, therefore, may just reflect the distinctive ways in which legitimating ideologies in those two settings are constructed.

The second major claim of this study is that the process of ideational development that judicial review triggers is not only distinct from everyday constitutional politics. It is also distinct from changes to a society's formal constitution.[11] This is in many ways a more startling finding. Notwithstanding all the effort put into the design of a new constitution, perhaps with the deliberate aim of transforming conceptions of the law/politics relation, a society's JR regime may not change. The main empirical evidence for this finding was presented in the Zimbabwe case study. At two moments of formal constitutional change in that country – the 1979 independence Constitution and the 2013 pro-democracy Constitution – a contemplated change to the dominant conception of law's appropriate relationship to politics did not occur. Rather, actors with an interest in perpetuating Zimbabwe's historically dominant JR regime – authoritarian legalism – were able to resist the con-templated change. The same lack of correspondence between changes to a

---

[8] Martin B. Carstensen and Viven A. Schmidt, "Power Through, Over and In Ideas: Conceptualizing Ideational Power in Discursive Institutionalism" (2016) 23 *Journal of European Public Policy* 318.

[9] Ibid 323.

[10] Ibid 326.

[11] Cf. Zachary Elkins, Tom Ginsburg, and James Melton, *The Endurance of National Constitutions* (New York: Cambridge University Press, 2009) 59–63 (distinguishing constitutional change from political regime change).

society's JR regime and its formal constitutional arrangements was witnessed in reverse during the *Lochner* era in the US. There, a major ideational transformation occurred without a formal constitutional change.

Sometimes, of course, the absence of any ideational change following a formal constitutional change may simply be a consequence of the fact that no such change was envisaged: the Constitution attempts to codify an existing conception of the law/politics relation and does so successfully. Australia provides the best example of this possibility, although Chapter 3 argued that the consolidation of its democratic legalist regime was not institutionally determined. Rather, it was the product of contingent events that triggered a self-reinforcing trajectory.[12]

In other situations, however, a new constitution and the political debate surrounding its enactment clearly do contemplate significant ideational change, and yet this change does not occur. Zimbabwe, Singapore, Hungary, and the OPT may all be cited as examples here. This raises the question of why that is so. What frustrates the best-laid plans of constitutional drafters in this respect? The answer, this study suggests, is that the existing JR regime provides resources to political actors opposed to ideational change that may be more powerful than a society's formal constitutional arrangements. That is particularly so where the exogenous shock that produces the formal constitutional change – the transition to majority rule in Zimbabwe, for example – is not accompanied by a desire on the part of political elites to drive the ideational change the constitution appears to usher in. Thus, in Zimbabwe after 1980, ZANU-PF had an interest in adapting the preindependence JR regime to its purposes rather than following through on the transformation to democratic legalism that the Constitution seemingly contemplated.

In practice, the tendency of formal constitutional change to produce ideational change depends on whether the conditions for JR-regime transformation are satisfied.[13] Where formal constitutional change *is* followed by ideational change, that is not because the constitution is self-executing in this respect. Rather, it is because the same social forces behind the formal constitutional change destabilize the existing JR regime to a sufficient degree to enable the contemplated ideational change to occur. For that change to take place, however, sympathetic legal and political actors must still drive it.

---

[12]   Another example of this possibility is the 2008 Myanmar Constitution, which codifies the idea of a "discipline-flourishing democracy" that has historical roots in the Burmese-socialist conception of the law/politics relation. See Chapter 6, Section 6.1.4.

[13]   See Chapter 6, Section 6.3.

Thus, in South Africa after 1994, the political process of overthrowing apartheid destabilized the existing authoritarian legalist regime. The transition to democratic legalism, however, would not have occurred without the concerted effort of a range of actors. In Zimbabwe, there was no such concerted effort, and consequently, no regime transformation.

To say that formal constitutional change does not necessarily produce ideational change, or that ideational change may occur without formal constitutional change, does not mean, of course, that the text of a constitution does not matter. This study's finding is not that it is culture all the way down and that attention to constitutional design is therefore a pointless exercise. All that follows is that constitutional designers need to pay attention to the possible lag-effect on their transformational ambitions of prevailing conceptions of the law/politics relation. Equally, when researching these phenomena, scholars need to maintain some sense of the ideational structures in which formal provisions are embedded. That point might appear obvious, but the current emphasis in the comparative judicial politics literature on large-N quantitative research runs the risk of a kind of neoformalism as scholars look to constitutional texts as readily measurable data.

In addition to these general findings, this study also generated some specific findings about each of the main JR-regime types and the process of transformation between them. Three of these findings are worth restating and elaborating: (1) democratic instrumentalism appears to be a relatively rare JR regime in practice, whereas an instrumentalist conception of law in authoritarian states is more common, though not often associated with judicial review; (2) subtype transformation may be as significant as wholesale transformation, and conforms to the same causal mechanism; and (3) vertical and horizontal JR-regime transformation in two-dimensional-matrix terms appear to be more ubiquitous than diagonal transformation.

7.1.1 *Findings Specific to Democratic and Authoritarian Instrumentalism*

This study did not conduct a comprehensive survey of all societies that have adopted systems of judicial review. The fact that there were only two democratic instrumentalist regimes in the fourteen societies discussed, however, suggests that this JR-regime type may be quite rare in practice. This finding was anticipated in the theoretical discussion. As noted there, democratic instrumentalism is a late-stage regime – the product of a long-term process of ideational development that depends on the prior existence of "autonomous law" in Nonet and Selznick's sense.[14] Crucially, too, for democratic instrumentalism to develop, growing cynicism about law's autonomy from politics must not precipitate a collapse back into the use of law for repressive purposes. Rather, law's politicality needs to be openly embraced, or at least grudgingly accepted, *under conditions of free democratic competition.*

That is likely to be quite a rare development in practice. It occurs, this study suggests, where one or the other of two rather unusual conditions is satisfied. Either there must be crossparty consensus about the legitimacy of using judicial review to pursue an ideologically motivated account of constitutional justice or there must be sustained public support for judges to play this kind of role. In the first case, the stability of democratic instrumentalism depends on each party in a competitive electoral system being assured that its turn to use judicial review to promote its preferred ideology will eventually come. In the second case, the stability of this regime comes from a self-reinforcing cycle of dependency in which a powerful constitutional court contributes to the perpetuation of the democratic pathologies that drive its public support. Both of those states of affairs are somewhat exceptional.

By contrast, the propagation of an ideology of law's instrumental subordination to overarching societal goals is a routine legitimation strategy of authoritarian power holders. The idea of "socialist legality" propounded in Eastern Europe under communism is an obvious example.[15] In contemporary China, the Communist Party seems to be defaulting back to this conception, after flirting with a turn to legalism under Deng Xiaoping.[16] What is less common in authoritarian states, however, is the combination of an instrumentalized conception of law with judicial review.[17] At least, this study has uncovered relatively few instances of that: in Zimbabwe, for a brief period from 1999 to 2008, the OPT after the Fatah/Hamas split in 2007, and Myanmar after 2008. A decision to establish judicial review, it seems, mostly implies some

---

[14]   Phillippe Nonet and Philip Selznick, *Toward Responsive Law: Law & Society in Transition* (New Brunswick, NJ: Transaction Publishers, 2001 [1978]).

[15]   See Gordon B. Smith, *Soviet Politics: Continuity and Contradiction* (London: Palgrave, 1988) 137–62.

[16]   Eva Pils, "China's Authoritarian Subversion of Legality and Ruling by Fear" unpublished paper presented at a Network for Interdisciplinary Study of Law seminar, UNSW Sydney (July 2017). Contemporary conceptions of the law/politics relation in Vietnam provide another example. See John Gillespie, "Changing Concepts of Socialist Law in Vietnam" in John Gillespie and Pip Nicholson (eds.), *Asian Socialism and Legal Change: The Dynamics of Vietnamese and Chinese Reform* (Canberra: ANU Press, 2005).

[17]   The power given to judges in Eastern European constitutions did not, with one exception (Yugoslavia), qualify as judicial review. See Inga Markovits, "Law or Order – Constitutionalism and Legality in Eastern Europe" (1982) 34 *Stanford Law Review* 513, 516.

commitment to law's separability from politics, even if that is just the distorted version of this ideal characteristic of authoritarian legalism.

The two exceptions to this rule were treated in Chapter 6 as distinct subtypes of authoritarian instrumentalism, one of which follows the rapid subordination of a partially independent judiciary (Zimbabwe and the OPT) and the other more sustained ideational work (Myanmar). The former subtype is the least stable of all the JR regimes considered in this study. It arises as part of a political containment strategy aimed at thwarting a threatened expansion of liberal political rights. In both Zimbabwe after 1999 and the OPT after 2006, pro-democracy groups began pushing the courts to enforce the ground rules for free democratic competition. In an effort to contain this development, authoritarian power holders staffed the courts with political loyalists. At the same time, they compensated for the lost legitimation benefits of a partially independent judiciary by ramping up ideological narratives explaining their entitlement to govern in the absence of an authentic democratic mandate. Neither of the resulting authoritarian instrumentalist regimes was very stable. In Zimbabwe, for example, ZANU-PF was forced to renegotiate its hold on power in 2008. While there were a range of reasons for that, one of them was that property rights, which had previously been reliably enforced, were no longer secure. A sphere of social life in which law had been allowed to rule was closed down and economic activities that had been premised on that understanding declined, eventually forcing a return to qualified rule of law.

The same politico-legal dynamic need not affect the second subtype. Where authoritarian instrumentalism is the product of sustained ideational work rather than a forced political containment strategy, economic actors may over time learn to work with a politically subordinated judiciary. In circumstances like that, authoritarian instrumentalist regimes may be more durable. Since judicial independence is not assumed, there can be no collapse in confidence of the sort that took place in Zimbabwe after 2000. Whenever the power holder in such a regime, however, attempts to open markets to foreign investment, as happened in Myanmar after 2008,[18] the demand for independent judicial review of property rights may spill over into a demand to expand law's sphere of authority to include liberal political rights. In that event, the authoritarian power holder must either stabilize the transition to authoritarian legalism, concede the demand for liberal political

---

[18] On Myanmar's economic reforms, see Marie Lall, *Understanding Reform in Myanmar: People and Society in the Wake of Military Rule* (London: C. Hurst & Co, 2016).

rights, or engineer the reconsolidation of a purely instrumentalist conception of law.[19]

7.1.2 Subtype Transformation under Democratic Legalism

If the sample in Chapter 6 is representative, democratic legalism may be the most common JR-regime type. All the Western European JR regimes, for example, could be fitted under this type and some of the Latin American as well.[20] That makes sense, since judicial review is typically associated with democracy rather than authoritarianism,[21] while legalism is the more usual ideological frame for law's claim to authority in a democracy.

The sheer volume and variety of democratic legalist regimes makes generalizing about their common dynamics somewhat hazardous. Chapter 6 tried to deal with this problem by distinguishing three subtypes: rights exclusion (subtype 1), substantive legalism (subtype 2), and deferential rights review (subtype 3). Each of these subtypes was defined by its specific variation on the characteristics common to this ideal type. Thus, subtype 1 maintains its commitment to law's separability from politics by excluding rights from the scope of judicial review. Subtype 2 is identified with a conception of a bill of rights as a logically coherent framework – a solution to the rights indeterminacy problem that sounds somewhat idealistic to Anglo-American ears. And subtype 3 counsels judges to be deferential when enforcing constitutional rights lest they intrude too far into areas of reasonable disagreement best left to democratic politics.

This classificatory scheme works up to a point, but it raises the question of whether the differences between these subtypes are more important than their similarities. And, if that is so, does proceeding on the converse assumption not skew the analysis? One issue that arose in Chapter 6, for example, was the phenomenon of transformation between these subtypes. In Colombia in 1991, the adoption of a new Constitution was associated with a change from democratic legalism subtype 3 to subtype 2.[22] If we assume that there was deferential

---

[19] This is one interpretation of what is going on in Myanmar at present, for example. After inviting foreign investment in 2010, the military is trying to stabilize a limited form of democracy with partial rule of law.

[20] For example, Costa Rica, Colombia, and Chile. On Colombia and Chile, see Chapter 6. On Costa Rica, see Bruce M. Wilson, "Enforcing Rights and Exercising an Accountability Function: Costa's Rica's Constitutional Chamber of the Supreme Court" in Gretchen Helmke and Julio Ríos-Figueroa (eds.), *Courts in Latin America* (New York: Cambridge University Press, 2011) 55.

[21] Cf. Ginsburg, *Judicial Review in New Democracies* 261–2.

[22] See the discussion in Chapter 6.

rights review under the Weimar Constitution,[23] a similar change could be said to have taken place in Germany after 1949. In Chile, at present, that country's long tradition of deferential rights review also appears finally to be transitioning to a more substantive version of legalism.[24] In Chapter 6, these developments were treated as adaptations of democratic legalism rather than examples of JR-regime transformation because the essential features of democratic legalism remained intact. There was no wholesale transformation in that sense between democratic legalism and another ideal type. But that could be said to be a purely definitional matter. If other features of these societies' JR regimes had been stressed – not their conception of law's autonomy, for example, but their conception of the role of courts in enforcing human rights – things would have been different. And if that is so, then does the dependence of the analysis on an arbitrary definitional choice not undermine the finding about the causal mechanism of JR-regime transformation?

The short answer to that question is "no." Largely because the causal mechanism of JR-regime transformation is expressed at a fairly high level of abstraction – exogenous shock followed by deliberate ideational work – it can accommodate the above examples. Thus, developments in Colombia after 1991, Germany after 1949, and Chile at present could all be seen either as adaptations of democratic legalism or transformations between subtypes of that regime. If viewed in the latter way, they still conform to the posited causal mechanism of JR-regime transformation since in all instances the exogenous shock condition was satisfied and there was deliberate ideational work. All that changes is that this ideational work needs to be viewed as driving a transformation to a new regime rather than adapting an existing one.

That explanation might be thought to be a little too convenient. If adaptations are transformations when looked at from a different angle then the causal mechanisms identified in this study are not hard-and-fast scientific rules but more-or-less persuasive, after-the-event explanations. But that is indeed what they are, and no greater claim for them is made than that.[25] This study has not developed any covering laws with predictive power; reading this book will not tell you what is likely to happen to the Hungarian JR regime in five years' time. The point has not been to build a science of JR-regime change in that sense,

---

[23] See the discussion of this point in Chapter 6.

[24] See Javier Couso and Lisa Hilbink. "From Quietism to Incipient Activism: The Institutional and Ideological Roots of Rights Adjudication in Chile" in Gretchen Helmke and Julio Ríos-Figueroa (eds.), *Courts in Latin America* (New York: Cambridge University Press, 2011) 99.

[25] The understanding of causal mechanisms presented here is derived from Jon Elster, *Alchemies of the Mind: Rationality and the Emotions* (Cambridge: Cambridge University Press, 1999) 1–47.

but to lay bare recurrent patterns in the development of conceptions of the law/politics relation in societies that provide for judicial review. This limitation does not mean that this study has no value. The insights it generates, Sections 7.2 and 7.3 will show, have real normative and practical implications. It just means that this study is not a manual on how to use judicial review to achieve desired ideational change. But the evolution of JR regimes is in any case too complex and contingent a phenomenon for that.

7.1.3 *Vertical and Horizontal versus Diagonal Transformation*

The conclusion to Chapter 6 noted that all the instances of JR-regime transformation identified in that chapter were either vertical or horizontal but not diagonal transformations in two-dimensional-matrix terms. At the instance of an exogenous shock, it would seem, either the legitimate scope of law's claim to authority may change, or the scope of a political authority claim, but not both at the same time. If shown to be generally true, that would be a significant finding. There is nothing in theory that precludes diagonal transformation, and thus its empirical absence tells us something important about the nature of JR-regime transformation.

One possibility is that the shock itself is always registered as a challenge to the scope of either a legal or a political authority claim, and thus the susceptibility to transformation is always along one dimension. In Zimbabwe after 1998, for example, the rise of the MDC destabilized authoritarian legalism by calling into question the legitimate scope of the courts' power to review political rights, and thus ZANU-PF's containment strategy targeted the independence that the judiciary had enjoyed up to that point. In India after 1977, too, it was legalism that was discredited by the Emergency and conceptions of law's autonomy that transformed. Things are not always that tidy, however. In the US after 1890, urbanization and industrialization processes challenged extant understandings of the authoritative scope of democratic political mandates. But the transformation that occurred was again a transformation in societal conceptions of law's autonomy. Thus, it appears that an exogenous shock that impacts the scope of one type of authority claim may be exploited to drive a change to the other.

Logically, four diagonal transformations are possible: from democratic legalism to authoritarian instrumentalism (DL>AI) or the reverse (AI>DL), and from authoritarian legalism to democratic instrumentalism (AL>DI) or the reverse (DI>AL). Of these four, AL>DI is precluded by the late-stage nature of democratic instrumentalism, as explained earlier. DL>AI is also unlikely because authoritarian backsliding from democratic legalism typically

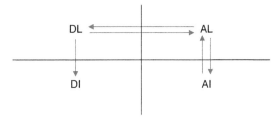

FIGURE 7.1: Most likely trajectories of JR-regime transformation

takes the form of a contraction of liberal political rights, rather than immediate and wholesale subordination of the judiciary. AI>DL is conceivable, especially since AI>DI is less so, but the absence of empirical examples suggests that the emergence of an ideology of law's autonomy from politics may be a necessary stepping stone to democratic legalism, which corresponds to the path followed by most countries in Western Europe. Finally, DI>AL is again conceivable – a populist political party could exploit a perception that judicial review has been politicized to amend the Constitution and restrict liberal political rights – but unlikely.

Based on this discussion, Figure 7.1 illustrates the most likely trajectories of JR-regime transformation.

Figure 7.1 expresses three tentative findings: that the path from authoritarian instrumentalism to democratic legalism likely passes through authoritarian legalism, that transformation from democratic legalism to democratic instrumentalism is a one-way ticket, and that shuttling back and forth between democratic and authoritarian legalism, on the one hand, and authoritarian legalism and authoritarian instrumentalism, on the other, may be the most common forms of JR-regime transformation.

7.2 NORMATIVE IMPLICATIONS

The two leading scholarly critiques of the moral justifiability of judicial review – by Jeremy Waldron and Richard Bellamy[26] – are premised on assumptions about the existence of traditions and institutions that do not hold in most parts of the world. Waldron explicitly recognizes this, and excludes dysfunctional democracies with weak judiciaries and minimal

---

[26] Jeremey Waldron, "The Core of the Case against Judicial Review" (2006) 115 *Yale Law Journal* 1346; Richard Bellamy, *Political Constitutionalism: A Republican Defence of the Constitutionality of Democracy* (Cambridge: Cambridge University Press, 2007).

commitment to rights from his analysis.[27] He hopes by this move, he says, to "identify a core argument against judicial review that is independent of both its historical manifestations and questions about its particular effects."[28] Whereas Larry Kramer's and Mark Tushnet's work on judicial review, Waldron notes, both make some telling points, they "entangle a theoretical critique of the practice with discussions of its historical origins and their vision of what a less judicialized U.S. Constitution would involve."[29] By contrast, Waldron says, he wants to "take off some of the flesh and boil down the normative argument to its bare bones so that we can look directly at judicial review and see what it is premised on."[30]

Waldron's methodological move succeeds in isolating an empirically stripped-down account of judicial review for normative assessment, but at the same time it introduces several problems into his argument that in the end undermine its persuasiveness and practical usefulness.[31] The first problem is that the assumptions Waldron says must hold if his argument is to apply depend on interpretive judgments about empirical states of affairs that are likely to be quite controversial. One of his assumptions, for example, is that "democratic institutions [are] in reasonably good working order."[32] That sounds straightforward, but Waldron then goes on to ponder whether New Zealand, because it has a unicameral legislature, might not qualify on this ground.[33] That query suggests that Waldron's threshold for democratic health might be quite high, excluding most societies in the world from the scope of his argument. Worse than this, Waldron's worry about New Zealand shows that the applicability of his argument to any particular society depends on the historically aware and sociologically informed assessments he wants to avoid.

The second problem with Waldron's argument is that the quality of democracy in a society may vacillate over time. This means that the moral justifiability of judicial review in that society vacillates, too, as its

---

[27] Waldron, "The Core of the Case" 1361–9. Bellamy's stated intention is to address judicial review's moral justifiability only in the context of settled democracies. His index contains references to the following countries: Australia, Canada, France, Germany, Italy, New Zealand, Norway, the UK, and the US.

[28] Waldron, "The Core of the Case" 1351.

[29] Ibid.

[30] Ibid.

[31] For a longer version of this response to Waldron, see Theunis Roux, "In Defence of Empirical Entanglement: The Methodological Flaw in Waldron's Case against Judicial Review" in Ron Levy and Graeme Orr (eds.), *The Cambridge Handbook of Deliberative Constitutionalism* (Cambridge: Cambridge University Press, 2018) 203.

[32] Waldron, "Core of the Case" 1360.

[33] Ibid 1361 n 47.

democratic institutions rise above and fall below Waldron's "reasonably good working order" standard. Further, once a society has adopted judicial review, it becomes impossible in practice to know whether any problems in the functioning of its democratic institutions are caused by judicial review or mitigated by it.[34] If democratic institutions are functioning badly, the case against judicial review supposedly does not apply. But what if they are functioning badly *because of judicial review*, which is a real possibility on Waldron's account? Should we then not get rid of judicial review? But how would we know for sure, given that we are dealing with a counterfactual? Conversely, if democratic institutions are in reasonably good order, Waldron's argument implies that judicial review should be disestablished. But what if those institutions are functioning well because of judicial review? Then, disestablishing judicial review might cause democratic institutions to fall below Waldron's standard, meaning that judicial review would need to be reestablished, and then disestablished again, ad infinitum.

Given these problems with Waldron's argument, there seems to be no alternative but to assess the moral justifiability of judicial review as a living, breathing institution – based on its actual sociological effects.

This study looks at only one of these effects: the impact of judicial review on conceptions of the law/politics relation. Clearly, a more diverse range of effects would need to be considered for a comprehensive assessment. The fact that the adoption of judicial review in a particular society might lead to the consolidation of a JR regime says nothing about the quality of democracy in that society or the existence of other morally desirable states of affairs. It is perfectly possible for a JR regime in a democratic society to consolidate and yet for the quality of democracy to be poor in certain respects. Equally, the contribution that judicial review makes to the stability of authoritarian rule may be benign or malign depending on the circumstances. In its capacity under certain conditions to legitimate authoritarian rule, judicial review could be said to morally unjustifiable. But it is not impossible that the provision of judicial review for purposes of authoritarian legitimation could create space for the assertion of political rights that eventually leads to democracy. And even if it does not have that effect, judicial review might safeguard the enjoyment of freedoms that would otherwise not exist. Its role in that respect might offset – if the moral calculus to determine such things could ever be designed – its contribution to authoritarian legitimation. Judicial review, in short, contributes to the stabilization of morally desirable but also undesirable states of affairs, and no conclusion about its justifiability follows from that.

---

[34] See Roux, "In Defence of Empirical Entanglement."

Nevertheless, there is something in the perspective adopted in this study that suggests that the argument that judicial review necessarily has a negative impact on the right to democratic self-government in well-functioning democracies may be overstated. The adoption of judicial review, as we have seen, sets in train a process of ideational development in which the legitimate scope of law's authority is determined by its interaction with claims to political authority. If that is so, then any attempt on the part of judges in a democracy to assert their powers of judicial review further than is morally justified by deficiencies in the democratic system is likely to trigger some sort of counterreaction. In the US, for example, the intrusion of the Supreme Court into controversial questions of public morality in the 1960s and 1970s triggered a counterreaction in the form of greater partisan-political control of judicial appointments. It took some time, but eventually a new accommodation between law and politics was reached in which judicial intrusion into policy questions that many commentators think ought to have been left to democratic politics was matched by an equal and opposite politicization of the judicial appointments process.

One does not have to go so far as to say that wherever judicial review is introduced, there is always a self-correcting tendency towards equilibrium – amounting to a scientific law – to see that morally unjustifiable judicial intrusions into democratic politics may have a sociological limit. It is enough that there are examples of cases where such overreach has been corrected to see that this is a feature of the institution that is at least worth bringing into the assessment of its moral justifiability. If judicial review is morally unjustified where democratic institutions are in reasonably good working order, and if judicial overreach may be corrected by tighter political control of the judiciary, then judicial review may function as a kind of safety valve on a constitutional system. Logically, judges might either get the moral calculus right, and calibrate the intrusiveness of judicial review to the degree of dysfunctionality of democratic institutions, or they might not. In the former case, judicial review would, on Waldron's account, remain justifiable. In the latter case, political actors – supported by the moral rightness of their cause – could curtail the scope of judicial review or otherwise ensure that it was made democratically accountable. Either way, it is better to provide for judicial review and have it available to protect the democratic system than not to have judicial review at all.

The point cannot end there, however, because, as this study has shown, it is possible for a JR regime to consolidate in a form where the right to democratic self-government is compromised in some way. That is obviously true of a JR regime that approximates one of the two authoritarian types.[35] But it may also be true of JR regimes that approximate one of the two democratic types. As noted already, the fact that claims to legal and political authority in such regimes might come to legitimate each other in a stable ideational complex says nothing about judicial review's impact on the quality of democracy in real terms. Indeed, a more sociological version of the Waldron/Bellamy critique might be to argue that the perniciousness of judicial review lies precisely in its capacity to legitimate, and therefore to stabilize, a constitutional system that may be suboptimal from the point of view of a commitment to democracy.

This study has found some evidence of this risk. As we saw in Chapter 4, several commentators are of the view that the Indian Supreme Court's power and prestige have come at the price of undermining the quality of India's democracy in certain respects.[36] Similar things have been said about the Colombian Constitutional Court, whose international reputation for bold and creative decision-making is matched by the apparent dysfunctionality of the democratic system in which it is operating.[37] On the basis of those examples, we may be tempted to join Waldron and Bellamy in thinking that, under certain conditions, judicial review either directly undermines democracy, or at least inhibits the people's representatives from addressing problems in the functioning of democratic institutions.

The problem with these sorts of examples, however, is that they are necessarily counterfactuals. As much as we might agree that judicial review in India or Colombia sustains certain pathologies in the functioning of the democratic system, the real question is what the quality of democracy in those two societies would be absent judicial review. Would either India or Colombia be in a better position? Would either still be a democracy? Those questions are imponderable. We simply do not know. All that we know is that India's democracy has survived against all odds,[38] and that it has survived in the presence of judicial review. The same is true of Colombia.

---

[35] The moral question there, as we have seen, is whether judicial review contributes to the perpetuation of what everyone agrees to be a morally unjustifiable state of affairs and whether, even if it does, things would be worse in the absence of judicial review.

[36] Balakrishnan Rajagopal, "Pro-Human Rights but Anti-Poor? A Critical Evaluation of the Indian Supreme Court from a Social Movement Perspective" (2007) 18 *Human Rights Review* 157; Lavanya Rajamani, "Public Interest Environmental Litigation in India: Exploring Issues of Access, Participation Equity, Effectiveness, and Sustainability" (2007) 19 *Journal of Environmental Law* 293.

[37] David Evan Landau, Beyond Judicial Independence: The Construction of Judicial Power in Colombia (*doctoral dissertation*, Harvard University, 2015) 31, 257, 284, 353.

[38] See Ashutosh Varshney, *Battles Half Won: India's Improbable Democracy* (New Delhi: Penguin, 2013).

Thus, we are again left having to assess the moral justifiability of judicial review on the basis of its actual sociological effects. That is a question, first, of our normative vantage point – what conception of democracy we adopt – and much will turn on our views on a range of questions, including: (1) what degree of individual rights protection our conception of democracy incorporates; (2) whether we think legislatures or judges are better at realizing these rights alone or in co-operation with each other;[39] (3) how much actual citizen participation is required in democratic decision-making and whether judicial review promotes or hinders such participation; (4) how much contemporary democratic control over the constitution is required as opposed to working within previously determined limits; and (5) whether we think constitutional practice – policy making and adjudication – allows the constitution to be changed over time even without formal constitutional amendment. After settling those normative priors, we would need to build a comparative understanding of the conditions under which judicial review promotes democracy in the sense defined. Only after all of that would we be able to build a general, sociologically informed case for or against judicial review. In relation to the moral justifiability of judicial review in any particular society, things would be easier, since we would then simply need to assess one particular set of sociological effects against our normative standard. But there would still be considerable problems in working out an agreed normative standard and in the interpretation of empirical data against that standard.

This study does not propose a normative standard or suggest a methodology for assessing the moral justifiability of judicial review, either in general or in relation to a specific society. All that it contends is that there are two stable ideational states into which a constitutional system that provides for judicial review in a democratic society may fall. While the impact of judicial review on the right to democratic self-government in those two stable states will vary from case to case, it is possible to say something in general terms about the moral merits and demerits of each, given what this study has revealed about their dynamics.

As to democratic instrumentalism, the principal appeal of this JR regime is its acceptance of the role of judicial ideology in constitutional adjudication. This stance, for many, has the virtue of greater candor about the process of legal reasoning in constitutional cases. In many instances, in rights adjudication in particular, formal legal norms will not dictate an answer, and judges will need to reason towards a conclusion by appealing to values. In democratic

---

[39] This is the nub of Richard Fallon's response to Waldron. See Richard H. Fallon Jr, "The Core of an Uneasy Case for Judicial Review" (2008) 121 *Harvard Law Review* 1693.

instrumentalist regimes, two or more ideologically motivated understandings of the constitution supply these values. In that situation, judges have no choice but to justify their decisions by presenting the best moral arguments for them from the particular ideological perspective they adopt. Over time, of course, that ideological perspective will write itself into a line of precedents and settled understandings of key constitutional terms.[40] Thus, even in democratic instrumentalist regimes, judges will be able to offer their arguments as legally authorized interpretations of the constitution rather than moral arguments pure and simple. But the law does not bind in the same way because other ideologies written into law are also available. In relative terms, therefore, judges in democratic instrumentalist regimes find it less necessary to pretend that their moral arguments are somehow just the law speaking through them.

This feature of democratic instrumentalist regimes provides a partial response to an argument both Waldron and Bellamy make about the way in which judges with the power of judicial review are inhibited by the technical demands of legal reasoning from giving the best account of rights. Legislatures are better moral reasoners, they say, because – unlike judges – they do not have to "focus[] on precedent, text, doctrine, and other legalisms."[41] This point both misses a vital distinction between legal reasoning in democratic instrumentalist as opposed to democratic legalist regimes, and downplays the potential constraining role of technical legal considerations in rights adjudication cases, which is one of the key reasons why judicial review might be morally justifiable.

In democratic instrumentalist regimes, as we have seen, judges have greater freedom to offer their decisions as the all-things-considered, morally preferred answer to a constitutional question, particularly when it comes to questions of rights. They are not moral reasoners pure and simple, to be sure, because their decisions are still couched in claims about the correct method of constitutional interpretation and what past precedents say. But the fact that there is less of a pretense in democratic instrumentalist regimes that the constitution itself provides the correct answer to rights questions, judges have more license to justify their decisions as morally attractive in themselves. Legal reasoning in US Supreme Court cases is noticeably less legalistic in that sense than it is on the German Federal Constitutional Court. At the very least, the charge that legalism gets in the way of moral reasoning cannot be made globally, but

---

[40]   See Duncan Kennedy, *A Critique of Adjudication (Fin de Siècle)* (Cambridge, MA: Harvard University Press, 1997).
[41]   Waldron, "Core of the Case" 1386. See also Bellamy, *Political Constitutionalism* 37.

needs to be adjusted to the varying degrees of legalism across different constitutional cultures.

Waldron and Bellamy's complaint about how legalism gets in the way of moral reasoning also downplays the constraining role of adherence to past precedent in rights cases. In a sense, they try to have it both ways by arguing, on the one hand, that law is sufficiently constraining of judicial discretion to make judges bad moral reasoners and, on the other, that law is insufficiently constraining to overcome the fact of reasonable disagreement about rights. The first of those arguments is better aimed at democratic legalist regimes, whereas the second is more apposite to democratic instrumentalist regimes. But both arguments cannot be correct. Either legalistic considerations *do* get in the way of moral reasoning, in which case judges are not the free-wheeling, anti-democratic actors that Waldron and Bellamy suppose, or legalistic considerations *do not* get in the way of moral reasoning, in which case judges may be better moral reasoners than they suppose.

In permitting judges to be more honest about the intrusion of political values into legal reasoning, democratic instrumentalist regimes in theory promote better public discussion of the values at stake, and this should have a positive effect on the richness of democratic discussion more generally. Functioning optimally, constitutional courts in democratic instrumentalist regimes are forums of public reason in which comprehensive conceptions of the good may be debated and their implications for public policy rationalized. Functioning badly, however, democratic instrumentalist regimes also pose certain risks. The first is exemplified by the American example, where two rival ideological understandings of the Constitution have become intractably entrenched as partisan gospel rather than revisable intuitions about the requirements of justice. Everything consequently hinges, not on the quality of moral reasoning within the US Supreme Court, but on which of the two main political parties has appointed a majority of its members. The second risk is exemplified by the Indian example, where a popular court has emerged in the context of a dysfunctional democracy and indirectly contributes to the democratic pathologies it claims to be addressing.

The downsides of democratic legalism are equally clear. The first is its suspension of disbelief in law's autonomy from politics. This stance may promote public confidence in judges as impartial arbiters, but it also entails a certain artificiality and lack of candor in the reasoning process. Recognition of this problem was the premise for the failed Mason Court revolution in Australia. It is also the problem that Karl Klare suggested would be a barrier to the realization of the 1996 South African Constitution's transformative promise. The lesson of this study is that it is hard to address this problem without some external challenge to legalism (like that which occurred in the US after 1890 and in India after 1977) to which advocates of greater transparency in legal reasoning may point.

The second downside of democratic legalism is its relative inability to support judicial attempts to adapt the Constitution to problems in the functioning of the democratic system that were not foreseen or explicitly catered to by the Constitution's framers. The South African case is illustrative here. The main threat to that country's constitutional project after the transition to democracy in 1994 has been the ANC's electoral dominance. The Constitutional Court's (otherwise sensible) embrace of democratic legalism has inhibited it from developing the substantive constitutional doctrines to counteract this threat that some commentators would like to have seen.[42] Nevertheless, the Court has been able to work incrementally within the parameters of legitimate legal reasoning in South Africa to address some of the problems attendant on the ANC's electoral dominance.[43]

Finally, democratic legalist regimes appear to be relatively more vulnerable to a contraction of liberal political rights in response to alleged national security threats. In effect, a commitment to law's separation from politics for sound democratic reasons may, under pressure of a perceived emergency, slide into the view that there are spheres of social life beyond the control of law. Lisa Hilbink's study of how judges capitulated to authoritarianism in Pinochet's Chile is the classic example of this in the comparative literature.[44] Her conclusion, though, is perhaps a little too strong. Rather than suggesting that "apoliticism appears to be the wrong ideal around which to construct a judiciary in service of liberal democracy,"[45] the Chilean experience suggests that democratic legalist regimes may simply be more susceptible to a transition to authoritarian legalism than JR regimes in which law's immersion in politics is more openly acknowledged. Without more examples, however, we cannot be sure.

---

[42] See Sujit Choudhry, "'He had a Mandate': The South African Constitutional Court and the African National Congress in a Dominant Party Democracy" (2009) 2 *Constitutional Court Review* 1; Samuel Issacharoff, "The Democratic Risk to Democratic Transitions" (2014) 5 *Constitutional Court Review* 1.

[43] See Theunis Roux, "The South African Constitutional Court's Democratic Rights Jurisprudence: A Response to Samuel Issacharoff" (2014) 5 *Constitutional Court Review* 33; Rosalind Dixon and Theunis Roux, "Marking Constitutional Transitions: The Law and Politics of Constitutional Implementation in South Africa" in Tom Ginsburg and Aziz Huq (eds.), *From Parchment to Practice: Implementing New Constitutions* (forthcoming).

[44] Lisa Hilbink, *Judges beyond Politics in Democracy and Dictatorship: Lessons from Chile* (New York: Cambridge University Press, 2007).

[45] Ibid 8.

7.3 PRACTICAL IMPLICATIONS

The practical implications of this study may be divided into three separate topics: constitutional-design implications, implications for judicial practice, and implications for social movements seeking to use judicial review to deepen democracy.

7.3.1 *Constitutional Design*

This study has shown that the mere adoption of a liberal-democratic constitution will not by itself produce the constitutional-cultural change that is one of the preconditions for its effective operation. Legal and political actors who share a given constitution's values and the vision of constitutional justice it propounds need to drive the process of ideational change through which institutional form becomes lived political reality. Constitutional design is in that sense a body of knowledge that needs to take account, not just of the interests that the new constitution regulates, but also of the dynamically evolving legal and political traditions on which the constitution draws and at the same time seeks to influence.

On that assumption, is there anything in this study that may be cashed out as practical advice to constitutional designers? What, in particular, does this study imply about two fundamental issues: (1) how to design a liberal-democratic constitution that makes it less likely that judges will overreach and undermine the quality of democracy, and (2) how to ensure that actors opposed to liberal-democratic ideals do not amend the constitution or so undermine its operation as to derail the constitutional project.

As argued in Section 7.2 above, this study's findings suggest that it is almost always better for constitutional designers to provide for judicial review than not. By operating as a safety valve, judicial review may help to maintain a healthy balance between curial power and democratic politics. Providing for judicial review may not really be a matter of choice, of course. The dynamics of the constitution-making process, as Tom Ginsburg's insurance theory posits,[46] may drive the adoption of judicial review whatever its merits. Equally, vested interests threatened by a transition to democracy may push to have judicial review included in a constitution to preserve their policy-making influence.[47] However, to the extent that a new democracy

---

[46]   Ginsburg, *Judicial Review in New Democracies*.
[47]   Hirschl, *Towards Juristocracy*.

contemplating how best to entrench liberal-democratic constitutionalism does have a choice, this study suggests that judicial review is a wise option.

But how long should a choice in favor of judicial review endure and how should its consequences be monitored? In an ideal Waldronian world, we would: (1) institute a system of judicial review if democratic institutions were not in "reasonably good working order,"[48] (2) monitor the changing quality of democracy, and (3) dispense with judicial review once democratic institutions reached the required performance threshold. In practice, however, it would be hard to determine whether this point had been reached. As noted in Section 7.2, the question is a counterfactual one in two respects: Would democratic institutions be in reasonably good working order if judicial review were not in place? And what would happen to the functioning of democratic institutions if judicial review were removed? There is also the problem that, on the logic of Waldron's argument, judicial review produces a kind of dependency effect in terms of which the destructive impact of this institution on the functioning of democratic institutions provides a moral justification for its continuation.

Given these problems, a preferable option would be to design a constitution that encouraged judges to adapt the intrusiveness of their review powers on democracy to the changing performance of democratic institutions. In a legal tradition in which it was acceptable for judges to engage in substantive political analysis of the threats facing democracy, it might not be necessary to specify the varying strength of judicial review according to democratic performance in so many words. Judges working in such a legal tradition would not be tied to the literal terms of their mandate, but would be free to justify intrusions into the democratic process by reference to the pathologies they were addressing.[49] In a more formalist legal tradition, however, the court's power to vary the intensity of judicial review might need to be expressly stated. Thus, for example, social rights could in such circumstances be formulated to indicate that the court could adjust the level of review according to its assessment of the performance of democratic institutions in realizing these rights.[50]

---

[48] Waldron, "Core of the Case" 1360.

[49] In the US, for example, the Supreme Court's three levels of scrutiny for equal protection clause violations could be said to conform to this intuition. Similarly, the idea of "representation reinforcing" review draws on the idea that the intrusiveness of judicial review should be adapted to the problems in the democratic system. John Hart Ely, *Democracy and Distrust: A Theory of Judicial Review* (Cambridge, MA: Harvard University Press, 1980).

[50] In using the term "reasonable," for example, section 26 of the 1996 South African Constitution gave the Constitutional Court an explicit, flexible discretion to adjust the level of review of the right to housing according to the performance of democratic institutions in realizing this right. Something like this idea is also contemplated in Mark Tushnet, *Weak Courts, Strong Rights:*

As a way of reinforcing this approach, the constitutional amendment procedure might be designed to allow Parliament to reduce the court's review powers in the event that the judiciary failed to respond to better-performing democratic institutions. Care would obviously need to be taken not to make the amendment procedure too easy to deploy, lest the threat of amendment be used to discourage judges from standing up to abuses of the democratic process, or to punish them when they did so. A supermajority requirement necessitating crossparty political support for any such amendment might work here.[51] Something like the Indian basic structure doctrine might also need to be constitutionally codified to ensure that any such amendment, even with the requisite supermajority, did not fundamentally disable judicial review.[52] If the constitutional amendment procedure were designed in this way, it might never need to be used because rational judges would preempt a threatened constitutional amendment by adapting the exercise of their review powers to the strength of the democratic coalition aligned against them.

Those two design features would help to support judicial review's function in maintaining an appropriate balance between curial power and democracy. What of the second question – the implications of this study for preventing a slide into illiberalism?

This issue has enjoyed a great deal of attention in recent literature.[53] In its most insidious form, the problem is one of democratically driven retrenchment of liberal constitutionalism rather than authoritarian takeover pure and simple. There is little that a constitution can do against a determined despot prepared to use force to secure power. But modern constitutional coups, the literature suggests, are not like that. Increasingly, they are staged by political parties with some degree of popular support and they respect constitutional form enough to amend provisions that stand in their way. The recent illiberal turns in Hungary and Poland have both taken that form,[54] and we may add, on

---

Judicial Review and Social Welfare Rights in Comparative Constitutional Law (Princeton, NJ: Princeton University Press, 2008).

[51] Section 74 of the 1996 South African Constitution, for example, ratchets up the size of the special majorities required for a constitutional amendment according to the seriousness of the perceived threat to founding democratic values.

[52] On the basic structure doctrine, see Chapter 4.

[53] David Landau, "Abusive Constitutionalism" (2013) 47 *University California Davis Law Review* 189; Aziz Huq and Tom Ginsburg, "How to Lose a Constitutional Democracy" (2018) 65 *UCLA Law Review* (forthcoming); Tom Gerald Daly, "Diagnosing Democratic Decay" paper presented at Gilbert & Tobin Centre of Public Law Comparative Constitutional Law Roundtable, UNSW, Sydney (August 2017); Richard Albert, "Constitutional Amendment and Dismemberment" (2018) 43 *Yale Journal of International Law* (forthcoming).

[54] On Hungary, see the discussion in Chapter 6. On Poland, see Daly, "Diagnosing Democratic Decay" 14–17.

the evidence of this study, also the return to one-party rule in Zimbabwe in 2013 and the 2007 amendment of the Supreme Constitutional Court Law in the OPT. In both those cases, political parties with authoritarian tendencies used an ostensible commitment to liberal constitutional form to entrench themselves in power. Is there anything that can be done to protect against that particular threat?

The obvious safeguard is the constitutional amendment procedure, but that is a specialized question to which this study has little to add.[55] The questions we can answer here are more general: How do we know the difference between a court bravely defending against illiberal backsliding and a court abusing its power of judicial review in ways that threaten democracy? And, even if we can't answer that question, how do we design a constitution that ensures that a court is defended in the first situation and curtailed in the second?

It was suggested above that a constitutional court that abused its powers might eventually trigger a counterreaction that brought the system back into balance. But that has not yet happened in the two instances of alleged judicial overreach discussed in this study – India and Indonesia.[56] In both those cases, constitutional courts struck back against attempted judicial accountability measures, and in neither case have the political branches thus far been able to do anything about it. Is this an acceptable outcome? Do we value curial power for its own sake? Or is the situation in India and Indonesia to be regretted?

The obvious answer to this question is that we need a normatively inflected conception of curial power – in effect, liberal-democracy-enhancing power. That is the sociological implication of Waldron and Bellamy's argument. Where a democratic system is dysfunctional, our normative preference is for a constitutional court that is able forcefully to intervene in national politics to help the democratic system function better. Provided that this was the purpose and effect of the court's intervention, we would tolerate a fair degree of intrusion into policy-making. Conversely, where a democratic system begins to function properly, our preference is for a court that is able to change tack – to promote democracy by respecting legitimately produced democratic outcomes. Initially forceful constitutional courts that made this kind of transition would experience a decline in power of sorts in as much as their direct policy-

---

[55] See Rosalind Dixon and David Landau, "Transnational Constitutionalism and A Limited Doctrine of Unconstitutional Constitutional Amendment" (2015) 13 *International Journal of Constitutional Law* 606.

[56] See the discussion in Chapters 4 and 6 respectively.

making role would diminish, but this would not provide cause for concern provided that: (1) their power to make policy was lost to the people's duly elected representatives acting in a way that respected the integrity of the democratic system; and (2) they retained some latent capacity to intervene should the democratic system again come under threat.

So much is relatively straightforward. The difficulty is that the nature of the power a court wields may morph over time, and thus the assessment of its performance must be sensitive both to the kind of power that the court is exercising and to its changing extent. The Indian Supreme Court, as we have seen, is today regarded as one of the most powerful constitutional courts in the world.[57] But the role it plays in India's democracy is not as uncontroversial as it used to be. Thirty years ago, there would have been little debate that the power it wielded was normatively desirable, giving voice as it did to democratically marginalized groups. Today, however, the assessment is more complex. While the Court is arguably more powerful than ever, it is no longer clear that its power is being deployed to desirable ends. According to one influential commentator, at least, the Court's intrusive intervention in policy-making is preventing the democratic system from correcting itself.[58] Similar concerns may be raised about the Colombian Constitutional Court, whose ongoing policy influence appears to be premised on the perpetuation, whether by the Court or simply in spite of what it is doing, of various democratic pathologies. Both the Indian Supreme Court and the Colombian Constitutional Court would thus score well on one kind of curial power rating (policy influence), but lower if that rating were targeted at assessing their contribution to improving the quality of democracy.

Understood in this way, the indicators for assessing the democracy-promoting performance of constitutional courts over time are: (1) the number and significance of decisions promoting the proper functioning of the democratic system; (2) the extent to which such decisions are obeyed and indeed have a positive impact on the democratic system; and (3) the changing quality of democracy in the country concerned and any evidence of a capacity on the part of the judges to adjust their policy-making role in line with improvements to the functioning of the democratic system.

How a court's performance registered in terms of these indicators would obviously be open to interpretation: one person's democracy-promoting

[57] Manoj Mate, "Public Interest Litigation and the Transformation of the Supreme Court of India" in Diana Kapiszewski, Gordon Silverstein, and Robert A. Kagan (eds.), *Consequential Courts: Judicial Roles in Comparative Perspective* (2013) 262.
[58] See Pratap Bhanu Mehta, "The Rise of Judicial Sovereignty" (2007) 18 *Journal of Democracy* 70.

decision might be another's usurpation of legitimately exercised democratic power. Differences like this would affect the assessment of a court's performance. There would be disputes and those disputes would themselves be the stuff of constitutional politics. In the end, they could not be bypassed or avoided. But the constitutional system could be set up to ensure as far as possible that the legislature, the executive, and the courts adjusted their behavior according to the above indicators. The system's tendency towards a normatively desirable law/politics equilibrium in that sense could be aided by wise constitutional design.

The key point would be to ensure that the court was responsive to democratic wishes without making it vulnerable to rights-disrespecting majoritarianism. The constitutional system would need to be able to differentiate in that sense between genuine concerns about the court's aloofness from public opinion and illiberal exploitation of populist sentiment. One stated reason for the move against the Polish Constitutional Court, for example, is that it had become distanced from the people – a forum for elites.[59] That feeling might have been manipulated by populist political leaders, but its negative impact on liberal democracy could have been mitigated by a number of fairly simple constitutional-design measures: ensuring that judicial selection procedures provided for meaningful public involvement; requiring judges to write decisions in plain language to be read by lay people as much as by lawyers; constitutionally guaranteeing and then legislating rigorous procedures for the ethical vetting of judges; and ensuring that judicial appointment rules provided for the selection of a demographically representative bench.

7.3.2 *Judicial Practice*

Even if all the provisions discussed in the previous section were included in a constitution, judges supportive of liberal-democratic constitutionalism would still need to act wisely. What does this study have to say about judicial practice in support of democracy and against illiberal backsliding?

Any developed politico-legal tradition, this study has shown, maintains an understanding of the appropriate relationship between law and politics – of the judiciary's legitimate sphere of authority as defined by past decisions, its remedial powers, and legitimate forms of legal reasoning. With the adoption of judicial review, traditional understandings of the boundary between law

---

[59] See Adam Czarnota, "Rule of Lawyers or Rule of Law: On the Constitutional Crisis and the Rule of Law in Poland" paper delivered at Australian National University conference on *Troubling the Rule of Law*, Kioloa (September 2017).

and politics become in many ways more important to respect, even as the introduction of judicial review provides a justification for reimagining them. Precisely because it threatens to politicize their role, courts with the power of judicial review need to work hard to maintain an impression of themselves as legal actors. The requirement that they remain within the culturally defined bounds of permissible legal reasoning exerts a moderately constraining influence on their capacity to respond to a changing political context. If new constitutional doctrines are required to combat emerging democratic pathologies, judges in formalist legal traditions, for example, may have to work towards those doctrines more systematically than judges in substantive traditions, where doctrines may be derived through substantive analysis of the threat posed to democracy by the political actors the court is trying to rein in.

The law/politics boundary as defined by past decisions, remedial powers, and legitimate forms of legal reasoning is not static or uncontested, this study has shown. Precedents and the scope of the court's remedial powers will be open to interpretation and development, particularly in a new constitutional democracy where judicial review has been introduced for the first time. Different forms of legal reasoning – more formalist and more substantive styles, for example[60] – will also be present in a single legal tradition, and it may be internally contested within that tradition which best serves the rule of law or best justifies the court's powers. Nevertheless, beneath these differences, there may be a dominant conception of the appropriate role of the court in developing new doctrines and asserting new powers that exerts a moderately constraining influence on what a court may do.

On this understanding, the main advantage of making provision for judicial review is that judges, in theory, have the capacity to adjust their role in the democratic system according to how well it is functioning. Where democratic self-government is threatened by the concentration of political power in a single political party, say, or by the emergence of anti-democratic groupings, courts may adapt their doctrines to address these pathologies. Where the democratic system is functioning well, courts may similarly show greater deference to democratically produced outcomes.

While the responsiveness of courts in this way to changes in the functioning of democratic institutions could be supported by certain constitutional-design features, as suggested above, there is an inbuilt pressure on judges in systems of judicial review to behave in this way. Courts that fail to adapt the exercise of

[60]   On the distinction between formal and substantive reasoning, see Patrick S. Atiyah and Robert S. Summers, *Form and Substance in Anglo-American Law: A Comparative Study of Legal Reasoning, Legal Theory, and Legal Institutions* (Oxford: Clarendon Press, 1987).

their review powers to the changing performance of the democratic system may lose legitimacy and become vulnerable to political clawback.[61] Courts' vulnerability to this kind of clawback acts as a self-regulating mechanism, helping to keep the constitutional system in balance. Waldron's nightmare scenario of disenfranchisement through judicial review ignores this dynamic aspect of constitutional systems and consequently overstates the threat to democracy that judicial review poses. The real problem is not the perpetuation of overzealous judicial review, but the fact that it is often difficult to know whether a particular clawback measure is a genuine response to judicial overreach by a democratically minded government or the beginning of an authoritarian assault on judicial independence. In Hungary, as seen in Chapter 6, the governing political party, Fidesz, has significantly curtailed the Constitutional Court's jurisdiction in what appears to be an attempt to redesign the democratic system to favor its continuation in power.[62] The repeated attempts in Indonesia to improve judicial accountability mechanisms are, by contrast, not so easy to attribute to authoritarian motives. That country's Constitutional Court's resistance to these measures, and its failure to adapt its practices to improvements in the functioning of democratic institutions,[63] looks more like an instance of what Stephen Holmes has called "halfway reform . . . when the judiciary manages to free itself from authoritarianism without adapting to democracy."[64]

7.3.3 *Social Activism*

It might be thought that this study is pessimistic about the possibility that judicial review under a liberal-democratic constitution could ever drive fundamental social and economic change. If constitutionalism is really about shifting conceptions of the legitimate reach of judicial power into politics,

---

[61] That, for example, is what was unsuccessfully attempted in India with the passage of the Constitution Ninety-Ninth Amendment Act (see the discussion in Chapter 4). A similar story may be told in Indonesia, where the Constitutional Court faced two major sets of amendments to its jurisdiction and powers in 2011 and 2013. See Theunis Roux and Fritz Siregar, "Trajectories of Curial Power: The Rise, Fall, and Partial Rehabilitation of the Indonesian Constitutional Court" (2016) 16 *Australian Journal of Asian Law* 1.

[62] Miklós Bánkuti, Gábor Halmai, and Kim Lane Scheppele, "Hungary's Illiberal Turn: Disabling the Constitution" (2012) 23 *Journal of Democracy* 138; Kim Lane Scheppele, "The New Hungarian Constitutional Court" (1999) 8 *East European Constitutional Review* 81.

[63] See Roux and Siregar, "Trajectories of Curial Power."

[64] Stephen Holmes, "Judicial Independence as Ambiguous Reality and Insidious Illusion" in Ronald Dworkin (ed.), From Liberal Values to Democratic Transition: Essays in Honour of János Kis *(Budapest: Central European University Press,* 2004) 3, 9.

then societies that adopt a liberal-democratic constitution are condemned at best to incremental change. What should be an occasion for great celebration is, on this understanding, but a pyrrhic victory. The real war is a war of ideas and that is a long-term campaign.

But that would be the wrong conclusion to draw. This study does not deny the transformational role of politics – the possibility of organizing against extant power structures and changing them. Nor does it deny that judicial review might play a role in such politics – in forcing power holders to pay greater attention to policy failures and bringing claims for the recognition of new ways of being human (identity politics) to the attention of both policy makers and the broader public. All that it claims is that the moment of constitution-making should not be seen as the endpoint of such political struggles, but as the formalization of a tradition of thinking about the organization of public power whose meaning and appropriateness will continue to be the subject of political debate.

For social movements in well-functioning democracies, the implication of this claim is that the long view matters. Groups organizing to drive a formal policy change, whether that be to the structure of social security benefits or the recognition of same-sex marriage, need to think not just about how to obtain the court order that will produce the policy change they are seeking, but about how that court order will be taken up in public discourse. The court order needs to be thought of as a constitutional-cultural moment, in that sense – as a public assertion of law's authority that has repercussions for the way the law/politics relation is understood. In just the same way that social movements need to be strategic about the political backlash their successful legal action may unleash,[65] so, too, do such groups need to be sensitive to the way the roles they are asking the court to fulfil impact societal understandings of the legitimate reach of judicial power.

That advice is not a plea for incrementalism, since fundamental policy change may still be effected through judicial review understood in this way. Rather, it is a plea for social movements to be sensitive to the politico-legal conjuncture – to the ideational setting in which they are operating and to the way public impact litigation feeds into the slower-moving contest of ideas over the law/politics relation. Is their case essentially one that the existing legitimation structure may accommodate – in which case it is about manipulating that structure to their advantage? Or is it one that cannot be accommodated within the existing legitimation structure, because the social and economic

[65] Reva B. Siegel, "Constitutional Culture, Social Movement Conflict, and Constitutional Change: The Case of the de facto ERA" (2006) 94 *California Law Review* 1323.

developments they are seeking to influence pose a challenge to that structure that requires it to be rethought?

What about authoritarian states? What does this study say about what pro-democracy groups should do in that setting? Is it again fatalistic and deterministic in the sense that fundamental change depends on external developments beyond these groups' control?

On the one hand, yes, because the clear finding of this study is that the transformation of an authoritarian JR regime does depend on an exogenous shock. In so far as that is true, pro-democracy groups should keep their powder dry and wait for an opportunity to exploit. But, again, this does not mean that political mobilization is futile. The shock that conditions JR-regime change is exogenous only in the sense of its being external to the extant legitimation structure. All other aspects of the governing power structure in an authoritarian state are still open to challenge by pro-democracy groups.

Having said that, this study does suggest that, when pro-democracy groups find themselves in a situation of authoritarian instrumentalism, there are some limits on how they should order their political goals. As noted in Section 7.1.3, this study suggests that the path to democratic legalism passes through authoritarian legalism: a commitment to law's autonomy needs to be built before there can be any progression to liberal democracy. Or to put the point in more conventional terms, liberal democracy depends on the enjoyment of political rights, and the enjoyment of political rights in turn depends on the existence of independent courts capable of enforcing them. Pro-democracy activists who find themselves in an authoritarian instrumentalist setting – current-day Myanmar, for example – would thus be advised to work first towards building a culture of respect for the rule of law before seeking to use judicial review to expand liberal political rights. This they might do by building courts' capacity impartially to decide issues not immediately threatening to power holders' interests, or indeed to decide issues that the power holder itself has handed over to the courts in its search for legitimation. An authoritarian power holder's quest for legitimation through judicial review may be strategically exploited in that sense to create a democratic opening. But such openings are always fraught and threatened by contraction. When the moment comes to expand the courts' remit to liberal political rights, democratic gains may be reversed, as happened in Egypt.[66] There is also the danger of low-equilibrium stabilization, where recourse to a partially independent judiciary plays a role in arresting the transition to full liberal democracy. Thus, it is always a

---

[66] Tamir Moustafa, *The Struggle for Constitutional Power: Law, Politics, and Economic Development in Egypt* (New York: Cambridge University Press, 2007).

strategic question for pro-democracy groups whether to play the legitimation game – to use the opening provided by judicial review to approach the courts to assert their power to control certain aspects of social life, on the understanding that this runs the risk of helping to consolidate an authoritarian legalist regime.

7.4 CONCLUSION

This has been a long book and it would be futile to conclude it by attempting a pithy summary of the argument. The modest aim has been to introduce a new perspective into the literature on comparative constitutionalism and judicial review, and to challenge some of the constitutional-cultural assumptions underlying the field by making those assumptions the very subject of analysis. The less modest aim has been to develop and test a typological theory of JR-regime change. The assessment of whether these aims have been achieved is now in other hands.

Bibliography

Abeyratne, Rehan, "Upholding Judicial Supremacy in India: The NJAC Judgment in Comparative Perspective" (2017) 49 *George Washington International Law Review* 569

Abualrob, Mohammad Hussein, "The Role of Constitutional Courts in Democratic Consolidation and State Formation in Palestine" (draft doctoral dissertation, UNSW Sydney, 2017)

Ackerman, Bruce, "Constitutional Law/Politics" (1989) 99 *Yale Law Journal* 453

Ackerman, Bruce, *We the People: Foundations* (Cambridge, MA: Harvard University Press, 1991)

Ackerman, Bruce, *We the People: Transformations* (Cambridge, MA: Harvard University Press, 1998)

Ackerman, Bruce, *We the People: The Civil Rights Revolution* (Cambridge, MA: Harvard University Press, 2014)

Adin, Aylin, "Judicial Independence across Democratic Regimes: Understanding the Varying Impact of Political Competition" (2013) 47 *Law & Society Review* 105

Agamben, Giorgio, *State of Exception* trans. Kevin Attell (Chicago: University of Chicago Press, 2005)

Albert, Richard, "Constitutional Amendment and Dismemberment" (2018) 43 *Yale Journal of International Law* (forthcoming)

Alexy, Robert, *A Theory of Constitutional Rights* trans. Julian Rivers (Oxford: Oxford University Press, 2002)

Altman, Scott, "Beyond Candor" (1990) 89 *Michigan Law Review* 296

Amaral-Garcia, Sofia, Nuno Garoupa, and Veronica Grembi, "Judicial Independence and Party Politics in the Kelsenian Constitutional Courts: The Case of Portugal" (2009) 6 *Journal of Empirical Legal Studies* 381

American Bar Association, *The State of Justice in Zimbabwe* (December 2004)

Aroney, Nicholas, "Julius Stone and the End of Sociological Jurisprudence" (2008) 31 *UNSW Law Journal* 107

Aroney, Nicholas and Haig Patapan, "The Gibbs Court" in Rosalind Dixon and George Williams (eds.), *The High Court, the Constitution and Australian Politics* (Melbourne: Cambridge University Press, 2015) 220

Arthur, W. Brian, *Increasing Returns and Path Dependence in the Economy* (Ann Arbor: University of Michigan Press, 1994)

Aspinall, Edward and Marcus Mietzner, "Indonesian Politics in 2014: Democracy's Close Call" (2014) 50 *Bulletin of Indonesian Economic Studies* 347

Atiyah, Patrick S. and Robert S. Summers, *Form and Substance in Anglo-American Law: A Comparative Study of Legal Reasoning, Legal Theory, and Legal Institutions* (Oxford: Clarendon Press, 1987)

Austin, Granville, *Working a Democratic Constitution: A History of the Indian Experience* (New Delhi: Oxford University Press, 1999)

Ayres, Philip, *Owen Dixon* (Melbourne: The Miegunyah Press, 2003)

Balbus, Isaac D., "Commodity Form and Legal Form: An Essay on the 'Relative Autonomy' of Law" (1977) 11 *Law & Society Review* 571

Bánkuti, Miklós, Gábor Halmai, and Kim Lane Scheppele, "Hungary's Illiberal Turn: Disabling the Constitution" (2012) 23 *Journal of Democracy* 138

Bar Human Rights Committee of England and Wales, *A Place in the Sun: A Report on the State of the Rule of Law in Zimbabwe after the Global Political Agreement of September 2008* (June 2010)

Barclay, Philip, *Zimbabwe: Years of Hope and Despair* (London: Bloomsbury, 2010)

Barrie, G. N., "Rhodesian UDI – an Unruly Horse" (1968) 1 *Comparative and International Law Journal of Southern Africa* 110

Baxi, Upendra, *The Indian Supreme Court and Politics* (Lucknow: Eastern Book Co., 1980)

Baxi, Upendra, "Taking Suffering Seriously: Social Action Litigation in the Supreme Court of India" (1985) 4 *Third World Legal Studies* 107.

Bayne, Peter, "Herbert Vere Evatt" in Tony Blackshield, Michael Coper, and George Williams (eds.), *The Oxford Companion to the High Court of Australia* (Melbourne: Oxford University Press, 2001) 251

Beatty, David M., *The Ultimate Rule of Law* (Oxford: Oxford University Press, 2004)

Belknap, Michael R., "Book Review" (1993) 98 *American Historical Review* 970

Bellamy, Richard, *Political Constitutionalism: A Republican Defence of the Constitutionality of Democracy* (Cambridge: Cambridge University Press, 2007)

Bennett, Andrew, "Process Tracing and Causal Inference" in Henry E. Brady and David Collier (eds.), *Rethinking Social Inquiry: Diverse Tools, Shared Standards* (Plymouth: Rowman & Littlefield, 2010) 207

Bennett, Andrew, "Causal Mechanisms and Typological Theories in the Study of Conflict" in Jeffrey T. Checkel (ed.), *Transnational Dynamics of Civil War* (New York: Cambridge University Press, 2013) 205

Berman, Sheri, *The Social Democratic Moment: Ideas and Politics in the Making of Interwar Europe* (Cambridge, MA: Harvard University Press, 1998)

Bhagwati, P. N., "Judicial Activism and Public Interest Litigation" (1984) 23 *Columbia Journal of Transnational Law* 561

Bhushan, Prashant, "Supreme Court and PIL: Changing Perspectives under Liberalisation" (2004) 39 *Economic & Political Weekly* 1770

Blackshield, Anthony R., "The Legacy of Julius Stone" (1997) 20 *University of New South Wales Law Journal* 215

Blackshield, Tony, "Legalism" in Tony Blackshield, Michael Coper, and George Williams (eds.), *Oxford Companion to High Court of Australia* (Melbourne: Oxford University Press, 2001) 429

Blyth, Mark, *Great Transformations* (New York: Cambridge University Press, 2002)

Blyth, Mark, Oddný Helgadóttir, and William Kring, "Ideas and Historical Institutionalism" in Orfeo Fioretos, Tulia G. Falleti, and Adam Sheingate (eds.), *The Oxford Handbook of Historical Institutionalism* (New York: Oxford University Press, 2016) 142

Bomhoff, Jacco, *Balancing Constitutional Rights: The Origins and Meanings of Postwar Legal Discourse* (Cambridge: Cambridge University Press, 2013)

Boulanger, Christian, "Europeanization through Judicial Activism? The Hungarian Constitutional Court's Legitimacy and the 'Return to Europe'" in Wojciech Sadurski, Adam Czarnota, and Martin Krygier (eds.), *Spreading Democracy and the Rule of Law? The Impact of EU Enlargement on the Rule of Law, Democracy and Constitutionalism in Post-Communist Legal Orders* (Dordrecht, NL: Springer, 2006) 263

Brown, Nathan J., "Constituting Palestine: The Effort to Write a Basic Law for the Palestinian Authority" (2000) 54 *Middle East Journal* 25

Bugarič, Bojan, "A Crisis of Constitutional Democracy in Post-Communist Europe: 'Lands in-between' Democracy and Authoritarianism" (2015) 13 *International Journal of Constitutional Law* 219

Bugarič, Bojan and Tom Ginsburg, "The Assault on Postcommunist Courts" (2016) 27 *Journal of Democracy* 69

Burnham, Walter Dean, "Constitutional Moments and Punctuated Equilibria: A Political Scientist Confronts Bruce Ackerman's *We the People*" (1999) 108 *Yale Law Journal* 2237

Bussiere, Elizabeth, "The Supreme Court and the Development of the Welfare State: Judicial Liberalism and the Problem of Welfare Rights" in Cornell W. Clayton and Howard Gillman (eds.), *Supreme Court Decision-Making: New Institutionalist Approaches* (Chicago: University of Chicago Press, 1999) 155

Butler, Anthony, "The Negative and Positive Impacts of HIV/AIDS on Democracy in South Africa" (2005) 23 *Journal of Contemporary African Studies* 3

Butt, Simon, *The Constitutional Court and Democracy in Indonesia* (Leiden: Brill Nijhoff, 2015)

Butt, Simon and Tim Lindsey, *The Indonesian Constitution: A Contextual Analysis* (Oxford: Hart Publishing, 2012)

Calda, Milos, "Constitution-Making in Post-Communist Countries: A Case of the Czech Republic" paper presented at the *American Political Science Association Convention*, Atlanta, Georgia, September 2, 1999

Capoccia, Giovanni and R. Daniel Kelemen, "The Study of Critical Junctures: Theory, Narrative, and Counterfactuals in Historical Institutionalism" (2007) 59 *World Politics* 341

Carruba, Clifford, Matthew Gabel, and Charles Hankla, "Judicial Behavior under Political Constraints: Evidence from the European Court of Justice" (2008) 102 *American Political Science Review* 435

Carstensen, Martin B., "Ideas are Not as Stable as Political Scientists Want Them to Be: A Theory of Incremental Ideational Change" (2011) 59 *Political Studies* 596

Carstensen, Martin B. and Viven A. Schmidt, "Power Through, Over and In Ideas: Conceptualizing Ideational Power in Discursive Institutionalism" (2016) 23 *Journal of European Public Policy* 318

Carver, Richard, "Zimbabwe: Drawing a Line Through the Past" (1998) 37 *Journal of African Law* 69

Catholic Commission for Justice and Peace in Zimbabwe, *Crisis of Governance: A Report on Political Violence in Zimbabwe* (Harare, 2000)

Cepeda-Espinosa, Manuel José, "Judicial Review in a Violent Context: The Origin, Role, and Impact of the Colombian Constitutional Court" (2004) 3 *Washington University Global Studies Law Review* 529

Cepeda Espinosa, Manuel José, "The Judicialization of Politics in Colombia: The Old and the New" in Rachel Sieder, Line Schjolden, and Alan Angell (eds.), *The Judicialization of Politics in Latin America* (New York: Palgrave Macmillan, 2005) 67

Cepeda Espinosa, Manuel José, and David Landau (eds.), *Colombian Constitutional Law: Leading Cases* (New York: Oxford University Press, 2017)

Chanock, Martin, *The Making of South African Legal Culture 1902–1936: Fear, Favour and Prejudice* (Cambridge: Cambridge University Press, 2001)

Chavez, Rebecca Bill, *The Rule of Law in Nascent Democracies: Judicial Politics in Argentina* (Stanford: Stanford University Press, 2004)

Chavez, Rebecca Bill, "The Rule of Law and Courts in Democratizing Regimes" in Gregory A. Caldeira, R. Daniel Kelemen, and Keith E. Whittington (eds.), *Oxford Handbook of Law and Politics* (New York: Oxford University Press, 2008) 63

Cheesman, Nick, *Opposing the Rule of Law: How Myanmar's Courts Make Law and Order* (Cambridge: Cambridge University Press, 2015)

Choudhry, Sujit, "Globalization in Search of Justification: Toward a Theory of Comparative Constitutional Interpretation" (1999) 74 *Indiana Law Journal* 819

Choudhry, Sujit, "Migration as a New Metaphor in Comparative Constitutional Law" in Sujit Choudhry (ed.), *The Migration of Constitutional Ideas* (Cambridge: Cambridge University Press, 2006) 1

Choudhry, Sujit, "'He had a Mandate': The South African Constitutional Court and the African National Congress in a Dominant Party Democracy" (2010) 2 *Constitutional Court Review* 1

Christiano, Tom, "Authority" in *The Stanford Encyclopedia of Philosophy* (Spring 2013 Edition), Edward N. Zalta (ed.)

Clayton, Cornell W. and Howard Gillman (eds.), *Supreme Court Decision-Making: New Institutionalist Approaches* (Chicago: University of Chicago Press, 1999)

Cohen-Eliya, Moshe and Iddo Porat, "American Balancing and German Proportionality: The Historical Origins" (2010) 8 *International Journal of Constitutional Law* 263

Cole, Daniel H., "'An Unqualified Human Good': E. P. Thompson and the Rule of Law" (2001) 28 *Journal of Law and Society* 177

Collier, Ruth Berins and David Collier, *Shaping the Political Arena: Critical Junctures, the Labor Movement, and Regime Dynamics in Latin America* (Princeton, NJ: Princeton University Press, 1991)

Coltart, David, *The Struggle Continues: 50 years of Tyranny in Zimbabwe* (Johannesburg: Jacana, 2016)

Compagnon, Daniel, *A Predictable Tragedy: Robert Mugabe and the Collapse of Zimbabwe* (Philadelphia, PA: University of Pennsylvania Press, 2011)

Coper, Michael and George Williams (eds.), *How Many Cheers for Engineers?* (Sydney: Federation Press, 1997)

Bibliography 333

Coppedge, Michael, *Democratization and Research Methods* (New York: Cambridge University Press, 2012)

Cotterrell, Roger, "The Concept of Legal Culture" in David Nelken (ed.), *Comparing Legal Cultures* (Aldershot: Dartmouth, 1997) 13

Cotterrell, Roger, "Comparative Law and Legal Culture" in M. Reimann and R. Zimmermann (eds.), *The Oxford Handbook of Comparative Law* (Oxford: Oxford University Press, 2006) 710

Couso, Javier, "The Judicialization of Chilean Politics: The Rights Revolution That Never Was" in Rachel Sieder, Line Schjolden, and Alan Angell (eds.), *The Judicialization of Politics in Latin America* (New York: Palgrave Macmillan, 2005) 105

Couso, Javier A., Alexandra Huneeus, and Rachel Sieder (eds.), *Cultures of Legality: Judicialization and Political Activism in Latin America* (Cambridge: Cambridge University Press, 2010)

Couso, Javier and Lisa Hilbink. "From Quietism to Incipient Activism: The Institutional and Ideological Roots of Rights Adjudication in Chile" in Gretchen Helmke and Julio Ríos-Figueroa (eds.), *Courts in Latin America* (New York: Cambridge University Press, 2011) 99

Cover, Robert M., *Justice Accused: Antislavery and the Judicial Process* (New Haven: Yale University Press, 1975)

Crouch, Melissa, "The Layers of Legal Development in Myanmar" in Melissa Crouch and Tim Lindsey (eds.), *Law, Society and Transition in Myanmar* (Oxford: Hart Publishing, 2014) 33

Czarnota, Adam, "Rule of Lawyers or Rule of Law: On the Constitutional Crisis and the Rule of Law in Poland" paper delivered at Australian National University conference on *Troubling the Rule of Law*, Kioloa (September 2017)

Dahl, Robert A., "Decision-making in a Democracy: The Supreme Court as a National Policy-Maker" (1957) 6 *Journal of Public Law* 279

Daly, Tom Gerald, *The Alchemists: Questioning our Faith in Courts as Democracy-Builders* (Cambridge: Cambridge University Press, 2017)

Daly, Tom Gerald, "Diagnosing Democratic Decay" paper presented at Gilbert & Tobin Centre of Public Law *Comparative Constitutional Law Roundtable*, UNSW, Sydney (August 2017)

Das, Gobind, "The Supreme Court: An Overview" in B. N. Kirpal et al. (eds.), *Supreme but not Infallible: Essays in Honour of the Supreme Court of India* (New Delhi: Oxford University Press, 2000) 16

Desai, Ashok H. and S. Muralidhar, "Public Interest Litigation: Potential and Problems" in B.N. Kirpal et al. (eds.), *Supreme but not Infallible: Essays in Honour of the Supreme Court of India* (New Delhi: Oxford University Press, 2000) 159

Deva, Surya, "The Indian Constitution in the Twenty-First Century: The Continuing Quest for Empowerment, Good Governance and Sustainability" in Albert H. Y. Chen (ed.), *Constitutionalism in Asia in the Early Twenty-First Century* (Cambridge: Cambridge University Press, 2014) 343

Dhavan, Rajeev, *The Supreme Court of India: A Socio-Legal Critique of its Juristic Techniques* (Bombay: Triphathi, 1977)

Dhavan, Rajeev, "Borrowed Ideas: On the Impact of American Scholarship on Indian Law" (1985) 33 *American Journal of Comparative Law* 505

Dhavan, Rajeev, "Introduction" in Mark Galanter, *Law & Society in Modern India* (Oxford: Oxford University Press, 1998) xiii

Diamond, Larry Jay, "Thinking About Hybrid Regimes" (2002) 13 *Journal of Democracy* 21

Dias, R. W. M., "Legal Politics: Norms behind the *Grundnorm*" (1968) 26 *Cambridge Law Journal* 233

Dixon, Owen, *Jesting Pilate and Other Papers and Addresses* (Melbourne: Law Book Co, 1965)

Dixon, Rosalind, "A Democratic Theory of Constitutional Comparison" (2008) 56 *American Journal of Comparative Law* 947

Dixon, Rosalind and David Landau, "Transnational Constitutionalism and A Limited Doctrine of Unconstitutional Constitutional Amendment" (2015) 13 *International Journal of Constitutional Law* 606

Dixon, Rosalind and Theunis Roux, "Marking Constitutional Transitions: The Law and Politics of Constitutional Implementation in South Africa" in Tom Ginsburg and Aziz Huq (eds.), *From Parchment to Practice: Implementing New Constitutions* (forthcoming)

Dorf, Michael C. and Charles F. Sabel, "A Constitution of Democratic Experimentalism" (1998) 98 *Columbia Law Review* 267

Dorsen, Norman, Michel Rosenfeld, András Sajó, Sandra Baer (eds.), *Comparative Constitutionalism: Cases and Materials* 1ed (St Paul, MN: Thomson West, 2003)

Dworkin, Ronald, *Law's Empire* (Cambridge, MA: Harvard University Press, 1986)

Dyzenhaus, David, *Hard Cases in Wicked Legal Systems: South African Law in the Perspective of Legal Philosophy* (Oxford: Clarendon Press, 1991)

Dyzenhaus, David, *Legality and Legitimacy: Carl Schmitt, Hans Kelsen and Hermann Heller in Weimar* (Oxford: Oxford University Press, 1997)

Dzinesa, Gwinyani A., *Zimbabwe's Constitutional Reform Process: Challenges and Prospects* (Institute for Justice and Reconciliation, 2012)

Eldredge, Niles and Stephen Jay Gould, "Punctuated Equilibria: An Alternative to Phyletic Gradualism" in Thomas J. M. Schopf (ed.), *Models in Paleobiology* (San Francisco: Freeman, Cooper & Co, 1972) 82

Elkins, Zachary, Tom Ginsburg, and James Melton, *The Endurance of National Constitutions* (New York: Cambridge University Press, 2009)

Ellmann, Stephen, *In a Time of Trouble: Law and Liberty in South Africa's State of Emergency* (Oxford: Clarendon Press, 1992)

Ellmann, Stephen, "To Resign or Not to Resign" (1997) 19 *Cardozo Law Review* 1047

Elster, Jon, *Alchemies of the Mind: Rationality and the Emotions* (Cambridge: Cambridge University Press, 1999)

Ely, John Hart, *Democracy and Distrust: A Theory of Judicial Review* (Cambridge, MA: Harvard University Press, 1980)

Emerton, Patrick and Jeffrey Goldsworthy, "The Brennan Court" in Rosalind Dixon and George Williams (eds.), *The High Court, the Constitution and Australian Politics* (Melbourne: Cambridge University Press, 2015) 261

Epperly, Brad, "Political Competition and De Facto Judicial Independence in Non-Democracies" (2017) 56 *European Journal of Political Research* 279

Epp, Charles R., *The Rights Revolution: Lawyers, Activists and Supreme Courts in Comparative Perspective* (Chicago: University of Chicago Press, 1998) 83

Epstein, Lee and Jack Knight, *The Choices Justices Make* (Washington, DC: Congressional Quarterly, 1998)

Epstein, Lee and Jack Knight, "Mapping Out the Strategic Terrain: The Informational Role of Amici Curiae" in Cornell W. Clayton and Howard Gillman (eds.), *Supreme Court Decision-Making: New Institutionalist Approaches* (Chicago: University of Chicago Press, 1999) 215

Epstein, Lee, Jack Knight, and Olga Shvetsova, "The Role of Constitutional Courts in the Establishment and Maintenance of Democratic Systems of Government" (2001) 35 *Law & Society Review* 117

Escresa, Laarni and Nuno Garoupa, "Testing the Logic of Strategic Defection: The Case of the Philippine Supreme Court – An Empirical Analysis (1986–2010)" (2013) 21 *Asian Journal of Political Science* 189

Escresa, Laarni and Nuno M. Garoupa, "Judicial Politics in Unstable Democracies: The Case of the Philippine Supreme Court, an Empirical Analysis 1986–2010" (2012) 3 *Asian Journal of Law & Economics* 1

Estlund, David M., *Democratic Authority: A Philosophical Framework* (Princeton, NJ: Princeton University Press, 2007)

Evans, Simon, "Appointment of Justices" in Tony Blackshield, Michael Coper and George Williams, *The Oxford Companion to the High Court of Australia* (Melbourne: Oxford University Press, 2001) 19

Falletti, Tulia G. and James Mahoney, "The Comparative Sequential Method" in James Mahoney and Kathleen Thelen (eds.), *Advances in Comparative-Historical Analysis* (New York: Cambridge University Press, 2015) 211

Fallon, Richard H., Jr, *The Dynamic Constitution: An Introduction to American Constitutional Law* (New York: Cambridge University Press, 2004) 81

Fallon, Richard H. Jr, "The Core of an Uneasy Case for Judicial Review" (2008) 121 *Harvard Law Review* 1693

Feldman, Noah, *Scorpions: The Battles and Triumphs of FDR's Great Supreme Court Justices* (New York: Twelve, 2010)

Fine, Robert, "The Rule of Law and Muggletonian Marxism: The Perplexities of Edward Thompson" (1994) 21 *Journal of Law and Society* 193

Finkel, Jodi S, *Judicial Reform as Political Insurance: Argentina, Peru, and Mexico in the 1990s* (Notre Dame, IN: University of Notre Dame Press, 2008)

Fiss, Owen M., "The Right Degree of Independence" in Irwin P. Stotzky (ed.), *Transition to Democracy in Latin America: The Role of the Judiciary* (Boulder, CO: Westview Press, 1992) 55

Fraenkel, Ernst, *The Dual State: A Contribution to the Theory of Dictatorship* (Oxford: Oxford University Press, 2017 [1941])

Freedom House, *Freedom in the World Report 2016*

French, Robert, "Judicial Activist – Mythical Monsters?" (2008) 12 *Southern Cross University Law Review* 59

Friedman, Barry, *The Will of the People: How Public Opinion Has Influenced the Supreme Court and Shaped the Meaning of the Constitution* (New York: Farrar, Straus and Giroux, 2009)

Fuller, Lon L., "The Forms and Limits of Adjudication" (1978) 92 *Harvard Law Review* 353

Gadbois, George H., Jr., *Judges of the Supreme Court of India: 1950–1989* (New Delhi: Oxford University Press, 2011)

Galanter, Mark, *Competing Equalities: Law and the Backward Classes in India* (Berkeley, CA: University of California Press, 1984) 484

Galanter, Mark, *Law & Society in Modern India* (Oxford: Oxford University Press, 1998)

Galanter, Mark and J. K. Krishnan, "'Bread for the Poor': Access to Justice and the Rights of the Needy in India" (2004) 55 *Hastings Law Journal* 789

Gallagher, Julia, "The Battle for Zimbabwe in 2013: From Polarisation to Ambivalence" (2015) 53 *Journal of Modern African Studies* 27

Galligan, Brian, *The Politics of the High Court: A Study of the Judicial Branch of Government in Australia* (Brisbane: University of Queensland Press, 1987)

Galligan, Brian, "Realistic 'Realism' and the High Court's Role" (1989) 18 *Federal Law Review* 40

Galligan, Brian, "The Barwick Court" in Rosalind Dixon and George Williams (eds.), *The High Court, the Constitution and Australian Politics* (Melbourne: Cambridge University Press, 2015) 201

Gappah, Petina, "Morgan Tsvangirai's messy love life is a gift to his enemies" *The Guardian* (September 20, 2012)

Gardbaum, Stephen, *The New Commonwealth Model of Constitutionalism: Theory and Practice* (New York: Cambridge University Press, 2012)

Gardbaum, Stephen, "How Do We and Should We Compare Constitutional Law" in Samantha Besson, Lukas Heckendorn, and Samuel Jube (eds.), *Comparing Comparative Law* (Geneva: Schulthess, 2017)

Garoupa, Nuno, Fernando Gomez-Pomar, and Veronica Grembi, "Judging under Political Pressure: An Empirical Analysis of Constitutional Review Voting in the Spanish Constitutional Court" (2013) 29 *Journal of Law and Economic Organization* 513

Garoupa, Nuno, Veronica Grembi, and Shirley Ching-pin Lin, "Explaining Constitutional Review in New Democracies: The Case of Taiwan" (2011) 20 *Pacific Rim Law & Policy Journal* 1

Gauntlett, Jeremy, "Zimbabwe: The War on Law" paper delivered at a seminar hosted by the Human Rights Lawyers Association and others (London, March 19, 2009) (published in December 2009 *Advocate* 44–47)

Geertz, Clifford, *The Interpretation of Cultures: Selected Essays* (New York: Basic Books, 1973)

George, Alexander L. and Andrew Bennett, *Case Studies and Theory Development in the Social Sciences* (Cambridge, MA: MIT Press, 2005)

Gerring, John, "The Case Study: What it is and What it Does" in Carles Boix and Susan C Stokes (eds.), *The Oxford Handbook of Comparative Politics* (New York: Oxford University Press, 2009) 90

Gibson, James L. and Gregory Caldeira, "Has Legal Realism Damaged the Legitimacy of the U.S. Supreme Court?" (2011) 45 *Law & Society Review* 195

Gillespie, John, "Changing Concepts of Socialist Law in Vietnam" in John Gillespie and Pip Nicholson (eds.), *Asian Socialism and Legal Change: The Dynamics of Vietnamese and Chinese Reform* (Canberra: ANU Press, 2005)

Gillman, Howard, *The Constitution Besieged: The Rise and Demise of Lochner Era Police Powers Jurisprudence* (Durham, NC: Duke University Press, 1993)

Gillman, Howard, "On Constructing a Science of Comparative Judicial Politics: Tate & Haynie's 'Authoritarianism and the Functions of Courts'" (1994) 28 *Law & Society Review* 355

Gillman, Howard, "The Court as an Idea, Not a Building (or a Game): Interpretive Institutionalism and the Analysis of Supreme Court Decision-Making" in Howard Gillman and Cornell W. Clayton, *The Supreme Court in American Politics: New Institutionalist Interpretations* (Lawrence, KS: University of Kansas Press, 1999) 65

Gillman, Howard and Cornell W. Clayton, *The Supreme Court in American Politics: New Institutionalist Interpretations* (Lawrence, KS: University of Kansas Press, 1999)

Ginsburg, Tom, *Judicial Review in New Democracies: Constitutional Courts in Asian Cases* (New York: Cambridge University Press, 2003)

Ginsburg, Tom, "The Global Spread of Constitutional Review" in Gregory A. Caldeira, R. Daniel Kelemen, and Keith E. Whittington (eds.), *The Oxford Handbook of Law and Politics* (New York: Oxford University Press, 2008) 85

Ginsburg, Tom, "The Politics of Courts in Democratization: Four Junctures in Asia" in Diana Kapiszewski, Gordon Silverstein, and Robert A. Kagan (eds.), *Consequential Courts: Judicial Roles in Global Perspective* (New York: Cambridge University Press, 2013) 45

Gleeson, Murray, "Judicial Legitimacy" (2000) 20 *Australian Bar Review* 4

Godwin, Peter, *The Fear: Robert Mugabe and the Martyrdom of Zimbabwe* (New York: Little Brown, 2011)

Goertz, Gary and James Mahoney, *A Tale of Two Cultures: Qualitative and Quantitative Research in the Social Sciences* (Princeton, NJ: Princeton University Press, 2012)

Goldsworthy, Jeffrey, "Realism about the High Court" (1989) 18 *Federal Law Review* 27

Goldsworthy, Jeffrey, "Reply to Galligan" (1989) 18 *Federal Law Review* 50

Goldsworthy, Jeffrey, "Australia: Devotion to Legalism" in Jeffrey Goldsworthy (ed.), *Interpreting Constitutions: A Comparative Study* (Melbourne: Oxford University Press, 2007) 106

Graber, Mark A., *Dred Scott and the Problem of Constitutional Evil* (New York: Cambridge University Press, 2006)

Graber, Mark A., "Constitutional Politics in the Active Voice" in Diana Kapiszewski, Gordon Silverstein, and Robert A. Kagan (eds.), *Consequential Courts: Judicial Roles in Global Perspective* (New York: Cambridge University Press, 2013) 363

Grey, Thomas C., "Judicial Review and Legal Pragmatism" (2003) 38 *Wake Forest Law Review* 473

Gubbay, Anthony, "The Light of Successive Chief Justices of Zimbabwe in Seeking to Protect Human Rights and the Rule of Law" 2001 Rothschild Foster Human Rights Trust Lecture

Gubbay, Anthony, "The Progressive Erosion of the Rule of Law in Independent Zimbabwe" Bar of England and Wales Third International Rule of Law Lecture, Inner Temple Hall, London (December 2009)

Guha, Ramachandra, *India after Gandhi: The History of the World's Largest Democracy* (London: Macmillan, 2007)

Gummow, William, "Law and the Use of History" in Justin T. Gleeson and Ruth C. A. Higgins (eds.), *Constituting Law: Legal Argument and Social Values* (Sydney: Federation Press, 2011) 75

Hailbronner, Michaela, *Traditions and Transformations: The Rise of German Constitutionalism* (Oxford: Oxford University Press, 2015)

Hall, Peter A., "Policy Paradigms, Social Learning, and the State: The Case of Economic Policymaking in Britain" (1993) 25 *Comparative Politics* 275

Halliday, Terence C. and Lucien Karpik, "Political Liberalism in the British Post-Colony: A Theme with Three Variations" in Terence C. Halliday, Lucien Karpik, and Malcolm Feeley (eds.), *Fates of Political Liberalism in the British Post-Colony: The Politics of the Legal Complex* (Cambridge: Cambridge University Press, 2012) 3

Halliday, Terence C., Lucien Karpik, and Malcolm Feeley (eds.), *Fates of Political Liberalism in the British Post-Colony: The Politics of the Legal Complex* (New York: Cambridge University Press, 2012)

Halmai, Gábor, "The Hungarian Approach to Constitutional Review: The End of Activism? The First Decade of the Hungarian Constitutional Court" in Wojciech Sadurski (ed.), *Constitutional Justice, East and West: Democratic Legitimacy and Courts in Post-Communist Europe in a Comparative Perspective* (The Hague: Kluwer Law International, 2002) 189

Hart, Henry M. and Albert M. Sacks, *The Legal Process: Basic Problems in the Making and Application of Law* (Foundation Press, 1994 [1958])

Hartmann, Bernd J., "The Arrival of Judicial Review in Germany Under the Weimar Constitution of 1919" (2004) 18 *Brigham Young University Journal of Public Law* 107

Hayne, Kenneth, "Owen Dixon" in Tony Blackshield, Michael Coper, and George Williams (eds.), *The Oxford Companion to the High Court of Australia* (Melbourne: Oxford University Press, 2001) 218

Helmke, Gretchen, *Courts under Constraints: Judges, Generals, and Presidents in Argentina* (New York: Cambridge University Press, 2012)

Hendrianto, Stefanus, *From Humble Beginnings to a Functioning Court: The Indonesian Constitutional Court, 2003–2008* (doctoral dissertation, University of Washington, 2008)

Hendrianto, "Institutional Choice and the New Indonesian Constitutional Court" in Andrew Harding and Pip Nicholson (eds.), *New Courts in Asia* (London: Routledge, 2009) 158

Hendrianto, Stefanus, "The Indonesian Constitutional Court at a Tipping Point," *International Journal of Constitutional Law Blog*, October 3, 2013

Heydon, J. D., "Theories of Constitutional Interpretation: A Taxonomy" (2007) (Winter) *Bar News: The Journal of the New South Wales Bar Association* 12

Hilbink, Lisa, *Judges beyond Politics in Democracy and Dictatorship: Lessons from Chile* (New York: Cambridge University Press, 2007)

Hilbink, Lisa, "Agents of Anti-Politics: Courts in Pinochet's Chile" in Tom Ginsburg and Tamir Moustafa (eds.), *Rule by Law: The Politics of Courts in Authoritarian Regimes* (New York: Cambridge University Press, 2008) 102

Hilbink, Lisa, "From Comparative Judicial Politics to Comparative Law and Politics" (2008) 18(12) *Law & Politics Book Review* 1098

Hilbink, Lisa, "The Constituted Nature of Constituents' Interests: Historical and Ideational Factors in Judicial Empowerment" (2009) 62 *Political Research Quarterly* 781

Hirschl, Ran, *Towards Juristocracy: The Origins and Consequences of the New Constitutionalism* (Cambridge, MA: Harvard University Press, 2007)

Hirschl, Ran, "The Judicialization of Politics" in Gregory A. Caldeira, R. Daniel Kelemen, and Keith E. Whittington (eds.), *The Oxford Handbook of Law and Politics* (New York: Oxford University Press, 2008) 119

Hirschl, Ran, *Comparative Matters: The Renaissance of Comparative Constitutional Law* (Oxford: Oxford University Press, 2014)

Hogg, Peter W. and Allison A. Bushell, "The Charter Dialogue between Courts and Legislatures (Or Perhaps the Charter of Rights Isn't Such a Bad Thing after All)" (1997) 35 *Osgoode Hall Law Journal* 75

Holmes, Stephen, "Judicial Independence as Ambiguous Reality and Insidious Illusion" in Ronald Dworkin (ed.), *From Liberal Values to Democratic Transition: Essays in Honour of János Kis* (Budapest: Central European University Press, 2004) 3

Horowitz, Donald L., *Constitutional Change and Democracy in Indonesia* (New York: Cambridge University Press, 2013)

Horwitz, Morton J., "The Rule of Law: An Unqualified Human Good?" (1977) 86 *Yale Law Journal* 561

Horwitz, Morton J., *The Transformation of American Law, 1780–1860* (Cambridge, MA: Harvard University Press, 1979)

Horwitz, Morton J., *The Transformation of American Law, 1870–1960: The Crisis of Legal Orthodoxy* (New York: Oxford University Press, 1992)

Horwitz, Morton J., *The Warren Court and the Pursuit of Justice* (New York: Hill and Wang, 1998)

Huq, Aziz and Tom Ginsburg, "How to Lose a Constitutional Democracy" (2018) 65 *UCLA Law Review* (forthcoming)

Human Rights Watch, *"Bullets for Each of You": State-Sponsored Violence since Zimbabwe's March 29 Elections* (June 2008)

Human Rights Watch, *"Our Hands Are Tied": Erosion of the Rule of Law in Zimbabwe,* (November 2008)

Iaryczower, Matías, Pablo T. Spiller, and Mariano Tommasi, "Judicial Decision-making in Unstable Environments, Argentina 1935–1998" (2002) 46 *American Journal of Political Science* 699

International Bar Association, *Report of IBA Zimbabwe Mission 2001* (London, 2001)

International Crisis Group, "Zimbabwe's Elections: Mugabe's Last Stand" *Africa Briefing* 95 (July 29, 2013)

Irving, Helen, *Five Things to Know about the Australian Constitution* (Melbourne: Cambridge University Press, 2004)

Irving, Helen, "The Dixon Court" in Rosalind Dixon and George Williams, *The High Court, the Constitution and Australian Politics* (Melbourne: Cambridge University Press, 2015) 179

Issacharoff, Samuel, "Constitutional Courts and Democratic Hedging" (2011) 99 *Georgetown Law Journal* 961

Issacharoff, Samuel, "The Democratic Risk to Democratic Transitions" (2014) 5 *Constitutional Court Review* 1

Issacharoff, Samuel, *Fragile Democracies: Contested Power in the Era of Constitutional Courts* (New York: Cambridge University Press, 2015)

Jackson, David F., "Brennan Court" in Tony Blackshield, Michael Coper, and George Williams (eds.), *Oxford Companion to the High Court of Australia* (Melbourne: Oxford University Press, 2001) 68

Jackson, Vicki C., "Constitutional Comparisons: Convergence, Resistance, Engagement" (2005) 119 *Harvard Law Review* 109

Jackson, Vicki C., *Constitutional Engagement in a Transnational Era* (Oxford: Oxford University Press, 2010)

Jackson, Vicki C., "Comparative Constitutional Law, Legal Realism, and Empirical Legal Science" (2016) 96 *Boston University Law Review* 1359

Jacob, Alice, "Nehru and the Judiciary" in Rajeev Dhavan and Thomas Paul (eds.), *Nehru and the Constitution* (Bombay: Triphathi, 1992) 63

Jacobs, Leslie Gielow, "Even More Honest than Ever Before: Abandoning Pretense and Recreating Legitimacy in Constitutional Interpretation" (1995) 2 *University of Illinois Law Review* 363

Jacobsohn, Gary Jeffrey, *Constitutional Identity* (Cambridge, MA: Harvard University Press, 2010)

Jakab, András and Pál Sonnevend, "Continuity with Deficiencies: The New Basic Law of Hungary" (2013) 9 *European Constitutional Law Review* 102

Kapiszewski, Diana, "Tactical Balancing: High Court Decision-making on Politically Crucial Cases" (2011) 45 *Law & Society Review* 471

Karekwaivanane, George H., "'It Shall be the Duty of Every African to Obey and Comply Promptly': Negotiating State Authority in the Legal Arena, Rhodesia 1965–1980" (2011) 37 *Journal of Southern African Studies* 333

Kennedy, Duncan, *A Critique of Adjudication (Fin de Siècle)* (Cambridge, MA: Harvard University Press, 1997)

Kildea, Paul and George Williams, "The Mason Court" in Rosalind Dixon and George Williams (eds.), *The High Court, the Constitution and Australian Politics* (Melbourne: Cambridge University Press, 2015) 244

King, Gary, Robert O. Keohane, and Sidney Verba, *Designing Social Inquiry: Scientific Inference in Qualitative Research* (Princeton, NJ: Princeton University Press, 1994)

Kirby, Michael, "A F Mason – From *Trigwell* to *Teoh*" (1996) 20 *University of Melbourne Law Review* 1087

Kirby, Michael, *Judicial Activism: Authority, Principle and Policy in the Judicial Method* (London: Sweet & Maxwell, 2004) 49

Klare, Karl E., "Legal Culture and Transformative Constitutionalism" (1998) 12 *South African Journal on Human Rights* 146

Klug, Heinz, *Constituting Democracy: Law Globalism and South Africa's Political Reconstruction* (Cambridge: Cambridge University Press, 2000)

Knight, Jack and Lee Epstein, "On the Struggle for Judicial Supremacy" (1996) 30 *Law & Society Review* 87

Kommers, Donald and Russell Miller, *The Constitutional Jurisprudence of the Federal Republic of Germany* 3rd ed. (Durham, NC: Duke University Press, 2012)

Kovács, Kriszta and Gábor Attila Tóth, "Hungary's Constitutional Transformation" (2011) 7 *European Constitutional Law Review* 183

Krasner, Stephen D., "Approaches to the State: Alternative Conceptions and Historical Dynamics" (1984) 16 *Comparative Politics* 223

Kriger, Norma J., *Zimbabwe's Guerrilla War: Peasant Voices* (Cambridge: Cambridge University Press, 1992)

Krygier, Martin, "Julius Stone: Leeways of Choice, Legal Tradition and the Declaratory Theory of Law" (1986) 9 *University of New South Wales Law Journal* 26

Krygier, Martin, "Law as Tradition" (1986) 5 *Law and Philosophy* 237

Lall, Marie, *Understanding Reform in Myanmar: People and Society in the Wake of Military Rule* (London: C. Hurst & Co, 2016)

Landau, David, "Abusive Constitutionalism" (2013) 47 *University California Davis Law Review* 189

Landau, David Evan, *Beyond Judicial Independence: The Construction of Judicial Power in Colombia* (doctoral dissertation, Harvard University, 2015)

Latham, R. T. E., *The Law and the Commonwealth* (Oxford: Oxford University Press, 1949 [1937])

Law, David S., "Generic Constitutional Law" (2005) 89 *Minnesota Law Review* 652

Law, David S. and Mila Versteeg, "The Declining Influence of the US Constitution" (2012) 87 *New York University Law Review* 762

LeBas, Adrienne, "The Perils of Power Sharing" (2014) 25 *Journal of Democracy* 52

Lee, H. P., "The Implied Freedom of Political Communication" in H. P. Lee and George Winterton (eds.), *Australian Constitutional Landmarks* (Melbourne: Cambridge University Press, 2003) 383

Legal Resources Foundation and the Catholic Commission for Justice and Peace in Zimbabwe, *Breaking the Silence, Building True Peace: A Report on the Disturbances in Matabeleland and the Midlands 1980 to 1988* (1997)

Leiter, Brian, "Rethinking Legal Realism: Toward a Naturalized Jurisprudence" (1997) 76 *Texas Law Review* 267

Leiter, Brian, "Legal Formalism and Legal Realism: What is the Issue?" (2010) 16 *Legal Theory* 111

Lembcke, Oliver W. and Christian Boulanger, "Between Revolution and Constitution: The Roles of the Hungarian Constitutional Court" in Gábor Attila Tóth (ed.), *Constitution for a Disunited Nation: On Hungary's 2011 Fundamental Law* (Budapest: Central European University Press, 2012) 269

Levitsky, Steven and Lucan A. Way, "The Rise of Competitive Authoritarianism" (2002) 13 *Journal of Democracy* 51

Levitsky, Steven and Lucan A. Way, *Competitive Authoritarianism: Hybrid Regimes after the Cold War* (New York: Cambridge University Press, 2010)

Lijphart, Arend, "Comparative Politics and the Comparative Method" (1971) 65 *American Political Science Review* 682

Llewellyn, Karl N., *The Common Law Tradition: Deciding Appeals* (Boston, MA: Little Brown, 1960)

Luhmann, Niklas, *Law as a Social System* trans. Klaus A. Ziegert (Oxford: Oxford University Press, 2004)

Mahoney, James, "Path Dependence in Historical Sociology" (2000) 29 *Theory and Society* 507

Mahoney, James, "Strategies of Causal Assessment in Comparative Historical Analysis" in James Mahoney and Dietrich Rueschemeyer (eds.), *Comparative Historical Analysis in the Social Sciences* (New York: Cambridge University Press, 2003) 337

Mahoney, James, "After KKV: The New Methodology of Qualitative Research" (2010) 62 *World Politics* 120

Mahoney, James and Dietrich Rueschemeyer (eds.), *Comparative Historical Analysis in the Social Sciences* (New York: Cambridge University Press, 2003)

Mahoney, James and Dietrich Rueschemeyer, "Comparative Historical Analysis: Achievements and Agendas" in James Mahoney and Dietrich Rueschemeyer (eds.), *Comparative Historical Analysis in the Social Sciences* (New York: Cambridge University Press, 2003) 1

Mahoney, James and Kathleen Thelen (eds.), "A Theory of Gradual Institutional Change" in James Mahoney and Kathleen Thelen, *Explaining Institutional Change: Ambiguity, Agency, and Power* (New York: Cambridge University Press, 2010) 1

Mahoney, James and Kathleen Thelen (eds.), *Advances in Comparative-Historical Analysis* (New York: Cambridge University Press, 2015)

Manyatera, Gift and Chengetai Hamadziripi, "Electoral Law, the Constitution and Democracy in Zimbabwe: A Critique of *Jealousy Mbizvo Mawarire v Robert Mugabe N.O and 4 Others* CCZ 1/13" (2014) 1 *Midlands State University Law Review* 72

March, James G. and Johan P. Olsen, "The New Institutionalism: Organizational Factors in Political Life" (1984) 78 *American Political Science Review* 734

Markovits, Inga, "Law or Order – Constitutionalism and Legality in Eastern Europe" (1982) 34 *Stanford Law Review* 513

Mason, Anthony, "The Role of a Constitutional Court in a Federation: A Comparison of the Australian and the United States Experience" (1986) 16 *Federal Law Review* 1

Massoud, Mark Fathi, *Law's Fragile State: Colonial, Authoritarian, and Humanitarian Legacies in Sudan* (New York: Cambridge University Press, 2013)

Mate, Manoj, "The Origins of Due Process in India: The Role of Borrowing in Personal Liberty and Preventive Detention Cases" (2010) 28 *Berkeley Journal of International Law* 216

Mate, Manoj, "Public Interest Litigation and the Transformation of the Supreme Court of India" in Diana Kapiszewski, Gordon Silverstein, and Robert A. Kagan (eds.), *Consequential Courts: Judicial Roles in Global Perspective* (New York: Cambridge University Press, 2013) 262

Mate, Manoj, "Elite Institutionalism and Judicial Assertiveness in the Supreme Court of India" (2014) 28 *Temple International & Comparative Law Journal* 360

Matondi, Prosper B., *Zimbabwe's Fast Track Land Reform* (London: Zed Books, 2012)

Maveety, Nancy and Anke Grosskopf, "'Constrained' Constitutional Courts as Conduits for Democratic Consolidation" (2004) 38 *Law & Society Review* 463

McCloskey, Robert G., *The American Supreme Court* (4th ed. revised by Sanford Levinson) (Chicago: University of Chicago Press, 2005)

Meerkotter, Anneke, "Trouble brewing in Zimbabwe – constitution-making in crisis" (August 31, 2012) available at www.polity.org.za/article/trouble-brewing-in-zimbabwe-constitution-making-in-crisis-2012-08-31

Mehta, Pratap Bhanu, "The Rise of Judicial Sovereignty" (2007) 18 *Journal of Democracy* 70

Mehta, Pratap Bhanu, "Can a Jurisprudence of Exasperation Sustain the Court's Authority" *Telegraph*, October 17, 2005

Mehta, Pratap Bhanu, "India's Judiciary: The Promise of Uncertainty" in Devesh Kapur and Pratap Bhanu Mehta (eds.), *Public Institutions in India: Performance and Design* (New Delhi: Oxford University Press, 2005) 158

Meierhenrich, Jens, *The Legacies of Law: Long-Run Consequences of Legal Development in South Africa, 1652–2000* (Cambridge: Cambridge University Press, 2008)

Meredith, Martin, *Mugabe: Power, Plunder, and the Struggle for Zimbabwe's Future* (New York: Public Affairs, 2002)

Merillat, H. C. L., "The Indian Constitution: Property Rights and Social Reform" (1960) 21 *Ohio State Law Journal* 616

Mietzner, Marcus, "Political Conflict Resolution and Democratic Consolidation in Indonesia: The Role of the Constitutional Court" (2010) 10 *Journal of East Asian Studies* 397

Mill, John Stuart, *A System of Logic* (Toronto: University of Toronto Press, 1974) [first published in 1843]

Mody, Zia, *10 Judgements that Changed India* (New Delhi: Sobhaa Dé Books, 2013)

Moustafa, Tamir, "Law and Resistance in Authoritarian States: The Judicialization of Politics in Egypt" in Tom Ginsburg and Tamir Moustafa (eds.), *Rule by Law Rule by Law: The Politics of Courts in Authoritarian Regimes* (New York: Cambridge University Press, 2008) 132

Moustafa, Tamir, *The Struggle for Constitutional Power: Law, Politics, and Economic Development in Egypt* (New York: Cambridge University Press, 2009)

Moustafa, Tamir, "Law and Courts in Authoritarian Regimes" (2014) 10 *Annual Review of Law and Social Science* 281

Moyo, Jason, "Mugabe outwits Tsvangirai on election date" *Mail & Guardian* (June 7, 2013)

Nardi, Dominic, "Discipline-Flourishing Constitutional Review: A Legal and Political Analysis of Myanmar's New Constitutional Tribunal" (2010) 12 *Australian Journal of Asian Law* 1

Nardi, Dominic J., "Finding Justice Scalia in Burma: Constitutional Interpretation and the Impeachment of the Myanmar Constitutional Tribunal" (2014) 23 *Pacific Rim Law & Policy Journal* 631

Nardi, Dominic Jerry, Jr., "How the Constitutional Tribunal's Jurisprudence Sparked a Crisis" in Andrew Harding (ed.), *Constitutionalism and Legal Change in Myanmar* (Oxford: Hart Publishing, 2017) 173

Ncube, Welshman, "State Security, The Rule of Law and Politics of Repression in Zimbabwe" *U-landsseminarets Skriftserie Nr 51* (University of Oslo Third World Seminar Series No 51, 1990)

Nelken, David, "Using the Concept of Legal Culture" (2004) 29 *Australian Journal of Legal Philosophy* 1

Nelken, David, "Comparative Legal Research and Legal Culture: Facts, Approaches and Values" (2016) 12 *Annual Review of Law and Social Science* 45

Neuborne, Burt, "The Supreme Court of India" (2003) 1 *International Journal of Constitutional Law* 476

Nijzink, Lia, "The Relative Powers of Parliaments and Presidents in Africa: Lessons for Zimbabwe?" in Norbert Kersting (ed.), *Constitution in Transition: Academic Inputs for a New Constitution in Zimbabwe* (Friedrich Ebert Stiftung, 2009) 160

Nonet, Phillippe and Philip Selznick, *Toward Responsive Law: Law & Society in Transition* (New Brunswick, NJ: Transaction Publishers, 2001 [1978])

Nussbaum, Martha, *The Clash Within: Democracy, Religious Violence, and India's Future* (Cambridge, MA: Harvard University Press, 2007)

Orren, Karen, *Belated Feudalism: Labor, the Law, and Liberal Development in the United States* (New York: Cambridge University Press, 1991)

Patapan, Haig, *Judging Democracy: The New Politics of the High Court of Australia* (Cambridge: Cambridge University Press, 2000)

Pierce, Jason L., *Inside the Mason Court Revolution: The High Court of Australia Transformed* (Durham, NC: Carolina Academic Press, 2006)

Pierson, Paul, "Increasing Returns, Path Dependence, and the Study of Politics" (2000) 94 *American Political Science Review* 251

Pierson, Paul, "Big, Slow-Moving, and ... Invisible: Macrosocial Processes in the Study of Comparative Politics" in James Mahoney and Dietrich Rueschemeyer (eds.), *Comparative Historical Analysis in the Social Sciences* (Cambridge: Cambridge University Press, 2003) 177

Pierson, Paul and Theda Skocpol, "Historical Institutionalism in Contemporary Political Science" in Ira Katznelson and Helen Milner (eds.), *Political Science: The State of the Discipline* (New York: W. W. Norton, 2002) 693

Pils, Eva, "China's Authoritarian Subversion of Legality and Ruling by Fear" unpublished paper presented at a Network for Interdisciplinary Study of Law seminar, UNSW Sydney (July 2017)

Pompe, Sebastian, *The Indonesian Supreme Court: A Study of Institutional Collapse* (Ithaca, NY: Cornell Southeast Asia Program Publications, 2005)

Popova, Maria, *Politicized Justice in Emerging Democracies: A Study of Courts in Russia and Ukraine* (Cambridge: Cambridge University Press, 2014)

Posner, Richard A., "Law as Politics: Horwitz on American Law, 1870–1960" (1992) 6 A *Critical Review* 559

Powe, Lucas A., Jr., *The Warren Court and American Politics* (Cambridge, MA: Harvard University Press, 2000)

Radbruch, Gustav, "Statutory Lawlessness and Supra-Statutory Law" (2006) 26 *Oxford Journal of Legal Studies* 1

Raftopoulos, Brian, "The Labour Movement and the Emergence of Opposition Politics in Zimbabwe" (2000) 33 *Labour, Capital & Society* 256

Raftopoulos, Brian, "The Global Political Agreement as a 'Passive Revolution': Notes on Contemporary Politics in Zimbabwe" (2010) 99 *The Round Table* 705

Raftopoulos, Brian, "The 2013 Elections in Zimbabwe: The End of an Era" (2013) 39 *Journal of Southern African Studies* 971

Ragin, Charles C., *Fuzzy-Set Social Science* (Chicago: University of Chicago Press, 2000)

Rajagopal, Balakrishan, "Pro-Human Rights but Anti-Poor? A Critical Evaluation of the Indian Supreme Court from a Social Movement Perspective" (2007) 18 *Human Rights Review* 157

Rajah, Jothie, *Authoritarian Rule of Law: Legislation, Discourse and Legitimacy in Singapore* (New York: Cambridge University Press, 2012)

Rajamani, Lavanya, "Public Interest Environmental Litigation in India: Exploring Issues of Access, Participation Equity, Effectiveness and Sustainability" (2007) 19 *Journal of Environmental Law* 293

Rajamani, Lavanya and Arghya Sengupta, "The Supreme Court" in N.G. Jaya (ed.), *The Oxford Companion to Politics in India* (New Delhi: Oxford University Press, 2010)

Ramachandran, Raju, "The Supreme Court and the Basic Structure Doctrine" in B.N. Kirpal et al. (eds.), *Supreme but not Infallible: Essays in Honour of the Supreme Court of India* (New Delhi: Oxford University Press, 2000) 107

Ranger, Terence, "Nationalist Historiography, Patriotic History and the History of the Nation: The Struggle over the past in Zimbabwe" (2004) 30 *Journal of Southern African Studies* 215

Rawls, John, "The Idea of Public Reason Revisited" (1997) 64 *University of Chicago Law Review* 765

Ritter, David, "The Myth of Sir Owen Dixon" (2005) 9 *Australian Journal of Legal History* 249

Robinson, Nick, "Expanding Judiciaries: India and the Rise of the Good Governance Court" (2009) 8 *Washington University Global Studies Law Review* 1

Robinson, Nick, "Structure Matters: The Impact of Court Structure on the Indian and U.S. Supreme Courts" (2013) 61 *American Journal of Comparative Law* 173

Roche, Declan, "Dietrich v The Queen" in Tony Blackshield, Michael Coper, and George Williams (eds.), *Oxford Companion to the High Court of Australia* (Melbourne: Oxford University Press, 2001) 207

Rosencranz, Armin and Michael Jackson, "The Delhi Pollution Case: The Supreme Court of India and the Limits of Judicial Power" (2003) 28 *Columbia Journal of Environmental Law* 223

Rosenfeld, Michel, "Comparative Constitutional Analysis in United States Adjudication and Scholarship" in Michel Rosenfeld and András Sajó (eds.), *The Oxford Handbook of Comparative Constitutional Law* (New York: Oxford University Press, 2012) 38

Roux, Theunis, "Transformative Constitutionalism and the Best Interpretation of the South African Constitution: Distinction without a Difference?" (2009) 20 *Stellenbosch Law Review* 258

Roux, Theunis, *The Politics of Principle: The First South African Constitutional Court, 1995–2005* (Cambridge: Cambridge University Press, 2013)

Roux, Theunis, "The South African Constitutional Court's Democratic Rights Jurisprudence: A Response to Samuel Issacharoff" (2014) 5 *Constitutional Court Review* 33

Roux, Theunis, "American Ideas Abroad: Comparative Implications of US Supreme Court Decision-Making Models" (2015) 13 *International Journal of Constitutional Law* 90

Roux, Theunis, "Constitutional Courts as Democratic Consolidators: Insights from South Africa after Twenty Years" (2016) 42 *Journal of Southern African Studies* 5

Roux, Theunis, "Comparative Constitutional Studies: Two Fields or One?" (2017) 13 *Annual Review of Law and Social Science* 123

Roux, Theunis, "In Defence of Empirical Entanglement: The Methodological Flaw in Waldron's Case against Judicial Review" in Ron Levy and Graeme Orr (eds.), *The Cambridge Handbook of Deliberative Constitutionalism* (Cambridge: Cambridge University Press, 2018) 203

Roux, Theunis and Fritz Siregar, "Trajectories of Curial Power: The Rise, Fall and Partial Rehabilitation of the Indonesian Constitutional Court" (2016) 16 *Australian Journal of Asian Law* 1

Russell, Peter H., "*Mabo*: Political Consequences" in Tony Blackshield, Michael Coper, and George Williams (eds.), *Oxford Companion to the High Court of Australia* (Melbourne: Oxford University Press, 2001) 450

Sadurski, Wojciech, *Rights before Courts: A Study of Constitutional Courts in Postcommunist States of Central and Eastern Europe* 2nd ed. (Dordrecht: Springer, 2014)

Sajó, András, "Reading the Invisible Constitution: Judicial Review in Hungary" (1995) 15 *Oxford Journal of Legal Studies* 253

Saller, Karla, *The Judicial Institution in Zimbabwe* 2 (Cape Town: SiberInk, 2004)

Sanchez-Urribarri, Raul A., "Courts between Democracy and Hybrid Authoritarianism: Evidence from the Venezuelan Supreme Court" (2011) 36 *Law & Social Inquiry* 854

Sanders, Elizabeth, "Historical Institutionalism" in Sarah A. Binder, R. A. W. Rhodes, and Bert A. Rockman (eds.), *The Oxford Handbook of Political Institutions* (New York: Oxford University Press, 2008) 39

Sanders, John T., "Political Authority" (1983) 66 *The Monist* 545

Sathe, S. P., *Judicial Activism in India: Transgressing Borders and Enforcing Limits* (New Delhi: Oxford University Press, 2002)

Saunders, Cheryl, "Book Review" (1988) 18 *Publius* 133

Saunders, Cheryl, "The Uniform Income Tax Cases" in H. P. Lee and George Winterton (eds.), *Australian Constitutional Landmarks* (Melbourne: Cambridge University Press, 2003) 62

Saunders, Cheryl, "The Use and Misuse of Comparative Constitutional Law" (2006) 13 *Indiana Journal of Global Legal Studies* 37

Saunders, Cheryl, *The Constitution of Australia: A Contextual Analysis* (Oxford: Hart Publishing, 2011)

Sawer, Geoffrey, *Australian Federal Politics and Law 1929–1949* (Melbourne: Melbourne University Press, 1963)

Sawer, Geoffrey, *Australian Federalism in the Courts* (Melbourne: Melbourne University Press, 1967)

Schauer, Frederick, "Formalism" (1988) 97 *Yale Law Journal* 509

Scheppele, Kim Lane, "The New Hungarian Constitutional Court" (1999) 8 *Eastern European Constitutional Review* 81

Scheppele, Kim Lane, "Constitutional Ethnography: An Introduction" (2004) 28 *Law & Society Review* 389

Scheppelle, Kim Lane, "Guardians of the Constitution: Constitutional Court Presidents and the Struggle for the Rule of Law in Post-Soviet Europe" (2006) 154 *University of Pennsylvania Law Review* 1757

Segal, Jeffrey A., "Separation-of-Powers Games in the Positive Theory of Courts and Congress" (1997) 91 *American Political Science Review* 28

Selznick, Philip, *The Moral Commonwealth: Social Theory and the Promise of Community* (Berkeley, CA: University of California Press, 1992)

Shapiro, Martin, *Courts: A Comparative and Political Analysis* (Chicago: University of Chicago Press, 1986)

Shapiro Martin, "The Mighty Problem Continues" in Diana Kapiszewski, Gordon Silverstein, and Robert A. Kagan (eds.), *Consequential Courts: Judicial Roles in Global Perspective* (New York: Cambridge University Press, 2013) 380

Shapiro, Martin and Alec Stone Sweet, *On Law, Politics, and Judicialization* (New York: Oxford University Press, 2002)

Shklar, Judith N., *Legalism: Law, Morals, and Political Trials* (Cambridge, MA: Harvard University Press, 1964)

Siegel, Reva B., "Constitutional Culture, Social Movement Conflict and Constitutional Change: The Case of the de facto ERA" (2006) 94 *California Law Review* 1323

Silverstein, Gordon, "Singapore: The Exception that Proves Rules Matter" in Tom Ginsburg and Tamir Moustafa (eds.), *Rule by Law: The Politics of Courts in Authoritarian Regimes* (New York: Cambridge University Press, 2008) 73

Sinha, Nilesh, "Just Deserts or Honor at Stake? India's Pending Judicial Standards and Accountability Bill," Int'l J. Const. L. Blog, February 2, 2013 (available at www.ico nnectblog.com/2013/02/just-deserts-or-honor-at-stake-indias-pending-judicial-stan dards-and-accountability-bill/)

Siregar, Fritz Edward, *Indonesian Constitutional Politics: 2003–2013* (doctoral dissertation, UNSW Sydney, 2016)

Skocpol, Theda, *States and Social Revolutions: A Comparative Analysis of France, Russia and China* (New York: Cambridge University Press, 1979)

Skocpol, Theda and Margaret Somers, "The Uses of Comparative History in Macrosocial Inquiry" (1980) 22 *Comparative Studies in Society and History* 174

Smith, Gordon B., *Soviet Politics: Continuity and Contradiction* (London: Palgrave, 1988)

Smith, Rogers M., "Historical Institutionalism and the Study of Law" in Gregory A. Caldeira, R. Daniel Kelemen, and Keith E. Whittington, *Oxford Handbook of Law and Politics* (New York: Oxford University Press, 2008) 46

Sokwanele, "Reflecting on Zimbabwe's Constitution-Making Process" (unpublished manuscript, August 2012)

Solidarity Peace Trust, *Subverting Justice: The Role of the Judiciary in Denying the Will of the Zimbabwe Electorate since 2000* (March 2005)

Solomon, David, *The Political High Court* (Sydney: Allen & Unwin, 1999)

Sólyom, László and Georg Brunner, *Constitutional Judiciary in a New Democracy: The Hungarian Constitutional Court* (Ann Arbor, MI: University of Michigan Press, 2000)

Southall, Roger, *Liberation Movements in Power: Party & State in Southern Africa* (Pietermaritzburg: University of KwaZulu-Natal Press, 2013)

Sridharan, Eswaran, "Behind Modi's Victory" (2014) 25 *Journal of Democracy* 20

Starr, Leonie, *Julius Stone: An Intellectual Life* (Melbourne: Oxford University Press, 1992)

Staton, Jeffrey K., *Judicial Power and Strategic Communication in Mexico* (New York: Cambridge University Press, 2010)

Stepan, Alfred, "India, Sri Lanka, and the Majoritarian Danger" (2015) 26 *Journal of Democracy* 128

Stolleis, Michael, "Judicial Review, Administrative Review, and Constitutional Review in the Weimar Republic" (2003) 16 *Ratio Juris* 266

Stone, Alec, *The Birth of Judicial Politics in France: The Constitutional Council in Comparative Perspective* (New York: Oxford University Press, 1992)

Stone Sweet, Alec, *Governing with Judges: Constitutional Politics in Europe* (Oxford: Oxford University Press, 2000)

Stone Sweet, Alec, "Path Dependence, Precedent, and Judicial Power" in Martin Shapiro and Alec Stone Sweet, *On Law, Politics, and Judicialization* (New York: Oxford University Press, 2002) 112

Stone, Adrienne, "Judicial Review without Rights" (2008) 28 *Oxford Journal of Legal Studies* 1

Stone, Julius, *The Province and Function of Law: Law as Logic, Justice and Social Control* (Sydney: Maitland, 1946)

Stone, Julius, *Legal System and Lawyers' Reasonings* (Stanford: Stanford University Press, 1964)

Stone, Julius, *Precedent and Law: Dynamics of Common Law Growth* (Sydney: Butterworths, 1985)

Streeck, Wolfgang and Kathleen Thelen, "Introduction: Institutional Change in Advanced Political Economies" in Wolfgang Streeck and Kathleen Thelen (eds.), *Beyond Continuity: Institutional Change in Advanced Political Economies* (New York: Oxford University Press, 2005) 1

Sudarshan, R., "Courts and Social Transformation in India" in Roberto Gargarella et al. (eds.), *Courts and Social Transformation in New Democracies: An Institutional Voice for the Poor?* (Aldershot: Ashgate, 2006) 153

Summers, Robert S., "Pragmatic Instrumentalism in Twentieth Century American Legal Thought – A Synthesis and Critique of our Dominant General Theory about Law and its Use" (1981) 66 *Cornell Law Review* 861

Tamanaha, Brian Z., *Law as a Means to an End: Threat to the Rule of Law* (New York: Cambridge University Press, 2007)

Tamanaha, Brian Z., *Beyond the Formalist-Realist Divide: The Role of Politics in Judging* (Princeton, NJ: Princeton University Press, 2010)

Tan, Kevin Y. L., "Constitutionalism in Burma, Cambodia and Thailand: Developments in the First Decade of the Twenty-first Century," in Albert Chen ed., *Constitutionalism in Asia in the Early Twenty-First Century* (Cambridge: Cambridge University Press, 2014) 219

Tate, C. Neal, and Torbjörn Vallinder (eds.), *The Global Expansion of Judicial Power* (New York: New York University Press, 1995)

Taylor, Robert H., *General Ne Win: A Political Biography* (Singapore: ISEAS Publishing, 2015)

Teitel, Ruti, "Comparative Constitutional Law in a Global Age" (2004) 117 *Harvard Law Review* 2570

Tendi, Blessing-Miles, "Robert Mugabe's 2013 Presidential Election Campaign" (2013) 39 *Journal of Southern African Studies* 963

Thelen, Kathleen, "Historical Institutionalism in Comparative Politics" (1999) 2 *Annual Review of Political Science* 369

Thelen, Kathleen, "How Institutions Evolve: Insights from Comparative Historical Analysis" in James Mahoney and Dietrich Rueschemeyer (eds.), *Comparative Historical Analysis in the Social Sciences* (New York: Cambridge University Press, 2003) 208

Thelen, Kathleen, *How Institutions Evolve: The Political Economy of Skills in German, Britain, the United States, and Japan* (New York: Cambridge University Press, 2004)

Thio, Li-ann, "Between Apology and Apogee, Autochthony: The Rule of Law Beyond the Rules of Law in Singapore" (2012) *Singapore Journal of Legal Studies* 269

Thompson, E. P., *Whigs and Hunters: The Origin of the Black Act* (New York: Pantheon Books, 1975)

Thompson, Elaine, "The 'Washminster' Mutation" in Patrick Weller and Dean Jaensch (eds.), *Responsible Government in Australia* (Richmond: Drummond, 1980) 32

Toohey, John, "A Government of Laws, and Not of Men?" (1993) 4 *Public Law Review* 158

Trubek, David M., "Max Weber on Law and the Rise of Capitalism" 1972 *Wisconsin Law Review* 720

Trubek, David M., "Complexity and Contradiction in the Legal Order: Balbus and the Challenge of Critical Social Thought about Law" (1977) 11 *Law & Society Review* 529

Tushnet, Mark V. (ed.), *The Warren Court in Historical and Political Perspective* (Charlottesville, VA: University of Virginia Press, 1993)

Tushnet, Mark, "The Possibilities of Comparative Constitutional Law" (1999) 108 *Yale Law Journal* 122

Tushnet, Mark, *The Constitution of the United States: A Contextual Analysis* (Oxford: Hart Publishing, 2009)

Tushnet, Mark, *Weak Courts, Strong Rights: Judicial Review and Social Welfare Rights in Comparative Constitutional Law* (Princeton, NJ: Princeton University Press, 2009)

Tushnet, Mark, *Advanced Introduction to Comparative Constitutional Law* (Cheltenham: Edward Elgar, 2014)

Tushnet, Mark, "Authoritarian Constitutionalism" (2015) 100 *Cornell Law Review* 391

Twomey, Anne, "McCloy v New South Wales: Out with US Corruption and in with German proportionality" AUSPUBLAW (October 15, 2015) https://auspublaw.org/2015/10/mccloy-v-new-south-wales/

Twomey, Anne, "The Knox Court" in Rosalind Dixon and George Williams, *The High Court, the Constitution and Australian Politics* (Melbourne: Cambridge University Press, 2015)

Unger, Roberto Mangabeira, *Law in Modern Society* (New York: Free Press, 1976)

Vanberg, Georg, *The Politics of Constitutional Review in Germany* (New York: Cambridge University Press, 2005)

Varshney, Ashutosh, *Battles Half Won: India's Improbable Democracy* (New Delhi: Penguin, 2013)

Varshney, Ashutosh, "Hindu Nationalism in Power" (2014) 25 *Journal of Democracy* 34

Versteeg, Mila and Tom Ginsburg, "Why Do Countries Adopt Constitutional Review?" *University of Virginia School of Law Public Law and Legal Theory Research Paper Series* 2013–29 2

Von Bogdandy, Armin, "Comparative Constitutional Law: A Continental Perspective" in Michel Rosenfeld and András Sajó (eds.), *The Oxford Handbook of Comparative Constitutional Law* (Oxford: Oxford University Press, 2012) 25

Von Soest and Grauvogel, "How Do Non-Democratic Regimes Claim Legitimacy?" German Institute of Global and Area Studies (August 2015) available at www.isn.et hz.ch/Digital-Library/Articles/Detail/?lng=en&id=193255

Waldron, Jeremy, *The Dignity of Legislation* (Cambridge: Cambridge University Press, 1999)

Waldron, Jeremy, "Foreign Law and the Modern *Ius Gentium*" (2005) 119 *Harvard Law Review* 129

Waldron, Jeremy, "The Core of the Case against Judicial Review" (2006) 115 *Yale Law Journal* 1346

Walker, Christopher J., "Toward Democratic Consolidation: The Argentine Supreme Court, Judicial Independence, and the Rule of Law" (2008) 4 *High Court Quarterly Review* 54

Walker, Kristen, "Anthony Mason" in Tony Blackshield, Michael Coper, and George Williams (eds.), *Oxford Companion to High Court of Australia* (Melbourne: Oxford University Press, 2001) 459

Waluchow, Wil J., *A Common Law Theory of Judicial Review: The Living Tree* (Cambridge: Cambridge University Press, 2007)

Weber, Max, *Economy and Society*, eds. Günther Roth and Claus Wittich (New York: Bedminister Press, 1968)

Wheeler, Fiona, "Book Review: *Owen Dixon*, Philip Ayres, The Miegunyah Press, 2003" (2003) 31 *Federal Law Review* 416

Wheeler, Fiona, "The Latham Court" in Rosalind Dixon and George Williams (eds.), *The High Court, the Constitution and Australian Politics* (Melbourne: Cambridge University Press, 2015) 159

White, G. Edward, *Earl Warren: A Public Life* (Oxford: Oxford University Press, 1987)

White, G. Edward, *Oliver Wendell Holmes: Law and the Inner Self* (Oxford: Oxford University Press, 1996)

Whittington, Keith E., *Political Foundations of Judicial Supremacy: The Presidency, the Supreme Court, and Constitutional Leadership in U.S. History* (Princeton, NJ: Princeton University Press, 2007)

Widner, Jennifer with Daniel Scher, "Building Judicial Independence in Semi-Democracies: Uganda and Zimbabwe" in Tom Ginsburg and Tamir Moustafa (eds.), *Rule by Law: The Politics of Courts in Authoritarian Regimes* (New York: Cambridge University Press, 2008) 235

Wild, Volker, *Profit Not for Profit's Sake: History and Business Culture of African Entrepreneurs in Zimbabwe* (Harare: Baobab Books, 1997)

Williams, David C., "What's So Bad about Burma's 2008 Constitution? A Guide for the Perplexed" in Melissa Crouch and Tim Lindsey (eds.), *Law, Society and Transition in Myanmar* (Oxford: Hart Publishing, 2014) 117

Williams, George, Sean Brennan, and Andrew Lynch, *Blackshield and Williams Australian Constitutional Law and Theory: Commentary and Materials* 6th ed. (Sydney: Federation Press, 2014)

Williams, John, "Lionel Keith Murphy" in Tony Blackshield, Michael Coper, and George Williams (eds.), *Oxford Companion to High Court of Australia* (Melbourne: Oxford University Press, 2001) 484

Wilson, Bruce M., "Enforcing Rights and Exercising an Accountability Function: Costa's Rica's Constitutional Chamber of the Supreme Court" in Gretchen Helmke and Julio Ríos-Figueroa (eds.), *Courts in Latin America* (New York: Cambridge University Press, 2011) 55

Winterton, George, "Garfield Barwick" in Tony Blackshield, Michael Coper, and George Williams (eds.), *Oxford Companion to High Court of Australia* (Melbourne: Oxford University Press, 2001) 56

Yap, Po Jen, *Constitutional Dialogue in Common Law Asia* (Oxford: Oxford University Press, 2015)

Young, Katharine G., *Constituting Economic and Social Rights* (Oxford: Oxford University Press, 2012)

Young, Katharine G., "On What Matters in Comparative Constitutional Law: A Comment on Hirschl" (2016) 96 *Boston University Law Review* 1375

Zamchiya, Phillan, "The MDC-T's (Un)Seeing Eye in Zimbabwe's 2013 Harmonised Elections: A Technical Knockout" (2013) 39 *Journal of Southern African Studies* 955

Zines, Leslie, "*Engineers* and the 'Federal Balance'" in Michael Coper and George Williams (eds.), *How Many Cheers for Engineers?* (Sydney: Federation Press, 1997) 81

Zines, Leslie, *The High Court and the Constitution* 5th ed. (Sydney: Federation Press, 2008)

Zines, Leslie, "Chief Justice Gleeson and the Constitution" in H. P. Lee and P. Gerangelos (eds.), *Constitutional Advancement in a Frozen Continent: Essays in Honour of George Winterton* (Sydney: Federation Press, 2009) 269

Index

A. C. Gopalan v. State of Madras, 168
A. D. M. Jabalpur v. Shivkant Shukla,
    164–165, 166
A. K. Gopalan v. State of Madras, 151, 188
Abbas, Mahmoud, 265, 266
Abdel Nasser, Gamal, 260
Ackerman, Bruce, 40
African National Congress (ANC), 25, 77, 200,
    208, 255, 290, 317
African Union (AU), 233, 238
    Chair, 195
Agamben, Giorgio, 71
Air Force Officers case, 217
Almira Patel v. Union of India, 181
ANC. See African National Congress (ANC)
Argentina, 28
Asia, constitutional courts, 28
Asmal, Kader, 208
Asshiddiqie, Chief Justice Jimly, 31,
    251–252, 275
association, implied freedom of, 132
Austin, Granville, 152, 160
Australia, 46
    Bill of Rights, absence of, 91, 93, 123
    Chifley ALP government, 112
    constitutional culture, 91, 93, 94, 105, 107,
        143, 145, 243
    constitutional democracy, 47
    constitutional law doctrine, 92
    constitutional politics, 92
    constitutionalism, 95, 124
        rights-based, 121, 144
    Convention Debates, 141, 142
    democratic legalism, 47, 81, 91, 92, 93, 94, 95,
        107, 109, 115, 118, 129, 133, 135, 141, 143,
        145, 243, 245–246, 282, 290, 302

democratic politics, 91, 105
doctrine of proportionality, 19
Engineers case. See Engineers case
federalism, 129
High Court. See High Court of Australia
judicial review regime, 47, 80, 94,
    140–145, 243
    consolidation, 26, 270, 302
    evolution, 290
    "exogenous shock," 94, 144, 282
    federalist, 91
    implied political values, enforcement
        of, 246
    increasing-returns path, 270
    threat to institutionalization, 99
    transformation, 133–134, 241, 282
law/politics relation, 11, 91, 93,
    94, 100, 107, 122, 135, 141, 144, 145,
    243, 290
legal independence from Britain, 93
legalism, 107, 139
    Dixonian consolidation, 114–120
Liberal Party, 101, 112, 113, 116
native title, 128
political values underlying democratic
    system, 134
representative and responsible government,
    139, 140, 282, 290
separation of law and politics, 93, 95, 105, 243
separation of powers, 134, 145
Australia Acts 1986, 123, 144
Australian Broadcasting Corporation v. Lange,
    282, 290
Australian Capital Television Pty Ltd
    v. Commonwealth, 125, 126, 127, 130, 131,
    133, 137

conceptual logic of typology, purpose of, 86
consolidation, 4, 10, 46, 49, 85, 86, 143, 241,
242, 244, 269–281, 293, 311, 312
adaptation, 272
adaptive continuity, 271, 274,
276, 278, 293
causal mechanism, 270, 271, 272, 274,
276, 297
counter-reaction, 271, 272, 279
law/politics relation, rival approaches, 275
new regime formation, 271, 272, 274,
275, 276
provisional pathways, 270, 271, 279
reversion to dominant type, 272, 293
constitutional culture, aspect of, 300
constitutional disagreement, effect of, 296
default, 240
democratic instrumentalism. *See* democratic instrumentalism
democratic legalism. *See* democratic
legalism
dynamic quality, 292
Egypt, in. *See* Egypt
environmental changes, adjustment to, 292
evolution, 10, 34, 51, 66–68, 85, 89, 143,
297, 308
"exogenous shock," 52, 140, 243, 281, 282, 283,
284, 286, 288, 294, 297, 299, 300, 307,
308, 327
"formal institutions" contrasted, 299
Germany, in. *See* Germany
Hungary, in. *See* Hungary
ideal types, 3, 44, 46, 50, 78, 85, 89, 242, 243,
244, 293, 297
ideal-typical, 11, 78
ideational power, 294, 301
incremental change, 11, 244
incremental development, 3, 49, 86, 292, 297
India, in. *See* India
Indonesia, in. *See* Indonesia
inertial quality, 293
Korea, 23
law/politics accommodation, 44, 45, 78, 84,
85, 90, 141
legal and political authority
changing conceptions of, 68–78
claims, 45, 46, 50, 313
conceptions, 51
legal and political authority claims, 67
legitimating ideologies, 299
legitimation logic, 300

Mongolia, 23
Myanmar, in. *See* Myanmar
nature of, 300
"new," 272
Occupied Palestinian Territories, in. *See*
Occupied Palestinian
Territories (OPT)
political transitions and constitutional
changes, survival during, 241
resistance to change, 89, 293
Singapore, in. *See* Singapore
sources of information about character, 65
South Africa, in. *See* South Africa
Taiwan, 23
transformation, 10, 46, 49, 85, 86, 87–89, 241,
242, 243, 244, 281–290, 293, 294, 297,
303, 307
causal mechanism, 4, 232, 241, 281, 282,
283, 284, 286, 287, 288, 303, 307
conditions, 283, 284, 289, 302
"exogenous shock," 297
exogenous trigger and agency, 300
ideational reconstruction, 281, 283
sub-types, under democratic legalism,
306–308
trajectories, 309
vertical, horizontal and diagonal, 294,
303, 308–309
wholesale, 11, 288, 294, 303
typological approach, 46
typological theory of change, 10, 35, 44, 47,
48, 89, 95, 242, 244, 269, 293, 328
United States, in. *See* United States (US)
within-regime incremental change, 11, 46,
243, 290–293, 294
Zimbabwe, in. *See* Zimbabwe
judiciary. *See also* judges
authoritarian instrumentalism, role in, 83
authoritarian legalism, role in, 82
constraints on, 30
impartiality, 55
power to strike down legislative and
executive conduct, 6
public confidence in, 55, 56
selection under democratic
instrumentalism, 85
*Jumbunna Coal Mine NL v. Victorian Coal
Miners' Association*, 106

Kabila, Laurent, 220
Karekwaivanane, George, 203